THE S. MARK TAPER FOUNDATION

IMPRINT IN JEWISH STUDIES

BY THIS ENDOWMENT

THE S. MARK TAPER FOUNDATION SUPPORTS

THE APPRECIATION AND UNDERSTANDING

OF THE RICHNESS AND DIVERSITY OF

JEWISH LIFE AND CULTURE

The publisher gratefully acknowledges the
generous contribution to this book provided
by the Jewish Studies Endowment Fund of
the University of California Press
Foundation, which is supported by a major
gift from the S. Mark Taper Foundation.

ADVENTURES IN YIDDISHLAND

POSTVERNACULAR LANGUAGE & CULTURE

ADVENTURES IN
YIDDISHLAND

JEFFREY SHANDLER

UNIVERSITY OF CALIFORNIA PRESS
BERKELEY   LOS ANGELES   LONDON

University of California Press, one of the most distinguished university presses in the United States, enriches
lives around the world by advancing scholarship in the
humanities, social sciences, and natural sciences. Its activities are supported by the UC Press Foundation and
by philanthropic contributions from individuals and institutions. For more information, visit www.ucpress.edu.

The author gratefully acknowledges permission for use
of the following: A version of chapter 1 was published
as "Imagining Yiddishland: Language, Place, and
Memory," in *History & Memory* 15, no. 1 (2003): 123–49.
Part of chapter 2 was adapted from "Beyond the Mother
Tongue: Learning the Meaning of Yiddish in America,"
in *Jewish Social Studies* 6, no. 3 (2000): 97–123. A
version of chapter 4 appeared as "Postvernacular
Yiddish: Language as a Performance Art," in *The
Drama Review* 48, no. 1 (2004): 19–43.

University of California Press
Berkeley and Los Angeles, California

University of California Press, Ltd.
London, England

Library of Congress Cataloging-in-Publication Data

Shandler, Jeffrey.
   Adventures in Yiddishland : postvernacular language
and culture / Jeffrey Shandler.
      p.   cm.
   Includes bibliographical references and index.
   ISBN 0-520-24416-8 (cloth : alk. paper).
   1. Yiddish language.   2. Yiddish language—Social
aspects.   3. Jews—Languages.   4. Language and
culture.   I. Title.
PJ5113.S53   2005
439'.1—dc22   2005005293

Manufactured in the United States of America

14   13   12   11   10   09   08   07   06   05
11   10   9   8   7   6   5   4   3   2   1

This book is printed on Natures Book, containing 50%
postconsumer waste and meets the minimum require-
ments of ANSI/NISO Z39.48–1992 (R 1997) *(Permanence
of Paper).*♾

FOR STUART

CONTENTS

List of Illustrations   ix

Acknowledgments   xi

Author's Note   xv

Introduction: Postvernacularity,
or Speaking of Yiddish   1

1. Imagining Yiddishland   31

2. Beyond the Mother Tongue   59

3. Founded in Translation   92

4. Yiddish as Performance Art   126

5. Absolut Tchotchke   155

6. Wanted Dead or Alive?   177

Notes   203

Index   243

ILLUSTRATIONS

Newsstand in Boro Park, Brooklyn   3

Workmen's Circle event, New York   5

Cover of a recording by klezmer band Huljet, Nuremberg, Germany   9

Cartoon by Zuni Maud in *Der groyser kundes*   14

"Yiddish Lesson" needlepoint canvas by Deco Point, Inc.   17

Actor Zvee Scooler, holding a copy of *Instant Yiddish*   24

Flier for Yiddishland Cafe, Toronto   35

Directional signs in Kinder Ring summer camp, Sylvan Lake, New York   38

Cover illustration of Leon Feinberg's *Yidish*   42

Map of Dobrzyn   44

Base map of the *Language and Culture Atlas of Ashkenazic Jewry*   45

Designs for Yiddishland stamps   52

Web page for the Japan Yiddish Club   55

Cover of *Yiddish with Dick and Jane*   60

"The Elephant," in *Zhargon-lehrer*   64

Children in a Yiddish school in Kovno, Lithuania   70

First lesson in *Di yidishe shprakh*   76

First lesson in *Yidish far onfanger*   77

Poster announcing Yiddish language instruction, Berkeley, California   88

Moritz Daniel Oppenheim's *Sabbath-Ruhe auf der Gasse*   96

"The Jewish Torah in Yiddish" cartoon   100

Page from a Yiddish translation of The New Testament   102

Cover of Yiddish translation of Dr. Seuss's *The Cat in the Hat*   118

Page from a Yiddish version of Will Eisner's *A Contract with God*   123

Bilingual announcement of a model East European
     Jewish wedding, New York   129

Performance of *Kheyder*, Belorussian State Yiddish Theater, Minsk   133

New World Angel leading the Ashkenaz Parade, Toronto   137

Great Small Works' *The Memoirs of Glückel of Hameln/Zikhroynes Glikl*   140

Poster announcing the International Yiddish Festival, Cracow   142

Yugntruf cartoon   148

Jewish Mood Cube   157

Advertisement for Absolut Vodka   159

Lapel button   161

Mr. Mahzel figurine   163

Refrigerator magnet with *Forward* logo   165

Yankee Yiddish Cocktail Napkins   167

GEFILTE fish plastic ornament   168

Look at the Schmuck on That Camel board game   171

Promotional brochure for the Folksbiene Yiddish Theatre, New York   181

Promotional card for Isle of Klezbos   187

"Kosher" set of "talking stickers"   195

Souvenir amulet   197

New Yorker cartoon   200

ACKNOWLEDGMENTS

It is difficult for me to say just when this project began. I am a native listener of Yiddish—that is, someone who regularly heard grandparents (native Yiddish speakers and immigrants from Eastern Europe) and, to a lesser extent, parents and other relatives converse in the language with one another but seldom with me. Consequently, I have been engaged with the issue of postvernacularity, albeit unwittingly, since childhood. I only began to address this issue—motivated, at the time, by a rather open-ended curiosity about Yiddish—in my mid-twenties, when I enrolled in an elementary class in the Yiddish summer program run by the YIVO Institute for Jewish Research in conjunction with Columbia University. During the ensuing years spent at YIVO and Columbia, I received more than a graduate training in Yiddish studies; I acquired an intellectual orientation to addressing scholarly questions that lie well beyond this field's conventional boundaries.

Moreover, I found myself in the midst of a remarkable community of scholars. It is my great privilege to have studied with Lucjan Dobroszycki, Benjamin Harshav, Mikhl Herzog, Barbara Kirshenblatt-Gimblett, Jack Kugelmass, Dan Miron, and Avraham Nowersztern and to have benefited from collegial contact with Dina Abramowicz, Zachary Baker, Adrienne Cooper, Jenna Joselit, Chava Lapin, Chana Mlotek, Deborah Dash Moore, Marek Web, and Bina Weinreich, among others in this community. In the spirit of intellectual rigor, creativity, and commitment that these mentors and their predecessors in the field of Yiddish studies inspire, I have pursued this project in the hopes that it will, in some small way, further their scholarly ideals.

Although I first thought of writing about contemporary Yiddish culture when considering possible topics for a dissertation, I didn't begin to formulate the agenda for this book until a few years after completing my doctorate. During a seminar at the Center for Judaic Studies at the University of Pennsylvania, where I had the good fortune to be a postdoctoral fellow, a spirited discussion among American and Israeli scholars about the curious nature of many Jews' attachment to Yiddish today—in particular, those who profess their love for the language but readily admit that they don't know it—first prompted me to consider addressing this and related phenomena, as well as their larger implications. The result is this book.

I began approaching the task of analyzing contemporary Yiddish culture through a series of separate research endeavors, some of which resulted in journal articles that, in altered form, have become chapters or parts of chapters of *Adventures in Yiddishland*. I thank the publishers of these journals for kindly granting permission to publish these revised texts in this volume. Substantive work on this project began while I was a Dorot Teaching Fellow at the Skirball Department of Hebrew and Judaic Studies at New York University, and I finished the manuscript as a faculty member of the Department of Jewish Studies at Rutgers University. I am grateful to my colleagues at both these institutions for their support of my research over the years. During this time I also benefited greatly from a number of opportunities to present parts of this study in a variety of scholarly settings: at "People and Things," the seminar on material culture in the Department of Anthropology at New York University; during the year of seminars on the study of performance at the Center for the Critical Analysis of Contemporary Culture at Rutgers, where I was an associate fellow; at conferences on Yiddish culture at the University of California Los Angeles, Northwestern University, and the Oxford Centre for Hebrew and Jewish Studies; as well as at seminars at the University of Illinois Urbana-Champaign, Princeton University, Ben-Gurion University of the Negev, and the Graduate Theological Union, Berkeley. I came away from the exchange with colleagues in each of these venues with fresh insights into the topic and its analysis.

Among the dozens of friends and colleagues who have contributed in one way or another to the completion of this book, I owe special thanks to Sally Charnow, Eve Jochnowitz, Barbara Kirshenblatt-Gimblett, Naomi Seidman, and Kalman Weiser, each of whom read a draft of the manuscript and offered invaluable suggestions for its improvement. Eve also graciously provided a trove of remarkable resources, and

I can't imagine ever having been able to realize this project without Barbara's probing insights, always generously offered, and her unfailing enthusiasm. Librarians Zachary Baker, Faith Jones, and Yermiyahu Aharon Taub not only answered numerous research queries but also brought to my attention wonderful resources that they discovered on their own. The clippings of material related to my work that Pamela Brumberg sent me over the years were also much appreciated and remain treasured tokens of her friendship and collegial support. Paul Glasser, Miriam Isaacs, Edward Portnoy, and Nina Warnke also gave generously of their time and expertise in response to various research problems.

For their kind advice, information, and assistance offered along the way, I wish to express my gratitude as well to Barbara Abrash, Natalia Aleksiun, Michael Alpert, Gulie Arad, Aviva Astrinsky, Sholem Berger, Robert Bernecky, Toby Blum-Dobkin, Alisa Braun, Sabina Brukner, Matti Bunzl, Hinde Ena Burstin, Yael Chaver, Jesse Cohen, Adrienne Cooper, Lynn Dion, Vivian Ducat, John Efron, Pearl Gluck, David Goldberg, Rachel Goldstein, Eric Gordon, Tresa Grauer, Janet Hadda, Jack Halpern, Mikhl Herzog, Jim Hoberman, Andrew Ingall, Jenna Joselit, Naomi Kadar, Ellen Kellman, Irena Klepfisz, Rebecca Kobrin, Szonja Komoroczy, Chava Lapin, Shira Leuchter, Olga Litvak, Ronny Loewy, Chana Mlotek, Zalmen Mlotek, Robert Neumann, Anita Norich, Sam Norich, Robby Peckerar, Wilbur Pierce, Alyssa Quint, Henia Reinharz, Jenny Romaine, David Roskies, Yankl Salant, Gitl Schaechter-Viswanath, Peter Schweitzer, Nancy Sinkoff, Lorin Sklamberg, Chaim Waxman, Marek Web, Bina Weinreich, Aviva Weintraub, Michael Wex, Adam Whiteman, Hana Wirth-Nesher, Edward Zaret, Froma Zeitlin, Eviatar Zerubavel, and Yael Zerubavel. I owe special thanks to Stan Holwitz at University of California Press for his thoughtful and attentive support of this project and to Randy Heyman and Suzanne Knott, who always responded promptly and graciously to my many editorial questions and production requests.

My ultimate thanks and profoundest indebtedness go to Stuart Schear, who, as life partner and fellow traveler in Yiddishland, has inspired my work and made the undertaking of this adventure a great joy.

AUTHOR'S NOTE

Yiddish and Loshn-koydesh terms are generally romanized according to the YIVO standard, except in citations, which preserve the romanization of the source. Yiddish terms are glossed the first time they appear in the text. All translations from Yiddish are mine, except where indicated. The spelling of Jewish authors' names generally conforms to the *Encyclopedia Judaica*.

POSTVERNACULARITY, OR SPEAKING OF YIDDISH

"I'm writing a book about Yiddish after World War II," I tell a colleague, whom I've known for years, when she asks what I've been doing lately. "It's a sad story," she replies. The fact is, I don't quite agree with her, though I refrained from saying so then. Hers is a response I hear often, especially from people who, like this colleague, are a generation older than I am and are native speakers of Yiddish. Their sense of its trajectory is different from mine, and while I have developed my own understanding of Yiddish language and culture, it is still very much indebted to theirs.

Nor are they the only ones who see the story of Yiddish in declinist terms. More often than not, discussions of Yiddish culture terminate in 1939, 1948, or some other date, with any later phenomena involving the language either characterized as vestigial or simply not mentioned at all. There are, in fact, compelling reasons for thinking of Yiddish culture as having terminated at some point in the middle to late twentieth century—as a result of the Holocaust, the Stalinist liquidation of Soviet Yiddish culture, the establishment of Hebrew as the official language of the State of Israel, as well as large-scale voluntary abandonment of Yiddish among Jews integrating into the cultural mainstreams of the Americas and Western Europe. As a consequence of these events, there has been a precipitous drop in the use of Yiddish, both in public Jewish culture and in Jews' private lives. On the eve of World War II the world's Yiddish speakers were reckoned at around 11,000,000; at the turn of the twenty-first century estimates are sometimes well under 1,000,000.[1] The inventory of current Yiddish books, newspapers, radio broadcasts, theatrical performances, children's schools, summer camps, and other cultural endeavors is a fraction of pre-war activity in the language.

Nevertheless, Yiddish has maintained a significant presence in Jewish life in the six decades since the end of World War II, albeit one quite different from that of the prewar era. Despite the great reduction in its use, there are still hundreds of thousands of Jews around the world who speak, read, or write it, at least some of the time, as a language of daily life. Yiddish also serves many others in different capacities—as a subject of study, as an inspiration for performers and their audiences, as a literature increasingly accessible through translation, as a selective vocabulary sprinkled through the speech of Jews and non-Jews, and as an object of affection.

Complicating the overall sense of Yiddish in decline are contemporary examples of linguistic maintenance and cultural creativity. Many *khareydim* (ultra-Orthodox Jews) not only continue to employ Yiddish as a language of daily life, but they use it to generate new cultural works, including children's literature, popular songs, and plays performed on certain festivals. Some observers of *khareydim* suggest that, as a result of their high birthrate and maintenance of a close-knit communitarian lifestyle, the number of Yiddish speakers has stabilized and may even be on the rise.[2] As a subject of humanistic scholarship, Yiddish language, literature, and culture have never before enjoyed the sustained support and extent of interest seen in recent decades, as Yiddish studies has become a presence in dozens of institutions of higher education in North America, Europe, and Israel. (For example, of the approximately two hundred doctoral dissertations and masters theses written in North American universities that deal in some way with Yiddish, about half were completed since 1990; only two were written before World War II.)[3]

Similarly, the preservation of Yiddish culture has attracted considerable support, exemplified by the National Yiddish Book Center (NYBC) in Amherst, Massachusetts. Founded in 1980 as an effort to collect abandoned Yiddish books and make them available to a new generation of readers, the NYBC has become a widely supported and admired institution—hailed in 1997 by one enthusiast as "the most exciting new venture in American Jewish institutional life" in nearly half a century—and has expanded its agenda beyond preserving Yiddish books to a larger mission of "reviving Jewish life."[4] Yiddish songs, folklore, and plays also currently enjoy a new popularity with audiences, Jewish and non-Jewish alike, at concerts and festivals held around the world. The interest in Yiddish among non-Jews—including scholars and performers in Germany, Ireland, Italy, and Japan, as well as throughout Eastern Europe and the Americas—is unprecedented in its range and scope.

Newsstand in Boro
Park, Brooklyn,
New York City's
largest hasidic
neighborhood,
2002.
Photograph by Stan
Sherer. Courtesy of
Stan Sherer.

Beyond evincing growth and innovation in the face of decline, these recent Yiddish cultural undertakings reveal a divergence between the reduced use of Yiddish
as a vernacular, on the one hand, and the proliferation of other forms of engagement with the language on the other. Not only have the circumstances in which
Yiddish is acquired, encountered, and employed changed profoundly in recent
decades, but so have notions of what might constitute Yiddish culture. Before
World War II it seemed self-evident that this culture comprised a range of activities—literature, the press, performing arts, pedagogy, scholarly research, political
activism, and so on—produced in Yiddish by and for Jews who were fluent, native
speakers of the language. Whatever modernist innovations this culture engaged, it
did so with an understanding of Yiddish as the centuries-old vernacular that distinguished—and, for some, even defined—Ashkenazim (that is, members of the
diaspora Jewish community originating in German lands during the Middle
Ages).[5]

After World War II, however, these ready connections among language, culture,
and people can no longer be assumed; their interrelation has changed in fundamen-

tal ways. By the turn of the twenty-first century, the notion of Yiddish as a contemporary Jewish language of daily life readily provokes fascination, incredulity, or amusement. For example, when New York City's Transit Authority programmed its MetroCard vending machines in 2004 to offer Yiddish as one of the language options at selected subway stations in Brooklyn neighborhoods with large Jewish populations, this development was reported in the local media, sometimes with piquant headlines ("Subway Learns Joy of Yiddish").[6] Other languages offered by these machines in various city neighborhoods—such as Greek, Korean, and Polish—received no such attention.

Moreover, Yiddish culture now has a sizeable constituency independent of a vernacular speech community. There are even many who profess a profound, genuine attachment to Yiddish who also admit that they don't really know the language; furthermore, they don't see their lack of fluency as interfering with their devotion. (In a recent mailing promoting its annual four-day gathering in the Blue Ridge Mountains of North Carolina, the Charlotte Yiddish Institute enthuses about the previous year's event: "It was the love [of] and interest in Yiddish, not the ability to speak or understand it, which created maximum joy for participants.")[7] While this disparity between enthusiasm and mastery can prove confounding, even distressing, for some champions of the language who are fluent speakers, it needs to be considered as a distinctive cultural phenomenon in its own right.

Indeed, having an affective or ideological relationship with Yiddish without having command of the language epitomizes a larger trend in Yiddish culture in the post-Holocaust era. In semiotic terms, the language's primary level of signification—that is, its instrumental value as a vehicle for communicating information, opinions, feelings, ideas—is narrowing in scope. At the same time its secondary, or meta-level of signification—the symbolic value invested in the language apart from the semantic value of any given utterance in it—is expanding. This privileging of the secondary level of signification of Yiddish over its primary level constitutes a distinctive mode of engagement with the language that I term *postvernacular* Yiddish. In the postvernacular mode, familiar cultural practices—reading, performing, studying, even speaking—are profoundly altered. Though it often appears to be the same as vernacular use, postvernacularity is in fact something fundamentally different in its nature and intent. And while it predates World War II, the postvernacular mode has had an increasing primacy in Yiddish culture since the war. Therefore, to understand the nature of Yiddish in recent years and to think about the possibilities of its future, the notion of postvernacularity is key.

Thus, during the past six decades, Yiddish hasn't simply dwindled, and it cer-

Workmen's Circle event,
New York, 1960s.
Courtesy of the Workmen's
Circle/Arbeter Ring.

tainly hasn't died, although it is often characterized in such terms. Rather, Yiddish has become something significantly different from what it once was. The questions this book seeks to address are, Just what is the nature of Yiddish at the turn of the millennium? In traversing the challenges of the past century or so, how have the language and its culture changed? And what does this transmigration reveal about the people who have engaged with Yiddish, both before the great breach in its history that occurred in the middle of the twentieth century and in the years since?

YIDDISH SEMIOTICS

Before we examine the nature of contemporary Yiddish culture in detail, several key, general issues need to be addressed. To begin with, one of the defining features of this language is that from its beginnings in towns along the Rhine and Danube Rivers as early as the ninth century to its use by millions of Jews across Europe and in immigrant centers around the world by the early twentieth century, Yiddish has never stood alone. Its speakers have always been in contact with non-Jews—indeed, Yiddish, like all other diaspora Jewish languages, is a product of Jewish-gentile interaction—and have always been multilingual, understanding, speaking, sometimes reading and even writing one or more of their neighbors' languages. This contact has shaped the content and structure of Yiddish, as has Jews' traditional internal bilingualism. This entails, in addition to command of a Jewish vernacular, knowledge of what Yiddish speakers term Loshn-koydesh—literally, the "language of holiness," referring to the Hebrew and Aramaic of Jewish scripture, ritual, and rabbinic scholarship. Not only do the lexicon and grammar of Yiddish reflect this range of multilingual interaction, but Yiddish speakers often demonstrate a "heightened . . . consciousness" with regard to the language's various components (Germanic, Romance, Semitic, Slavic) and its "hybrid or fusion nature."[8]

The linguistically contingent status of Yiddish is epitomized by the earliest dated record of a Yiddish sentence, which appears in the Worms *makhzer* (holiday prayer book) of 1272. This sentence—actually a rhymed couplet—is inscribed in lozenges embedded within larger letters spelling a Loshn-koydesh word. The Yiddish text appears to be in an embryonic state, dependent on the Loshn-koydesh that contains (and nurtures?) it. At the same time, the Yiddish words disrupt, and even seem on the verge of escaping from, their Loshn-koydesh womb, as they playfully voice a benediction that elaborates the value of the sacred text in which they appear in the language and behavior of everyday life: *Gut tak im betage / s'ver dis makhzor in bes hakneses trage:* "A good day is given the man who bears / Into the synagogue this Book of Prayers."[9]

As communities of Ashkenazim extended their geographic range over the centuries into an international diaspora, Yiddish has been situated in a series of multilingual constellations. Each of these entails a particular set of languages, in which their juxtaposition informs the significance of what is said or written in each one, beyond its primary semantic level of meaning. Literary scholar Benjamin Harshav terms this secondary, symbolic level of significance, which Yiddish always possesses as a result of never standing alone, the "semiotics of Yiddish."[10]

Consider, for example, the long and complicated relationship between Yiddish and German. The two languages have a fundamental connection, given that Yiddish is a Germanic language (i.e., its Germanic component, related to various dialects of Middle High German, comprises the preponderance of its lexicon and grammar). The history of debating the origins of Yiddish is tied to competing theories about when (or even if) it can be properly regarded as a language separate from German.[11] The earliest speakers of what has come to be called Yiddish (they did not refer to it as such) were not merely vague regarding what it was they were speaking but apparently conceptualized language identity differently than would become the case in the modern era.

But by the Enlightenment the notion that Jews in German lands spoke something significantly different from their neighbors was evident to both Jews and non-Jews. In their pioneering scholarship on language and culture, Johann Gottfried von Herder and Wilhelm von Humboldt defined Jews as outsiders—on linguistic, cultural and, what would eventually be termed racial, grounds—in relation to the nascent idea of German nationhood. In this context, notes literary scholar Jeffrey Grossman, Yiddish "came to function as a synecdoche for the otherness of Jewish culture, language, traditions, and society." By resisting assimilation into a homogenous nation, Yiddish speakers—and the language itself—came to be regarded as "a disruptive, disordering, or anarchic element in German culture."[12]

German Jews more famously became pioneers of the Haskalah (the Jewish Enlightenment movement), epitomized by the philosopher Moses Mendelssohn. Although he spoke and wrote Yiddish, Mendelssohn disparaged it as an impure language that lacked beauty and coherence. In what became the predominant view of the Haskalah, not only did Yiddish, as a means of communication, hinder its speakers, but it had perforce a morally deleterious influence on them. The language, notes historian Steven Aschheim, "became synonymous with *Unbildung* [lack of cultivation], [the] counter-example of what the new German Jew had to become."[13] Abandoning Yiddish for German soon stood as a hallmark of enlightened, integrationist German Jews. Consequently, the extent to which traces of Yiddish lingered among them ineluctably became a focus of modern German anti-Semitism and Jewish self-hatred. The instrument of comic mockery of German Jews, Yiddish was also perceived more ominously as the Jews' covert language. As cultural historian Sander Gilman has noted, this notion had telling ideological implications: "Even if Jews could speak perfect grammatical, syntactic, and semantic German, their rhetoric revealed them as Jews." Such an understanding of Yiddish as an insidious cultural force would eventually inform Nazi anti-Semitism. The Nazis' "racial linguistics was a continuation of the long tradition of viewing the Jews' discourse as polluted" and, therefore, as a threat to the cultural health of Germans.[14]

Conversely, Yiddish writers in nineteenth-century Eastern Europe often turned to German as a model for refining their language into a proper vehicle for modern literary expression. (Indeed, the German model of vernacular language as providing "those modes of shared sensibility from which a nation-state could evolve" was paradigmatic for East European Jews and non-Jews alike as they sought to articulate nationalist identities in the nineteenth century.)[15] The prolific Yiddish writer Isaac Meir Dik, for example, who wrote hundreds of titles published from the 1840s to the 1890s, would, in the course of his narratives, render traditional Yiddish terms and phrases, mostly from the language's Loshn-koydesh component, into modern German equivalents.[16]

Later authors and champions of Yiddish stigmatized such practice as *daytshmerish*, an overreliance on literary German. In the early decades of the twentieth century, notes linguist Christopher Hutton, debating *daytshmerish* came to symbolize pro-Yiddish activists' efforts "to assert the identity of Yiddish as an autonomous linguistic entity."[17] For some engaged in creating standards for Yiddish as a *kultur-shprakh* (language of "high" culture), *vos vayter fun daytsh* (the further from German [the better]) became an ideological as well as an instrumental watchword.

Such concerns were soon overwhelmed by the Nazi era's transformation of German-Jewish relations throughout Europe into a life-and-death struggle. During the Holocaust and its immediate aftermath, some Jews assailed German as the epitome of "Aryan" savagery, just as they saw Yiddish as a metonym for the millions of Jewish victims. In a poem he wrote during World War II, the American Yiddish poet Yankev Glatshteyn voiced his outrage at Germany's mass murder of European Jewry by ascribing to Yiddish and German contrary moral characters and by despairing that the civility and creativity of "our well-kept tongue" had been rendered speechless by the savagery of "your *Blutwurst Sprache* [blood sausage language]."[18]

More recently, the affinity of the two languages has fostered new appreciation—albeit circumspectly, given their fraught history. For example, when young American musicians involved in the klezmer revival began performing in Germany in the 1980s, they soon discovered that they could sing and speak to audiences there in Yiddish without providing the extensive translation that their (often largely Jewish) audiences in the United States usually required. Before long, young German musicians took up playing klezmer and performing Yiddish songs themselves.[19]

The liner notes to the 1993 recording *Beyond the Pale* by the klezmer band Brave Old World address the complicated challenge of performing in Germany, noting archly that there "the population speaks a corrupted Yiddish, which they write in the alphabet of Christians." In his lyrics to the album's concluding song, "Berlin 1990," band member Michael Alpert articulates both the uneasiness and the attraction generated by the encounter of American-born Jewish klezmer musicians with Germans, especially their youth, during that nation's dramatic transformation:

Nor nokh alts, oy, farbindn zikh
undzere tsvey felker,
a farbotene libe, fun reshoim geshtert,
Tsi libe, tsi sine,
Zi hersht vi bashert.

Yet something still draws together
Our two peoples;

Cover of the premiere recording of Huljet (Yiddish for "carouse"), a klezmer band based in Nuremberg, Germany, 2000. The text of the accompanying booklet begins: "Sind Sie Jude?—Nein?—Und warum machen Sie dann Klezmer?" (Are you a Jew? No? Then why do you play klezmer?)
Courtesy of Huljet.

A forbidden love, disrupted by evildoers,
Be it love or hate,
It is as if fated.[20]

During the past century, Yiddish has taken on very different symbolic meanings within the multilingual constellation of the Jewish settlement in Palestine and, since 1948, the State of Israel. There Yiddish is juxtaposed against modern Hebrew, the official national language and now prevailing Jewish vernacular, as the traditional Jewish language of diaspora.[21] Consequently, Yiddish has become emblematic of a way of life rejected and superceded by Zionism.[22] There is a considerable history of Zionist derision and even persecution of Yiddish in the pre-State era, which continued for years after the State of Israel was established. In Palestine under British mandate rule, Hebraists denounced Yiddish as a language lacking in linguistic, cultural, or social integrity (a discourse similar, and to an extent indebted, to the German assault on Yiddish) and indelibly marked with the stigma of exile. They occasionally vandalized Yiddish printing presses and torched newsstands that sold Yiddish newspapers.[23] And in 1930 a screening of an early Yiddish "talkie" in Tel Aviv provoked some in the audience to spatter the screen with ink and to hurl "foul-smelling objects" in protest, leading to arrests by British police. The film was later screened "after cutting out the talking and singing parts"—in effect, quelling what was denounced as "the deliberate impertinence of a jargon [i.e., Yiddish] performance."[24]

Official policy in Israel has consistently denied the value of Yiddish as a Jewish vernacular within its borders (although Ashkenazim have spoken Yiddish in the region for centuries).[25] During the war crimes trial of Adolf Eichmann in 1961, for example, the Israeli government refused to translate the proceedings into Yiddish or to offer daily press briefings in the language (these were made available in English, French, and German), despite the extensive international Yiddish press covering the event. Israeli officials argued that "Yiddish journalists ought to know Hebrew" and that they "can translate on their own from the other languages," like the Yugoslavian or Polish journalists covering the trial.[26] State-run institutions have occasionally accorded Yiddish an emblematic, vestigial status, especially in connection with the Nazi destruction of European Jewry. Thus, signage in the original museum at Yad Vashem, which opened in Israel's official Holocaust memorial complex in 1973, identified sections of its exhibition chronicling Nazi Germany's persecution of European Jewry in Yiddish and English as well as Hebrew (the building's emergency exits, however, were marked only in Hebrew and English).

Recently in Israel, Yiddish has received more beneficent official recognition as an important resource of Jewish heritage. In January 1993 the Knesset convened a special session dedicated to Yiddish language and culture. This homage to Yiddish, "after years of denial and negation" on the part of the state, included speeches by Knesset members Abraham Burg, Ovadia Eli, Dov Shilansky, and Shevah Weiss, among others, who "spoke in praise of Yiddish and expressed their love for it." Complicating this official demonstration of respect were the diverging perspectives it offered on the language. Whereas Shilansky "spoke with great emotion of the Yiddish language and its beauty, clinging to the memory of the past," offering what amounted to a eulogy for the language, Minister of Education and Culture Shulamit Aloni declared, "It is too early to mourn over the Yiddish language. It is necessary to cultivate it. . . . Its riches must not be lost." One feature common to all the speakers at this event was that they made their remarks in Hebrew.[27]

Juxtaposed against official state attitudes toward Yiddish, whether negative or positive, folkloric evidence demonstrates how alternative valuations of Yiddish in Israel have persisted informally. For example, in his celebratory volume *The Joys of Yiddish*, published in the United States in 1968, Leo Rosten included the following joke: "On a bus in Tel Aviv, a mother was talking animatedly, in Yiddish, to her little boy—who kept answering her in Hebrew. And each time the mother said, 'No, no, talk Yiddish!' An impatient Israeli, overhearing this, exclaimed, 'Lady, why do you insist the boy talk Yiddish instead of Hebrew?' Replied the mother, 'I don't want him to forget he's a Jew.' "[28]

The state's official equating of Hebrew, Israeli, and Jewish identities is also re-fracted through the prism of Yiddish in another joke, which explains that the He-brew word *b'diyuk* ("precisely," as in *b'sheva v'hetsi b'diyuk*, "at precisely 7:30") is really an acronym for *biz di yidn veln kumen* (Yiddish for "until the Jews come").[29] In this bit of comic wordplay Yiddish offers a linguistic undoing of Hebrew mean-ing and signifies the cultural subversion of a precise, standard time by a subjective, alternative "Jewish time." Or consider the phenomenon of Arab dealers in second-hand goods who troll the streets of Israeli cities in horse-drawn wagons, shouting *"Alte zakhn, alte zakhn, alte zakhn!"* (Yiddish for "old clothes"). Here, Yiddish per-sists in Israel as a token of exile, signifying an archetypal Jewish profession of the European diaspora, though it has been mapped onto a different people and thereby configures them as local emblems of a way of life that Israeli Jews have left behind.

There may also be a new generational divide in Israeli attitudes toward Yiddish, according to journalist Efrat Shalom, reporting in 2003 on younger Israelis who are drawn to Yiddish as part of a larger reclaiming of "Ashkenazism." Among these is author Nir Baram, who compares the fate of Yiddish under Zionism with that of Mizrahi ("Oriental," i.e., non-European diaspora Jewish) culture: "Unlike the Mizrahi culture, which was clearly oppressed, the Zionist Ashkenazim murdered their own culture with their own hands. . . . Ironically, it's the Mizrahi campaign [to assert its distinctive diaspora cultures within Israel] that is leading the cultural lib-eration of the Ashkenazim." Shalom notes that Baram's thesis angered older Is-raelis, who, in Baram's words, "felt the need to defend the basic Zionist narrative." In Israel, he maintains, "the Ashkenazim were the first to wipe out their past. Now, my generation wants to continue the historical continuum."[30]

YIDDISH ON TRIAL

Within any given constellation of languages the choice to speak, write, or perform in Yiddish (or to refrain from doing so) has always been invested with meaning, be-yond the content of what is actually being uttered. (For instance, a live recording of a recital in the United States by cantor Moshe Koussevitzky begins with him an-nouncing in English that he will sing the aria "Rachel, quand du Seigneur" from Jacques Fromenthal Halévy's opera *La Juive*. "In Yiddish," Koussevitzky adds, after a pause, and the audience stirs with laughter, then applause.)[31] While this added semiotic value has always been present in the history of Yiddish, it became especially charged following the advent of the Haskalah. Until this period, notes linguist Max Weinreich, Ashkenazim "were attached to Yiddish not by a formulated ideology, but because it was their own indigenous possession."[32] Thereafter, however, a modern consciousness about Yiddish evolved, responsive to new scrutiny of the paradigms and contingencies defining Jewishness, and the significance of Yiddish in Jewish life could no longer be regarded as self-evident. The language became the subject of extensive public discussion, as established patterns of Ashkenazic multiglossia gave way to a much more open and contentious configuration of language use. This was especially the case in Eastern Europe, home since the eighteenth century to a Jewish population of unprecedented size.

As Harshav notes, the symbolic meaning of Yiddish was dramatically transformed during the "modern Jewish revolution"—the abrupt, intense, and multivalent response of East European Jews to the waves of anti-Semitic violence and punitive legislation that followed the assassination of Czar Alexander II in 1881. Constituting "a major watershed in the history of Jewish culture and consciousness," this response was anything but uniform, but its impact was "so immense that [it] undermined all certainties of the Jewish community in Eastern Europe,"[33] compelling millions to question every aspect of Jewish life, from what constitutes a proper sociopolitical vision of Jews as a people to how a Jew should eat, dress, and talk. The question of language was vital to this revolution, linking its national and personal dimensions; the choice of proper language(s) for the modern Jew—with possibilities that included Hebrew, Yiddish, German, Russian, Polish, Hungarian, English, and Esperanto, among others (and combinations thereof)—was one of the most widely and passionately debated issues of the period.

From the late 1800s until the end of World War II the discourse about Yiddish ranged widely, from ardent advocacy to equally passionate repudiation. A common assumption in this discussion, regardless of the esteem accorded to the language, was that there were millions of Jews, the majority of the world's Jewish population, whose first language was Yiddish more or less by dint of birth. Hence, for the foreseeable future there would continue to be a sizeable population of Yiddish speakers—most of them living in Eastern Europe, where they had made their home for centuries, along with significant immigrant communities established in Western Europe and the Americas. This was an unprecedented phenomenon in Jewish history: never before (or since) have so many Jews, and such a widely dispersed preponderance of their world population, been united by their knowledge of a Jewish vernacular. Indeed, it was this large population of native speakers of Yiddish (more, on the eve of World War II, than there were native speakers of, say, Czech, Dutch, or Greek) that provided the foundation for Yiddishism.[34] The ideology—or, rather, cluster of ideologies—of Yiddishism centered on the notion that Yiddish, as a *folkshprakh* (a Yiddish term for "vernacular language," literally, "the people's language"), was an essential, definitional feature of a modern Jewish nation.

Conversely, the great extent of this vernacular community also prompted vehement attacks on Yiddish. These came from Jews who championed Hebrew as their modern vernacular or who advocated linguistic assimilation into German, Russian, Polish, or another major national language. Other Jews assailed Yiddish as the instrument of a pernicious ideology, be it hasidism, communism, or Jewish nationalism. Although this may be a difficult notion to grasp from our current perspective, since Yiddish seems to be, if anything, endangered rather than dangerous, defending the language from attack by both Jews and non-Jews was a constant of modern Yiddish culture in its heyday. At the end of the nineteenth century the philologist Leo Wiener observed that "there is probably no other language in existence on which so much opprobrium has been heaped."[35]

As Wiener wrote these words in his landmark study of modern Yiddish literature, this new culture was burgeoning in the face of extensive state restriction. The majority of the world's Yiddish speakers then lived in the Russian Empire, where they had been forbidden to run modern schools or perform plays in Yiddish, since these were suspected of serving as vehicles of sedition. Under czarist rule, Jews seeking to issue books and periodicals were subject to state censorship (as was all publishing in Russia), and they had to comply with specific constraints on the operation of Jewish presses.[36]

Although World War I brought an end to these restrictions, East European Yiddish speakers encountered both new obstacles and unprecedented opportunities in the interwar years. Provisions in the Versailles Treaty stipulated that minorities in Eastern Europe's new republics, including Jews, would be afforded considerable cultural autonomy. These provisions included the right to establish trade unions, political parties, schools, presses, and cultural institutions run in their own languages. However, efforts to implement Yiddish in public culture met with frequent government resistance, including in the Polish Republic, home to the largest Jewish population in interwar Europe.[37]

During the 1930s, state-endorsed and -supported Yiddish cultural institutions that had been established in Soviet Russia in the previous decade came under increasingly oppressive governmental control, sometimes at the hands of fellow Jews in leadership positions in the Russian Communist Party. Following World War II,

אוּן עֶר הֶערט זײ װי דעם קאָטער אוּן לעכם!

"And he pays them no heed and lives!" This cartoon by Zuni Maud was published in the American Yiddish humor magazine *Der groyser kundes* (The Big Prankster) in 1921. The boy, with a hat labeled "Yiddish" and a book labeled "Jewish History," strides past adults representing Hebrew, French, English, German, Spanish, Russian, and Polish, who say, "He won't amount to anything; his sort can't survive." In the background, ghosts haunt the tombstones of Chaldean, Latin, and Aramaic.

leading figures of Soviet Yiddish culture were arrested and later executed for their involvement in efforts that had come to be denounced as acts of anti-Soviet nationalism and treason. Prominent Yiddish writers who were among the defendants in the 1952 secret trial of the Jewish Anti-Fascist Committee were coerced into renouncing their life's work as interfering with Jewish assimilation into the Soviet mainstream. At one point during the proceedings the principal defendant, Solomon Lozovsky, observed: "What is on trial here is the Yiddish language."[38]

During the Holocaust, Yiddish became a powerful signifier of an exigent, ineluctable Jewishness in the struggle for survival. Writing in Vilna in the spring of 1940, educator Chaim Kazdan exhorted fellow Yiddishists to respond to an urgent need for reading material by fellow Jews caught in the upheavals of war:

Those who are already familiar with Yiddish literature as well as those who have only just now come to Yiddish and all forms of Yiddish secular culture—those among the refugees [from western Poland] who have only just begun speaking Yiddish and are trying to integrate themselves into the Yiddish milieu—are all seeking companionship in the Yiddish book. . . . Now more than ever our literature is called upon to strengthen the spirit, to solidify the masses, to raise the level of culture in our environment.[39]

From our postwar perspective it is apparent that, just as the atrocities that awaited Europe's Jews during World War II were beyond their imagination, Yiddish speakers could not fathom the devastating effect that the Holocaust would have on the language and its culture. Writing in the *Jewish Daily Forward* at the end of 1941, weeks after the United States' entry into the war, Max Weinreich considered its consequences for Yiddish. While anticipating that the language would reflect the "terrible upheavals" of the war, he situated this notion within the larger historical dynamic of Yiddish and remarked that, in general, "languages are always changing, especially in extraordinary times." Noting that predictions, positive as well as negative, of the impact World War I would have on Yiddish had all proved to be inaccurate, Weinreich refused to speculate about the particular consequences of the current war. "It will be a completely different world," he observed. "Jews fleeing demolished areas will encounter one another, and many Jews will immigrate to new places."[40] Though he resisted forecasting the nature of postwar Yiddish, Weinreich appears to have anticipated that the impact of World War II on the language and its speakers would be similar in scope to that of the previous war. The upheavals of warfare would disrupt usage but would also result in reconfigurations with the potential to foster linguistic and cultural innovations. The enduring viability of Yiddish and of its core community of speakers in Europe, however, was beyond questioning.

YIDDISH AS MARTYR

With the revelations of the Holocaust this assumption was abruptly and cruelly undone. The great majority of Jews murdered during World War II spoke Yiddish; within less than a decade the number of Yiddish speakers in the world had been cut in half. Along with the extensive loss of life came the widespread destruction of Jewish communal infrastructure in Eastern Europe, compounded by its regulation or liquidation at the hands of various postwar communist-bloc governments. Yiddish proved to be newly problematic for East European Jewish survivors of the Holocaust. In the late 1940s an American visitor to Poland reported that "Jews were afraid to speak Yiddish in public" and that they were told "it was 'inadvisable' for Jews to provoke Poles by speaking Yiddish on the public streets."[41] What had been the central locus of Yiddish culture for half a millennium was now perceived as a haunting void. Recent immigrant communities, most only one or two generations old, regarded before the war as adventive outposts of Yiddish culture, now bore the onus of its endurance.

As but one consequence of this catastrophic loss of life and sudden reconfiguration of Jewish demographic and cultural centers, the significance of Yiddish was radically altered. In addition to new multilingual constellations in which Yiddish speakers found themselves (such as the arrival of a sizeable postwar community in Australia), the situation of Yiddish in existing milieus was transformed. This was especially true in the United States, where Jews—most of whom were Yiddish-speaking immigrants or their descendants—suddenly confronted the fact that they were not only the world's largest and most prosperous Jewish community but also its most continuous and, albeit by default, its most authoritative one. As historian Jonathan Sarna writes, "Whereas before [World War II], the Jews of Europe represented the demographic and cultural center of world Jewry, now that designation fell to America."[42]

The signal changes of life in postwar America—large-scale embourgeoisement, internal migration from cities to suburbs, expanded access to higher education—had a profound impact on the nation's Jews. These and other factors contributed to a paradigmatic shift in their sense of self, which sociologist Nathan Glazer characterized in 1957 as a move from Jewishness (i.e., Jews understood as an ethnic group—or, as Glazer termed it, "secular culture and quasi-national feeling") to Judaism (Jews defined as a religious community).[43] The postwar years also witnessed a widespread desire on the part of American Jews to be seen, by other Americans as well as by themselves, as well integrated into the national cultural mainstream. For many American Jews during the early postwar years, Yiddish was an embarrassing vestige of immigrant difference. With the onset of the Cold War, the antireligious stance and left-wing associations of many secular Yiddishists came to be seen as especially problematic. The establishment of the State of Israel also fostered a surge in American Jews' interest in studying modern Hebrew. These changing circumstances and perspectives contributed to postwar American Jews' extensive abandonment of Yiddish as a vernacular. At the same time, these developments prompted a new self-consciousness about the loss of the language.

Needlepoint canvas by Deco Point, Inc., 1959. The words taught in this "Yiddish Lesson" exemplify the wide symbolic range of Yiddish in postwar America: as a signifier of piety and sentiment, on the one hand, and of excess and disparagement on the other.

The neglect of Yiddish became a topic of interest in itself, notably in works of American Jewish literature and in humor that played with the disparity between different generations' knowledge of the language. In 1946 humorist Sammy Levenson published "A Guide to Basic Yiddish," one of the earliest mock Yiddish-English dictionaries (a genre that would proliferate in ensuing decades). Levenson prefaced this inventory of selected Yiddish terms with comic glosses (e.g., "YONTEFDIK [festive:] Tight shoes"; "KOVED [honor:] Allowing the other guy to pay the check") by explaining:

[Today's] grandchildren speak very little Yiddish. Generally speaking, they know less of Yiddish than their grandparents knew of English. This dictionary contains remnants of grandpa's Yiddish which still circulate among the younger generation of American-Jews. They are retained because they are sweet and colorful. They are richly idiomatic and "hit the spot." Besides, many of us have a sentimental attachment for them as for grandma's candlesticks or grandpa's old watch. They "belonged" to our people. They are precious because the places like

Jewish Poland where people used them most as their very own are fewer and the people who sang to their children in Yiddish and worked in Yiddish and made love in Yiddish are nearly all gone.[44]

This trope of recounting the decline of Yiddish in postwar America as an ambivalent sign of cultural loss has continued through the turn of the millennium. In 2000 *New York Times* columnist Clyde Haberman observed that while "a fair amount of Yiddish . . . has become mainstream in America, . . . the Yiddish that Americans tend to know (most Jews included) consists of only a word here, a word there, and often those words are exceedingly vulgar. Yet clueless speakers casually toss them out all the time, and now and then they land in hot water." Even as he noted the lost popular awareness of Yiddish as a language of high culture, Haberman himself could not resist the appeal of its "joke potential," dubbing this problem, "with apologies to the late lexicographer Leo Rosten, the Oys of Yiddish."[45]

Paradoxically, at the same time that Yiddish was becoming, for many Jews, a lost language, it also gained new value as a signifier of loss. This association was forged during World War II, when Yiddish was quite literally "written . . . with blood," as Hirsh Glik, a poet of the Vilna Ghetto, famously stated in his "Partisans' Hymn." Not merely a metaphor, this image can be seen in one of the most chilling photographs taken during the Holocaust: as one of photographer Hirsh Kadushin's neighbors lay dying in the Kovno Ghetto, he wrote on the floor in his own blood the words *Yidn nekome!* (Jews—revenge!).[46]

After the war, the sudden absence of Yiddish speech became, especially for Jewish survivors of the Holocaust, a compelling metonym for the tragic loss of its speakers. This development invited some to make special efforts to restore the use of Yiddish as a gesture of rebuilding or of memorialization. Thus, Samy Feder, who in 1945 established a Yiddish theater troupe among Jewish survivors in the liberated concentration camp Bergen-Belsen, recalled, "I was deeply moved when several Jewish girls came to see me and begged me with tears in their eyes to let them join the troupe. They could speak no Yiddish at all, but they were stagestruck. When I told them that we were going to produce our plays in Yiddish, they promised to learn Yiddish in a very short time. . . . How could I send them back?"[47] Similarly, in a 1961 collection of Yiddish poetry in English translation the anthologist, Joseph Leftwich, cited as evidence of the postwar renewal of Yiddish belles lettres the words of an unnamed survivor of Nazi persecution: "Yiddish, which I hardly knew before, the language of my parents and grandparents, has become my most sacred credo, . . . and I swear that if there is anything I can write out of my experiences, it will be written in Yiddish, the language hallowed by our millions of martyrs."[48]

Such devotion to Yiddish as an act of remembrance and of a defiant Jewish persistence in the face of genocide elides the fundamental questioning of the language's future, which was pervasive, if often tacit, in early postwar Yiddish culture. This issue was addressed by some of its finest authors, such as Glatshteyn, who interrogated the viability of Yiddish poetics in the very act of writing powerful new verse.[49] Abraham Sutzkever, who settled in Palestine in 1947 and would eventually emerge as the doyen of Yiddish poetry in Israel, challenged the new state's dismissal of Yiddish. In a poem written in 1948, he asked that if someone knows "exactly in what region" the fruits of Yiddish culture

> Are straying to their sunset—
> Could he please show me
> *Where* the language will go down?
> Maybe at the Wailing Wall?
> If so, I shall come there, come,
> Open my mouth,
> And like a lion
> Garbed in fiery scarlet,
> I shall swallow the language as it sets.
> And wake all the generations with my roar![50]

YIDDISH AS A POSTVERNACULAR

In the postwar era, those who have maintained a commitment to Yiddish as a *kulturshprakh*, such as Glatshteyn and Sutzkever, have done so not only in the face of political or ideological opposition, as was the case in prewar years. They have been obliged as well to assert their devotion in the face of the increasingly pervasive notion that Yiddish is moribund—a language whose speech community is dwindling, whose function as the basis of a Jewish national ideology or simply as a Jewish vernacular is passé. Increasingly, devotees of Yiddish have not been able to take for granted their rationales for maintaining the language and must assert explicitly their motives for what was once thought to be self-evident. Thus, the certificate of incorporation of the Forward Association, which has published its Yiddish newspaper for over a century, made no mention of the organization's commitment to Yiddish when the document was originally drafted in 1901, nor did it include any mention of Yiddish when it was amended in 1911 or again in 1949. In 1967, however, an amendment to the Forward Association's by-laws stated that its "particular objects and purposes" include "the promotion and development of the use, understanding, and appreciation of the Yiddish language."[51] This change exemplifies the shift of Yiddish from an implicit vernacular to a reification of heritage, wherein the language is perceived as both threatened and valued. (Historian David Lowenthal writes, "Endangered dialects are not yet priced alongside Old Master paintings in Sotheby's salesbooks, but their collectors and protectors talk the same legacy lingo.")[52]

In recent years the viability of Yiddish, especially among generations born after World War II, has become newsworthy in itself. In the United States the devotion of a young Yiddishist to the language has been a recurring subject of features in English-language periodicals.[53] Even Yiddish publications treat the intergenerational maintenance of the language as a phenomenon of note. In 2003 the *Forverts* (the Forward Association's Yiddish-language weekly) reported on the debut of two student journals in Yiddish—*Dos naye dor* (The New Generation), issued in Mexico City, and *Di yunge gvardye* (The Young Guard), published on the Internet in Melbourne, Australia—under the headline "Two New Yiddish Journals by and for Young People!" and ended its report with the wish that "these new youth publications have many young readers!"[54]

Though perceived largely in terms of loss, the current state of Yiddish—increasingly self-conscious, contingent, and tenacious—has also opened up new cultural possibilities for the language. Indeed, the symbolic values invested in Yiddish have expanded greatly and have done so precisely because of the prevailing sense that it is no longer what it once was, with this disparity inspiring innovation. Thus, Yiddish is no longer employed in films as it was in the several dozen features made in Eastern Europe and the United States during the 1930s, in which "everyone—cantors, seamstresses, psychiatrists, police offers, judges, Negro servants, Polish aristocrats, Ukrainian peasants, even anti-Semites—not only speaks Yiddish but inhabits an imaginary world in which Yiddish is the predominant, sometimes the sole language and where Yiddish speakers' sensibilities are central."[55] However, Yiddish continues to be heard occasionally (almost always as one of two or more languages spoken) in films made after World War II, and use of the language is imbued with a range of symbolic values: it is affectionately recalled as a once-scorned Old World vernacular (e.g., in Joan Micklin Silver's 1975 film *Hester Street*); invoked archly as the native tongue of an exoticized American Jewish middle class (by Ken Jacobs in his 1975 film *Urban Peasants: An Essay in Yiddish Structuralism*); deployed with heavy irony as the lingua franca of the Holocaust (in Andres Veiel's 1994 film *Bal-agan* [Chaos]); or celebrated as the language of improbable Jewish romance (most provocatively in Jean-Jacques Zilbermann's 1998 film *L'homme est une femme comme les autres* [released in English as *Man Is a Woman*], in which the sheltered daughter of hasidim and a secular gay Jewish man bond, albeit briefly, through their common love of Yiddish culture). In perhaps the most telling illustration of the self-consciousness with which Yiddish is uttered in post-Holocaust films, Emmanuel Finkel turned his search for elderly Yiddish speakers to perform in his features *Madame Jacques sur La Croisette* (1995) and *Voyages* (1999) into a documentary about the audition process (*Casting*, 2001).

Innovations in the meta-meaning of Yiddish take place today in traditionally ob-servant Jewish venues as well. For example, in 2003 recordings of Rabbi Mordechai Pinchas Teitz's *Daf Hashavua* (Page of the Week), a weekly half-hour radio pro-gram devoted to Talmud study originally aired on WEVD (in New York City) from 1953 to 1988, were made available for sale. Tapes of the rabbi's lectures were advertised as offering the experience of a *gemore shier* (Talmud study session) con-ducted "in a pure Yiddish," providing an opportunity for students to be transported "across centuries of learning." When these lessons originally aired, Yiddish served as the traditional vehicle for the study of sacred texts written in Hebrew and Ara-maic. (While this practice continues in some yeshivas, most Talmud scholars con-duct their studies in English, modern Hebrew, or another vernacular.) Now the Yid-dish of *Daf Hashavua* is offered as having scholarly value in itself, since it embodies the heritage of East European rabbinical erudition and is imbued with a level of sanctity of its own. Whereas Hebrew, the promotion explains, "is *lashon ha-kodesh* [the language of holiness], Yiddish is *l'shon ha-k'doshim* [the language of those who are holy]." Indeed, the recordings of *Daf Hashavua* are promoted not only to "those who want to hear a brilliant, classical *litvishe shiur* that will re-create the study in Lithuanian yeshivos" but also to "those who want to learn a pure, elegant Yiddish."[56]

Conversely, there are those who turn to Yiddish as a symbol that looks not to the past but to the future, not inward to Jewish tradition but outward, beyond its cul-tural boundaries. Thus, in a commentary on National Public Radio in 2002, writer David Mickel analogized Yiddish and the language of hip-hop, characterizing them as codes that are similarly arcane and playful:

It occurred to me that hip-hop has become this generation's Yiddish. . . . With the right inflection, rap expressions like "shizzle my nizzle," "big ups" and "off the hizzy" almost sound Yiddish. They're as fun and clever as they are confusing, but that's the point. You aren't supposed to understand them, or at least your parents aren't. Like the Yiddish of my youth, rap today has become the private language for kids, but fear not. For just as oy vay and schlep have become commonplace, so, too, will "hoop-de" and "holla back." Then you, too, can get busy with the meshuggeh bling bling that's playing the dozens to your favorite bubelah. Understand, right?[57]

As much as these and other contemporary cultural endeavors differ in the symbolic values that they invest in Yiddish, they share the same mode of engagement with the language—namely, as a postvernacular. As it implies, the term *postvernacular* relates to Yiddish in a manner that both is other than its use as a language of daily life and is responsive to the language having once been a widely used Jewish vernacular. Postvernacularity is, therefore, a relational phenomenon. It always entails some awareness of its distance from vernacularity, which is usually contemplated in terms of retrospection—even as vernacular Yiddish continues to be maintained by Jewish communities around the world. What most distinguishes postvernacular Yiddish is its semiotic hierarchy; unlike vernacular language use, in the postvernacular mode the language's secondary, symbolic level of meaning is always privileged over its primary level. In other words, in postvernacular Yiddish the very fact that something is said (or written or sung) in Yiddish is at least as meaningful as the meaning of the words being uttered—if not more so.

Postvernacular Yiddish relates to vernacular Yiddish much as other "post-X" phenomena do to their respective "X's": postmodernism, poststructuralism, post-feminism, post-Zionism, or what historian David Hollinger terms postethnicity. "Post-X's" do not simply supercede "X's"; as Hollinger notes, they "build upon, rather than reject" their respective "X's."[58] A "post-X" is a response or reaction to "X" and exists in a dialogic, interdependent relationship with "X." In positing postvernacularity as a model for understanding Yiddish in the post-Holocaust era, I claim neither that vernacular Yiddish is a thing of the past nor that we should look forward to such a day when that would be the case. Rather, I argue that postvernacular Yiddish is a phenomenon whose origins can be seen taking shape during the efflorescence of modern Yiddish culture at the turn of the twentieth century. Postvernacularity has since moved to the foreground of Yiddish culture, largely as a consequence of the destruction and attrition of the majority of the world's native Yiddish speakers in the middle decades of that century. Moreover, as is the case with other "post-X" phenomena, I argue not only that postvernacular Yiddish is dependent on vernacular Yiddish, past and present, but also that contemporary vernacular Yiddish culture is itself shaped in response to postvernacular phenomena.

The notion of postvernacular Yiddish may well seem unsettling, especially to those committed to maintaining Yiddish as a language of daily life. I do not propose postvernacularity as a critique of this commitment but rather as a model for thinking about modes of engaging with Yiddish that have figured throughout the history of its modern culture, before as well as after World War II, across the Jewish ideological spectrum—and have even played a formative role in Yiddishism. In this respect, postvernacularity is a phenomenon not only of Yiddish but of other languages as well—such as Ainu, Irish, and Navajo—whose "native" communities have grappled with language maintenance in the face of challenges posed by various social, political, and cultural forces.[59]

Moreover, postvernacular Yiddish should be considered in light of the extent to which nonvernacular languages have been a vital part of the Jewish past since the Babylonian exile, which transformed the ancient Israelites' Hebrew from a language of daily life into a language of scripture and worship. Subsequently, Judeo-Aramaic has functioned as a postvernacular language for hundreds of years, studied by students of the Talmud and employed in the writing of Jewish marriage contracts and bills of divorce, among other uses; rabbinic Hebrew, traditionally used for Jewish legal responsa and commentaries on sacred texts, has always been a nonvernacular language; modern Hebrew began as a protovernacular during the Haskalah and only became a language of daily life in the twentieth century. Other diaspora Jewish languages are also engaged in the postvernacular mode, such as Albert Memmi's reflections (originally written in French) on his mother tongue, "the Judeo-Arabic dialect of Tunis, a crippled language . . . hardly understood by the Moslems and completely ignored by everyone else," or the vestigial role of Piedmontese Judeo-Italian locutions among Primo Levi's ancestors, recounted in the first chapter of his memoir *Il sisteme periodico* (The Periodic Table).[60]

Postvernacular engagements with language inevitably engender different kinds of cultural practices from those of the native speaker or even the schooled vernacular speaker. In this regard, postvernacularity can be a liberating concept, prompting possibilities of language use other than the vernacular model of full fluency in an indigenous mother tongue. Thus, postvernacularity has important implications for the interrelation of language, culture, and identity—indeed, for the notion of what might constitute a "speech community"—especially for a language such as Yiddish, which has been so extensively and exclusively associated with Ashkenazic folkhood.

Yiddish actor and radio announcer Zvee Scooler in the studio of radio station WEVD, New York City, in the mid-1960s, holding a copy of *Instant Yiddish*. This sound recording, scripted by Fred Kogos, features Scooler and actress Maria Karnilova in a series of lessons in conversational Yiddish. The album jacket explains that "you don't have to be Jewish to speak Yiddish." Courtesy of the Theatre Collection, Museum of the City of New York.

To understand postvernacularity it is therefore essential not to regard it as any less valid than vernacular engagement with language. In particular, postvernacular Yiddish is distinguished from its vernacular use, as well as from the use of other languages of daily life employed by Jews today, by virtue of its being motivated so prominently by desire. Increasingly, speaking, reading, writing—even hearing—Yiddish has become an elective act. Relatively few Jews now use Yiddish because it is the only language that they have for communication with other Jews, nor is Yiddish thrust on its speakers by any polity. Rather, those who use Yiddish (including a noteworthy number of non-Jews) do so voluntarily, as communities, as families, and as individuals. Understanding postvernacular Yiddish, then, requires investigation into the desires of those who choose to pursue it. What is it that draws people to sign up for Yiddish language classes, to attend Yiddish festivals, to organize Yiddish conversation groups, to support the rescue of abandoned Yiddish books, to purchase mock Yiddish dictionaries, to compose pious songs and plays in Yiddish, to subscribe to Yiddish periodicals, to translate works of world literature into Yiddish, or to tune into Yiddish radio programs via the Internet? The great variety of activities and agents involved in postvernacular Yiddish culture suggest a complex of motives; taken together, what do they reveal about Jewish culture at the turn of the twenty-first century, especially at a time when those who remember prewar Yiddish culture make up an aging, declining population?

. . .

These are daunting questions to tackle, and not merely because Yiddish culture has become so diverse, at times even contradictory, in its range of practices. The greatest challenge, I believe, is to assess recent Yiddish culture without judging it from pre-Holocaust perspectives. This challenge calls for a special effort to discuss what contemporary Yiddish culture *is*, rather than what it *isn't*. That being said, it would be naïve to sever all consideration of post-Holocaust Yiddish culture from its prewar past, especially because the contemporary culture is shaped to such a great extent by efforts to engage with Jewish life "before" (not only before World War II, but also before the Bolshevik Revolution, World War I, the era of mass immigration to America, the Haskalah, the advent of hasidism, the Cossack massacres in Ukraine, the arrival of Jews in Poland, the Crusades). Taking into account the extensive retrospection of contemporary Yiddish culture calls for careful consideration of the "past" and "present" as constructs. The boundaries separating them, which seem etched indelibly into the history of Yiddish—especially by the Holocaust—need to be scrutinized to determine whether they are as definitive as they seem. In fact, some issues that one might expect to have arisen only after the Holocaust—such as concerns about the decreased use of Yiddish and the loss of it as an idiomatic and indigenous vernacular—turn out to have been expressed with as profound a sense of urgency well before World War II. But what does it mean to voice such anxieties at, say, the turn of the twentieth century as opposed to at the turn of the twenty-first?

Not only do these issues need to be situated in historical context; their intentions require analysis as well. Worries about the decline of a language are inevitably tied to extralinguistic concerns. For generations, much of the discussion of Yiddish has been in part a symbolic endeavor, in which the language stands in for Jewish culture or politics more generally or for Jewish people themselves. For example, the enduring fascination with non-Jews who know Yiddish, while Jews' command of the language is in decline (recently exemplified by the attention to U.S. Secretary of

State Colin Powell's knowledge of the language or singer Madonna performing Yiddish songs), betokens larger questions about Jewish literacy and identity.[61] An analysis of the state of Yiddish in recent times is also, therefore, an examination of what now constitutes Jewish culture as a set of definitional practices.

Moreover, this analysis makes for a revealing case study of how people conceptualize the interrelation of language, culture, and identity when the widely held notion that these are somehow mutually constitutive has been disrupted. For the people in question, this situation raises provocative questions: When a language no longer seems inevitable, rooted, indigenous, but appears instead to be fading, moribund, or even dead, what are the implications for its attendant culture? Conversely, when they perceive their culture as being in crisis, neglected, or vanquished, what do they see as the consequences for the culture's relationship to language? Studying this phenomenon calls for interrogating these questions and addressing others as well: How are the people in question affected by these pronouncements of loss, by the undoing of the definitional ties that bind them to a certain language and culture? As a result of this disruption, how do these people reconceptualize language and culture, so that they might still be meaningful in relation to one another and meaningful to this people's collective sense of self?

These questions speak to a growing challenge for humankind generally, as we confront language loss on a global scale with unknown consequences for the richness and variety of human culture.[62] With regard to Yiddish, this investigation has a specific urgency now, with the approach of yet another threshold in the language's turbulent annals—the eventual passing of the last native speakers of Yiddish who acquired and used the language in prewar Eastern Europe. Well before World War II, Eastern Europe was widely regarded as the Yiddish "heartland," even as millions of its inhabitants fled geographically, ideologically, and linguistically. The value then invested in Yiddish Eastern Europe as an indigenous fountainhead of Jewish linguistic and cultural authenticity was evinced by writers' and researchers' repeated efforts to document this way of life, which was perceived, since the mid-nineteenth century, as being ever on the verge of disappearing.[63] Even so, the extensive devastation of people, places, and institutions wrought so swiftly and cruelly during the Holocaust is of such a magnitude that all previous notions of loss in this culture—including the extensive upheavals of World War I—pale in comparison. If the finality of the Holocaust for "authentic" Yiddish seems to many to be self-evident, how have those committed to Yiddish answered this most daunting challenge in its long history, and how might they continue to do so in the future?

Ascertaining the nature of something as protean as postvernacular Yiddish calls for an equally adventurous, expansive approach, looking across cultural genres, languages, ideologies, and national boundaries, as well as drawing on resources from various scholarly disciplines. *Adventures in Yiddishland* examines an array of cultural undertakings in Europe, the (former) Soviet Union, the Americas, Palestine/Israel, and elsewhere throughout the twentieth century and into the present, as practiced in Jewish communities ranging from ardent secularists to *khareydim* and among non-Jews as well. The analysis is informed by the work of historians, literary scholars, linguists, sociologists, anthropologists, folklorists, and an array of cultural theoreticians.

However, this book does not strive to offer a comprehensive inventory or chronicle of Yiddish activities of the past six decades. Rather, the approach is selective, focusing on particular phenomena that best demonstrate the use and significance of Yiddish as a postvernacular language (as opposed to, say, centering the study on those examples of Yiddish culture considered to be the most popular or accomplished). Moreover, this book's selective approach reflects a special interest in tracking the dynamics of postvernacular Yiddish. In particular, this focus entails a shift away from Eastern Europe and toward other centers of Yiddish culture, especially in America, as the geography of Yiddish was reconfigured over the course of the past half-century. My focus on Yiddish in America reflects a larger reconfiguring of the global Jewish diaspora following World War II, which placed the United States at its center—even as it was juxtaposed against a new center of Jewish life in Israel.[64] Related to this geographical development is an equally important shift in the international vernacular shared by the majority of the world's Jews from Yiddish to English over the course of the twentieth century.[65]

Adventures in Yiddishland organizes the analysis of postvernacular Yiddish according to key activities that span the full spectrum of modern Yiddish culture. Each chapter focuses on a particular activity, broadly defined—such as Yiddish pedagogy (chapter 2) or practices of materializing the language (chapter 5)—and examines how it has been engaged across temporal, geographical, generic, and ideological boundaries. While linked to the others as part of a multifaceted approach to the larger topic at hand, each chapter constitutes a self-sufficient study with its own parameters, gauged to its particular subject. Thus, the examination of translation (chapter 3) traces the dynamics of translating literary works into and from Yiddish from the sixteenth century to the present, in order to consider how changes in writing, reading, and publishing practices are implicated in the shifting meanings assigned to Yiddish as a literary language. In contrast, the analysis of performing Yiddish (chapter 4) concentrates on very recent phenomena, since these evince an unprecedented degree of self-consciousness with regard to the challenges of employing this language in performance.

Chapter 1 of *Adventures in Yiddishland* considers the vital role that the imagination plays in facilitating postvernacular Yiddish culture by focusing on how the idea of Yiddishland has been articulated, both explicitly and implicitly, in twentieth-century Jewish culture. The conjuring of Yiddishland proves to be a wide-ranging enterprise, manifest in political and literary writing, as well as in an array of cultural phenomena, including maps, children's games, public displays, and websites. These practices, and their implications of associating notions of territoriality and sovereignty with language use, change fundamentally after World War II; taken together, though, these various Yiddishlands reveal both the power and the limitations of the imagination to create a virtually indigenous place for Yiddish.

The second chapter traces the dynamics of Yiddish-language pedagogy. Long regarded as something Ashkenazim acquired "natively," Yiddish became a subject taught in classrooms to young Jews at the turn of the twentieth century, a development that epitomizes its speakers' engagement in the "modern Jewish revolution." The advent of Yiddish pedagogy thus marks both a new valuation of the language as a *folkshprakh* and, at the same time, the destabilization of this notion, epitomized by the advent of Yiddish studies in universities in Europe, Israel, and North America after World War II. Yiddish pedagogy also provides a strategic opportunity for tracking shifting notions of the symbolic value of the language as it passes from one generation to the next, configured variously as an emblem of emergent Jewish nationalism, an exercise of homage to ethnic heritage, or, among *khareydim,* a bulwark securing religious tradition.

Chapter 3 considers the role that literary translations from and into Yiddish have played in the conceptualization of Yiddish culture, beginning with the earliest works of Yiddish literature in print and concluding with certain recent translations of works of world literature into Yiddish, which exemplify postvernacularity's distinctive privileging of a language's symbolic level of meaning. Translations also provide the opportunity to consider the significance of Yiddish in relation to other languages. The presentation and reception of all the texts in question demonstrate cultural negotiations at linguistic frontiers, in which the act of translation takes on the contradictory symbolic values of continuity and homage, versus rupture and betrayal. These issues assume added importance in the post–World War II era, given postvernacular Yiddish culture's inherent reliance on other languages as means of communication at the primary level.

In the fourth chapter the role that a wide variety of public performances—including festivals, concerts, workshops, and retreats—play in contemporary Yiddish culture is scrutinized. These events transform the vernacular use of Yiddish through practices in which the language, rather than serving as a means of performance, has become the performance's end. Often this transformation entails the professionalization of speaking Yiddish as a performance skill; at other times, it involves complementing or even replacing spoken Yiddish with other forms of communication, including nonverbal ones, such as instrumental music or dance. The study of these recent events reveals how, in the postvernacular mode, the uttering of Yiddish is an increasingly self-conscious practice, since saying something in Yiddish has become a noteworthy activity above and beyond what is being said.

Chapter 5 analyzes the wide-ranging material culture of Yiddish produced in post–World War II America, focusing on comic, lowbrow items (T-shirts, coffee mugs, novelty items, etc.). These realia provide an opportunity to consider how, as the language is atomized into a limited number of isolated words, vernacular Yiddish has been both fetishized and mocked. This practice, also manifest in a sizeable inventory of comic Yiddish dictionaries, expands the meaning of individual words and idioms while telescoping the meaningfulness of Yiddish as a full language, transforming it into a signifier of the carnivalesque in contemporary Jewish life. In addition to the insights these objects offer into the meaning of Yiddish in American Jewish popular culture during the past six decades, they demonstrate how new, growing forms of Jewish culture—here, the creation, promotion, purchasing, and collecting of objects—interface with cultural practices that have atrophied—in this instance, Yiddish fluency.

The final chapter interrogates the theorizing of Yiddish, beginning with its pervasive characterization as a moribund language—a trope that began to be sounded just as Yiddish culture flourished with unprecedented innovation and energy at the turn of the twentieth century. In addition to analyzing the implications of this problematic trope's long-standing appeal, this chapter considers a variety of recent alternative models for discussing the state of Yiddish. These appear in analytic and conjectural writings and also emerge from various cultural practices, including those of two disparate contemporary American Jewish subcultures examined here: ultra-Orthodox yeshivas and queer Jews. The chapter concludes with a summary of the contributions that postvernacularity offers as a model for characterizing the nature of contemporary Yiddish and thinking about the possibilities of its future.

In sum, *Adventures in Yiddishland* strives to assess changes that Yiddish has undergone since the end of World War II and to offer perspectives on the nature of the language now, at another threshold moment in its remarkable history. I hope that this book will provide insights to scholars studying this as well as other languages and to all those pursuing their own adventures in the realm of Yiddish.

CHAPTER ONE

IMAGINING YIDDISHLAND

The postvernacular mode prompts us to rethink the possibilities of language. The implications of this exercise are of particular importance to Yiddish, since ideas about what roles it might play in Jewish culture shifted radically during the past century. Once widely regarded as a central force, in mid-century Yiddish was abruptly displaced. Other linguistic prospects—especially the establishment of the State of Israel, with Hebrew as its official language, and the greater importance of English as a language for Jewish culture internationally—just as swiftly came to the fore. In the post–World War II era, testing this new configuration of what does—and does not—seem possible for Jewish language has at times proved remarkably daunting, challenging even the powers of the imagination.

Thus, one of the more surprisingly provocative phenomena of Yiddish culture since World War II is a small paperback entitled *Say It in Yiddish*, a phrase book for travelers. This volume, part of a Dover Publications series (which includes over two dozen languages, among them modern Hebrew, Indonesian, and Swahili), first appeared in 1958 and is still in print. The book was edited by linguist Uriel Weinreich, then Atran Chair of Yiddish Studies at Columbia University, and his wife, folklorist Beatrice Weinreich.

Almost forty years after its publication, *Say It in Yiddish* became the subject of some controversy, when author Michael Chabon discussed it in an essay that appeared in 1997, first in *Civilization*, a periodical published in association with the Library of Congress, and then, in abbreviated form, in *Harper's Magazine*.[1] In his essay, originally titled "Guidebook to a Land of Ghosts," Chabon both mocks and mourns *Say It in Yiddish*, which he introduces as "the saddest book that I own" and characterizes as a "tragic . . . joke," an "absurd, poignant artifact of a country that never was." Unaware of the potential audience for this volume, whether in the 1950s or today, he tries in vain to conjure imaginary environments in which a traveler might talk to an auto mechanic, dentist, or hair dresser in Yiddish. Accompanying illustrations by cartoonist Ben Katchor depict invented urban scenes with a telephone booth, cinema, bus, ferry, and factory, all sporting signs in Yiddish.[2] "This country of the Weinreichs is in the nature of a wistful fantasyland," Chabon argues, a counterfactual Europe where "the millions of Jews who were never killed produced grandchildren, and great grandchildren." Finding this vision "heartbreakingly implausible," he wonders, "Just what am I supposed to do with this book?"[3]

Chabon does not appear to have researched the history of *Say It in Yiddish;* had he done so, he would have learned that it was created not at the Weinreichs' initiative but at the request of Dover's founder and president, Hayward Cirker. Cirker envisioned the phrase book as being of practical value; Yiddish was widely spoken in Israel in the late 1950s, and there were substantial Yiddish-speaking communities in Paris, Montreal, Mexico City, Buenos Aires, and other places where someone who knew only English and had limited or no knowledge of Yiddish might find the volume useful. Moreover, Beatrice Weinreich recalls, Cirker regarded *Say It in Yiddish* as a symbolic gesture of his devotion to a language that he had learned as a child at home and in schools run by the Workmen's Circle.[4]

Say It in Yiddish is, arguably, an exercise in artifice—but then, the same can be said for any such phrase book offering travelers the false promise that it provides sufficient skills for conversing in a language they don't know. Even so, this book stands out as an example of the powerful and contentious role of the imaginary in Jewish culture, for *Say It in Yiddish* and its reception constitute an implicit exercise in imagining Yiddishland.[5] In his incredulous response to the book Chabon envisions a post-Holocaust milieu saturated with spoken Yiddish not simply as counterfactual but as untenable. His is not the reaction of an ideologist—say, a Hebraist or Zionist who cannot accept another vision of Jewish cultural or political nationalism as valid. Indeed, Chabon's essay evinces neither any particular Jewish ideological convictions nor any awareness of the range and tenacity of Yiddish in the six decades since World War II. On the latter issue, Chabon was taken to task by several impassioned letters to the editor printed in *Civilization* and *Harper's*. The authors of these letters argue that this "imaginary state" of Yiddish does, in fact, exist. One author, a resident of

Brooklyn's Boro Park, explains that *"Say It in Yiddish* is available in practically every bookstore" there and that she uses Yiddish "to communicate with my neighbors, children on the street, my grocer, the bus driver for the local private bus service, and the electrician who rewired my apartment. . . . We even have Yiddish-speaking cash machines at fourteen branches of our local bank."[6]

This and similar responses to Chabon's essay are not merely ripostes from devoted Yiddishists defending the viability of their beleaguered tongue. For what Chabon challenges, ultimately, is not the language's legitimacy or popularity, but rather the ability to conjure a homeland for Yiddish, with its implications of indigenousness, territoriality, and even sovereignty. To conjure this homeland is to flout the language's widespread association with marginality, mutability, or obsolescence, situating it—not only through one's use of Yiddish, but through one's convictions and, indeed, one's imagination—in a place of its own, in Yiddishland.[7]

Say It in Yiddish is neither the oldest nor the most recent example of imagining Yiddishland, which I define as a virtual locus construed in terms of the use of the Yiddish language, especially, though not exclusively, in its spoken form. (I once heard a student at the commencement of the YIVO Institute's Summer Program in Yiddish Language, Literature and Culture at Columbia University—in the late 1980s, I think—define Yiddishland as a place that comes into existence whenever two or more people speak Yiddish.)[8] The term *yidishland* does not appear in any Yiddish-language dictionary, and, while its meaning seems self-evident, it carries some noteworthy connotations.[9] To begin with, it resonates with a productive idiom in the language: *a(n)* X *fun* X-*land,* which means, according to Uriel Weinreich's *Modern English-Yiddish Yiddish-English Dictionary,* a "genuine, excellent, [or] outstanding" X (Weinreich offers the example *"a kukhn fun kukhnland"*—literally, a cake from cakeland—"an excellent cake").[10] Following this model, the phrase *yidish fun yidishland* would mean "genuine Yiddish" or perhaps "the epitome of Yiddish, Yiddish at its best," implying that *yidishland* is the language's ideal locus, a Yiddish utopia. (The meaning of this idiom can also be ironic, as is apparently the case in the earliest oblique reference to Yiddishland I have found. In a letter written in 1888 from Y. L. Peretz to Sholem Aleichem, the former describes the latter as an author whose "aim is to write for the public, which speaks *zhargon* [jargon, i.e., Yiddish] *fun zhargonen-land.*")[11]

At the same time, the term Yiddishland infers a highly contingent tenacity inherent in any spatial entity defined by language use. This notion has provocative implications, especially for Yiddish in its postvernacular mode: Does Yiddishland flicker on and off during a conversation, vanishing during pauses and interruptions?

What is the status of Yiddishland in a conversation in which one party speaks Yiddish and the other responds in another language? Does talking to oneself in Yiddish constitute Yiddishland, or is some sort of community, even a community of two, required? And what about thinking or dreaming in Yiddish?

Examples of the use of the term Yiddishland are noteworthy not only in their quantity but also in their variety and, moreover, in the range of implications inherent in their use. What does it mean, for example, when Benjamin and Barbara Harshav write of early-twentieth-century American Yiddish poets and their devotees that, for them, "literature was 'everything.' It was a substitute for religion and statehood, it was a state in itself, 'Yiddishland' "?[12] Or when film critic J. Hoberman describes Yiddish film as "not just a national cinema without a nation-state, but a national cinema that, with every presentation, created its own ephemeral nation-state. . . . Yiddish was not just a language and a folk culture but an entire Jewish world, a '*Yidishland*' "?[13] Or when Abraham Burg, at the time chair of the Education Committee of the Knesset, stated, as part of the Israeli legislature's "Homage to Yiddish" during a special session convened in 1993, that such terms used by Israeli Hebrew speakers as "Mapainik" (member of the Labor Party), "shvitzer" (show-off), and "kumsitz" (get-together) have "come from Yiddishland"?[14] And what is the significance of the Yiddishland Cafe run by the Workmen's Circle in Toronto, or of a recording label for Yiddish folksongs called Yiddishland Records, or of an email appeal from the Yiddishist organization Yugntruf to make reservations for its annual end-of-summer retreat in the Berkshires, *"kedey tsu voynen in 'yidish-land' af der vokh"* ("in order to live in 'Yiddishland' for the week")?[15] What do these and other uses of the term, whether direct or oblique, suggest about the power—and the limitations—of the imaginary to endow this language with the symbolic value of a native, sovereign territory? In the post-Holocaust era, how does conjuring Yiddishland defy the widespread consignment of Yiddish to obsolescence? And how can Yiddishland provide a home for this language in its postvernacular mode, wherein its secondary, meta-level of meaning is privileged over its significance as a language of Jewish daily life?

"THE KINGDOM OF THE YIDDISH WORD"

Imaginary engagement with Yiddishland is part of an extensive discourse linking language and homeland. This subject has proved especially productive in the modern era, involving Jews concerned with issues other than Yiddish (for example, literary scholar George Steiner's discussion of "the 'textuality' of the Jewish condi-

Flier announcing the grand opening of the Yiddishland Cafe, organized by the Workmen's Circle in Toronto, Canada, 1996.
Courtesy of the Toronto Workmen's Circle.

tion" as a sense of "at-homeness in the word" in his essay "Our Homeland, the Text"), and, of course, many people other than Jews, especially immigrants and refugees. Czesław Miłosz, for instance, wrote in Berkeley, California, of Polish: *"Moja wierna mowo, . . . Byłaś moją ojczyzną"* ("Faithful mother tongue, . . . You were my native land").[16]

At the same time, imagining Yiddishland must be considered within the larger issue of language and nationalism particular to the modern Jewish experience. In its earliest manifestations, the notion of Yiddishland is a product of the new ideas about Yiddish and its role in Jewish life that emerged in Eastern Europe at the turn of the previous century, ideas that gave rise to Yiddishism. Its adherents championed their native language as a distinctive cultural repository to be cultivated rather than condemned. Their commitment to a modern, often radically secularized, Jewish culture that placed Yiddish at its center was rooted in the language's long-standing East European indigenousness. Even so, Yiddishists offered as thoroughly transformed a vision of Jewish vernacularity as did Hebraists or linguistic assimilationists.

The very fact that the nativeness of Yiddish needed to be defended in Eastern Europe at this time evinces the extent to which the language debates of the era were tied to larger questions of modern Jewish nationhood, including questions about place. While the revival of a vernacular Hebrew came to be linked especially with Zionist plans to create a new Jewish state, Yiddishism was generally tied to a validation of Jewish life in diaspora, centered in Eastern Europe. The Jewish Workers' Bund—a socialist, secular, Yiddishist, pro-diaspora political party established in Russia in 1897 that would achieve its greatest influence in interwar Poland—articulated this notion most forthrightly in the first decades of the twentieth century. Through the diaspora nationalist principle of *doikeyt* (literally, "hereness" in Yiddish), Bundists asserted the right and the value of Jews to live "here"—that is, wherever they found themselves and, while engaging in modern international socialist activism, to maintain a distinctive secular culture, marked as Jewish by its own vernacular. In its very articulation, *doikeyt* implies Yiddishland.[17]

No more elaborate vision of the geopolitical implications of Yiddish can be found than in the writings of pioneering secular Yiddishist ideologist Chaim Zhitlowski; these are among the earliest published evocations of Yiddishland. In his 1913 essay "In a yidisher medine" (In a Jewish/Yiddish State), Zhitlowski characterizes the time and place of his childhood as a model of Jewish cultural and socioeconomic autonomy centered on the Yiddish language:

> I spent my childhood years in a purely Jewish/Yiddish environment *[in a reyn yidisher svive]*. Had I not known that, in theory, we Jews lived in diaspora, and had I been asked to characterize my life's experiences as they appeared at first glance, I would then have had a right to say that I live in a Jewish/Yiddish country *[a yidish land]*. For there was so little sense of exile in our region of Belorussia in the years between 1865 and the end of the 1870s . . . [that it seemed as though we Jews] did not live in exile among the Russians, but perhaps quite the opposite—that the Russians with whom we interacted lived in exile among us, in our own Jewish/Yiddish country *[in unzer eygn yidish land]*. . . . We Jews [were] the ruling people, if not in the political sense, then at least in the economic, national, and cultural sense. . . . [Many of the non-Jews with whom we dealt] spoke the ruling language of the land—Yiddish—and in fact quite a fine Yiddish, spiced with appropriate idioms.[18]

Zhitlowski roots his vision of Yiddishland in a personal remembrance of a specific historical and geographical locus, which serves as a model for how Yiddish might function, in later times and other places, as the basis of an autonomous Jewish cultural community with the attributes, if not the actuality, of nationhood. This exercise in conjuring Yiddishland exemplifies Benedict Anderson's notion of "imagined communities" as fundamental to the nature of nationalism. Anderson is quick to point out that the role played by the imagination here ought not to be disparaged as falsehood but, rather, is inherent in the process: "All communities larger than primordial villages of face-to-face contact (and perhaps even these) are imagined. Communities are to be distinguished not by their falsity/genuineness, but by the style in which they are imagined."[19] Central to the style of Zhitlowski's imagined community, distinguishing it from most of the places that Anderson discusses, is the strategic use of the term *yidish* in this passage. For Zhitlowski, the tautology of language and people embodied in this term (which is undone in English, Hebrew, and other languages that distinguish between "Yiddish" and "Jewish") epitomizes the power of language to realize Jewish sovereignty in the face of the widespread perception of Jews as a people without a land.

Indeed, one of the particular challenges of imagining Yiddishland is the question of how one might either situate it in some geographically specific locus or develop an alternative vision that somehow thrives despite geography. Birobidzhan—the Soviet Union's Jewish Autonomous Region, formally established in far eastern Russia on the Manchurian border in 1934—might seem to be a case of Yiddishland realized, however incompletely and problematically (and if so, one might also include other Jewish agricultural colonies founded by Yiddish-speaking Jews elsewhere in the Soviet Union, as well as in the Americas). Yiddish did not merely figure in propaganda on behalf of this most elaborate effort to establish a Soviet alternative to a Zionist homeland in Palestine (indeed, one Soviet official adapted Zionist rhetoric in formulating recruiting slogans for Birobidzhan, such as *"Tsu a yidish land"* [To a Jewish/Yiddish land]).[20] The language also "was intended to serve as the bedrock of a secular, proletarian Soviet Jewish culture and community."[21] In its heyday, Birobidzhan boasted a Yiddish theater, library, school system, and even a Yiddish teachers' college. The region published its own Yiddish newspaper, and all official documents (including postmarks) were to be in both Russian and Yiddish. One of Birobidzhan's main thoroughfares was named after Sholem Aleichem, and public signage on buildings and streets included their Yiddish names printed in the *alefbeys* (the Jewish alphabet).

But if Yiddishland is understood as a site, whether actual or virtual, defined by language use, Birobidzhan and other such settlements do not meet this primary criterion in its strictest sense. For in these instances, turf, not language, is the defining matrix. It is not simply that Birobidzhan constituted an imposition of territorial autonomy from outside the community (i.e., Stalin's answer to Zionism) or that the stature of Yiddish as an official language was never fully realized there. The pres-

Directional signs in Yiddish
and English, Kinder Ring
summer camp, Sylvan
Lake, New York, 2000.
Photograph by Jeffrey Shandler.

ence of Yiddish in Birobidzhan was not what called it into existence as a Jewish territory but rather what was called on to mark it as such.[22] Similarly, Jewish agricultural colonies in Ukraine (Dzhankoiia), Argentina (Moisésville), or the United
States (Woodbine, New Jersey), where Yiddish was spoken during the early twentieth century, did not constitute Yiddishlands any more (or less) than did urban immigrant enclaves in New York City's Brownsville, London's Whitechapel, or the
Marais in Paris. Whatever their impulses toward socioeconomic autonomy, the establishment of these Jewish agricultural colonies was not driven by Yiddish; rather,
the language followed along as a consequence of being the communities' vernacular. The rise and fall of these sites as Jewish settlements or territories did not depend
on, nor were they necessarily concomitant with, the use of Yiddish.

By contrast, Yiddishist summer camps in the Americas are closer to the essence
of Yiddishland as communities that, however temporary and limited in scope, come
into existence out of a commitment to the language. Historian Jenna Joselit characterizes these camps as the "equivalent of a *shtetl*": "campers encountered a world in
which . . . buildings and walkways carried the names of legendary Jewish person-
alities" and Yiddish could be "heard on the baseball diamond and on the stage."[23]
Some of these camps—Kinderland, Boiberik (the name of Sholem Aleichem's fic-

tional Ukrainian resort community), Nit Gedayget (literally, "Don't worry," named after a fictional Soviet agricultural colony in works by Yiddish writer Peretz Markish)—bear names that invoke both territoriality and playfulness. The names of other camps—Nayvelt (New World) in Ontario and Yidishland in Argentina—are more forthrightly utopian.[24]

While not as turf-centered as political Zionism or Territorialism, Yiddishland nevertheless has delimited geographic and demographic implications that distinguish it from, say, the imagined nationless, panethnic utopia of Esperantists. At the same time that notions of Yiddishland often evoke expansive political and cultural impulses (as is the case in progressive Yiddishist summer camps), they remain tied to some retrospective notion of folkhood rooted in Eastern Europe. However, this geographic specificity has become increasingly attenuated over time, as the political, social, and economic map of Eastern Europe has been repeatedly redrawn. In addition, generations of migration, both within this region (as many Jews moved from small towns and villages to major cities) and outward to other countries and continents, have taken Jews far from milieus where the language and its speakers thrived for centuries. These developments have prompted speakers of Yiddish to reconfigure its relationship to former notions of home, often relying on language to compensate for geographical disorientation and displacement—even within the East European "heartland" of Yiddish. In this respect, Yiddish has faced a challenge different from that confronting such minority European languages as Catalan or Welsh, whose speakers for the most part continue to live in highly localized, indigenous regions. In such cases, the physical landscape plays a key role in maintaining a language (as when residents use it to name rivers, towns, streets, subway stations, and so on), and linguistic projects, such as securing state funding for native-tongue schooling, are often bound up with struggles to maintain cultural or political autonomy.[25] By contrast, Yiddishland is defined by geographical instability and contingency.

Therefore, the willfully paradoxical existence of Yiddishland is exemplified as much by the utopian exercises of agricultural colonies and summer camps as by interwar Yiddishists' devotion to the city of Vilna—an important center of Ashkenazic life and culture since the sixteenth century and, according to legend, proclaimed the Jerusalem of Lithuania by no one less than Napoleon—as "the capital of Yiddishland." In an enthusiastic report for the Warsaw cultural weekly *Literarishe bleter* on the YIVO Institute's 1935 international conference—characterized as "a lively, colorful map of Yiddishland, with representatives from America, Palestine, Lithuania, Estonia, Argentina, Rumania, France, Austria"—Yankev Botoshanski notes that the ideals of Yiddishism under discussion at the conference have no better advocate than the city where the institute was then headquartered. Vilna "represented and demonstrated 'Yiddishland,' which appeared, despite all crises and assaults, to be alive."[26]

The tenacity of Vilna's interwar Yiddishist culture seems only to have enhanced its reputation as a "citadel of Yiddish" among admirers and critics alike. During her studies at YIVO the year before the outbreak of World War II, historian Lucy Dawidowicz characterized this "autonomous Yiddish realm that happened to be located in Poland" as an exception in Polish Jewry's commitment, both symbolic and instrumental, to the language. Moreover, she concluded (though perhaps only after the war) that this Yiddishist vision was an untenable fantasy promoted by ideologists: "The YIVO has created an illusion, at least in Vilna, that there's a Jewish people which earns its daily bread in Yiddish and takes pleasure in using its own language for matters of mind and spirit. I know that it's only an illusion because the headlines in the daily papers belie it every day."[27]

As a locus defined by language, Yiddishland flourished most readily during the pre–World War II era on the printed page and in the minds of an extensive and widely scattered readership. Though the term *yidishland* appears seldom in Yiddish prose, when it does its meaning is self-evident. Thus, Dovid Gubalnik's introduction to a Yiddish translation of Juliusz Słowacki's long narrative poem *Ojciec Zadżumionych* (Father of the Lepers), published in 1938 in Beresteczko, Poland, praises the work of the translator, "because he has brought to the Yiddish reader one of the most ingenious poems in world literature and thereby enriched the literature in translation in Yiddishland."[28] That same year, Yitskhok Grudberg reported in *Literarishe bleter* on the dearth of organized Yiddish culture in Vienna, characterizing it as "a declining city in Yiddishland."[29]

Literary images of Yiddishland are articulated most extensively and imaginatively in poetry. Yiddish poems written about the Yiddish language (a remarkably extensive subgenre of Yiddish belles lettres) frequently employ territorial images of Yiddish, explicitly or implicitly identified as Yiddishland.[30] In his undated poem titled "Yiddish" (probably written in the 1930s), the American Yiddish poet Abraham Reisen lauds the language as a portable homeland. Reisen's Yiddishland is realized in the familiar sounds of spoken and sung Yiddish as well as in its press and literature ("Peretz, Mendele, all the rest, / They're my home—my Yiddishland"), which provide the author with a universal sense of at-homeness ("I'm not a stranger anywhere, / With Yiddish as my guide").[31]

The Yiddish language and its attendant culture are characterized in more specifically geographical imagery in A. Almi's 1930 poem, also titled "Yiddish": "An empire of scattered, beautifully blossoming islands. . . . / Its playful streams and rivers / Course through the great oceans." These lines lead to a gazetteer of the Yiddish-speaking diaspora that starts in Eastern Europe and extends outward to the Americas, Africa, and Asia:

Along the Vistula, along the Dniester and the Dnieper,
Along the Thames, Hudson, Mississippi,
On the plateau, in the chain of the proud Andes . . .
In Siberia and in the splendid Caucasus . . .
In the tropical heat of Africa and in Rio de Janiero,
In Mexico, in Cuba and Canada—
Yiddish . . . makes the rockiest soil bear fruit.

Almi's poem ends with the author's wish to "rise up to the greatest heights" so as to observe this "scattered empire," with its "blossoming islands, rivers, gulfs, streams."[32] Other interwar Yiddish poems offer similar visions of Yiddishland, chronicling its centuries-old history and inventorying its international diaspora, bravely championing the tenacity of the language (and, implicitly, of its speakers) in the wake of recent decades of upheaval and in the face of looming danger in its East European heartland. These poems epitomize literary scholar Sidra Ezrahi's observations about the particular value of creating "imaginative space" in modern Jewish letters. She argues that "writing the exile," the literary project of such pioneering authors of modern Yiddish literature as Sholem Yankev Abramovitsh and Sholem Aleichem, was "more than a response to displacement," becoming "in itself a form of repatriation, of alternative sovereignty."[33]

Poetic conjurings of Yiddishland continued to appear after World War II, as can be seen in one of the more elaborate self-reflexive literary works in Yiddish, Leon Feinberg's cycle of fifty poems—again, titled *Yidish*—which praises this "language of languages" as it chronicles its literary riches, from the works of sixteenth-century Venetian poet Elijah Levita to those of Abraham Sutzkever. On the cover of this work, published in New York in 1950, the title *Yidish* appears superimposed on a map of the world, on which various cities (including Montreal, Mexico City, Kiev, and Warsaw) are identified. Beneath this appears a quatrain, limning the worldwide dimensions of a valiantly defiant Yiddishland:

ל. פיינבערג

פּאָעמע

פֿון ווילנע ביז בוענאָס־איירעס,
פֿון תּל־אָביב אַן ביז גױאָרק ·
האָט אױסגעשפּרײט זיך—נס פֿון דורות—
דאָס קיניגרײך פֿון י י ד י ש ־ װאָרט.

Cover illustration of Leon Feinberg's narrative poem, *Yidish*, published in New York in 1950.

From Vilna to Buenos Aires,
From Tel Aviv to New York,
The miracle of generations has spread—
the kingdom of the *Yiddish* word.[34]

"THE NATIONAL LANGUAGE OF NOWHERE"

Feinberg's poems notwithstanding, imagining Yiddishland has become a very different sort of cultural exercise after World War II. Before the war notions of Yiddishland were tied, directly or indirectly, to the existence of an extensive speech community centered in Eastern Europe. Despite the upheavals of mass emigration, war, and the demands of the modern Jewish revolution, this was still a place that millions of Yiddish-speaking Jews called home, and it appeared that they would continue to do so. But after the Holocaust, conjuring Yiddishland has become more of an exercise in memory, one that entails imagining a speech community in situ (however it might be configured) in the absence of its centuries-old East European center and, sometimes, in the absence of Yiddish speakers as well. Postwar examples of Yiddishland therefore constitute a new order of cultural endeavor; they chart the range and dynamics of what Yiddish has come to signify in Jewish life after the Holocaust, as they demonstrate the strengths and limitations of this construct of the cultural imaginary.

Whereas prewar Yiddishlands projected utopian visions rooted in a vernacular actuality, postwar Yiddishlands often must engage imaginatively with vernacularity itself. Consequently, many of them are realized in different cultural genres and practices from those of the prewar era. In particular, more recent examples of Yiddishland frequently entail some extralinguistic activity or involve language use differently. This development does not simply reflect a decline in the use of Yiddish; it also testifies to the advent of new ways of engaging with the language that do not rely, as prewar examples typically did, on a shared fluency in Yiddish as a vernacular. In most postwar examples of Yiddishland, Yiddish is engaged, albeit often implicitly, as a postvernacular language. These efforts foreground the symbolic worth of Yiddish, sometimes overwhelming its use as the traditional everyday language among Ashkenazim.

Despite—and also precisely because of—the extensive physical destruction of the European Yiddish environment during World War II, construing the language in geographic terms flourished in the early postwar years. Two very different kinds of mapping projects undertaken at the time offer complementary topographical visions of Yiddishland. First are the maps of individual towns that appear in hundreds of *yisker-bikher*, collaboratively produced memorial books, most of them written entirely or in part in Yiddish, which recall prewar Jewish life in East European cities and towns. These volumes began to be produced in large numbers by immigrants and survivors from these communities after World War II. As anthropologists Jack Kugelmass and Jonathan Boyarin observe, these maps vary considerably in appearance: "Sometimes these are regional, showing the relation of the town to neighboring locations. Others are free-style, schematic representations of the town's layout. For smaller communities, these may show each house and be numerically coded to match a listing of each homeowner's name. Others show cows, crosses, gravestones and the like to represent the locations of pastures, churches, and cemeteries."[35] A common feature of these maps is that they are almost all drawn entirely from memory. Moreover, they all chart local Jewish geography, prominently indicating its landmarks—synagogues, cemeteries, schools, bathhouses, kosher slaughterhouses, and the like—some of which might never appear on an official municipal map of the same locality. Some of these maps also give the Yiddish names that were used for streets and other geographic features, which likewise often differ from their official names in Polish, Russian, and so forth. Typically reproduced on the

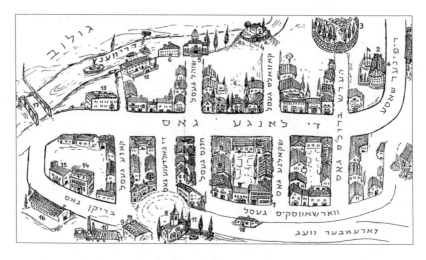

Map of Dobrzyn, from *Ayarati: sefer zikaron le-ayarot Dobrzyn-Golub* (My Town: Memorial Book for the Towns of Dobrzyn-Golub), published in Israel by the Association of Former Residents of Dobrzyn-Golub in 1969.

endpapers of *yisker-bikher,* these maps enclose the volumes' memoirs, photographs, and lists of names within the frame of an implicit, localized Yiddishland.

In contrast, the *Language and Culture Atlas of Ashkenazic Jewry (LCAAJ)*—delineates Yiddishland on a grand scale. This elaborate research project was initiated by Uriel Weinreich at Columbia University in the late 1950s.[36] Working with responses from over six hundred native informants to an extensive questionnaire (some 220 pages long), the *LCAAJ* maps regional variations in Yiddish language and culture across the European continent, ranging from phonological, lexical, and grammatical differences in dialect to an array of folkloric beliefs and practices (e.g., whether or not it was local practice to put sugar in gefilte fish and what games of chance were played on Hanukkah). While the *LCAAJ*'s central intellectual goal is to demonstrate the diachronic substructure inherent in the configuration of modern European Yiddish dialects, the project also makes an important symbolic statement about the territoriality of Yiddish. Writing about the *LCAAJ* in 1963, Weinreich noted that it had been rejected for funding under the National Defense Education Act: "Show us the country in which Yiddish is an *official* language, say the strategists in Washington, and we will gladly include it in the list of critical tongues along with Gujerati, Khalkha, Twi, and the like. But merely because an exclusive Yiddish area does not appear on any administrative map, is the humanistic relevance of this culture to be denied?"[37]

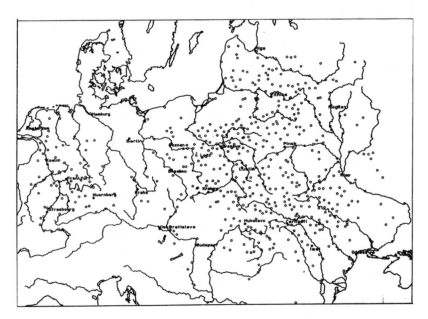

Base map of the *Language and Culture Atlas of Ashkenazic Jewry.* Each dot locates the hometown of one of the hundreds of European Jewish informants interviewed about their local Yiddish dialect and Jewish folkways.
Courtesy of Max Niemeyer Verlag and the editors of the *Language and Culture Atlas of Ashkenazic Jewry.*

Weinreich went on to argue that it is precisely the "lack of a self-contained territory" that endows the project "with exemplary value for a particularly crucial problem in social history: the effect of communication channels and barriers on the diffusion of cultural innovations. . . . The geographic fragmentation of a culture and a language thus yields an opportunity to reconstruct the influences of neighboring localities upon one another." The Ashkenazim of Europe provide "a rare instance of [such] temporal and spatial overlapping on a sweeping scale." Moreover, Weinreich argued, preliminary data demonstrated that cultural "variation is not individual or local, but conforms to definite regional patterns" and that this has implications for understanding the relationship of culture and territory not just for this subject, but for social science in general. In addition to giving Yiddishland an impressive geographic measure—characterized as "eventually coming to occupy a European area second in size only to the Russian one"—the *LCAAJ* situates the language's diasporic territoriality as strategic to understanding the interrelation of Ashkenazic society with its European neighbors across time and space.[38]

During the early postwar years the physical reality of East European Jewish life was rendered ethereal by popular works of nostalgia and beatific elegies—for example, Abraham Joshua Heschel's assertion in his 1950 book, *The Earth Is the Lord's,* that these Jews "lived more in time than in space."[39] The maps in *yisker-bikher* and in the *LCAAJ* not only offer reminders of the geographic presence of millions of Yiddish-speaking Jews throughout prewar Eastern Europe from a displaced, retrospective vantage, but they also provide imaginings of a pre-Holocaust Yiddishland on the local and continental scale.[40]

Mapping Yiddishland has taken other, more playful forms in recent years—most literally in the case of two Yiddish-language children's board games sold in Brooklyn, Montreal, and other major hasidic communities. The board of *Handl erlikh* (Deal Honestly) mimics the familiar layout of *Monopoly*; the game links adventures in real estate (here, too, players buy and charge rent for properties on which they erect little plastic houses and hotels) with lessons in proper social and business conduct (players must tithe all income, for instance).[41] The game's instruction booklet explains that it will "implant in children good character and reverence for God. Whoever deals honestly will have much success."[42] But whereas other imitations of *Monopoly* replace the streets of Atlantic City with those of New York, Chicago, or some other city, *Handl erlikh* enables players to acquire property from an international roster of sites located in a hasidic Yiddishland, both past (Cracow, Kuźnica, Leżajsk, Lublin, Rymanów) and present (Antwerp, Boro Park, London, Monsey, Montreal). Even as it assumes that its young players are fluent in Yiddish, *Handl erlikh* does not take language use for granted. The game reinforces the hasidic commitment to Yiddish as the proper Jewish vernacular by penalizing players for speaking either English or modern Hebrew—indeed, these are two of the more egregious sins for which a player is punished on the game's *kheẓhbn-hanefesh* (personal reckoning) cards.[43]

Kfitses haderekh (Shortcut), a Yiddish-language board game created in the mid-1990s, enables players to travel via airplane over a map to similar sites, including Muncacz, Czernowitz, Warsaw, Łódź, Budapest, Prague, and Frankfurt, thereby emulating the legendary shortcuts once taken by *rebeyim* (hasidic leaders) as they moved from one site of hasidic pilgrimage to another. The game's cards send players on virtual journeys, while imparting lessons in proper pious conduct (a sample travel tip is "Be sure to have your *tales* [prayer shawl] and *tfiln* [phylacteries] with you always") and introducing the history and geography of the pious Yiddish-speaking diaspora. In addition to cities and towns renowned as pre-Holocaust centers of hasidism are Vilna—home to "the holy Vilna Gaon," a champion of anti-hasidic rabbinism—and Raduń, where "the holy Hafez Hayyim," another influential Lithuanian talmudist, "taught about the harshness of slander."[44] In its reconfiguration of Europe (the game's map bears scant resemblance to a modern map of the same area), *Kfitses haderekh* enables players to explore the continent as a locus of Ashkenazic piety over the centuries, its contours limned by Yiddish and the religious communities that have thrived on the continent in this Jewish vernacular.

A very different kind of vicarious travel to a past Yiddishland—a place that can be reached "without passport or visa, without fear of being turned away, simply by turning back the clock"—is facilitated by Gérard Silvain and Henri Minczeles's 1999 volume titled *Yiddishland*, which reproduces photographs of prewar East European Jewish life found on hundreds of vintage postcards. Vestiges of an earlier era of tourism, these images are offered as documents of a lost world—indeed, even the acts of collecting and reprinting them are characterized as a cultural salvage operation: "Although Yiddishland had disappeared by the end of the Second World War, it lives on thanks to the millions of postcards found in attics and family archives or sold during publishers' stock clearances or liquidations. Despite their frozen imagery, these small cards faithfully re-create the immutable rhythms of the *shtetl*."[45] Silvain and Minczeles not only employ the term Yiddishland to define a place, a time, and a people (the book includes a map of Yiddishland's East European "heartland"); they also invest it with a complex symbolic value as a site of memory. In their prefatory remarks the authors describe Yiddishland as phantasmic (suggesting that it may or not be a "mythic country"), transcendent ("the intellectual luggage Jews took with them all over the world"), appealingly unofficial ("a territory without borders, army, or flag"), and evanescent (always "fragile and vulnerable").[46]

By rendering Yiddishland—a sense of place defined by speech—into a visual idiom, these maps, games, and cards all transform the significance of the concept as they translate its form. At the same time, there are telling differences between examples of Yiddishland that assume fluency in the language and those that do not. The Yiddishlands of *Handl erlikh* and *Kfitses haderekh* emphasize the continuity of observant Jewish life in the twentieth century, rooted in Yiddish as a shared language and in a familiarity with East European geographical sites as indexes of the teachings and practices of hasidism and other *khareydim*. Silvain and Minczeles's *Yiddishland*, in contrast, memorializes a break in continuity, revisiting pre-Holocaust Eastern Europe as the locus of a lost culture epitomized—indeed, defined—by its abandoned vernacular. Silvain and Minczeles's book, which addresses its reader in French (in its original edition) and through the complex semiotics of postcards, must therefore define its subject and its significance: "Yiddishland . . . is a cultural concept emanating from Yiddish. . . . Around the Yiddish language, there was Yiddishkeit, a pluralist cultural amalgam. Yiddishland was more than a country, it was an unknown continent."[47]

This need to define Yiddishland explicitly is a significant development of the postwar era; it evinces the advent of a postvernacular culture, in which efforts to conjure Yiddishland take place in languages other than Yiddish. Indeed, when the term Yiddishland is used in these other languages—especially those that have separate words for "Yiddish" and "Jewish"—it exposes the undoing of the tautological link between people and language implicit in Yiddish. At the same time, the separation of "Yiddish" from "Jewish" also has culturally liberating possibilities for imagining Yiddishland, which can become a locus of cultural alternatives to prevailing notions of Jewishness. Consider, for example, the following anecdotes, originally related in Yiddish by Abraham Sutzkever during a public program held in the poet's honor at New York's YIVO Institute in 1986:

> I remember, several years ago, when the Manger Prize was awarded in Tel Aviv, a young Hebrew poet—the daughter of Yiddish writer Leyb Rokhman, who signs her work "Miriam"—greeted those assembled in Yiddish and said the following: "Hebrew has a fatherland, and Yiddish is itself a fatherland."
>
> A similar incident—years ago I was strolling with a Yiddish writer, Yisroel Kaplan . . . around Jaffa. . . . We were speaking, of course, . . . in Yiddish. Two small children passed by, and they looked at us strangely. . . . A little girl . . . approached us, and she asked me [in Hebrew] what language we were speaking. My companion replied, "In Yiddish." "Oh," she said, "Now I understand. You've come from the Land of Yiddish [fun land Yidish]." It's . . . true: There is a land "Yiddish"; there is a fatherland "Yiddish."[48]

Even as they demonstrate how Yiddish has been separated from Israeli notions of Jewishness, these anecdotes evince the capacity for transforming what Yiddish can signify when it is no longer synonymous with Jewishness and no longer a prevailing Jewish vernacular. It has frequently been observed that, over the course of the twentieth century, "Hebrew and Yiddish have all but changed roles as Hebrew has become a spoken, accessible language and Yiddish has become the language that is primarily read by scholars and students."[49] This is a broad characterization of a more nuanced reality (in particular, contrasting Yiddish as an unofficial, diasporic lingua franca with Hebrew as a state-mandated language points up telling differences). Nevertheless, this observation testifies to a profound transformation of the meaning as well as use of these languages in relation to one another.

The notion of Yiddish and Hebrew having, in effect, traded places within the constellation of modern Jewish multilingualism, at least within the State of Israel, has particularly important implications for conceptualizing Yiddishland in the postwar era. At the beginning of the twentieth century Yiddish was rooted in an actual place—Eastern Europe, home to millions of Jews, the great majority of whom spoke and declared Yiddish as their mother tongue—while Hebrew belonged to the realms of Jewish imagination—both the Jewish state of the future promoted by political Zionists and the virtual realm of cultural Zionism. At the end of the century Hebrew had become the official language of an actual place—the State of Israel—while Yiddish had become the language of several imaginary worlds: the imagined milieu of East European Jewry before World War II (which is not entirely coterminous with the actual Eastern Europe, past or present); the diaspora of hasidim and other Ashkenazic *khareydim;* and secular Yiddishlands, both transcontinental and localized.

The realization of the Zionist "poetics of return" with the establishment of Israel poses a special challenge to the notion of Yiddishland, given what Sidra Ezrahi characterizes as a repudiation of the inherently mimetic nature of diasporic culture "in favor of a reclamation of 'original space.' " This development, she argues, "also activates, at the deepest level, a mechanism for renouncing the workings of the imagination, the invention of alternative worlds."[50] Conversely, the persistence of the idea of an indigenous place for Yiddish becomes much more provocative when juxtaposed against the actuality of a Hebrew-speaking Jewish polity.

For precisely this reason, however, the geographic uncanniness of Yiddish—what author Michael Wex archly terms "the national language of nowhere"—is essential to its appeal.[51] While imagining Yiddishland is not necessarily an anti-Zionist project, it does offer an alternative model of Jewish at-homeness, one that can exist not only instead of the State of Israel but also alongside and even within it. Indeed, the ways that Yiddishlands conceptualize Jewishness in spatial terms are radically different from political Zionist visions. Poems and maps of Yiddishland do not rejoice in the amassing of turf—in contrast, say, to early Jewish National Fund maps showing how many dunams of land its contributions had purchased in Palestine—but instead celebrate the great distances among its many outposts. Nor does Yiddishland paint an agrarianist vision of homeland; unlike the idyllic fields and orchards once depicted on Zionist fund-raising brochures, Yiddishland is in essence a cosmopolitan utopia. Almost all its major centers are cities, or, more specifically, urban neighborhoods, ethnic enclaves thick with Jews, their newsstands, theaters, cafés, union halls, schools, synagogues, bookstores—and their speech.

Thus, the virtual geographies of Yiddishland, whether they be projects of secular Yiddishists or of hasidim, are all conceived as existing somewhere beyond the shtetl. (This is true as well for *yisker-bikher,* which, even as they mourn the destruction of actual shtetlekh, acknowledge the existence of virtual shtetlekh, each town having its own diaspora, constituted by *landsmanshaftn* [immigrant mutual aid societies], communal cemetery plots, informal networks of immigrants and survivors, as well as the *yisker-bukh* itself.) The provincial market town in which the preponderance of East European Jews lived for centuries before the Holocaust is a locus left behind by Yiddishland—just as it is by Zionism, though their respective retrospections on the shtetl are quite different. The shtetl is Zionism's anti-home; in conjurings of Yiddishland, it is the Ur-home. As is true of modern Yiddish culture generally, the notion of Yiddishland emerged—and perhaps could only emerge— once Jews had begun to move out of shtetlekh, geographically as well as ideologically. Originally conceptualized as a point of common departure for modern East European Jews, the shtetl subsequently became a prime locus of symbolic return— especially after the Holocaust, when it came to be hallowed, in the words of linguists Gennady Estraikh and Mikhail Krutikov, "as the lost Yiddishland."[52]

VIRTUAL SHTETL

It is therefore a paradox of the postwar era that, as Jewish Eastern Europe has become ever more remote, the desire not merely to imagine it but to pay it a visit has grown stronger. Realizing this desire informs many of the most recent efforts at conjuring Yiddishland. As examples of postvernacular Yiddish culture, these undertakings typically depend on more than language, whether spoken or written, to facilitate the experience of inhabiting an imagined realm defined by the use of Yiddish. Increasingly, territoriality no longer suffices as a metaphor. Conjuring Yiddishland often pays at least as much attention to place (however limited and temporary) and the journey required to get there as its does to language.

Hence, the growing prominence of realizing the quest for Yiddishland in performance—such as Gernot Steinweg and Rea Karen's 1996 film *Reise nach Jiddischland* (Journey to Yiddishland), which follows a German Jewish boy's interest in learning to speak Yiddish with his grandparents, who live in Tel Aviv, or Nikolai Borodulin's "Trip to Yiddishland," an interactive program for American children and their parents, which "acquaints the participants with the life and customs of East

European Jews through Yiddish language and songs, visual aids, arts and crafts projects."[53] Often these enterprises rely on music, theater, dance, and other activities to provide an experience that stands in for lost time, place, and mores. The same applies to pursuits organized around quotidian Yiddish speech, such as Yugntruf's annual *yidish-vokh* (Yiddish week) retreat or Yiddish *shmues-krayzn* (conversation clubs), which meet weekly or monthly in many communities. These are all what sociologists term "time-out" activities—that is, events that take place outside the normal routine, which functions in some other language. In each instance, special arrangements must be made to create temporary environments in which Yiddish is once again, whether actually or symbolically, a community vernacular.

Similar to performed Yiddishlands (discussed in detail in chapter 4) are those centered on display, exemplified by the current headquarters of the National Yiddish Book Center (NYBC), built in the mid-1990s. Self-described as "a true *lebedike velt* [living world]," the NYBC is dedicated to making "the past thousand years of Jewish history come alive." The architecture of this implicit Yiddishland strives to transcend, even defy, the limits of space and time. The building's design pays homage to the wooden synagogues of northern Poland, perhaps the best-known example of shtetl architecture, and the structure is situated so that, according to its architect, Allen Moore, "once you start walking toward the building, you turn your back on the 20th century." (One NYBC board member characterized it as placing "an East European village on a New England campus.")[54] Yet even as it invokes a premodern, Old World diaspora, the NYBC constitutes a contemporary Yiddishland imagined in sovereign terms. (What, after all, is the nation that the *National* Yiddish Book Center serves?)[55]

A more explicit example of Yiddishland on display is a proposal made in the late 1990s by Eric Gordon, director of the Workmen's Circle in Los Angeles, to "mount a Yiddishland show," inviting people to "submit designs for a Yiddishland flag, a 'national' seal, an anthem, put them on display, [and] declare a winner," which would be determined by "panels of experts."[56] Such enterprises demonstrate the transvaluation of Yiddish from its status little more than a century ago as a vernacular struggling for recognition of its legitimacy to its current worth as a prized object of heritage. Indeed, they exemplify folklorist Barbara Kirshenblatt-Gimblett's characterization of heritage as a "mode of cultural production" that creates "something new" from the sites, objects, events, and practices of the past, transforming their value and giving them "a second life."[57]

The second life of heritage productions is, inevitably, never the same as the first. In the case of contemporary postvernacular Yiddishlands, their transvaluation of

Designs for Yiddishland stamps, created by Adam Whiteman of New York City in 1999. Whiteman's papercuts, a traditional East European Jewish folk art medium, depict Mirele Efros, Yosl Ber, and Gitl Puriskevitsh, three characters from Yiddish literature.
Courtesy of Adam Whiteman. All Rights Reserved.

Yiddish as heritage entails both gains and losses. On the one hand, Yiddishlands are often imagined in the postwar era as more exclusively Yiddish-speaking environments than were the original sites being invoked. A recent example of this dynamic was realized on the site of a former epicenter of prewar Yiddishland: *S'iz geven a nes* (It Was a Miracle), a musical revue about Jewish life in Eastern Europe before the Holocaust and in Israel afterward, staged by Warsaw's Ester-Rokhl Kaminska State Yiddish Theater in 1998.[58] The shtetl marketplace setting for the production's first act depicted all the signs for the various shops in Yiddish, although in actual shtetlekh such signage was usually in the local non-Jewish language.[59] During the late 1990s Yiddish speakers could also visit towns in Ukraine (including Pereyaslav, Uman', Berdychiv, Bratslav, Medzhybizh, Nemyriv, Vinnytsa) as part of a tour "In the Footsteps of Hassidic Masters and Yiddish Authors." Led in Yiddish by folklorist Dov Noy for the World Council for Yiddish Culture, the tour was, in essence, a pilgrimage to landmarks, both secular and sacred, of Yiddishland.[60] These and similar phenomena resonate with literary scholar Dan Miron's observation that Jewish literature on the shtetl, beginning in the latter half of the nineteenth century, tends to portray it as an "exclusively Jewish enclave . . . a *yidishe melukhe* [Jewish kingdom]" with non-Jews on the periphery or altogether absent. Miron characterizes this "radical Judaization" of the shtetl as responsive to "a compelling cultural need for such a belief."[61]

On the other hand, while some efforts to conjure Yiddishland entail what might be termed a "radical Yiddishization" of the East European Jewish past, the converse is also possible—a Yiddishland without Yiddish, wherein the language is invoked rather than used, becoming a signifier almost completely devoid of vernacular value but heavy with meta-meaning. Consider, for example, the Shtetl Museum, "an open-air Museum of East-European Jewish history and culture in the form of a life-size Shtetl," currently under construction on a sixty-seven-acre site in Rishon LeZion, the fourth largest city in Israel.[62] Scheduled to be completed in 2010, the Shtetl Museum will be a living history museum, modeled on Colonial Williamsburg or Plimoth Plantation, in which reenactors in period dress perform the daily tasks of a bygone way of life while also interacting with tourists.

This juxtaposition of the quotidian past and the touristic present poses a number of challenges for living history museums in general.[63] For the Shtetl Museum, it raises a particular problem: How will visitors and reenactors understand one another? In Plimoth Plantation, for example, Pilgrim reenactors speak various dialects of seventeenth-century English among themselves and when talking to visitors.[64] If the Shtetl Museum seeks to restore a similar linguistic authenticity, then its Jewish reenactors would speak a Lithuanian dialect of Yiddish most of the time, which most tourists would find unintelligible. Should the reenactors, then, speak modern Hebrew, the official language of the country in which the Shtetl Museum is being built? Or should they speak English, which has superceded Yiddish as the vernacular used by most of the world's Jews? (According to Yaffa Eliach, who conceived of the Shtetl Museum, as of December 2003 the issue of language use had yet to be resolved.)[65] That this most elaborate effort to provide entrée into the shtetl, "the lost Yiddishland," will in all likelihood do so without its original vernacular—indeed, the project has been elaborately conceived and initiated without tackling the question of language—testifies to a remarkable shift in contemporary Jewish culture more generally. Here, debating language is no longer a foremost defining issue; its former primacy in modern Jewish life (including that of the shtetl during the first decades of the twentieth century) has yielded to the importance of a totalizing, multisensory experience of place.

Most of the recent efforts to visit Yiddishland are tied, one way or another, to Eastern Europe. In some instances, elements of the East European terrain, actual or virtual, figure as reifications of Yiddish or of the people who once spoke Yiddish there, becoming what travel writer Ruth Ellen Gruber terms "a virtual Jewish world."[66] At the same time, Yiddishland is also flourishing in a new venue that privileges language over landscape: the Internet. Indeed, as virtual geographies defined by means of communication, the Internet and Yiddishland would seem to have a special affinity.

Since the advent of the Internet, Yiddish has been used and discussed on web-sites, discussion lists, online publications, and blogs. Here, too, Eastern Europe is sometimes invoked, as is the case at *Shtetl: Yiddish Language and Culture*. Online since July 1994, this "virtual shtetl" provides a wide range of information about Yiddish, East European Jewry, and Judaism through pages labeled "Synagogue," "School," "Post Office," "Station," and "Library."[67] The website thus uses the East European market town as its model for social intercourse and the exchange of goods and resources "in an effort to give the spatiality of information greater palpability and vividness."[68] More as a literary than as a geographical entity, Eastern Europe is invoked by *Mendele: Yiddish Literature and Language*.[69] The name of this listserv, es-tablished in 1991, pays homage not only to a foundational figure in modern Yiddish literature but also to the role of the itinerant book peddler as the creator and dis-seminator of a novel Yiddish discourse for a new community of readers. Like its namesake, Mendele Moykher-Sforim (Mendele the Book Peddler, the literary per-sona of writer Sholem Yankev Abramovitsh), the listserv is a virtual entity. And, like the written works ostensibly composed and distributed by Abramovitsh's Mendele, the postings on *Mendele* constitute a new hybridization of oral and writ-ten language, as is the case with much of what appears on Internet listservs and bul-letin boards generally. This development may also reflect the changing interrelation of oral and written language for Yiddish speakers today, especially those whose re-lationship with the language is postvernacular. As Jonathan Boyarin notes, the lan-guage is increasingly "spoken the way it is written, not written as it is spoken, be-cause the basic means of communication of today's secular Yiddish is writing, not speech."[70]

The notices that appear on *Mendele*—queries about the meaning of Yiddish terms or sources of Yiddish texts, announcements of Yiddish cultural events and new publications, as well as exchanges (sometimes very passionate) on the current state of Yiddish—evince a new kind of Jewish vernacularity responsive to this novel medium. *Mendelistn*, as users of this listerv are sometimes termed, variously communicate in Yiddish, English, sometimes French, German, or other languages. These are used alone or in combinations (most frequently, Yiddish plus one other language) that can be either redundant (some *Mendelistn* diligently submit their en-tire postings in one language followed by a complete translation in another) or mac-aronic. All communications are typed in the Roman alphabet, which, of course, has special implications for those postings in Yiddish. Users of the listserv romanize Yiddish according to a variety of systems: some follow the YIVO standard, others

Web page for the Japan Yiddish Club, 2003.
Courtesy of Jack Halpern.

are clearly soi-disant, with some of these reflecting the authors' spoken dialects.[71] The new kind of Jewish communication that *Mendele* demonstrates straddles not only the border between oral and written language but also other linguistic boundaries. English is the language in which the listserv functions (i.e., in which it gives instructions to subscribers, is accessed from its online archive, etc.), while Yiddish figures on the listserv both as a means of communication and as its end, treated variously as a whole language or as a fragment of one, by users ranging from accomplished stylists and fluent speakers to those with only rudimentary skills in Yiddish or none at all. As is typical of postvernacular Yiddish culture, discussions *about* Yiddish, rather than *in* Yiddish, are foremost—indeed, definitive—in this enterprise.

As it unites widely scattered participants and archives their exchanges, *Mendele* simultaneously facilitates and attenuates a sense of community rooted in the Yiddish language. Cyberspace can provide valuable communion for Yiddish speakers, some of whom increasingly find themselves lacking direct personal contact with others conversant in the language. This medium also offers some Yiddish speakers a public forum for self-expression that obviates social protocols. Such is the case with a small number of Hasidic bloggers who exploit the anonymity of cyberspace to offer personal reflections, sometimes sharply critical, on their local communities, thereby avoiding censure for their outspokenness.[72] The Internet also expands the parameters of other media and cultural institutions—for example, by providing access to local Yiddish radio broadcasts or offering online instruction in the language.[73] To some extent, these developments extend the diasporic nature of Yiddish, elaborating its long-standing pattern of gathering and redistributing communications.

At the same time, the Internet points up the limits of this medium for facilitating a culture centered on the notion of oral communication as realizing, or at least evoking, a traditional communal intimacy. Much of what is posted on Yiddish websites facilitates other encounters—for example, promoting "live" events such as concerts, plays, conferences, lectures, and conversation circles—rather than serving solely as encounters complete in themselves. Yugntruf uses the Internet to solicit volunteers to visit and converse with elderly, homebound Yiddish speakers and to promote its "Yiddish Community Stipends." These "help qualified applicants partially defray the costs associated with moving closer to other Yiddish-speaking individuals or families," thereby supporting "the creation of Yiddish-language communities" among "those who are committed to speaking Yiddish on a daily basis."[74] Indeed, by virtue of its extraordinary capacity for interaction, the Internet highlights the importance—and, in some places, the growing paucity—of human contact in the Yiddish-speaking world. Thus, even as Yiddishland is defined by language, its existence ultimately entails something extralinguistic: the familiar, intimate social encounter implicated in speaking Yiddish.

In this regard, Yiddishland is akin to the phenomenon of playing "Jewish geography," which Boyarin defines as "the social activity of establishing links with fellow Jews, usually upon first meeting them, by elaborating with them an informal account of shared family, friendship, or community ties." This practice differs from "classical cartographic geography" in that it is "person-centered, concerned with establishing networks outward and back to the person," and as such is "shaped by social and cultural interests." Boyarin notes a paradox in playing "Jewish geography" on the Internet: "The game depends on finding people who were in the same place at the same time. But playing it via computer requires neither. . . . Since one can communicate via electronic mail with anyone from anywhere, the point is less establishing new and lasting links than renewing one's sense of being a part of a network that will follow you wherever you go, if you continue to help maintain it."[75] Similarly, the Internet is a means, but not an end, in the conjuring of Yiddishland, which also centers on the agents of speech and their interrelationships, defined with regard to (if not necessarily by means of) Yiddish speech. Yiddish language may be what identifies Yiddishland, but ultimately it is composed of speakers.

As epitomizing phenomena of postvernacular Yiddish culture, Yiddishlands look to the past as they project into the future. Yet far from being exercises in cultural continuity (though they are often vaunted as such), they entail radical transformations of the language itself and its symbolic value in Jewish life across geographic, temporal, and cultural boundaries. The transvaluations of Yiddish in all these imaginings of Yiddishland demonstrate a break with prewar environments in which the language served millions of Jews as a vernacular. Not so much a failure to reconstruct, or even to recall, the place of Yiddish in prewar Eastern Europe, these are instead deliberate efforts to offer visions of the Jewish past that speak to the needs and desires of the present. Moreover, these inventions sustain the process of defining and redefining the meaning of Yiddish that has been a hallmark of modern Ashkenazic Jewish life since well before the Holocaust. Common to all these imaginary projects, prewar and postwar, is a cultural yearning or dissatisfaction of some kind; desires to see Jewish life transformed are projected onto the language and its potential for symbolic meaning. These dissatisfactions thrive on remembrance of the past, even as they react against it.

The proliferation of Yiddishlands now being written, performed, displayed, and otherwise conjured by Jews around the world testifies to the power of this language, at once enduring and mutable, as a symbolic force in Jewish culture in the post-Holocaust era. Loosed from its prewar geographic, demographic, and cultural moorings, Yiddish acquires new symbolic significance even as its primary semiotic value as a vernacular is in decline. How can these diverging tendencies be sustained simultaneously, and what are the limitations of their range—even in as elastic a venue as Yiddishland?

Perhaps with these questions in mind, Boyarin cautions against "the ironic or nostalgic discourse of a lost or dreamed Yiddishland. It's better to keep in mind the Yiddish-nowhere-land."[76] Still, why is the notion of imagining Yiddishland so attractive, especially at the turn of the millennium, and for such a diverse range of individuals and communities? The answer may lie in the way that Yiddishland sustains contradictory impulses, capable of embodying progressivism as well as retrospection, appealing to the traditionally devout as well as the ardently secular, and elevating Yiddish to sovereign status at the same time that it flouts conventional notions of nationhood. And perhaps this is why, for those who have not made the imaginative leaps that it demands, Yiddishland can seem offensive or preposterous, for part of its appeal is precisely its unrealness. But failing to appreciate the value inherent in conjuring Yiddishland is to discount the vital role that the imaginary can play in modern Jewish culture, especially in its ability to redress extensive rupture, displacement, and loss with liberating possibilities for cultural creativity.

CHAPTER TWO

BEYOND THE MOTHER TONGUE

A friend of mine once told me that for years she had wanted to learn to speak Yiddish. Several times she had asked an aunt of hers, who was a native speaker and active in New York's Yiddish cultural scene, to give her lessons—but the aunt kept putting her off. Finally, my friend offered to do her aunt a favor, provided she would give her Yiddish lessons in exchange. The favor done, my friend asked her aunt to hold up her end of their agreement. And so the aunt invited her into the kitchen, where they sat down at the table. "Sit up straight," the aunt told her. "Open your mouth, relax your jaw." She did so. "All right," the aunt said. "The Yiddish should start coming out very easily now."

At this point, of course, my friend realized that she was never going to get any Yiddish lessons from her aunt and demanded to know why her aunt refused to satisfy her request. Her aunt replied that she felt that unless one grew up with the language and spoke it regularly in an active cultural environment, it was simply impossible to learn Yiddish.

As a language teacher I have had similar encounters with older native speakers who, for example, dropped in on my class to see how it was possible to teach Yiddish in a school setting. Some expressed genuine incredulity that texts exist for teaching Yiddish to college students—or, for that matter, that Yiddish can be learned from a book. "You have to grow up with Yiddish," they contend. "It's *mame-loshn* [literally, "mother tongue," often used as an affectionate term for Yid-

Cover of Ellis Weiner and Barbara Davilman's *Yiddish with Dick and Jane,* published in 2004, a parody of the popular mid-twentieth-century "Dick and Jane" primers. The humor of this mock textbook relies, in part, on the notion that a Yiddish primer is inherently risible. Designed by Chika Azuma. Courtesy of Little, Brown and Company.

dish]; you can only learn it from your mother." Yiddish speakers, they insist, "are created in the bedroom, not in the classroom."

Such sentiments may exasperate Yiddish teachers or cause would-be students of the language to despair. But, in fact, learning Yiddish in a classroom as a second language is not inherently harder (or easier) than it is for any other language. The speaker of a second language inevitably has a different relationship with it than does a native speaker. This is not a question of relative degrees of literacy or fluency; classroom-taught speakers of a second language can, and not infrequently do, surpass native speakers in their command of vocabulary, grammar, style, and, sometimes, even idiom. Rather, this difference is a matter either of psycholinguistics—

because "the language-specific learning mechanisms available to the young child simply cease to work for older learners"—or of sociolinguistics—because older learners of a second language "do not have the social opportunities, or the motivation, to identify completely with the native speaker community, but may instead value their distinctive identity as learners or as foreigners."[1]

That being said, skeptics' remarks directed at those who would learn Yiddish as something beyond their mother tongue should not be dismissed completely. Though they are wrong about the feasibility of learning Yiddish in a classroom, they voice a very real anxiety in response to the dissolution of centers of modern Yiddish culture, especially in Europe, and to the steep decline in the number of native Yiddish speakers in the six decades since the Holocaust. These developments have powerful extralinguistic implications, involving both external persecutions and intrinsic disjunctures, and are projected, especially by aging native speakers of Yiddish, onto the present and future state of the language as a Jewish vernacular. How, these remarks imply, can a classroom simulate *di yidishe gas* ("the Jewish street," i.e., a Jewish neighborhood), or a teacher replace a *yidishe mame*?

Yiddish has a relatively brief and yet very contentious history in the language classroom, making it a key locus for understanding the language in postvernacular mode. The dynamics of Yiddish-language pedagogy reveal shifting notions about how one can (and cannot) master the language, and to what end one might wish to do so, responsive to unprecedented Jewish self-consciousness about language use. Once a skill taken for granted, learning to read, write, or even speak Yiddish became an increasingly deliberate undertaking during the previous century, as Ashkenazic communities around the world, ranging from hasidim to communists, established classes, trained teachers, and published textbooks to teach the language. These recent innovations in the long history of Yiddish have had important consequences for its symbolic meaning, challenging long-held assumptions about how one acquires the traditional vernacular of Ashkenaz. Indeed, Yiddish pedagogy emerged as a strategic venue for formulating and communicating new ideas about the value of the language as it has become increasingly postvernacular.

TEACHING *ZHARGON*

According to a proverb, there is no need for instruction in Yiddish; it is *di shprakh vos redt zikh*—the language that "speaks (by) itself." While Yiddish is over a thousand years old, efforts to offer Jewish children formal instruction in the language are, by and large, an innovation of the past century. There are many other vernaculars for which this pattern holds true, of course. Yet the case of Yiddish is distinguished by general concepts of Jewish literacy and by the configuration of language use among Ashkenazim—in particular, their traditional internal Jewish bilingualism. Max Weinreich argued that this complementary relationship of Yiddish and Loshn-koydesh is not based on semantics—say, the "secular" versus the "holy," as is often assumed—but is rather a matter of function. Traditionally, Yiddish is the primary spoken language, Loshn-koydesh basically (although not exclusively) the written language.[2]

This distinction is reflected in the practices of Ashkenazic literacy, including rituals, dating back to the late Middle Ages, that celebrate a boy's introduction to learning the *alefbeys*. These rituals entail a richly textured array of practices—such as wrapping the boy in a *tales* and carrying him aloft, feeding him special cakes or eggs inscribed with Hebrew texts following his first lesson—which were claimed to be *mineg avoyseynu*, the "custom of our ancestors." Historian Ivan Marcus notes that these rituals thereby imbue this moment with symbolic value that extends beyond the boy's personal history to a "communal affirmation" of Jewish peoplehood.[3]

Unmentioned in Marcus's study of these rituals (and, of course, in his medieval sources) is their implicit involvement of Yiddish. Whatever instructions were given to the boy—"now say this; now do this"—would not have been uttered in Hebrew, but in the language he and his family spoke at home, which we now refer to as Yiddish. This bilingual (or, more accurately, diglossic) pattern has persisted in traditional Ashkenazic education: the pedagogical objective of the *kheyder* (the school where Jewish children begin their traditional religious education) is to teach young boys (and, at times, girls) to read the Hebrew of the Bible and prayer book, but the language of instruction was (and, in some instances among Ashkenazic *khareydim*, still is) Yiddish. This pattern continues as the (male) student matures and enters the *besmedresh* (study house, for adult scholars), where traditional study of the Talmud rests on the foundation of translating the original Loshn-koydesh into the vernacular.

Its primary association with orality notwithstanding, Jews have been reading and writing Yiddish for centuries. A popular Yiddish readership developed following the advent of the printed Yiddish book in the sixteenth century, which engendered a sizeable vernacular literature with its own genres, audiences, and notions of literacy. However, there was no institutionalized instruction in reading Yiddish in traditional Ashkenaz. This was simply a by-product of Hebrew literacy, given the cultural imperative of learning Hebrew as an instrument of divine service and the fact that the two languages use the same alphabet (though employing some of the letters in different ways). Traditional Yiddish literacy was neither mandated nor ritualized; as Weinreich noted—perhaps with old images of the *kheyder* in mind—"No one was ever flogged for not knowing Yiddish."[4] Indeed, the earliest instructional manuals for Yiddish—such as Wilhelm Christian Just Chrysander's *Unterricht vom Nutzen des Judenteutschen* (Instruction in the Use of Judeo-German [i.e., Yiddish], 1750) and Gottfried Selig's *Lehrbuch zur gründlichen Erlernung der jüdisch-deutschen Sprache* (Textbook for the Complete Acquisition of the Judeo-German Language, 1792)—were written by and for Christian humanists.[5]

The first texts specifically designed to instruct Jews in some form of Yiddish literacy are *brivnshtelers*—letter-writing manuals, which began to appear in the early nineteenth century.[6] These books do not teach how to speak or read Yiddish; they assume their user is fluent in the language and familiar with the *alefbeys* for reading Loshn-koydesh. Rather, *brivnshtelers* explain how to write in Yiddish—specifically, offering models of correspondence for occasions ranging from business transactions to courtship. These books formalized a widespread practice in nineteenth-century Eastern Europe, in which Jewish parents sought to provide their children with a modicum of "practical" (as opposed to devotional) education and hired a tutor to teach them "at least how to write a letter in the Jewish jargon"—that is, in Yiddish—as well as "to learn a little Russian, arithmetic," and perhaps "a little German as well."[7] (Tsvi-Hirsh Goldshteyn-Gershonovitsh's preface to his 1890 *brivnshteler*, from which these lines are cited, provides a vivid portrait of these tutors, often minimally skilled and so preoccupied with dashing from the home of one student to the next that their instruction was barely worth the tuition of three or four rubles a month.)

Their very specific scope notwithstanding, *brivnshtelers* mark a threshold in Yiddish pedagogy. Sample texts that students were to practice copying—including poems, discourses on the natural sciences, as well as model missives, some of which contain lessons in moral conduct—constitute pioneering efforts in using Yiddish as a vehicle for modern education. Moreover, these manuals evince a concern with normativizing Yiddish orthography and grammar, reflecting its growing importance among its speakers as a language of modern letters.[8]

Over the course of the nineteenth century new notions of Yiddish literacy evolved in Eastern Europe as a consequence of the Haskalah and the subsequent rise of Jewish nationalist movements in the century's final decades, during which the question of what language(s) a Jew ought to speak, read, and write engendered an unprecedented self-consciousness about the meta-significance of language. Though it varied from ignoble to exalted, the status of Yiddish remained a charged issue

"The Elephant," one of a series of illustrated lessons on natural history, in Yoyne Trubnik's *Zhargon-lehrer* (Jargon [Yiddish] teacher), a "practical textbook for mastering . . . the Yiddish language easily in a short time," published in Warsaw in 1886. In addition to explaining Yiddish orthography, this volume offers humorous anecdotes, proverbs, and samples of correspondence.

throughout this period. Moreover, ideological principles often clashed with actual circumstances. While most *maskilim* (followers of the Haskalah) reviled Yiddish, they were sometimes obliged to use the language to reach their readers—even as they argued that Yiddish epitomized all that was wrong with traditional Ashkenazic life and strove to hasten the language's demise. Conversely, among those who subsequently championed Yiddish as a distinctive Jewish national resource were some individuals who did not know Yiddish well enough to articulate these sentiments in the language itself. By the turn of the twentieth century, the notion of a self-evident Yiddish vernacularity among its millions of speakers in the Russian and Habsburg Empires had already been problematized extensively.

Most advocates of Yiddish did not focus on its pedagogy at first. As young adults primarily concerned with forging a new Jewish national consciousness in terms that were largely outside the legal possibilities of their circumstances, Yiddishists initially focused on endeavors involving their own cohort, especially publishing and political organizing. Nevertheless, occasional efforts were made throughout the nineteenth century to situate Yiddish in a modern school, though such institutions remained exceptional and marginal until the First World War. Laws in the Russian Empire expressly forbade schooling, other than religious instruction, in minority cultures' native languages. Moreover, most East European Jews elected to give their children a traditional education in a *kheyder* or from a tutor. Though it was repeatedly assailed by *maskilim* for its primitive physical conditions and harsh, often inept teachers, who provided a limited, retrograde education, the *kheyder* proved remarkably resilient. Indeed, as historian Steven Zipperstein notes, it became an object of Jewish national sentiment, even among some champions of modernity.[9]

A small, relatively affluent, assimilationist Jewish elite enrolled its children in state-run or private schools where the language of instruction was Russian or, for those Jews living in the Habsburg Empire, German. These institutions promoted linguistic and cultural integration into the imperial mainstream and disparaged the use of Yiddish inside the classroom as well as outside it. By the 1880s even Russians noticed that "once a Jew has an education . . . he very rarely speaks Yiddish."[10] At the same time, some maskilic experiments in modern Jewish education—notably, Joseph Perl's Öffentliche Israelitische Hochschule (Israelite Public High School), established in Tarnopol in 1809—offered instruction in reading and writing Yiddish. However, in such cases it was treated, in effect, as a foreign language—analogous to, say, the school's teaching of French—rather than as the students' native tongue. At the same time, Yiddish apparently served as a de facto vernacular in these early maskilic schools, especially for beginning students, who arrived knowing little, if any, German or Russian.[11]

By the turn of the twentieth century there were several isolated attempts in Eastern Europe to establish modern schools in which Yiddish served as the language of instruction—for example, a school founded by Noah Mishkowsky in Mir in 1898, or one that the Yiddish writer Abraham Reisen recalled seeing in operation in Warsaw the following year.[12] However, according to Chaim Kazdan, a pioneer of modern Yiddish education, "these efforts arose more from social, populist impulses, rather than from purely pedagogical, Yiddishist, nationalist ones. They were more rudimentary in origin, and not of an organized, communal character."[13]

These schools also lacked textbooks, Kazdan notes, as further evidence of the embryonic, provisional nature of Yiddish education at the time. In fact, several Yiddish primers were published in the Russian Empire during the first decade of the twentieth century, and they testify to the pedagogical and cultural novelty of the enterprise. Though the earliest of these texts indicate that they were intended for private as well as classroom study, they are clearly modeled on introductory texts used in modern European classrooms to bring children across the threshold of literacy in their native language.[14]

Thus, in contrast to traditional Ashkenazic practices marking the child's first lesson in the *alefbeys*, formal initiation into Yiddish literacy was conceived as a decidedly modernist practice. It was not celebrated in terms of time-honored family ritual but embodied by a textbook encountered in a novel setting—the modern Jewish school. The newness of the enterprise was of symbolic importance in itself—if not for the children, then certainly for their parents. Similarly, Yiddish primers (like instructional books for children generally) ultimately reveal more about the aspirations of the adult community than they do about its children's actual experience.

Prefatory remarks in Moyshe Fridman's Yiddish primer *Hayehudiye* (The Jewess), published in Odessa in 1904, explain that, for years, Jewish children have struggled to learn to read Yiddish as a consequence of learning to read Loshn-koydesh. His book, however, is written especially for the student who wishes to learn to read Yiddish "in a short time and without torment." This student "need only learn [the letters] *mem* [M] and *pasekh-alef* [A] and then can read *mama*, and so on." *Hayehudiye* proceeds from words to phrases, then to short texts; "soon one can read a whole book or . . . newspaper." Moreover, because Yiddish contains so many Loshn-koydesh words, Fridman explains that, once one has learned to read Yiddish, "it isn't so hard to read from a prayer book when one has to pray"—thereby inverting the traditional hierarchy of Ashkenazic literacy.[15]

Y. Pirozhnikov's primer *Reyshis mikro* (Beginning Reading), published in Vilna in 1906, configures Jewish bilingual literacy differently. The book is in two parts: the first teaches children *ʒogn ivre* (how to read Loshn-koydesh aloud), employing what is touted as an innovative, effective method of calibrated exercises. The book's second part is "dedicated to our so-called 'mother-tongue,' i.e., *ivre-taytsh* [the archaic form of Yiddish used for translating sacred texts], or plain-old *ʒhargon*." The author not only problematizes the identity of Yiddish but addresses the reader's anticipated ambivalence about it:

Whatever one's opinion of this language, it must be admitted that most Jewish children understand no other language than *ʒhargon*. Only in this language does the child first hear his mother speak; only in this language does he learn the Torah, Rashi commentaries, and even the Talmud in *kheyder*. Only in this language can a Jew write someone a letter, conduct his business and keep his accounts, and for most Jews this is the only language in which they can read a newspaper and discover what's going on in the world.

Despite the ubiquity of Yiddish usage, Pirozhnikov argues, "there is hardly a Jew who can write this language without making terrible mistakes." Widespread native knowledge thus legitimates the value of Yiddish but is not sufficient for it to function as a modern language. Anticipating his critics' assumptions—"I know there will certainly be those who will say, 'What do you mean by this? Learning *zhargon*, a language of exile, which has no grammar' "—Pirozhnikov insists on the importance of treating Yiddish as a respectable modern language: "The truth is, that in recent years our *zhargon* . . . has become more and more the equal of others; even now it is nothing to be ashamed of."[16]

The obstinate nature of Yiddish pedagogy at the turn of the twentieth century was bound up in the larger social upheavals taking place in the Russian Empire. Advocacy for Yiddish-language schooling increased during the general expansion of political activism around the 1905 Revolution and its aftermath. At the time, legislation allowed some ethnic minorities living under czarist rule to establish schools in their native languages, but Jews were still forbidden to do so, since these institutions were suspected of fomenting sedition. (Perhaps such fears were not entirely unfounded. In at least one instance, a dissident message does appear to have been embedded within a reading exercise in an early Yiddish primer. A lesson in *Di folkssphrakh*, published in Warsaw in 1909/10, teaches students the use of the letter *yud* [Y] as a consonant by introducing two new words—*yid* [Jew] and *pistolyet* [pistol]—followed by these provocative sample sentences: *"Di nakhtigal yomert. Dizer yingl hot a pistolyet. Kinder! Yogt zikh nit. Der may kumt shoyn on. Der vind voyet."* [The nightingale moans. This boy has a pistol. Children! Don't rush. The month of May has arrived. The wind howls.])[17]

In fact, calls for Yiddish-language education had begun to figure in revolutionary Jewish political agendas. Organs of the Jewish Workers' Bund featured a series of articles debating at length the idea of educating children in Yiddish. Maria Yakovlevna Frumkin (known by the nom de guerre Esther) offered the party's most extensive theorization of the issue in her 1910 book *Tsu der frage vegn der yidisher folkshul* (On the Question of the Jewish Public School), in which her advocacy of

Yiddish-language education linked linguistic awareness with political conscious-ness: "It's natural that the Jewish masses, the most oppressed of all the oppressed, don't have a sufficiently developed consciousness to value their language and to un-derstand that they can *also* be educated in our mother tongue. It's natural that they don't care about pedagogical rules and don't know that their children can *only* be ed-ucated in our mother tongue, as is our due."[18] That year the Bund issued an official resolution at its eighth conference, calling for the creation of "state schools for each national group in its native language." The party expressed its commitment to Yiddish-language pedagogy in universal terms, situating the school as a site for en-acting "national cultural autonomy" and characterizing the cause of education in one's mother tongue as revolutionary: "All persecution of the use of one's native language in public life—at assemblies, in the press, and in public and private schools—should be abolished."[19] The Bund's notion of what was at stake in Yid-dish education was rooted in more than theory: in 1907, several dozen progressive Jewish teachers, most of them Bundists, had convened a conference in Vilna. Be-cause such proceedings were illegal, the participants were all arrested, and they con-tinued their conference in prison.[20]

To a considerable extent, Yiddishists' ideological objectives for mother-tongue schooling were the same as their aspirations for Yiddish literature, press, political activism, and other public cultural endeavors. What distinguished Yiddish-language education was its focus on the next generation of Jews. In Yiddishist ped-agogy, children figured as the proving ground for the reinvention of Jewish life, and through them ideologists projected visions of a radically transformed Jewry within a revolutionized Eastern Europe.

During the years between the two Russian revolutions, members of other Jew-ish political parties—the Fareynikte, the Folkspartey, Sejmists, Socialist-Territorialists—also called for Yiddish-language education. In addition to peda-gogues, prominent Jewish activists, scholars, and writers (including historian Simon Dubnow and author Y. L. Peretz) spoke out on behalf of establishing a modern ed-ucation in Yiddish for East European Jewish children.[21] Even some Zionists—most of whom championed the revival of Hebrew as a modern language and called for its use in the modern Jewish classroom—endorsed instruction in Yiddish at least as a temporary measure, given its widespread familiarity among diaspora Jews. In a se-ries of articles on "Yiddish and Its National Value," published in the Russian Yid-dish press in 1905–1906, Zionist leader and educator Joseph Lurie suggested that there was more than an expedient value in Yiddish-language schools, writing that they were possible "if we only remain steadfast to the basic notion that our people's language is Yiddish and Jews ought to be educated in this language. This is not a dream, nor is it a bizarre claim. Our interests, the survival of our people, demand it."[22] Nevertheless, at this time the modern Yiddish-language school was more publicly visible as an ideologically charged ideal than as an actual institution.

FROM *FOLKSHPRAKH* TO *KULTURSHPRAKH*

The establishment of modern Yiddish-language schools in Eastern Europe on more than a sporadic, underground basis only began during World War I and was due more to the ad hoc demands of German occupying forces in Russian Poland than to the will of Yiddishists. Hirsz Abramowicz, who became a leading figure in Jewish vocational education in interwar Poland, recalled:

> The Germans banned Russian as the language of instruction in schools. Each national minority was expected to run its schools in its own mother tongue. Yiddish schools sprang up spontaneously, but the transition to Yiddish as the language of instruction was by no means a simple matter. There were not enough textbooks, and they did not exist on subjects for which there was virtually no Yiddish terminology. Few teachers were really fluent in Yiddish and not all parents were pleased that it was being used as the language of instruction. However, the commandment of the time was: Mother tongue! Yiddish![23]

After the Versailles Treaty and the consolidation of Bolshevik rule in Russia, modern Yiddish-language schools became fixtures of life for many thousands of young Jews in Eastern Europe for almost two decades. This brief period, celebrated as the heyday of secular Yiddish education, was distinguished as much by a complex of new challenges as it was by its unprecedented accomplishments. In the newly established Republics of Poland and Lithuania (and, to a lesser extent, in other East European nations), Yiddish was the language of instruction in a variety of institutions, ranging from the Orthodox Beys Yaakov girls' schools to the socialist, secularist Tsentrale Yidishe Shul-Organizatsye (Central Yiddish School Organization). Such schools were part of a wider array of educational options for young Jews in these countries. They included schools in which the language of instruction was modern Hebrew and that were also pursuing newly won opportunities to flourish legally, as well as state or private schools run in the national language. In Soviet Russia, where Yiddish received official recognition as the language of the Jewish national minority, state-funded and -supervised Yiddish-language schools were es-

Children in a Yiddish school in Kovno (Kaunas), Lithuania, in 1932. The Yiddish text printed on their paper headbands reads: "We, students in the first preschool class of the Kovno Jewish Commercial High School, are holding a great celebration to mark our learning to read and write."
Courtesy of the Archives of the YIVO Institute for Jewish Research, New York.

tablished almost immediately after the founding of the Jewish Commissariat in 1918. Both Jewish politics and Soviet educational philosophy, notes historian David Shneer, "made the language of instruction the sine qua non of the 'new education' for national minorities."[24]

Education was but one component of secular Yiddish culture's efflorescence during the interwar years. New opportunities for Yiddish publishing, scholarship, political activism, and performance, as well as pedagogy fulfilled long-awaited and much-debated agendas for developing what sociolinguist Joshua Fishman terms "high-culture functions for a language of everyday life."[25] These innovations made new demands on Yiddish; as Abramowicz indicated, Yiddish publications, its speakers, and the language itself were seen—even by their champions—as being in need of betterment.

Yiddishists responded to this challenge by stepping up efforts to normativize the language, creating standards in its orthography, lexicon, and grammar and implementing them through newly established institutions. The YIVO Institute for Jewish Research, founded in Vilna in 1925, assumed the role of a Yiddish language academy as part of its philological research activities (though its authority was frequently challenged or simply ignored by Polish Jews).[26] In the Soviet Union, language reform was a matter of state policy and reflected Soviet ideology.[27] As linguist Christopher Hutton notes, normativization entailed conflicting valuations of Yiddish. On the one hand, the language was prized as a *folkshprakh*—"an essentially natural phenomenon, rooted organically in the historical consciousness of its speakers and expressing their unity." On the other, in conceiving the language as a *kulturshprakh*, its advocates had come to see Yiddish as "a social institution that must be regulated to ensure its effective functioning and its preservation as a cultural symbol or artifact."[28]

Schools, Hutton notes, proved a strategic venue for language normativization: "Language planning is in general best adapted to prescribe usage for formal situations such as schools and universities, governmental and public functions."[29] For Yiddishists, the classroom became the venue par excellence for enacting a modernist transformation of traditional Ashkenazic culture. Shneer notes that in the Soviet Union "teachers as a social group embodied the synthesis that linguists were looking for in language—the group that could incorporate high Yiddish into the vocabulary of the masses through the school, and the group that interacted with the masses and could bring their vocabulary back to the Yiddish intelligentsia."[30]

Paradoxically, schools that were established to fulfill a vision of "natural" education in the Jews' mother tongue and to forge a new generation of modern Yiddish speakers also proved to be sites of unprecedented linguistic contestation. Even before World War I it was becoming apparent that there was a growing disparity between East European Jews' declared native language (according to the 1897 census, some 97 percent of Jews living under Russian rule reported Yiddish as their mother tongue) and the language(s) they actually used in daily life.[31] This was especially true among younger and more urbanized Jews.

Yiddishist ideology, rooted in convictions that the traditional Ashkenazic vernacular sufficed to define Jewish identity on a personal as well as national scale, did not accommodate well the complex, rapidly changing multilingualism of its constituency, even as Yiddishists sought to employ the language as an instrument for achieving social reform. For growing numbers of East European Jews caught up in the modernizing transformations of their society, Yiddish was a language one left behind. Thus, recalled Abramowicz, the Vilna Jewish Technical School, which employed Yiddish as the language of instruction, was organized by an engineer, Matthias Schreiber, who—like most of his generation of Jewish intellectuals in Vilna—was thoroughly Russified and knew no Yiddish himself. Nevertheless,

Schreiber "learned Yiddish and produced excellent technical handbooks . . . on mechanics, technology, and various branches of applied physics . . . in correct and, at the time, strictly scientific Yiddish." Not only were the school's instructors, most of whom "had very little acquaintance with Yiddish," obliged to learn the language; their students, who came from all over Poland, "were often completely [linguistically] assimilated [to Polish] and knew no Yiddish. Schreiber allowed them a specified period of time in which to acquire the language."[32]

Nor was the shift away from Yiddish as a vernacular among Polish Jewish youth considered a problem only among secularists. In 1931 Sarah Schenirer, who founded the Beys Yaakov school system in 1917, issued an appeal to its Orthodox female students and teachers to refrain from speaking Polish and exhorted them to maintain Yiddish as a matter of upholding traditional religious devotion: "Be resolute and from this day forward speak only Yiddish and call each other only by your Jewish names! Think of ways to carry this out: perhaps by choosing someone in each group to be on guard and remind the others, perhaps by putting up large signs that say 'Speak Only Yiddish!' . . . Keep a daily account of what you have been doing to improve the situation of Yiddish."[33] And while Yiddish was officially vaunted as "the embodiment of the Jews as a nation" in the Soviet Union, Yiddish education never attracted a majority of Jewish students there.[34] Gennady Estraikh notes that "parents quite often regarded Yiddish schools as a link in the 'poverty chain': educational disadvantage could be linked with employment disadvantage," and some protested against forcing their children to attend these institutions. "Even for many employees of Jewish institutions Yiddish was often confined to their professional activity, while every day, in their family life, they used Russian and sent their children to Russian schools."[35]

World War II rendered the question of the feasibility of Yiddish-language schooling in Eastern Europe tragically moot. Soviet Yiddish culture enjoyed a brief reprieve from Stalinist oppression during the war, but this did not extend to Yiddish schools; nor were they revived when Yiddish culture was rehabilitated under Khrushchev. A Yiddish primer published in Birobidzhan in 1982 was apparently the first such textbook issued in the Soviet Union since the 1940s.[36] Romania's Yiddish schools were taken over by the state in 1948, and their agenda was directed at promoting Romanian patriotism and Marxist indoctrination, as well as combating "the bourgeois mentality of Zionism."[37] In postwar Poland, a decimated Jewish community soon established an array of communal institutions, including a small number of Yiddish schools, which eventually came under state control. There Yiddish schooling remained in operation until the anti-Semitic expulsions of the late 1960s, which reduced the number of Polish Jews to a few thousand. The commitment to Yiddish in early post–World War II Poland was as much symbolic, a desire to continue the "chain of the generations," as it was instrumental. Many pupils, who had spent the war years in hiding or removed from the Jewish community, knew no Yiddish, and it was difficult to find qualified Yiddish-speaking teachers among the survivors.[38]

LANGUAGE OF HERITAGE

A major factor contributing to the destabilization of East European Jewry at the turn of the twentieth century was the departure of about one-third of its population—some two million men, women, and children—from the early 1880s until the start of World War I, most of them bound for the United States. Immigration was thus an ongoing option for Yiddish speakers over the span of a generation. Whether or not they chose to leave their homes, all members of this community were affected by the knowledge that it was possible, and there were few East European Jews without a close relative or acquaintance who had decided to immigrate.

Once in America, immigrant Jews found themselves in radically altered circumstances. These had an impact on every aspect of their daily lives, including the challenge of encountering a different and unprecedented multilingual constellation, which presented new possibilities and challenges for Yiddish. Consequently, Yiddish education would take a very different path in the United States (and, later, elsewhere in the Americas) from concomitant developments in Eastern Europe. The most significant difference, though not articulated as such, was a sense from the start that in America Yiddish pedagogy would have to grapple with the daunting idea that Jewish children were encountering the language as something other than a vernacular, even though many of them lived in Yiddish-speaking families and communities. Indeed, American Yiddish pedagogy reveals an ongoing, albeit often implicit, engagement with the issue of postvernacularity, starting in the early twentieth century.

Upon their arrival in the United States, Yiddish speakers swiftly created a distinctive immigrant culture. Thanks to new political and economic circumstances, American Yiddish culture often flourished in ways that were not feasible in Eastern Europe. Yet unlike Yiddish theater, political activism, or press, Yiddish education did not develop straightaway in America. During the period of mass immigration, American Yiddish culture focused on the concerns of young adults, the core cohort group of the immigrant community. The relationship of the immigrants' young children to Yiddish attracted little attention at the time. The issue of receiving a public school education in one's mother tongue, which was to become a central concern in Eastern Europe, was moot in America; in the United States almost all immigrant Jewish children attended public schools and were taught exclusively in English. Those who received a Jewish education at the turn of the century usually did so in Orthodox talmud torahs and other afternoon or weekend schools. (Here, especially at first, Yiddish was often the language of instruction, following the model of the East European *kheyder*.)[39] Although many immigrant Jewish radicals, like their European counterparts, embraced Yiddish as a language of political activism for their cohorts, they did not necessarily envision forging a link between the language and their progeny. In the first Sunday schools established by several New York City branches of the Workmen's Circle in 1906, children of Yiddish-speaking immigrants were given a left-wing, internationalist political education in English.[40]

Formal Yiddish-language instruction for immigrants' children did not begin in the United States until the final years of mass immigration, when the first secular Yiddish school system, the Labor Zionist Farband schools, was founded in 1910. Other schools followed at the end of World War I: the non-Zionist, socialist Workmen's Circle schools in 1918, and the nonpolitical, secularist Sholem Aleichem Folks-institut in the same year. In 1930 an ideological split among left-wing secularists led to the establishment of a new Yiddish school system by the communist International Workers Order (IWO). By the mid-1930s, almost 10 percent of American children (and some 20 percent in New York City) who received some kind of formal Jewish education attended one of these secular Yiddish schools.[41]

At the same time, the first American Yiddish primers, which were published in the mid-1910s and early 1920s, indicate that the language was also taught in talmud torahs. These schools accounted for the Jewish education of over one half of American Jewish children during the interwar years.[42] Though the number of these talmud torahs offering Yiddish language instruction is not known, the frequent reprinting of some of the textbooks intended for this venue indicates that they were used by tens, if not hundreds, of thousands of children during the interwar years.[43]

Learning Yiddish was of particular significance in talmud torahs to the extent that they were training Jewish boys for bar mitzvah ceremonies. During the early decades of the twentieth century, delivering a speech in Yiddish emerged as "the most prominent" of innovative American Jewish "folk practices" associated with this coming-of-age ritual, notes Jenna Joselit.[44] Published volumes of sample speeches helped establish protocols for this new custom, which incorporated into an increasingly elaborate public performance of entry into Jewish manhood the demonstration of one's ability to speak in Yiddish as a rite of passage in itself.

The emergence of Yiddish education at this time among both secular and Orthodox Jews suggests that it was responsive not so much to any particular ideology as it was to the immigrant generations' shared sense of disjuncture from the Old World in the wake of World War I and the subsequent end of mass immigration. This impulse was fundamentally different from the concomitant development of Yiddish-language schooling in Eastern Europe. Teaching Yiddish to their American-born children was implicated with immigrants' need to forge new understandings of Yiddish as an object of cultural heritage, articulating connections between the immigrants' Old World past and their visions for the future of Jewish life in America.

This development is borne out, for example, by the foreword to Leon Elbe's *Di yidishe shprakh* (The Yiddish Language). Published in New York in 1914, it claims to be the first American Yiddish primer and was intended for use in Farband schools as well as in talmud torahs. The foreword's author, journalist Joel Entin, articulates the great symbolic value invested in this modest volume:

> Above all, I hope that our "Moyshelekh and Shloymelekh," our younger generation, on whom we place all of our hopes, will be drawn through this book to something of their own, something intimate and familiar; that they will find herein the voices of their people, of their past and present; that not only will this book acquaint them with the Yiddish language and foster a love of its literature, but that through it they will be filled with love for our people and its existence.[45]

In America Jewish children were to learn Yiddish not toward some political or socioeconomic end, as was the case in Eastern Europe, but for the sake of their cultural enrichment. Entin suggests that while Yiddish embodies an affective spirit of Jewish collective identity, young American Jews lack this feeling, due to an insufficient familiarity with Yiddish as a language of daily life, and that therefore some effort needs to be made to help them acquire it.

Working within the limitations of a text written for someone who has yet to cross the threshold of literacy, the first lesson in *Di yidishe shprakh* addresses this daunting challenge obliquely. The lesson introduces the fundamentals of the mechanics of reading Yiddish, presenting a selection of six letters of the alphabet, the forming of syllables and words, the use of punctuation, and the difference between print

First lesson in Leon Elbe's *Di yidishe shprakh* (The Yiddish Language), first published in New York in 1914.

and script. Much of this lesson reflects established methods of teaching children the *alefbeys* for reading Hebrew; but the selection of the four first words taught here—*kar* (tram), *rak* (crayfish), *bok* (he-goat) and *rod* (wheel)—stands out. The first two words, *kar* and *rak*, offer a lesson in the important issue of the direction in which to read Yiddish, from right to left, with accompanying pictures that underscore the consequences of misreading. The implicit contrast is, of course, with the left-to-right direction of English, the language that the student was learning to read at the same time in public schools. The child's introduction to Yiddish literacy thus also constitutes a tacit lesson in linguistic and cultural juxtaposition. There is further implicit instruction in the symbolic meaning of Yiddish to be found within the first words taught here. Together with their attendant images, they delineate something of the length and breadth of the language, which both looks back to the East Euro-

First lesson in B. Ostrovski and S. Hurvits's *Yidish far onfanger* (Yiddish for Beginners), first published in New York in 1930.

pean Old World (the goat being a common metonym of shtetl life) and embraces the modern urban milieu of streetcars.

Exploiting the symbolic potential of the first word or words that a Jewish child is taught to read is by no means an innovation of modern Yiddish pedagogy. Memoirs of *kheyder* instruction report first lessons in which children learn one or more words embodying abstract moral and pious values.[46] Whereas Yiddish primers published in Eastern Europe begin with a variety of first words, their American counterparts show a decided preference for certain first words. These choices suggest a shared awareness of the primers' symbolic value as they address the challenge of teaching Yiddish to children who do not necessarily know the language, even nominally, from home.

The most common first word taught in American Yiddish primers is *mame* (sometimes spelled *mama*), appearing in a half-dozen of the texts published between the 1920s and 1940s. To read the word *mame*, the student needs to learn three letters—*mem, pasekh-alef,* and *ayin.* Before the word *mame* is presented, these books introduce the *pasekh-alef* by accompanying the letter with a picture of a mother lulling a child to sleep. In some instances, the letter's sound ("a" as in "far") is explicitly defined in an accompanying text as the mother's crooning *(a-a-a-a)* to her baby. The word *mame* may also be preceded by repeated syllables *(ma, me)* wrought out of the letters used to spell it.[47]

Linked with the visual image of mother and child, these devices invoke the widely held notion of the "natural" process of native language acquisition, beginning with a parent's nonsensical "baby talk" and progressing to more meaningful language skills that pass between parent and child. (According to linguist Steven Pinker, this notion of language acquisition is itself a cultural myth. Human language, he argues, is instinctual: "Children actually reinvent it, generation after generation—not because they are taught, . . . but because they just can't help it.")[48] With such a beginning, these primers symbolically replicate the ostensibly organic manner of Yiddish as akin to acquiring maternal nurturing. In doing so, these texts celebrate an idealized heritage of intergenerational linguistic and cultural continuity that the very books in which they appear have, in fact, disrupted and revolutionized. These primers symbolically obviate their modern classroom setting by simulating the "natural" acquisition of a native tongue, starting with one of the first words that children usually learn to say. Even though Yiddish vied with English as the primary language for these children of immigrants, it was, at least symbolically, still to be regarded as their *mame-loshn.*[49]

Cultural subversion of a different kind is at work in the case of the second most common first word taught in American Yiddish primers—*shul*—which is defined in secular Yiddish primers as "school."[50] Here, too, is a symbolic lesson, meaningful less for children than for their parents: not only is one taught that *shul* means "school," but also, implicitly, that *shul* does not mean "synagogue" (which is, in fact, the much older meaning of the word). This first lesson becomes the foundation for later instruction, which presents Yiddish as the center of a secular culture that radically redefines Jewish identity and practice. Yiddish functions here as a marker of Jewish religious heritage as well as of its subversion, thereby extending the language's semiotic value as a sign of revolution.[51]

Beyond their first pages, American Yiddish primers of the interwar years offered language instruction as they provided lessons in a culture alternative to that embodied by the American public school and the English language. At the same time that textbooks teaching American children to read English shifted their focus from reading content to the process of reading itself, American Yiddish primers were explicitly, sometimes emphatically, ideological. As they taught the fundamentals of Yiddish as a language of daily life, these books also provided their young readers with a charged sense of the symbolic value of Yiddish as the embodiment of distinctive cultural principles. The texts in these books positioned their young readers in a world of historical depth and cultural breadth, according to their various ideologies: Yiddish textbooks used in Orthodox talmud torahs included Bible stories and other readings that validate religious traditions, while primers issued by the Farband promoted Labor Zionist ideals.[52]

The most vivid examples of fusing Yiddish language literacy with ideological instruction are found in textbooks published by the IWO in the 1930s. Unlike most children's textbooks in any language or culture, they offer a harshly critical perspective of the children's environment and, moreover, teach their young readers to become active participants in a radical transformation of their world.[53] This can be seen even before opening the 1932 primer *Arbeter-shul* (Workers' School): in the cover illustration, a boy and a girl wear neckerchiefs (a sign that they are members of the Pioneers, a communist youth movement) and hold aloft a banner that says *"Mir lernen un kemfn"* (We learn and struggle). The letters of the *alefbeys* on the banner are wrought out of hammers and sickles—a deft semiotic fusion of Yiddishism and communism. *Arbeter-shul* is also demonstrably antireligious and anti-Hebrew; in one short text a boy tries to convince his friend not to go to Hebrew school but to attend the workers' school.[54]

Yiddish primers published during and shortly after World War II testify to the war's profound transformation of American Yiddish culture, evincing signal sociological and ideological changes. For example, the poem "Mayn land Amerike" (My Country, America) in *Mayn yidish bukh* (My Yiddish Book)—published in 1944 by the Jewish People's Fraternal Order (JPFO), a secular, left-wing Yiddishist organization, following its break with the IWO—celebrates the United States as a homeland for all classes, races, and ethnic groups. *In der heym un in der shul* (At Home and at School), published by the Workmen's Circle in 1951, places a story about children playing baseball opposite another story about a tailor, the latter clearly a nod to the immigrant, working-class heritage of the students' forebears. Like Elbe's 1914 primer, this textbook seeks to position Yiddish as a language embracing the Jewish past as well as its present.[55]

But American Yiddish pedagogues confronted more fundamental changes in the postwar era. In 1950 educator Khayem Bez addressed the challenge that secular Yiddish schools faced in teaching the grandchildren of immigrants, asking "how such a child should be integrated . . . into the [Jewish] national community through Yiddish; how our people's language should become, in time, the child's own."[56] In Bez's view, Yiddish schools faced the daunting task of teaching Yiddish to children for whom the language might not seem to be self-evidently "their own." Moreover, the challenge of forging such an attachment to Yiddish was vital in preventing these American Jewish children from feeling estranged from their own people.

Authors of Yiddish textbooks were already answering the call for pedagogical reform. In the preface to *Der nayer onfanger* (The New Beginner)—a revised version of *Der onfanger,* one of the most frequently reprinted Yiddish primers of the interwar years—author Yankev Levin writes in 1945 that, increasingly, students know little, if any, Yiddish, and often their parents have limited knowledge as well. These children can't be taught by the same methods (hence the revised book), because they don't arrive with the same "mental baggage" as children whose mother tongue is Yiddish. Yet Levin is loath to characterize Yiddish as a "foreign language" for this growing number of American Jewish children; somewhere in the recesses of their consciousness, he asserts, lies their cultural heritage, like buried treasure, which will be revealed when they hear Yiddish spoken. Nevertheless, he concedes, Yiddish is *not* their mother tongue, but a *second* language, and must be taught as such.[57] Levin's remarks testify both to lingering notions that Yiddish was still essentially *di shprakh vos redt zikh* and to the looming challenge of how to transmit the heritage understood as inherent in Yiddish when this assumption of its nativeness gives way to a new, postvernacular configuration—one in which Yiddish cannot even be symbolically represented as the mother tongue.[58]

While Levin advocated structured conversational drills in class to compensate for the lack of hearing Yiddish at home, other primers of the period evince more profound shifts in pedagogical approach, which were less a matter of methodology than of recognizing a signal shift in American Jewish literacy. Consider, for example, the JPFO's *Mayn yidish bukh* (My Yiddish Book), a revised version of *Mayn alefbeys* (My Alphabet), a primer originally published by the IWO in the mid-1930s.[59] The new version replaces the original first lesson, which had introduced students to seven words in a simple Yiddish rhyme, with a rhyming English-language text that includes only two Yiddish words:

This is a school,
We call it "a shul"
You will learn Yiddish in the shul.

In Yiddish you will learn
to read and write
And to recite.
And when you know it better
You can even write a letter!
It will please your Mom and Dad,
And everybody will be glad.[60]

The introductory presentation of Yiddish shifts from that of a full language to one that has been atomized and absorbed by another, integral language, which the revised primer implicitly recognizes as the students' vernacular. Indeed, rather than being acquired from conversational give-and-take with family members and close acquaintances, Yiddish is transformed into a classroom exercise in heritage, undertaken to please one's parents. Other changes took place in postwar Yiddish textbooks: simplified vocabularies, shorter readings, and the discontinuation of advanced-level readers. These changes signal not merely the reduction of pedagogical goals but also the need to establish, through pedagogy, a new relationship with Yiddish for future generations, who no longer encounter it, even indirectly, as a language of daily life.

The attrition of vernacular Yiddish speakers in postwar America was compounded by a much greater sense of cultural disjuncture. Assumptions about Yiddish embodying a vibrant sense of Jewish peoplehood had been abruptly undone by the Holocaust, and the primacy of Yiddish as a Jewish vernacular was swiftly superceded by English and, in Israel, by modern Hebrew. At the same time, the secondary significance of Yiddish as a vestige of a "lost" culture flourished. The desire to forge a symbolic attachment of some kind to the language and to the bygone Old World it embodies has persisted among many American Jews, even as their commitment to maintaining Yiddish fluency has faded. Thus, a 1959 study commissioned by the American Association for Jewish Education reported that twice as many Jewish community leaders thought "familiarity with the Yiddish aspect of Jewish culture" was "indispensable" to American Jewish schooling as compared to the number who thought "making Yiddish a second spoken language" or the "ability to read Yiddish literature" to be essential.[61]

More recent Yiddish textbooks address students who are at an even greater distance from the language and the culture it has come to symbolize. The Workmen's Circle's 1971 edition of *Yidishe kinder* (Jewish Children) includes several prefatory pages in English that explain not only why students are studying Yiddish but also what Yiddish is, thereby explicitly transforming the vernacular of the past into an object of heritage for the present and acknowledging its postvernacular status for the students: "Yiddish is the language that millions of Jews speak and write, and in which they create their rich culture. . . . In this book you will also find interesting stories about the Jewish holidays, stories that every Jewish boy and girl should know. Knowing them is like receiving a gift, for your life will be much richer with this knowledge."[62] Like *Mayn yidish bukh*, this introduction also explains (in English) that Yiddish is read from right to left. So, too, does *The Yiddish Alphabet Book* (published in 1979 in Palo Alto, by a press with no affiliation to any Yiddish cultural organization), which teaches readers only one or two words per letter of the *alefbeys*. This book proffers "a glimpse through a half-opened door at a wonderful, warm world which awaits the explorer of Yiddish," while making only a nominal attempt to bring the reader into this world.[63] Yiddish is no longer presented as a language to be mastered, even symbolically, but to be appreciated for its affective value through a highly selective sampling. Indeed, as the illustration that accompanies the letter *lamed* (L) and the word *lerer* (teacher) demonstrates, the volume's implicit expectation is that the reader will sooner explore other linguistic worlds: the teacher is depicted writing on the blackboard not in Yiddish, but in modern Hebrew.

LANGUAGE OF CHOICE

The trajectory of Yiddish education does not end here. While the teaching of the language to children in afternoon and weekend schools, whether religious or secular, has declined in the post–World War II era, Yiddish is taught to growing numbers of children in hasidic day schools and young adults in universities. These trends, responsive to different demographic and cultural developments, have each fostered new notions of the symbolic meaning of Yiddish for future generations.

In the immediate postwar years hasidim, who had been rooted in Eastern Europe for generations, rapidly established new communities in an international diaspora that includes Antwerp, Jerusalem, London, Melbourne, Montreal, and especially Brooklyn. Neighborhoods of this New York City borough emerged as the new epicenter for most of the major hasidic groups that survived the war. Postwar hasidic communities comprise a new American Yiddish-speaking population with its own valuation of the language and its own way of teaching it. As linguist Dovid Katz has noted, there is virtually no contact between the writers and teachers of Yiddish in the secular and hasidic communities, which are separated by a cultural "iron curtain."[64]

At the same time, the juxtaposition of secular and hasidic approaches to Yiddish pedagogy articulates the range of the language's meta-value in the postwar era. Comparing the two demonstrates how instruction in the same language in communities that, though sometimes geographically proximate, are culturally segregated responds differently to divergent ideological, pedagogical, and sociolinguistic factors. Yet the comparison also reveals the extent to which these diverging approaches to Yiddish pedagogy are nonetheless similarly responsive to the decline in Yiddish vernacularity and the concomitant expansion of its postvernacular mode in the second half of the twentieth century.

Although Yiddish has played an important role in hasidic education from the movement's inception, formal Yiddish-language instruction in schools directly run by hasidic communities is a postwar phenomenon. In the United States the teaching of Yiddish was typically inaugurated only after these communities were established and an American-born generation had matured.[65] This development conforms with linguist Miriam Isaacs's observation of a shift in the significance of Yiddish among postwar hasidim from an "immigrant language" to what she terms a "minority language."[66]

Since the 1970s Jewish bookstores catering to hasidim in the Brooklyn neighborhoods of Crown Heights, Williamsburg, and Boro Park have featured a growing inventory of Yiddish pedagogical materials for children, including primers, readers (many recounting the deeds of prewar *rebeyim*), and books teaching holiday customs and daily pious conduct, some in the form of coloring books and activity books.[67] In addition, a few titles deal with what might be thought of as secular subjects, such as the lavishly illustrated *Oylem umloye* (The World and All That's in It), published in 1999. However, as the foreword to this multivolume children's encyclopedia makes clear, learning about world geography and zoology is intended to inspire the reader "to love and revere the Creator," citing Maimonides, the Psalms of King David, and Jewish lore about Adam as prooftexts.[68] *Oylem umloye* is issued by a press based in Jerusalem, with an office in Lakewood, New Jersey—illustrative of the international network of Yiddish publications circulating among ultra-Orthodox centers in North America, Western Europe, and Israel.

Several of these hasidic children's publications are especially designed to teach the Yiddish language. Typically, as the workbook *Di yidishe shprakh, undzer tsirung* (The Yiddish Language, Our Jewel) states in its preface, they link "teaching children how to write Yiddish without mistakes" with "inculcating values of devotion to God and good conduct."[69] Some books, such as *Yidish leyenbukh far lererin* (Yiddish Reader for the Female Teacher), one of a series of readers for use in the Beys Rokhl schools run by Satmar hasidim, are specifically intended for young girls.[70]

These books exemplify a pattern, noted by observers of post–World War II hasidic communities, of distinctions in their use of Yiddish along gender lines.[71]

Postwar hasidic education formalizes this distinction by schooling boys and girls separately and according to different curricula that reflect the discrete futures envisioned for these children—professionally, socially, intellectually, and spiritually—as pious Jewish men and women. In the education of boys and young men, Yiddish continues to figure as the traditional language of devotional study of the Talmud and other sacred texts. In girls' schools, however, the language has been curricularized to provide a separate, appropriate voice for their religious instruction. In 1958 author and journalist Ascher Penn described the advent of hasidic girls' schools in postwar New York, noting that the center of their curriculum was Bible study conducted in Yiddish. According to one of the schools' directors, this practice achieved two goals: "First, it maintains the familiar tradition of [Bible] study, and, second, it also teaches the girls the Yiddish language, in an indirect manner. Yiddish is the best means of linking the students to the older generation. . . . Even their American-born parents, who cannot speak Yiddish well themselves, understand the language to a considerable extent, and the Yiddish that their children learn in schools has great meaning for these estranged parents."[72] The Yiddish language is not offered as a subject of study in itself, but, following the traditional pattern of the *kheyder*, is acquired as a by-product of study centered on sacred texts in Loshn-koydesh. Yet at the same time, the language is valued as a sign of cultural continuity, including for those who are not fluent native speakers and who might even provide a corrective model for their parents (whose knowledge of Yiddish might have been limited, in many cases, as a result of their experiences in Europe during World War II and its aftermath).[73]

Isaacs notes that the commitment of hasidic communities to teaching Yiddish to their children constitutes a "new stability" for the use of the language; indeed, she argues that, given the sharply rising population of postwar hasidim, "there is increased likelihood of Yiddish growth with greater distance from the immigrant generation." At the same time, she notes that the "need to articulate the appropriateness of Yiddish" in current pedagogical materials indicates an unprecedented awareness of language choice and its inherent significance.[74] In this respect, Yiddish is constituted as the embodiment of heritage—which, David Lowenthal notes, "reflects not just habit but conscious choice"—for postwar American hasidim as much as for prewar East European Jewish immigrants.[75]

Such developments imply that postwar hasidim are, in their own way, engaging with Yiddish as a postvernacular language. Consider, for example, special features for juvenile readers in *Mayles* (Virtues), a monthly Yiddish-language family magazine that began publication in Monsey, New York, in the 1990s. As Katz observes, these lessons are intended "for the hasidic child who thinks in Yiddish," and they indicate both what the child reader is expected to know and what the extent of his fluency may eventually include.[76] Thus, vocabulary enrichment units on terms related to theater (e.g., *shpiln a role* [playing a role], *hinter di kulisn* [behind the curtains]) and music (*kapelye* [orchestra], *marsh* [march], *notn* [notes]) suggest that the scope of language use in the children's cultural world will extend beyond the home and the traditional use of Yiddish in the study of sacred texts.[77]

Despite the hasidic commitment to maintaining Yiddish as a language of daily life, such efforts to enhance the community's command of the language, especially among its younger generation, do not meet with universal approval. A letter to the editor printed in *Mayles* in 2002 criticizes the magazine's explanations of Yiddish grammar and glossaries of Yiddish terminology as a dangerous trend toward "Yiddishism." In this context, Yiddishism is denounced not only for its secular associations but also as an undue devotion to Yiddish for its own sake, regardless of one's religiosity. ("Who says that there has to be a Yiddish word for everything?" asks the letter's author. "Not all languages are equally rich.")[78] Rather, Yiddish is properly valued for its delimited role as a traditional vehicle of hasidic lore, as a linguistic gatekeeper that limits hasidic access to the larger world, and, hence, as a language of daily life that increasingly distinguishes hasidim from other Jews.

Simultaneous to the development of hasidic Yiddish pedagogy in post–World War II America is the advent of teaching the language in American universities as part of the emergence of Jewish studies as an academic discipline generally. Remarkably, this realization of early-twentieth-century Yiddishists' aspirations for recognition of the language's academic legitimacy has sometimes been a source of discomfort, even for its practitioners. Writing on the subject of Yiddish in the university in the mid-1970s, literary scholar Leonard Prager asserted that "there *is* something incongruous in removing Yiddish to a university, and something disturbing as well." Here Yiddish pedagogy is extracted from the context of a Jewish community and the agenda of intergenerational continuity. At the same time, the university setting is not a cultural or ideological vacuum. (Indeed, Yiddish studies programs at universities may be thought of as Yiddishlands, tenaciously staking out a place for the language somewhere in the intellectual terrain of the humanities.) Prager himself claimed that "all Yiddish scholars, regardless of ideology, value the fruits of Yiddish creativity and the great marvel of the Yiddish language itself. Their very enterprise argues some mode of 'survival' for Yiddish."[79]

This notion is manifest in the opening pages of Uriel Weinreich's *College Yiddish*, the earliest such textbook for the English speaker.[80] First published in 1949, when it was used in only a handful of settings, it is still in print and remains a classroom standard. (Prager asserted that, "had we not been fortunate enough to possess" this landmark text, "Yiddish might not have penetrated the university at all.")[81] Designed for the American undergraduate, *College Yiddish* assumes fluency in English and a familiarity with basic grammatical terms. However, it does not anticipate the student's prior knowledge of the *alefbeys*, how Yiddish uses the alphabet, or Yiddish phonetics (all of which are explained in prefaces). Moreover, the text does not assume that its reader is a descendant of Yiddish speakers any more than a book teaching, say, Italian to English speakers assumes that the students are of Italian ancestry. As a work of humanistic scholarship, *College Yiddish* makes no explicit claims to fostering Jewish identity, solidarity, or continuity; it does not strive to reify Yiddish as heritage. Instead, its foreword by linguist Roman Jakobson speaks of the importance of promoting a standard language to ensure the maintenance of Yiddish as a *kulturshprakh:* "Under conditions of diaspora, a rigorously unified standard is even a much more vital premise for the being and development of a cultural language than it is in a closely knit speech community. There cannot be approximate knowledge of a literary language for its users. Full mastery or illiteracy—*tertium non datur.*"[82]

And yet, *College Yiddish* does celebrate the "marvel of Yiddish," if obliquely so, as an emblem of Jewish tenacity. Its first lesson begins with a reading in Yiddish on Jewish population. Though articulated in the dispassionate, third-person voice of an encyclopedia entry, the lesson makes a charged statement for the late 1940s—a quiet, self-reflexive affirmation of the endurance of Yiddish among Jews around the world: "Today Jews are a people numbering eleven million. Jews live on every continent. . . . Jews speak Yiddish in many countries. . . . Yiddish unites Jews of every country."[83]

At the turn of the millennium, dozens of institutions of higher learning in the United States offer Yiddish-language instruction.[84] Establishing Yiddish as part of a liberal arts education has important new pedagogical and cultural implications for the language in its postvernacular mode. Rather than a first language, here Yiddish is almost always a second, and sometimes a third or fourth, language studied (if not mastered). Moreover, it is increasingly likely to be a second Jewish language learned, after modern Hebrew, which has become a pervasive presence in American Jewish education in the post–World War II era, taught in Jewish day schools, afternoon and weekend synagogue schools, summer camps, and educational programs for Jewish youth visiting Israel. While learning Hebrew is typically a fixture of an American Jewish childhood (and not infrequently ends with Jewish rites of passage into adolescence), taking a class in Yiddish now marks for some a voluntary step in the formation of one's Jewish adult self, along with other college studies and activities, such as attending Hillel programs, joining a Jewish political group or chorus, or living in a kosher dormitory.

In the mid-1970s, Prager saw the rise of Yiddish studies on university campuses as part of a larger cultural transformation distinctive to the United States: "The young, especially in America, spurred on by identity problems and temperamentally predisposed to value what their parents may have scorned, are more likely to be without preconceived [negative] notions as to the nature and status of Yiddish. In an educational environment where virtually everything may be studied and where Black America has been vigorously transvaluing a largely sordid past, it is no wonder that Yiddish, too, should enter the curriculum."[85] Indeed, while many college students are still attracted to Yiddish as an embodiment of Jewish heritage, for others learning the language has a subversive cachet, offering alternatives to American Jewish social and cultural conventions. Students are now often drawn to Yiddish as a Jewish signifier of the diasporic, politically progressive, culturally avant-garde, feminist, or queer, the language emblematic of what one observer has described as a new, Jewish "twenty-something in-your-face radicalism."[86]

Thus, whereas prewar talmud torahs and secular Yiddish schools responded largely to the concerns of teachers and parents, today's university-based Yiddish studies programs reckon with the interests of young adult students. The move of Yiddish into the academy has other implications as well: university programs can be situated far from any sizeable Yiddish-speaking community, and the field is open, both in principle and in practice, to non-Jews and Jews alike. In this way, the long-standing issues for Yiddish of diaspora and cultural borders take on new configurations, as do notions of learning the language as an engagement with heritage.[87]

The postwar advent of Yiddish education at the university level now extends to institutions of higher learning in Israel and across Europe. Especially noteworthy is the return of Yiddish pedagogy in former Soviet republics and Warsaw Pact nations since the late 1980s. Classes in Yiddish language, literature, and culture are taught at universities and other venues in Warsaw, Kiev, Moscow, and Vilnius, among other cities, often with financial and scholarly support from the United States and Israel. This instruction has been offered, for example, by Project Judaica, established in 1990 by the Jewish Theological Seminary of America and the YIVO In-

RESIST!
THE MAJOR LANGUAGES

Subvert the dominant language.

REGISTER FOR YIDDISH TODAY!

Introductory Yiddish • Yiddish 1 • CC# 38103

Yiddish is the millennium-old language of the Jews of Central and Eastern Europe. At the beginning of the twentieth century, there were over 15 million speakers of Yiddish, now there are around three million. Come explore the riches of Yiddish culture next semester.

Printed with the support of the Institute of European Studies

Poster announcing Yiddish language instruction at the University of California, Berkeley, 2004. Designed by Robby Peckerar. Courtesy of the Program in Jewish Studies, University of California, Berkeley.

stitute in conjunction with the Russian State University for the Humanities in Moscow to institute university-level Jewish studies programs in Russia.

This undertaking is intended for local Jewish students as part of a larger revival of Jewish religious and cultural life in postcommunist Eastern Europe; other contemporary efforts to teach Yiddish address Eastern Europe's non-Jewish population as well. Magdalena Sitarz's textbook, *Jidysz: Podręcznik nauki języka dla początkujących* (Yiddish: Language Instructional Manual for Beginners), published in Cracow in 1995, reflects an "interest in Yiddish from a basically Polish point of view," notes literary scholar Monika Adamczyck-Garbowska. The textbook explains to the " 'average' Pole who would like to learn this language . . . that studying Yiddish can be a fascinating adventure for everybody, not only because the language contains so many Slavic elements, but because 'Yiddish is first of all a means to a better knowledge and understanding of a people that lived in Poland for many centuries and who had an important share in the development of 'our culture.' "[88]

An intensive Yiddish studies program in Vilnius, established in 1998, extends its appeal even further by offering its setting to foreign students as an "authentic habitat." The English-language promotional brochure for the Vilnius Program in Yiddish boasts "a unique opportunity to enter the world of Yiddish. . . . Encounter the historical Yerusholayim d'Lita, work with native East European Yiddish speakers. . . . Participate in the living encounter with the breathtaking expanse of Yiddish."[89] These claims of environmental authenticity rest on top of Vilne/Wilno/Vilnius's complex, heterogeneous history of political and cultural discontinuity and reconstitution. Vaunted as a *milieu de mémoire*, the erstwhile Jerusalem of Lithuania as invoked here is more exemplary of historian Pierre Nora's denatured, self-consciously constructed *lieux de mémoire*.[90]

The program's faculty also embodies complexities that problematize this image of indigenous authenticity. Some of the instructors hail from America, Israel, or Western Europe, while others who reside in Lithuania or Russia were trained abroad. And consider the personal history of Anna Verschik, who has taught Yiddish language at the Vilnius program since its inception, as reported in a 2003 bulletin: though a native of Leningrad and a native speaker of Russian, "in her childhood Anna often heard her grandmother conversing in Yiddish with older family members—in the Belorussian dialect of Shklov; and, as she herself puts it, she 'got the general idea.' From that time, Yiddish remained latent within her." After spending summers in the Estonian Soviet Socialist Republic, Anna was attracted to its distinctive culture and decided to make it her home: "At the age of eleven, she also understood that a language does not just 'come' to you, you have to learn it. She began studying Estonian, which by now has become her 'mother tongue.'" Verschik discovered that in Estonia "there existed a kind of solidarity with Jews as yet another persecuted people of the Soviet empire, and this further strengthened Anna's sense of belonging." When one of her professors, a non-Jew who knew Yiddish, asked whether she spoke the language, Verschik "discovered—thanks to grandmother Sonia—that she could." This eventually led her to pursue graduate studies in Yiddish linguistics. "Today," the bulletin explains, "her cultural identity is Yiddish and Estonian."[91] Vershik's relationship to Yiddish (or, for that matter, to Estonian) challenges conventional notions of a naturalized "mother tongue." Yet at the same time it is emblematic of the deliberate, inventive forging of identity that can thrive in the possibilities of postvernacular language.

Learning a language in a classroom is not in itself a sign of postvernacularity, of course. But in the case of a language such as Yiddish—which for centuries was acquired almost exclusively by Ashkenazic children as their first language from their families and from other Jews in their immediate environment—the introduction of classroom instruction has radically altered both the community's functional relationship to the language and its semiological value. This development contrasts with the concomitant invention of modern Hebrew education. Learning Hebrew from a textbook in a classroom was not in itself a departure from Jewish tradition; on the contrary, what was revolutionary was the notion of learning Hebrew as a mother tongue. (Consider, for example, the "magical quality" of Eliezer Ben-Yehuda's account in his autobiography of his son's birth as the advent of the first native speaker of modern Hebrew.)[92]

Jewish nationalists' appeals for mother-tongue schooling in Eastern Europe a century ago sought to build on the foundation of Yiddish as a *folkshprakh*—a language that defined peoplehood politically and culturally with a distinctive primacy for this diaspora, minority community. Indeed, the Yiddish classroom served as a prototype in miniature of an imagined Jewish nationhood; pictures of Yiddish writers and Yiddishist ideologists hung on classroom walls where, in state-run schools, portraits of national leaders would be displayed. Yet even in its heyday, mother-tongue pedagogy created unprecedented challenges, both practical and theoretical, for Yiddishists, as social and cultural upheavals, large-scale population shifts, and the redrawing of the political map of Eastern Europe destabilized their assumptions about Jewish vernacularity. In America, learning Yiddish has, from the start, been largely a response to its postvernacular status, though acknowledging this has proved daunting for those who advocate the maintenance of Yiddish, whether they are ardent secularists or devout hasidim.

Linguist Yudel Mark observed in 1947 that Yiddish education "was not built on tradition. . . . It was free from the burden of superfluous accumulation but it also did not have the benefit of established forms," and in the course of its existence it "passed through a number of transmigrations."[93] The history of teaching Yiddish over the span of the past century demonstrates the mutability of linguistic continuity as a consequence of war, revolution, immigration, and genocide, and also as a result of linguistic persecution, regulation, and neglect. At the same time, this history testifies to the tenacity of Jewish communities as they strive to renegotiate their ties to the language both instrumentally and symbolically.

At the beginning of the twentieth century, Yiddishists envisioned a radical transformation of Jewish peoplehood, centered on the language that was and, they assumed, would remain their mother tongue. The Yiddish classroom emerged as a strategic proving ground for this vision of a new, modern Jewish vernacular culture, to be realized through future generations. One century later, the aspirations of Jews to transform the language yet again into something beyond a mother tongue involve similar leaps, both of imagination and of action. Now the classroom is a site for looking back in time as much as forward, for looking toward traditional cultural origins as much as away from them. Instead of serving as a venue for elevating a language of daily life to a *kulturshprakh*, Yiddish education, now secured in institutions of "high" culture, facilitates subjunctive ventures into the retrieval of "lost" Jewish vernacularity.

CHAPTER THREE

FOUNDED IN TRANSLATION

> "One language has never been enough for the Jewish people."
> —SHMUEL NIGER, *Bilingualism in the History of Jewish Literature*

This piquant observation by Yiddish literary critic Shmuel Niger (né Charney; one language was apparently not enough for him even nominally) suggests that code-switching—moving back and forth between one language and another—constitutes a definitional Jewish activity. Indeed, most Jewish cultures have routinely entailed code-switching, not only as practitioners shift from one task to another but also within their performance of a single activity, be it devotional study, prayer, writing belles lettres or personal correspondence, singing songs, relating folktales—even in daily conversation. In the course of these language shifts, translating from one language to another occurs regularly—sometimes explicitly and methodically (as in the case of the traditional *gemore shier,* or bilingual prayer books), sometimes more freely and obliquely (for instance, in multilingual jokes or macaronic songs). In such milieus, translation is not, as the Italians famously say, an act of betrayal *("traduttore, traditore")*. On the contrary, in translation Jewish culture is not lost but found. Thus, in his memoir of "discovering Yiddish in America," literary scholar and translator Richard Fein writes, "Some form of translation, or removal from the original, has become a factor in my identity, as I struggled to touch a source that announced itself while it was hidden from me."[1]

In Yiddish culture translation plays a foundational role. Because Yiddish is a language that never stands alone, translations both into and out of it provide strategic opportunities for considering the shifting linguistic and cultural frontiers of Ashkenaz. More than items of linguistic or literary interest, translations can be regarded as sites of cultural engagement that reveal the contingent nature of Yiddish in relation to other languages at a given time and place. The frontiers of Yiddish culture are dynamic both geographically and socially; in addition to changes in language use, they articulate shifting notions of Jewish literacy, fluency, and vernacularity. In this respect, Yiddish exemplifies literary theorist Homi Bhabha's characterization of translation as a strategic, formative locus of culture: "it is the 'inter'—the cutting edge of translation and negotiation, the *in-between* space—that carries the burden of the meaning of culture."[2]

In Jewish cultures, translation not only negotiates transmigrations across Jewish-gentile borders, it also engages the definitional practice of having more than one Jewish language. Traditional internal Jewish bilingualism entails more than a complementary use of two languages. They are also sometimes employed redundantly, while at other times their interrelation is ludic. Much traditional textual study, prayer, or storytelling entails repeating a Loshn-koydesh text in the Jewish vernacular either orally or in print, a practice hearkening back to ancient times with the establishment, following the Babylonian exile, of public readings of scripture in both Hebrew and in a vernacular translation.[3] Though the languages interrelate within a hierarchy that privileges the sacred Hebrew original over its translation into the vernacular, this ritualized duplication is a mutually reinforcing practice. Worshipers are expected to be competent in both languages and to understand each one in relation to the other. At the same time, such redundancies can reveal slippages between two Jewish languages, exposing both resonant connotations and divergent nuances that inspire insight into the texts and enhance engagement with them.[4]

Jewish code-switching also generates language play that deftly manipulates the tension between the components' parities and divergences. (Thus, *targem*, the Yiddish term for the Aramaic translation of the Bible, generates the humorous idiom *targem-loshn*, meaning "gibberish.") Sometimes this activity extends beyond language to other cultural practices, imbuing them with additional semiotic value. In his history of the Yiddish language, Max Weinreich cites several examples of these—the custom of eating cabbage soup (an allusion to German *Kohl mit Wasser* [cabbage with water]) in western Ashkenaz on the holiday of Hoshanah Rabbah, when the Hebrew prayer *Kol mevaser* is recited; illustrations of hare hunting in sixteenth-century Passover Haggadahs that create a pun by juxtaposing the Yiddish phrase *yog'n hoz* with the Hebrew acronym *YaKNeHoZ*, which reminds readers of the order for the five blessings recited when the seder falls on Saturday night—as evidence of how "language is a cofashioner of life, a cocreator of values."[5]

Since the beginnings of modern Yiddish belles lettres in the mid–nineteenth century, translation practices involving Yiddish—both as a target language (i.e., translating into Yiddish) and as a source language (translating from Yiddish)—generate innovative meanings out of code-switching, as they engage new kinds of texts and create new kinds of readers. In particular, translation practices can be seen as exemplary Jewish engagements with modernity—both expanding the frontiers of Yiddish literacy and presenting it with unprecedented potential for its dissolution.

In postvernacular Yiddish, translation is a constant, if often tacit, presence. Because it does not engage Yiddish as an everyday language or mother tongue, postvernacular Yiddish by definition is encountered through or along with some other semiotic system. Moreover, the symbolic value of Yiddish in its postvernacular mode also requires translating. Consequently, translation is an issue engaged in every chapter of this book. Even so, translating warrants consideration as a cultural practice on its own, focusing on the changing role of literary translations in Yiddish culture and on those moments when the process of translation becomes a subject of attention itself.

The translation practices in postvernacular Yiddish culture prove to be as diverse as they are abundant, responding to the disparity between erstwhile assumptions of Yiddish as vernacular and some new relationship with the language—as exoticism, as heritage, as fantasy. Therefore, to appreciate the significance of literary translation in Yiddish culture of the post-Holocaust era, it is essential to consider translation in light of its formative role in Ashkenaz from its earliest days through the efflorescence of modern Yiddish belles lettres.

ENGENDERING THE VERNACULAR READER

Much of the earliest textual evidence for Yiddish is associated with translation, such as the Old Yiddish glosses that appear in the commentaries of the eleventh-century rabbinical scholar Rashi, for whom these words served to explicate obscure Loshn-koydesh terms in scripture in the vernacular of medieval Ashkenazim living in northwestern Europe. Most of the earliest works of Yiddish literature, especially those that appeared following the advent of printing, are translations. Prominent among these are Yiddish versions of the Bible, legends, ethical guides, liturgy, and other texts originally written in Loshn-koydesh. The earliest of these works, which began to appear in the mid-1500s, render in print the centuries-old oral practice of translating sacred texts into the vernacular, the foundation of traditional Jewish scholarship. Translations of secular literature from non-Jewish sources—from

Aesop's fables to the romance of King Arthur—also appear among early printed Yiddish books.[6]

At the time, the language into which these works were rendered was most often referred to as *taytsh*. Use of this term indicates that Ashkenazim knew "of a proximity of their language to German *[Deutsch]*, but that they had no particular interests in stressing the uniqueness of their language by means of the name."[7] Significantly, *taytsh* also came to function as a noun in Yiddish, defined as "meaning"; it served as the base of the verbs *(far)taytshn* (to translate, to interpret), *oystaytshn* (to construe), and *zayn der/di taytsh* (to denote, to mean), as well as of the idiom *staytsh?* (How is that possible?). This vocabulary evinces a semiological encoding of Yiddish as the linguistic vehicle of Ashkenazic vernacular translation—that is, as the means of conveying texts from various other languages, sacred as well as gentile, into the familiar voice of home, where their meaning becomes indigenous.

As is true of translation generally, Yiddish renderings of texts, regardless of their source, entail transforming as well as transferring their meaning. The meta-value of early Yiddish translations is distinctive, for they constitute a popular Ashkenazic literature that radically altered prevailing notions of Jewish literacy, erudition, and devotion. Coinciding with the democratizing effect of the printing press, these books created new communities of Jewish readers and, moreover, new notions of what it meant to read as a Jew, defined by Jewish vernacular language and conduct. Writing from the vantage of the twentieth century, literary scholar Israel Zinberg saw this phenomenon as playing a definitional role in Jewish national consciousness: "The fact that the printing press first provided the possibility that the vernacular, with its oral folklore, be raised to the level of folk-*literature*, which becomes an important factor in national culture, called forth a complete revolution in Jewish cultural life."[8]

The most popular work of traditional Yiddish literature, the *Tsenerene* (believed to have been first published around 1600 and still in print, over two hundred editions later, at the turn of the twenty-first century), integrates Bible text with translation, various commentaries, and folklore, all in a running stream of vernacular language. This format not only made sacred texts and commentaries accessible to readers outside the rabbinic elite, but it also facilitated the independent study of these core works of Jewish sacred literature, free from any prescribed time, setting, ritual, or social configuration as required in the communal, male-centered synagogue or *besmedresh*.

The notion that the *Tsenerene* engendered a form of scriptural study and literacy with special significance for women is embedded in its title, which references a verse

Photogravure of Moritz Daniel Oppenheim's 1866 painting *Sabbath-Ruhe auf der Gasse* (Sabbath Rest on the Street), which depicts the archetypal Ashkenazic matriarch's Saturday afternoon pastime of reading the *Tsenerene* or a similar Yiddish book published especially for the pious female Jewish reader. The image hints at the strategic role of female readers in the transformation of Jewish literacy during the Haskalah. At the extreme right, inside the house, a younger, more fashionably dressed woman can be glimpsed reading a different, smaller book—perhaps a work of secular literature—by herself.

from the Song of Songs: *"Tsene urene bnos Tsiyen"* (Go forth and see, daughters of Zion [3:11]). Though they were not the only members of the Ashkenazic community to read the *Tsenerene*, women served as the model readers of vernacular Jewish literature as a whole. Indeed, the female reader's emblematic stature with regard to Yiddish literacy is inscribed in these texts through the use of *vaybertaytsh* (women's Yiddish), the appellation given to the distinctive typeface used in printing most of these early Yiddish books.

Max Weinreich argued that, in the seventeenth century "the woman provided a kind of permission for Yiddish in writing."[9] The title pages of some of these early

Yiddish works do indicate that they are especially intended for women, but others explain that they are for "common people," both male and female, or state they are for "women and men that are like women, that is, that they are uneducated."[10] More than simply indexing a female readership, ideal or real, Yiddish translations of Loshn-koydesh texts fostered a gendering of language and literacy that troubles the simple binary of male/female or Hebrew/Yiddish.[11] The gendering of Yiddish devotional literature is of special interest in this regard, as anthropologist Chava Weissler notes. Beginning in the seventeenth century, the development of Yiddish *tkhines*, liturgical works largely written for a female reader, from kabbalistic Hebrew petitional prayers, demonstrates how translation into the vernacular contributed to the evolving of a novel devotional culture centered on the tasks and concerns of daily life.[12]

The vernacular Ashkenazic reader also embodied a new kind of erudition, distinct from that of rabbinic authorities. Consider, for example, the agenda of the *Mayse-bukh* (Book of Tales), a popular compendium of over three hundred morally edifying tales and legends, most translated from rabbinic sources. The introduction that appears on the first pages of the oldest extant edition of the *Mayse-bukh*, printed in Basel in 1602 (the first edition is believed to have appeared around 1580), assures the reader that

> even if one knows much *Gemara*, he will bring out of [the *Mayse-bukh*] midrashim and stories and legends, so that the whole world will be astonished at him and every man will say: "I believe he knows the whole Torah on one foot. As he has such great erudition in the *Gemara*, I believe he knows the whole Torah. Who has seen his like?" To every situation he gives a law to be carried out in practice applicable to the case. At times one will encounter a tale that will make him abandon his bad thoughts and bad deeds. For many a parable and tale teaches persons much good; it keeps many a man with God and with honor.[13]

Notwithstanding the fact that the *Mayse-bukh* offers a highly limited sampling of Jewish lore, its readers are promised erudition that is the equal of the rabbinate. At the same time, mastery of this knowledge is to be manifest differently than that of the rabbis, who demonstrate their command of sacred texts by making authoritative rulings on matters of Jewish law. In contrast, the *Mayse-bukh* indicates that the vernacular readers' erudition is realized through other actions, which take place in the course of daily life: first, through their ability to cite elucidating texts appropriate to the occasion at hand and second, through their own ethical conduct as well as that of fellow Jews whom they enlighten.

The importance of these early Yiddish translations of scripture, prayer, and lore for gaining insight into Jewish popular religion and cultural history cannot be underestimated: from the sixteenth century into the twentieth, these works (some of which are still in print and are read in certain communities of Ashkenazic *khareydim*) defined a distinctive corpus of knowledge and a means of acquiring and acting on it for what was, at one time, the majority of the world's Jews. Their translation into Yiddish encoded the reading of these works and the implementing of their teachings as practices of daily life for "ordinary" people.

REVOLUTIONIZING THE JEWISH READER

Translating world literature into Yiddish during the flourishing of modern Yiddish belles lettres in the late nineteenth to mid-twentieth century wrought a different but equally profound transformation of Jewish literacy and erudition. Earlier in the history of Ashkenaz, Yiddish versions of Jewish scripture, liturgy, and compendia of customs and morally instructive tales reconfigured the traditional interface between the learned elite and the rest of the community. Yiddish renderings of European, American, and Asian fiction, poetry, drama, as well as works of philosophy, history, and the social sciences revolutionized the notion of secular literacy in the Jewish vernacular as much as did the works of Yiddish literary patriarchs Sholem Aleichem and Y. L. Peretz and their fellow writers.

In the history of modern Yiddish literature translations also serve as landmarks of a new cultural era. Scholars have long cited Mendel Lefin's renderings of books from the Hebrew Bible into Yiddish—and the controversies they engendered among his fellow *maskilim* in the early decades of the eighteenth century—as a watershed in the development of modern Yiddish letters. Historian Nancy Sinkoff notes that while the contention over Lefin's use of Yiddish is distinctive to the context of early *maskilim* in Polish borderlands, it foreshadows later debates over the "language question" for East European Jews, which "represented larger issues in the articulation of what . . . *maskilim* meant by becoming modern."[14] Renderings of modern world literature into Yiddish appeared sporadically during later decades of the Haskalah. Often—as in the case of Isaac Meir Dik's *Di shklaferay* (Slavery, 1868) or Sholem Yankev Abramovitsh and Yehude-Leyb Binshtok's *Der luftbalon* (The Hot-air Balloon, 1869)—these works were freely reworked adaptations that sometimes failed to acknowledge their source texts (here, Harriet Beecher Stowe's *Uncle Tom's Cabin* and Jules Verne's *Cinq semaines en ballons* [Five Weeks in Balloons]).

By the turn of the twentieth century, Jewish publishing houses and periodicals in

Europe and America were regularly issuing Yiddish translations from Russian, German, Polish, English, and French, as well as from other European and, occasionally, non-Western languages. A 1910 advertisement for Farlag "Progres" in London announces the press's forthcoming translations of Byron's *Cain*, Maeterlinck's *Marie Magdeleine*, Wilde's *The Picture of Dorian Gray*, and works by Dostoyevsky, Poe, Spinoza, and Strindberg.[15] In 1925 a catalog of titles sold by Farlag B. A. Kletskin, a major publisher of Yiddish books in Poland, features dozens of authors in translation, among them Artsibashev, Defoe, Gogol, Hugo, Kipling, Lao-tzu, Molière, Shaw, Twain, Wyspiański, and Zola.[16] Some Yiddish translations of world literature were as widely available as the works of major Yiddish writers. Most famous, perhaps, are the collected works of Guy de Maupassant, translated by novelist Leon Kobrin, in a fifteen-volume set offered as a premium to subscribers to the *Jewish Daily Forward* during the 1910s.[17]

Many leading Yiddish poets and prose writers also worked as translators during this period. Most often such efforts were regarded, like their journalism, as a means of supporting their "true" literary vocation, but some of these authors—most notably, the American poet known as Yehoash (né Solomon Bloomgarden)—achieved equal renown as translators. Among his accomplishments are masterful renderings of *Hiawatha* and *The Rubaiyat of Omar Khayyam* (from Edward Fitzgerald's English version) into Yiddish verse, as well as what is considered the crowning achievement of Yehoash's literary career: a translation of the entire Hebrew Bible into modern Yiddish.

This profusion of literary translations exemplifies modern Yiddish vernacularity at its zenith, evincing a culture that strove to offer comprehensive access to the wealth of world cultures through Yiddish, just as each major European language served its readership. The endeavor presupposed a critical mass of Yiddish readers who were eager for this literature and either had no recourse to encountering it in any other language or whose fluency in Yiddish exceeded their abilities to read other languages. In addition to being a market-driven phenomenon, publishing Yiddish translations of world literature was implicated in ideological concerns. Literary scholar Ellen Kellman notes that these translations comprised a considerable percentage of Yiddish publishing in interwar Eastern Europe—over one fourth of Yiddish titles issued in Poland, Lithuania, and Latvia in 1922, for example. Yiddishists debated the significance of the popularity of world literature in Yiddish translation. Some expressed concern that Jewish youth often seemed to prefer reading these books over original Yiddish works and worried about "the alarming rate at which young Polish Jewish readers were switching to Polish al-

"The Jewish Torah in Yiddish." This cartoon, which appeared in *Der groyser kundes* (The Big Prankster) in 1926, depicts the poet Yehoash as Moses (and as Dante), descending Mount Bronx to present his translation of the Hebrew Bible to awestruck onlookers.

together." Others, however, argued that issuing more Yiddish translations of world literature would, in fact, help "combat the encroachments of . . . language assimilation."[18]

To the extent that these publications addressed the translator's task explicitly, it was as a rule understood conventionally (and naïvely) as providing a Yiddish-language equivalent of the source text. Thus, of his Bible translation, Yehoash wrote, "My goal was a faithful, clear, and readable translation of our 'great book' in the language in which the greatest number of our people speak and think."[19] At the same time, of course, there is a symbolic value implicit in this translation. Far from being the first rendering of Hebrew Scriptures into Yiddish, *Targem Yehoash* stands in contrast to the various traditional Yiddish versions as a modern literary effort, demonstrating the belletristic capacity of Yiddish with respect to this foundational Jewish text and its history of renderings in the vernacular of Ashkenaz.

The use of Yiddish as a point of entry into world literature is rich with meta-value that redounds onto both the target language and the works being translated. Sometimes this issue is taken up explicitly in prefaces to these publications, which call attention to the merits of these undertakings and stress their significance as contributions to Yiddish letters, simultaneously reinforcing and transforming the language's literary range. Author Moyshe Olgin's preface to his 1919 Yiddish translation of Jack London's *The Call of the Wild* hails the novel's representation of "wild nature, the experience of nature through action, the awakening of the primitive" as a unique achievement. "In our Yiddish literature we can't conceive of such a work," he writes, "and it is thus a thankful task to make *The Call of the Wild* accessible to the Yiddish reader."[20]

Other translators position their efforts as defiant acts of linguistic and cultural legitimization. Solomon Judson introduces his 1910 translation of Goethe's *Die Leiden des jungen Werther* (The Sorrows of Young Werther) by first noting that "this book, which we provide here to the Yiddish reader, is recognized throughout the literary world as a work of genius, a work of art of the first rank." He continues: "When I told a few of my acquaintances that I intended to translate *Werther* into Yiddish, they scoffed. . . . First of all, they said, it is technically impossible to translate such a wealth of feeling and thought into impoverished Yiddish. Secondly, they said that the Yiddish reader would not understand the book, because it is too profound." To these challenges Judson responds: "A book that the Chinese read 125 years ago can certainly be translated into Yiddish today. . . . I am full of hope that there will be enough Yiddish readers who will not only understand this book but will also treasure and love it."[21] Judson vaunts his work as an achievement that flouts those skeptics who doubt the capacities of his readers and their native tongue. At the same time, he charges his readers both with the importance of Goethe's work generally and with the special onus of its appreciation by Yiddish speakers, whose embrace of *Werther* constitutes a defense of their language and its people.

Perhaps no single work proves more inherently provocative in Yiddish translation than the New Testament—and yet when Henry Einspruch's rendering, *Der bris khadoshe*, appeared in 1941, writer and critic Melekh Ravitch exhorted the Yiddish audience to read it. Ravitch hailed the translation as a "beautiful" and "nuanced" effort, a work that was important to add to the Yiddish literary canon, something that no "intelligent Jew" could "afford to ignore."[22] Remarkably, Ravitch's evaluation of the text separates its belletristic value from its provenance—*Der bris khadoshe* was published by American missionaries seeking Jewish converts to Christianity. The critic thus argued for expanding Jewish cultural boundaries while flouting the publisher's expectations that reading the New Testament in Yiddish would promote the

First page of the Epistle to the Hebrews, from the second edition of Henry Einspruch's Yiddish translation of the New Testament, published in Baltimore in 1959. The artwork bordering the text, like other illustrations in the volume, is the uncredited work of Ephraim Moses Lilien, culled from other Yiddish publications.

abandonment of Judaism. In a deft act of subversion, Ravitch transformed the emblematic meaning of this translation from a challenge to Jewish religious convictions into a validation of the capacity of secular Yiddish literary art.

Though appearing to lead Yiddish readers on a very different cultural trajectory—away from traditional Jewish erudition instead of closer to it—early-twentieth-century translations of modern secular literature facilitate a "category of cultural encounter" similar to older Yiddish renderings of scripture, prayer, and lore. Both kinds of texts institute a distinctive class of readers within Jewish society who engage with a body of knowledge in their vernacular instead of in those languages that are known, within their communities, only by an elite. Just as full and authoritative fluency in Loshn-koydesh was the proprietorship of the rabbinate, literary command of European languages was confined to those Yiddish-speaking Jews who, by dint of economic standing or ideological conviction, received a Western education (true of a small minority of East European Jews before World War I). Even as the ranks of Jews fluent in major European languages grew during the interwar years, Yiddish translations of world literature remained instrumental for a sizeable audience and attracted still other readers as symbolic efforts of Yiddishism. If, in the seventeenth century, the iconic reader of traditional Jewish literature in Yiddish was a woman, the iconic reader of modern world literature rendered in the language during the first decades of the twentieth century was a young member of the proletariat. In both instances, reading works that had been translated into Yiddish situated readers "in their socially determined echelon. It enlightened them and deprived them, liberated them and confined them." As is the case in colonial societies, as discussed by literary scholar Sukanta Chaudhuri, these translations "confirmed the gap" between cultural echelons "in the very process of bridging it."[23]

REROUTING JEWISH LITERACY

It is instructive in a different way to juxtapose the first published translations into Yiddish with twentieth-century translations of modern Yiddish literature into other languages, which have, in their own way, also forged new notions of Jewish literacy and vernacularity. Together, these two kinds of translations—involving early Yiddish as target language and modern Yiddish as source language, respectively—bracket the history of Yiddish literature, since they take measure of the language's changing role in vernacular Jewish writing and reading.

Translations of Yiddish literature are of special importance for understanding the symbolic transformation of the language following the Holocaust. Before World War II, the audience for Yiddish literature consisted primarily of native speakers who read it in the original. With limited exceptions—Sholem Asch's novels in English translation, Leyb Kvitko's children's books in Russian translation—few people read works of Yiddish literature in the modest number of translations then available.[24] Not long after the war the opposite became true. Today Yiddish literature is much more widely available and read in English, French, German, Hebrew, and Russian, among other languages, than in the original. This is, of course, true of literary works originally written in other "smaller" languages (consider, for example, how for generations Henrik Ibsen's dramas have been read by many more people in translation than in Norwegian). In the case of Yiddish literature, however, translating it into other languages has both marked and facilitated an abrupt shift in Jewish vernacularity.

Indeed, postwar translations of Yiddish always entail extraliterary and extralinguistic concerns that are tied to a larger sense of crisis responsive to the Holocaust. Even when these concerns are tacit, they frame the publishing and reading of Yiddish literature in translation, endowing individual works and anthologies, authors' lives and careers, as well as the practice of reading itself, with new meanings quite apart from their original valuations in Yiddish. Far from a problematic "distortion" of original value or intent, these changes comprise an important site of cultural productivity in itself. As Walter Benjamin observed, a translation issues from the "afterlife" of the original. "In its afterlife—which could not be called that if it were not a transformation and a renewal of something living—the original undergoes a change."[25]

Most significant, the translation of Yiddish literature after World War II produces a shift in the meta-meaning of the source language. Each author's choice of writing in Yiddish, from among the various languages available to him or her, has a definitional meta-value, which is inherent in all modern Yiddish writing before the Holocaust (and, in a different way, is also true for postwar Yiddish writing). Postwar translations of these same works engage a different symbolic issue—namely, the significance of what has been written in Yiddish apart from its being in this language. In other words, as the original works implicitly respond to one question— Why elect to write in Yiddish?—these works in translation address a different implied question: What, if anything, remains of the meta-meaning of Yiddish after the text has been rendered in another language?

Sometimes this new value ascribed to Yiddish literature in postwar translations expands on the already charged significance of its having been written in Yiddish; at other times, a new symbolic meaning of Yiddish supersedes the old one. Often the translation of Yiddish is regarded as having double-edged consequences: on the one hand, expanding the reach of Yiddish writers beyond the limits of a diminished Yiddish readership and on the other, undoing the close bond among the language, its literature, and its readership.

Translations of Yiddish literature into English illustrate this phenomenon particularly well, in part because of their extensive inventory (appearing, on an ongoing basis and in growing numbers, from the late nineteenth century to the present). Moreover, they are especially significant in light of the shift from Yiddish to English as the leading international vernacular among Jews over the course of the past century. Consequently, rendering Yiddish literature into English engages extraliterary issues of cultural transformation that are key for understanding postvernacular Yiddish culture.[26]

The earliest translations of modern Yiddish literature into English typically present this literature as evidence of a vibrant, exotic culture. In 1899 philologist Leo Wiener published a pioneering study of modern Yiddish literature that includes a chrestomathy sampling the poetry, prose, and drama of fifteen writers, from Lefin to Peretz. Wiener explained in his introduction to the volume that "the purpose of this work will be attained if it throws some light on the mental attitude of a people whose literature is less known to the world than that of the Gypsy, the Malay, or the North American Indian."[27] Thirteen years later, translator Helena Frank presented her collection of *Yiddish Tales* as an effort to demystify "that strangely fascinating world so often quoted, so little understood (we say it against ourselves), the Russian Ghetto."[28] And in 1926 author Dorothy Canfield Fisher introduced a volume of stories by Sholem Aleichem rendered into English by admitting that "like many Americans . . . I had more notions, blurred and inaccurate though they might be, about life in Thibet *[sic]* than about life among . . . the orthodox Russian Jews in this book."[29] Not unlike works of Asian literature translated into West European languages during the age of empire, these texts "use translation as a trope for a cultural encounter" that projects "a subaltern culture into a hegemonic situation."[30]

On the eve of World War II, translations of Yiddish literature take on a very different and more urgent symbolic worth. In the preface to the 1939 edition of *The Golden Peacock*, an anthology of Yiddish poetry in English translation published in England, editor Joseph Leftwich positions translation generally as an activity of historical, social, and even moral importance. He argues that "the translator, by making accessible the work of other peoples and ages, diffusing thought and suggesting new ways of thinking, influences the whole course of civilisation." Translation is also, he posits, a distinctive virtue of Jews as cultural middlemen, who served, for example, as "the chief interpreters to Western Europe of Arabian learning." Leftwich's claims defy the period's rising tide of anti-Semitism, in which an unprecedented number of Europeans had come to see Jews as inimical to Western civilization. (Elsewhere in his preface, he cites author Israel Zangwill: "The question is sometimes raised . . . whether Jews are Europeans. They are more, for they have helped to make Europe.")[31]

That same year, Sholem Asch—regarded for decades as both "a leading light" and "the spoiled playboy" of Yiddish literature—published *The Nazarene*, the first of his three novels on the subject of Jesus.[32] These works (the others are *The Apostle*, 1943, and *Mary*, 1949) inaugurated protracted and passionate debates about Asch's "sympathetic use of Christian subject matter." As literary scholar Anita Norich notes, critical reception of *The Nazarene* was divided between the Yiddish readership, which generally deplored the work, and a more sympathetic audience, Jewish and Christian, who read the novel in English; each group of readers "seem to have encountered a different text."[33]

In addition to its unusual subject matter for a Yiddish writer, *The Nazarene* was distinguished by being published in book form in English translation (the work of Maurice Samuel) before first appearing, as most of Asch's novels had previously, serialized in the Yiddish press. *The Apostle* and *Mary* were issued only in English translation, though Asch had written them in Yiddish. For his Yiddish readers, prior publication in English was, in itself, tantamount to apostasy. In this respect, the reception of *The Nazarene* resonated with its plot. The novel traces the complicated relationship between Viadomsky, an anti-Semitic Polish intellectual, and Asch, the novel's narrator, who translates for Viadomsky the "lost" gospel of Judas Iscariot from Hebrew into Polish. Both within the novel's narrative and without, translation is implicated in a complex of acts of transgression and betrayal that extend across centuries.

Though some denounced Asch for having written "an insidious piece of proselytizing fiction," Norich argues that Yiddish readers were ultimately outraged less by theological issues than by "the rendering of Yiddish into a more readily accessible and translatable culture."[34] (In the wake of the controversy, for example, parents in Brooklyn refused to send their children to a secular Yiddish school named after Asch until it was renamed.)[35] Thanks to both the form and the content of these novels, Yiddish—or at least its iconic value for a generation of American Yiddishists—"was thus completely and successfully erased," and at the start of World War II the implications of this act of erasure "were more terrifying than they had ever been."[36]

During the war Maurice Samuel rendered the work of another widely popular—but quite uncontroversial—Yiddish writer into English. With his volume *The World of Sholom Aleichem*, first published in 1943, Samuel went far beyond translating the author's prose by creating a hybrid work that presents biographical material about Sholem Aleichem, historical and cultural background of East European Jewry at the turn of the twentieth century, and retellings of parts of Sholem Aleichem's writings, all fused into a highly synthetic text that defies easy classification.[37] Samuel's rationale for this radical approach to rendering Sholem Aleichem to readers of English was that his book is not merely a literary endeavor but rather "a sort of pilgrimage among the cities and inhabitants of a world which only yesterday—as history goes—harboured the grandfathers and grandmothers of some millions of American citizens. As a pilgrimage it is an act of piety; on the other hand it is an exercise in necromancy, or calling up the dead. . . . For that world is no more." Samuel not only conflated the life, milieu, and literary output of Sholem Aleichem as he rendered it into English, he also recast Sholem Aleichem's stories as the raw data of social science, arguing that "we could write a *Middletown* of the Russian-Jewish Pale basing ourselves solely on the novels and stories and sketches of Sholem Aleichem, and it would be as reliable a scientific document as a 'factual' study."[38] Barbara Kirshenblatt-Gimblett characterizes Samuel's effort to translate literature into anthropology as "an early example of the popular arts of ethnography" undertaken by American Jews in the middle decades of the twentieth century in an effort to reanimate the "vanished world" of prewar East European Jewry.[39]

In fact, during the early postwar years, Sholem Aleichem's writings are cited repeatedly as a test case for the ability of English-language translations to serve as both a memorial and a conduit to the prewar East European Yiddish past.[40] Long considered challenging works to translate for linguistic reasons, Sholem Aleichem's prose is imbued with the added value of heritage by postwar translators, such as Curt Leviant, writing in 1959:

> To his generation, to those who spoke Yiddish and lived in its world, Sholom Aleichem mirrored what was known. For the succeeding generations, for those who neither speak nor read Yiddish, but have a faint memory of it and long to know its culture, Sholom Aleichem opens a door to a world unknown and, with laughter and tender pathos, shows us the spirit of our forebears and their heartbeat, which has been the key of our survival.[41]

At the same time, others found in English-language translations of Sholem Aleichem's prose an implicit critique of the postwar American Jewish reader. Such a meaning is beyond the original agenda of the author's works, of course (even through Sholem Aleichem offered some pointed critiques of immigrant Jewish life in his prose). Rather, this reading emerged from their translation and, moreover, from reflecting on the implications of the art of translation itself. In providing access to Sholem Aleichem's work, such readings called attention to the disparity between his first readers and those encountering him a half-century later in English. Thus Alfred Kazin wrote, in his introduction to the Modern Library edition of selected stories by Sholem Aleichem, published in 1956:

> This is the great thing about the Jews in this book. They enjoy being Jews, they enjoy the idea of belonging to the people who are called Jews—and "their" Sholom Aleichem, perhaps more than any other Jewish writer who has ever lived, writes about Jewishness as if it were a gift, a marvel, an unending theme of won-

der and delight. . . . The secret of this enjoyment consists not so much in physical solidarity and "togetherness," as in the absence of loneliness, as in the fact that
a deep part of your life is lived below the usual level of strain, of the struggle for
values, of the pressing and harrowing need—so often felt in America—to define
your values all over again in each situation, where you may have even to insist on
values themselves in the teeth of brutish materialism."[42]

Implicitly, Yiddish—as written by Sholem Aleichem, as read and spoken by his original readership—is the code of bygone Jewish cultural confidence and intimacy, of a
communal and moral strength Kazin sees as lacking among postwar American Jews.

Renderings of works originally written in Yiddish after the Holocaust into other
languages often prompt a special sensitivity to the implications of their translation.
The best-known example is doubtless the prose of the most popular postwar Yiddish author, Isaac Bashevis Singer. The English-language versions of Singer's
works, on which he typically worked closely with his translators, are frequently
characterized as "second originals," not only because of their often considerable differences from the Yiddish, but because they, in turn, serve as the basis for the most
criticism and further translation. This phenomenon has prompted a corrective impulse among some scholars of Yiddish literature, who assert that Singer "belongs
first and foremost to Yiddish language and culture and only secondarily to the broad
and great stream of twentieth-century American literature." Literary scholar Seth
Wolitz characterizes this as the author's "ambivalent dual position" and attributes it
"entirely . . . to the surgical skills of translators, publishers, editors, and, indeed,
Singer himself, who was never opposed to any changes in his English translations
that would enhance his popularity among readers."[43]

Public attention to Singer's relationship with translation—and with his translators—has been unusually extensive; in addition to considerable discussion by critics
and scholars, it has been the subject of works of fiction, film, and memoir.[44] In this discussion Singer is sometimes characterized as violating the social contract implicit in
translation (mistreating his translators, misleading his readership), and cavils directed
at translations of his work are often part of a larger disapproval of him as a writer. In
this discussion literary, linguistic, historical, ethnic, and ethical issues have all become
implicated in the act of translation. Historian Eli Lederhandler, for example, argues
that Singer "could assert moral purpose on behalf of his medium. But . . . , by con-
sciously placing Yiddish behind the oriental screen of translation, he discreetly hid its
particularism and sought to use it for a purpose far more ambitious than commemo-
ration."[45]

A similar question regarding the moral consequences of translating from Yiddish in the postwar era concerns one of the most widely read works of Holocaust literature—Elie Wiesel's autobiographical novel *Nuit*, which he edited and translated into French (the source of the text published in English, as *Night*, in 1960) from a considerably longer Yiddish original, *Un di velt hot geshvign* (And the World Was Silent), first issued in 1956. As Naomi Seidman has observed, a comparison of the Yiddish and French versions reveals a "cultural translation" of a text originally intended for a Jewish audience (with "its own set of cultural conventions") reworked for a French Catholic readership (epitomized by the author François Mauriac, who first read Wiesel's translation, helped see it published, and wrote its introductory essay). The resulting text constitutes a "negotiation" of memory to suit a different audience, a "compromise between Jewish expression and the capacities of non-Jewish readers." In particular, the translation into French entailed suppressing the original text's account of the Holocaust survivor's desires for revenge, thereby silencing as well the "desire for an audience he also mistrusts and hates." For Seidman, this strategy, which provided Wiesel with "a language to talk about the Jewish genocide that could hold the attention of Jews and Christians," also prompts troubling questions regarding the moral and political consequences of translation: "Was it worth translating the Holocaust out of the language of the largest portion of its victims and into the language of those who were, at best, absent, and at worst, complicitous in the genocide? . . . In the complex negotiations that resulted in the manuscript of *Night*, did the astonishing gains make good the tremendous losses?"[46] Seidman's hesitance to answer these questions intimates that the moral value invested in translation, however realized, might never be sufficient to redress the great wrongs that prompted the need for Wiesel's writing in the first place.

The extraliterary consequences of translating are further elaborated in anthologies of literature in translation. Some collections of modern Yiddish belles lettres endeavor to translate not only a corpus of texts but also the experience of reading Yiddish as a Jewish vernacular activity for readers who are at a cultural as well as a linguistic remove. Such is the case with Irving Howe and Eliezer Greenberg's influential collection *A Treasury of Yiddish Stories*, first issued in 1954 and still in print at the turn of the millennium. At the same time that the editors remind readers of the daunting chasm that stands between them and the original milieu of Yiddish literature—they dedicate their volume "to the Six Million"—Howe and Greenberg offer words of encouragement. The epigraph to the anthology's introduction is Franz Kafka's famous assertion that "you understand Yiddish better than you suppose."[47]

Striving to provide readers with a point of entry into the vanquished culture of

Eastern Europe's Yiddish-speaking Jews—which they characterize as "a kind of nation, yet without nationhood," whose mores and sensibilities are "probably without parallel in Western history"—Howe and Greenberg transform the reading of the various works in their collection by organizing them into a sequence of sections that forms a hypertext narrating the emergence, efflorescence, and destruction of Yiddish modernism. Howe and Greenberg link fifty-two discrete works by twenty-three authors, from Mendele Moykher-Sforim through Chaim Grade, in an intertextuality of the editors' own making, crossing generational, geographic, and stylistic boundaries as they fashion these works into chapters of a master narrative that traces pathways leading toward, and then away from, "Maidanek and Auschwitz."[48]

In their effort to reanimate the lost world of East European Jews, the editors of *A Treasury of Yiddish Stories* also strove to reconstitute an audience for Yiddish literature in light of the relationship that it had, at its acme, with a reading public understood simply as "the folk." The challenge for the anthologists—and for their readers—is nothing less than the forging of a new conceptualization of Jewish vernacularity in the American post-Holocaust milieu, in which fluency in Yiddish and the cultural literacy of prewar Yiddish-speaking Jews are no longer central. The works included in the volume cannot, therefore, stand on their own, as they are understood to have done previously; readers require supporting material (including extensive introductions and a glossary), as well as an overarching meta-narrative to contextualize individual works. Significantly, the anthology situates them not so much in some kind of experiential context as in a historical and cultural intertextuality with each other.

INVENTING TRANSLATIONS

Prominent among the new meanings that Yiddish literary anthologies forge from the works they collect is their phenomenologizing of Yiddish literature as a discrete body of work that is the equivalent of national, monolingual literatures. Given the complexly fluid, multilingual character of Yiddish-speakers' diaspora of literary cultures, the notion of "Yiddish literature" as a corpus analogous to that of, say, Polish, Hungarian, or Russian is not unproblematic.

Whereas in other contexts, modern writers who are accomplished in more than one European language are considered exceptional figures (e.g., Vladimir Nabokov, Samuel Beckett), it is much more common for Yiddish authors to have also written and published, at times extensively and masterfully, in one or more other languages.

The luminaries of modern Yiddish literature—including its three *klasiker* ("classic" writers) Abramovitsh, Sholem Aleichem, and Peretz—typically began writing in maskilic Hebrew or a European language, and critics often characterize these authors' subsequent shift to Yiddish as a definitive step in their artistic development. Sometimes Yiddish writing comprises a distinct period or genre in an author's mature career (e.g., that of Uri-Zvi Greenberg, Judd Teller); in other cases the interrelation of Yiddish and other languages in an author's work proves more complicated. The poet Morris Rosenfeld, for example, championed Yiddish when writing in the language while, at the same time, intimating its limitations in some of his English verse.[49] A number of authors—including Abramovitsh, Joseph Hayyim Brenner, and Singer—translated their own works into or from Yiddish, creating new versions of their original texts as they shifted from one language (and readership) to another.[50] In the case of one of the most celebrated works of modern Yiddish literature, S. Ansky's drama *The Dybbuk*, the text has a complex history involving three languages and, arguably, more than one author. Originally written in Russian, the play was translated into Yiddish by Ansky (incorporating substantial input from the renowned stage director Konstantin Stanislavski), then into Hebrew by Hayyim Nahman Bialik, then back into Yiddish by Ansky (after the first Yiddish version was lost), this second Yiddish version bearing the influence of Bialik's Hebrew rendering.[51]

Multilingualism is also an explicit feature of individual works in Yiddish as much as it is of authors' literary careers. These works tacitly problematize the notion of "Yiddish literature" by making code-switching (and the internalized translating that this entails) part of the texture of Yiddish belles lettres. A considerable number of modern Yiddish writers produced macaronic texts—the most elaborate, perhaps, being Isaac Euchel's *Reb Henekh*. This late-eighteenth-century satirical drama features a range of characters, both Jews and non-Jews, each of whom speaks a different language, including French, English, and variants of German and Yiddish. Each Jewish character's idiolect situates him or her somewhere along a spectrum ranging between a traditional and a maskilic sensibility.[52] Sholem Aleichem's stories and monologues regularly play with the borders between Yiddish and other languages (Loshn-koydesh, Russian, Ukrainian, German, English) that Yiddish speakers engaged. These issues not only present the translator with practical challenges (for example, how to represent Sholem Aleichem's English-Yiddish speech play when rendering into English his stories about immigrant life in America); they pose larger questions about conceptualizing as a monolingual literature literary phenomena rooted in a range of multilingual milieus.

Much of modern Jewish writing in other languages endeavors to realize the multilingual context of Yiddish speakers in a different literary matrix. Again, American works written in English provide especially rich examples. Abraham Cahan's 1896 novella *Yekl* and Henry Roth's 1934 novel *Call It Sleep* are the best known and most elaborate examples to be found in Anglo-Jewish writing of the immigrant and early postimmigrant periods.[53] More recently—even as Yiddish retreats from vernacular familiarity for the majority of American Jews—as literary scholar Hana Wirth-Nesher notes, the language has increasingly figured as a "signifier of difference in a cultural landscape that legitimizes and even requires difference."[54] Here the resistance of Yiddish to translation figures as an emblem of Jewish challenge to complete assimilation. The impulse to render Yiddish speakers' multilingualism in English-language texts informs much of American Jewish writing of the past century, found in various configurations in the work of its most accomplished literary figures (e.g., Saul Bellow, Bernard Malamud, Grace Paley, Philip Roth) as well as popular and lowbrow comic writing (Milt Gross's books of dialect humor, Leonard Ross's *H*Y*M*A*N K*A*P*L*A*N* stories). So pervasive is a Yiddish inflection of some kind that it can be considered a defining feature of this subgenre of American literature for much of the twentieth century.

Translating Yiddish has become a literary subject in itself, engaging the limitations of the act of translating as well as its opportunities. Some of the most self-reflexive of such efforts can be found in the recent work of American Jewish poets. Irena Klepfisz's 1990 collection *A Few Words in the Mother Tongue* concludes with a selection of poems that integrate romanized Yiddish words and phrases into English text. Some of these poems are, in effect, bilingual works, the Yiddish translated into English phrase by phrase—for example, in the section of Klepfisz's poem "*Di rayze aheym* / The Journey Home" titled "*Zi flit* / She flies":

> *Zi flit*
> *vi a foygl*
> > like a bird
> *zi flit*
> *ibern yam*
> > over the sea
> *iber di berg*
> > over the mountains
> *Tsurik*
> > *tsurik* back
> > > back

For the reader who knows no Yiddish, Klepfisz's bilingual text functions as a pedagogical device. For the reader fluent in both languages (and their attendant cultures) these poems invoke the traditional Jewish practice of pedagogical translation. Here, though, English replaces Yiddish as the vernacular, Yiddish replaces Loshn-koydesh as the language in need of translation, and the instruction concerns not scripture but linguistic and cultural memory. Other poems in this collection deal more explicitly with the challenge of translation. In "Fradel Schtok" Klepfisz meditates on the cultural and personal implications of language shift through the voice of a Yiddish writer who in 1907 immigrated from her native Galicia to New York at the age of seventeen:

> Think of it: *heym* and *home* the meaning
> the same of course exactly
> but the shift in vowel was the ocean
> in which I drowned.

Yiddish is part of Klepfisz's own complex multilingual experience. Thus, of her memories of Friday nights as a young girl in New York City she writes, in another poem in this collection: "Erev shabes was plain fraytik / or more precisely: *piontek* [i.e., *piątek*, Polish for "Friday"]."[55] Other American Jewish poets, responding to their own relationships to Yiddish, present it as a lost language and as a sign of loss. John Hollander, in "On a Stanza of H. Leyvick," invokes New York's immigrant Yiddish poets, contrasting their authorial voices—"writing in a language that today / Is sentenced to an early death"—with that of Hollander's fellow American-born, "de-Yiddished" poets. "And yet," he wonders, whether their English "was just a dying / Yiddish, . . . now already in need / Of too much glossing."[56] The tension between notions of Yiddish as lost and as enduring finds resolution of a sort in the meta-language of poetry; linguistic self-consciousness both stymies the writer (who fears his own verse may, like that of his Yiddish forebears, become lost in translation) and stimulates his literary creativity. In calling the reader's attention to the disparity between Jewish poets writing in Yiddish and in English, Hollander exposes gaps—generational, linguistic, artistic—that animate American Jewish life. The breakdown of Yiddish language at the center of the poem generates, in response, new cultural energy.

Similarly, Jacqueline Osherow's 1996 poem "Ch'vil Schreibn a Poem auf Yiddish" relates, in English, her desire to write in a language in which, as the title intimates, she is not fluent. However, by virtue of the inherent elusiveness of this language, her hypothetical Yiddish poem would defy being rendered into the language in which she does write: "I want to write a poem in Yiddish / and not any poem, but . . . / a poem so Yiddish, it would not / be possible to translate." Here, Yiddish is powerful in its obscurity, and the esoteric nature ascribed to it extends from the author's own lack of language to the absoluteness of her imagined poem—defying not only translation and reproduction but also mortality:

> my Yiddish poem can never be taken down,
> not even by a pious scribe
> who has fasted an entire year
> to be pure enough to write my Yiddish poem,
>
> which exists—doesn't he realize?—
> in no realm at all
> unless the dead still manage to dream dreams.[57]

Osherow's yearning for Yiddish is implicitly juxtaposed with her native fluency in English. The expressive possibilities with which English provides her are taken as self-evident; they are only problematic in that they are somehow insufficient in relation to Yiddish, which lies beyond the poet's grasp (even in translation). This tacit questioning of whether English monolingualism suffices for the American Jewish author echoes throughout post-Holocaust writing. Author Cynthia Ozick, for example, notes anxiously that "since the coming forth from Egypt five millennia ago, mine is the first generation [of Jews] to think and speak and write wholly in English."[58]

Although it was written in the late 1960s, Ozick's short story "Envy; or, Yiddish in America" remains one of the best-known disquisitions—in English or any other language—on postwar Yiddish culture in the United States and on the strategic role translation plays therein. Ozick portrays a dwindling, aging circle of American Yiddish writers as hapless beings who have outlived a culture characterized as "lost, murdered . . . —a museum."[59]

The only hope her protagonist, the poet Edelstein, sees for himself, his work, and for Yiddish is translation into English, for this has enabled his rival, the prose writer Ostrover, to become a celebrity with American audiences. Edelstein sets out to find a translator (in vain, it turns out) not only because he envies Ostrover's success, but also because of the promise that translation offers as a means of liberation, transformation, and, ultimately, immortality. At the same time, Edelstein is suspicious of translation, contemptuous of its readership (deriding the publishers of Ostrover's work in English as "Jews without tongues"), and he relativizes "death through forgetting" and "death through translation."[60]

Even as it equivocates between translation as a vehicle for survival and as an act of betrayal, "Envy" obliquely invites readers to pursue various translation exercises of their own. In the narrative, Ostrover mocks Edelstein through a short story à clef, in which both the envious poet and their common language are thinly disguised in the most transparent of literary veils. Ostrover writes: "Satan appears to a bad poet. 'I desire fame,' says the poet, 'but I cannot attain it, because I come from Zwrdl, and the only language I can write in is Zwrdlish. Unfortunately no one is left in the world who can read Zwrdlish. That is my burden. Give me fame, and I will trade you my soul for it.' "[61] Just as Zwrdlish is obviously Yiddish, it is clear (to Ostrover's fellow Yiddishists as well as to the readers of "Envy") that the "bad poet" is Edelstein. This easy bit of encoding and decoding invites readers to approach "Envy" itself as a story à clef. And so it is frequently explained that the two rival authors, Ostrover and Edelstein, are portraits of two actual Yiddish writers: Isaac Bashevis Singer and Yankev Glatshteyn, respectively.[62] According to Ozick, however, the story found its inspiration elsewhere: in the plight of Hebrew writers in mid-twentieth-century America who, unlike their Yiddish counterparts, bemoaned the fact that they had almost no readership.[63] Ozick, in effect, translated their dilemma into the postwar despair of Yiddish writers.

Although "Envy" appears to present the movement from Yiddish to English as an inevitable, if not entirely felicitous, outcome of postwar American Jewish life, the story also suggests opportunities to reverse the path of translation. By offering samples of Edelstein's poetry in English, Ozick implies the existence of their Yiddish originals:

How you spring out of the ground covered with poverty!
In your long coats, fingers rolling wax, tallow eyes.
How can I speak to you, little fathers?
You who nestled me with lyu, lyu, lyu,
lip-lullaby, jabber of blue-eyed sailors,
how am I fallen into a stranger's womb?[64]

Indeed, a reader who knows Yiddish can (re)construct the "original" poems, thus:

Vi ir shpringt aroys fun der erd, badekt mit dales!
In di lange khalatn, velgern vaks di finger, kheylevene oygn.
Vi ken ikh mit aykh redn, tatelekh?
Ir, vos hot mikh getulyet mitn lyu-lyu-lyu,
Lipn-viglid, plapleray fun bloy-oygike matrosn,
Vi bin ikh arayngefaln in a fremdn shoys arayn?[65]

Ozick thus invites readers to imagine the preservation, in English, of "lost" Yiddish works that never existed and, moreover, to engage in a fictional act of cultural retrieval by "undoing" their translation. The appeal of these virtual texts lies in their elusiveness, thereby suggesting a complement to Edelstein's envy of Ostrover's success in translation—namely, the monolingual English reader's envy of those who have access to the abstruse milieu of Yiddish. (As Ozick has Ostrover tell his rival, "It doesn't matter what you speak, envy sounds the same in all languages.")[66]

DREAMING THE QUOTIDIAN

The implicit allure in Ozick's short story of recovering lost Yiddish originals—including those that never actually existed but can only be imagined as such—epitomizes postvernacular Yiddish culture. Indeed, nothing better exemplifies Yiddish in its postvernacular mode than a spate of recent translations into Yiddish that seem to realize the impulse suggested by Ozick's story.

Consider, for example, one of the more widely publicized phenomena in Yiddish letters at the turn of the millennium: *Vini-der-Pu*, a Yiddish version of A. A. Milne's 1926 children's classic, *Winnie-the-Pooh*, issued in 2000 by Dutton. Reviewing the book for the *Forverts*, Anita Norich notes that Leonard Wolf's translation is "consistent and very close to the English original, but with a genuine Yiddish flavor."[67] This last point is demonstrated by the occasional deftly idiomatic substitution, such as replacing Pooh's refrain "rum-tum-tidl-um-tum" with *"haydl-didl, haydl-didl dam"* or changing "Cottleston pie" into *"varshever tort* [Warsaw cake]." However, Norich tells her Yiddish readers, "It's a shame that one can barely read [the book]," because the text is printed in romanized Yiddish (more specifically, the first paragraph of each chapter is printed in *alefbeys*, followed by the full chapter rendered in YIVO's standard romanization). "This raises a question," Norich continues: "For whom was this book made?" She is not the only one to have asked this. "Who's this book for, anyway?" asks an anonymous reviewer on the amazon .com website, who suspects that "most purchases . . . will be as 'gag' gift[s]" and then wonders, "Why go to the effort of translating if you're not going to present the finished product in a form Yiddish speakers can actually comprehend???"[68]

These questions raise issues about readability that are worth interrogating in themselves. Nevertheless, one could also raise such questions about several similar titles that have appeared in recent years: Yiddish versions of two German children's classics—Wilhelm Busch's *Max und Moritz* (as *Shmul un Shmerke*) and Heinrich Hoffman's *Struwwelpeter* (as *Pinye shtroykop*)—both the work of translators Charles Nydorf and Elinor Robinson; *Der kleyner prints*, Shloyme Lerman's translation of Antoine de Saint-Exupéry's *Le Petit Prince* (The Little Prince); *Der ẓeyer hungeriker opfreser*, Marcia Gruss Levinsohn's rendering of Eric Carle's *The Very Hungry Caterpillar;* or Sholem Berger's Yiddish version of Dr. Seuss's *The Cat in the Hat* (as *Di kats der payats*).[69] These works call to mind other similar translations into Yiddish, including Marie Jaffe's 1965 anthology *Gut Yontif Gut Yohr* (Happy Holiday to You)—which features renderings of Clement Moore's "A Visit from St. Nicholas," six haiku, and verses by Shakespeare, Longfellow, Dickinson, and Whitman, among others—or Yiddish versions of Gilbert and Sullivan operettas, some dating back to the 1950s and recently in vogue again as performance pieces.[70]

All these works differ in form, content, and function from the conventional protocols of literary translations, including the many renderings of world literature into Yiddish published since the nineteenth century, as described above. What sort of translations are these, especially if, as Norich and others suggest, they aren't really readable—and moreover, aren't actually *meant* to be read? If that is how they are perceived, then what might their value as literary efforts or as cultural artifacts be?

Translations of world literature into Yiddish for its vernacular readership have continued to appear in the decades following World War II, though the number of these works is, of course, much reduced.[71] In his foreword to Hersh Rosenfeld's translation of the Finnish epic *Kalevala*, published in 1954, historian Jacob Shatsky welcomes the availability of this work for the Yiddish reader, noting that "before the catastrophe of Hitler, Yiddish literature produced many able translations of poetry, prose, and even scholarly writing from other languages. The situation has, sadly, changed for the worse. Therefore every [Yiddish] translation from world literature is a prized item and a cause for celebration."[72] Like postwar translations from Yiddish, these translations into Yiddish take on new emblematic meanings responsive to the Holocaust. Sometimes the transvaluation of Yiddish itself is implicated in the significance ascribed to these postwar efforts. Thus, a critic reviewing Gisela Skilnik's 1974 Yiddish translation, from the German, of Nellie Sachs's Holocaust poetry praises Skilnik's effort as "rescu[ing] this intimately Jewish tragedy from the exile of a foreign language."[73]

די קאַץ
דער
פּאַיאַץ

DI KATS
DER
PAYATS

The Cat in the Hat by Dr. Seuss
in Yiddish

פֿון ד"ר סוס
ייִדיש: שלום בערגער

Fun Dokter Seuss
Yidish: Sholem Berger

Cover of Sholem Berger's Yiddish translation of Dr. Seuss's *The Cat in the Hat*. As in most other recent translations of children's literature into Yiddish, the book presents the text both in the *alefbeys* and in romanization.

But postvernacular translations into Yiddish are emblematic undertakings of another kind. Not only are their symbolic meanings often different from those of vernacular translations, but their meta-value has a distinctive primacy. Their creators do not, as those of vernacular translations conventionally do, desire that their efforts be invisible as translations—that is, that "the structures of the [source language] will be preserved as closely as possible but not so closely that the [target language] structure will be seriously distorted."[74] On the contrary, recognition of their work as transformations of the original texts into Yiddish versions is key. These translators intend for readers to center their attention not on the original works but on the very act of these works' being rendered into Yiddish. Therefore, appreciation of the cultural value of these translations is heightened by—indeed, to a considerable degree is dependent on—foreknowledge of the original works. Also, these translations' semantic divergences from the originals are considered as meaningful as those instances where the two versions conform, if not more so.

While these postvernacular translations into Yiddish are united in foregrounding the act of translation, their cultural implications are varied. First, some of these translations constitute symbolic acts of collecting Yiddish—that is, reifying Yiddish as a curiosity, an esoteric linguistic specimen that can be included within an inventory of other literary languages. Consider the case of Shloyme Lerman's *Der kleyner prints*. An engineer by profession, Lerman is an amateur translator, who, as he reports, was motivated to render *Le Petit Prince* into Yiddish as a life-long devotee both of his first language and of St. Exupéry's book. Having collected translations of *Le Petit Prince* in ninety different languages, he wanted to add Yiddish to the inventory.[75] (The German press that publishes *Der kleyner prints* also issues the book in various German dialects, including Pälzisch, Hessisch, Fränkisch, Schwäbisch, and Plattdüütsch.)

Second, postvernacular translations can constitute symbolic demonstrations of the target language's facility, range, or viability. Wolf's *Vini-der-Pu* calls to mind another postvernacular rendering of Milne's book, *Winnie ille Pu*, a Latin translation by Alexander Lenard issued in 1960. This publishing phenomenon—the book made the *New York Times* bestseller list for several months—prompted an editor of the *Christian Science Monitor* to write that "there is some thought of removing Latin from the list of dead languages."[76] The status of Latin as a dead language continues to be debated; Yiddish certainly is not one but is often spoken of as moribund or as a signifier of demise. Consequently, Wolf's *Vini-der-Pu* has been cited as demonstrating the viability and vivacity of Yiddish. In press interviews, Wolf characterized his effort as "a sign of hope that Yiddish will not be forgotten" and as "counteract[ing] what he considers a widespread misperception that Yiddish is a language linked with tragedy." Seeing *Vini-der-Pu* as a strategic opportunity to transform the meta-value of Yiddish, Wolf stated, "I think it would be good for people to discover that Yiddish can be used in such an affectionate way and not only as a historical demonstration of pain."[77]

Third, a distinctive and often salient feature of many postvernacular translations is their Judaization of source texts. This practice is not unique to recent, postvernacular translations into Yiddish. Elijah Levita's *Bove-bukh* (Book of Buovo), his 1507 rendering of *Buovo d'Antona* into Yiddish, creates a distinctive variant of this Italian epic poem for an Ashkenazic audience, most notably through the deletion of Christian references and the occasional creation of Jewish ones.[78] For example, in the *Bove-bukh* Princess Druzane "laments . . . that in her wandering life she has not had the opportunity to circumcise her children, and [her] father consoles her: 'Do not worry; tomorrow I will arrange a great circumcision feast.' " Israel Zinberg also identifies in the Yiddish "reworking" of *Buovo d'Antona* a distinct rhetorical framing of its narrative—a "light, mocking tone. . . . In the Yiddish *Bove-bukh* is felt not the representative figure of the Renaissance but one of the clever jesters of the Jewish ghetto who . . . mocks the foreign world of chivalry."[79]

Recent postvernacular translations employ Judaization to articulate various relations between the source text (and, implicitly, its language and culture) and a projected sensibility of the Yiddish reader. Frequently this relationship is parodic; but unlike, say, some of the macaronic Yiddish-English parodies of Borsht Belt–era entertainers created a half century earlier, these texts are not self-mocking. Rather, they constitute acts of cultural subversion, staking a claim on a cultural territory or sensibility widely thought of as alien to or incompatible with Yiddish. Thus, literary scholar Ruth Wisse identifies "the day Isaac Rosenfeld, with the help of Saul Bellow, composed a Yiddish parody of [T. S. Eliot's] 'The Love Song of J. Alfred Prufrock' " as the moment when "American Jewish letters gave notice of its independence from Anglo American modernism."[80]

Al Grand's Yiddish versions of Gilbert and Sullivan operettas are another case in point: in a foreword to the libretto of *Di Yam Gazlonim* (The Pirates), Grand's 1988 adaptation of *The Pirates of Penzance*, science fiction author and avid Savoyard Isaac Asimov contrasts the "quintessentially *Victorian* British" sensibility of Gilbert and Sullivan with that of diaspora Jewry as "the difference between the serene masters of the globe and a people who have had to live in the hidden nooks and crannies of the land, waiting always for the blow to fall." How, then, Asimov wonders, is it possible to fit Gilbert's lyrics or Sullivan's "cheerful, bouncy, busy" music to "the Jewish experience?"[81]

Grand's translation includes Yiddishized characters' names—Frederic becomes Fayvl, Mabel becomes Malke—and inserts Jewish idioms throughout: Fayvl does not start out as a would-be apprentice to a navigator but is an erstwhile yeshiva student; the pirates don't quaff sherry but feast on bagels and seltzer. Set to Sullivan's music—with rhymes sometimes as clever as those in Gilbert's original lyrics— Grand's text offers a celebratory performance of linguistic virtuosity and cultural assertiveness that flouts Asimov's depiction of the great disparity between the omnipotent British Empire at its acme and the abject Jewish diaspora epitomized by

Yiddish.[82] This agenda is sometimes made explicit; for example, in *Di Yam Gazlonim* the chorus "Hail, Poetry" becomes a paean not to the muse but to *yidishkeyt*—literally, "Yiddishness" or "Jewishness"—here invoking pride in Ashkenazic folkhood embodied in language:

Shray hoykh un klor far Yidishkayt!!
Mit shtolts in harts zol klingen vayt!
Lebn zol dos folk vos lakht un zingt!
Hert tsu, oy velt, a lid bay undz—es klingt![83]

[Shout loud and clear for *yidishkeyt!*
May it resound far and wide with pride in one's heart!
Long live the people who laugh and sing!
Listen, O World, to the sound of our song!]

Nydorf and Robinson's translation of *Max und Moritz* similarly Judaizes not just the title characters' names; Itsik, the tailor in episode three (originally named Meister Böck), makes, among other things, *shabesdike kapotes* (special long coats worn by hasidic men on the Sabbath and holidays), and the teacher in episode four, Reb Uri-Fayvish (originally Lehrer Lämpel), who in the German original plays the organ in church on Sunday, has become an organist in a *templ* (a Reform synagogue) on Saturday.[84] As with Zinberg's analysis of the Judaizations in the *Bove-bukh*, these recent examples suggest that translation into Yiddish also entails an extralinguistic transformation of the original text's narrative milieu into a Jewish one. There is no reason, of course, why a Yiddish text cannot represent church organists or sherry-swilling pirates; such subjects are not beyond the language's capacity (as both original works of Yiddish literature and vernacular translations of world literature into the language amply demonstrate). But a distinctive feature of most postvernacular translations is a reworking of the original work's fictional world into a Yiddish world. Such efforts suggest that inherent in Yiddish is a distinctive cultural sensibility that cannot help but Judaize whatever enters its semiotic field. As cultural practices of the post-Holocaust era, postvernacular translations project the power of Yiddish to inflect as Jewish the unexpected; they defiantly expand the scope of Yiddish in the face of prevailing notions that its sphere is shrinking.

At the same time, the Judaization of these works is never complete. What these translations offer is not so much a transformation as a negotiation, albeit often a playful one, between two cultures. In contemporary postvernacular translations, as in parodies, familiarity with the original work is key. Their significance emerges from the interplay of sameness and difference between the original and the re-worked or parodic version. In postvernacular Yiddish translations this interplay often involves nonlinguistic elements: in the Gilbert and Sullivan operettas, it is re-alized in performance, juxtaposing the Yiddish lyrics with the original music. Sim-ilarly, the interplay in the recent translations of children's literary classics is height-ened by publishing the Yiddish renderings along with the books' original illustrations. Indeed, the fact that the recent spate of postvernacular Yiddish trans-lations includes a preponderance of works of children's literature is noteworthy for linking Yiddish with playfulness of a particular kind. These publications imply a common exercise in imagining a Yiddish-speaking childhood—connoting "natu-ral" language acquisition, innocence, amusement, and fantasy—which, however it is envisioned, is at odds with any actual child's experience.

So compelling is the symbolic value of translation in postvernacular Yiddish cul-ture that occasionally the act of translating has been provocatively reconfigured or even imagined (what Chauduri terms an "anticipated translation").[85] Consider the case of Will Eisner's landmark graphic novella of 1978, *A Contract with God*, ren-dered into Yiddish (as *An opmakh mit Got*) in 1984 by Bobby Zylberman. In a fore-word to the Yiddish edition, Eisner writes: "The text originally employed in the cre-ation of this story . . . was English. But in addressing it to the reader I intended to convey a feeling of Yiddish. So that, one might say, this was . . . the language of its true origin." At the same time, then, this Yiddish rendering both is and is not a trans-lation. Indeed, Eisner characterizes Yiddish as the book's "underlying language," inflecting his artwork, which is "executed in Yiddish in the first place. It needs no translation!"[86]

Eisner's remarks recall other earlier instances of Yiddish imagined as revealing an "underlying" original. Writing in the 1970s, Irving Howe remembered Isaac Rosenfeld "once explaining to me with comic solemnity that Chekhov had really written in Yiddish but [the English translator] Constance Garnett, trying to render him respectable, had falsified the record. Anyone with half an ear, said Rosenfeld, could catch the tunes of Yiddish sadness, absurdity, and humanism in Chekhov's prose."[87] Nor are such projections confined to East European writers. In a 1951 essay in *Commentary* actor George Ross argued that, while watching Joseph Buloff's pro-duction of *Toyt fun a Salesman*, he felt that "this Yiddish play is really the original, and the Broadway production [of *Death of a Salesman*] was merely—Arthur Miller's translation into English."[88] Such postulations of nonexistent Yiddish Ur-texts that lie hidden beneath actual English originals imagine Yiddish as an ex-tralinguistic phenomenon, a fundamental as well as a transcendent essence that can

Panel from Will Eisner's graphic novel *A Contract with God,* translated into Yiddish by Bobby Zylberman. In addition to this version, printed in romanized Yiddish, the translation was also published in the *alefbeys.*
Courtesy of Will Eisner Studios, Inc.

persist despite the absence of actual language. As an idiom or sensibility, Yiddish can thrive without lexicon or syntax; indeed, its "spirit" can inhabit the form of another language. The implicit metaphors are both biological—language as DNA—and supernatural—language as dybbuk.

Perhaps the most unusual and semiologically provocative permutation of Yiddish translation in the postvernacular mode is *On Foreign Soil*, Martin Green's 2000 rendering of Falk Zolf's Yiddish memoir *Af fremder erd*, originally published in Yiddish in 1945. The translation begins almost entirely in English, with individual Yiddish terms introduced (romanized, but in a contrasting font) and glossed according to a variety of strategies within the text:

> Kamenetz was also known throughout the region for its old, historical walled tower, or sloup, which with its size and height, reminded one of der bavel-Turem. According to old legends, it was built by a long-ago Lithuanian duke. And so that it should be **shtark** un' fest and remain standing "oyf eybick un'

eybick", they made the mortar with egg-yolks instead of water. And so it was takkeh as **strong** as a festung (fortress) and its pointed tower seemed to reach **azh** kayn himmel (**all the way** to the sky).[89]

As one gets further into *On Foreign Soil,* more and more Yiddish is incorporated:

But the khazen-shoykhet could not be hurried. Everyone had to wait for him. And in the "waiting", iz eppis geve'en **aza min** shtille, farborgene hanoyeh; eppis **a kind of** nekummeh-gefiel, as though he were saying: "You see! Ihr darft mikh nokh hobben . . . ihr muzt nokh alle on-kummen tsu mir!"[90]

By the end of the book, the English translation all but disappears into a romanized Yiddish "original":

Der alter balebus, Harkavey, an oyf-geregter un a tse-raytzter, hot arum-geshpannt hin un tsurick ibber'n kantor. Suddenly he stopped next to me un a zog geton: "Bistu shoyn a bavaybter?"[91]

Presented to the reader as a pedagogical device, the text offers the promise of lin-guistic and cultural continuity, though it actually embodies quite the opposite. Green writes: " 'Oyf Fremder Erd' is available to the English-speaking reader in a unique form that transports him back in time . . . to experience firsthand what life was like in Old Russia. . . . The extensive use of Yiddish words and expressions makes the story real in a way that would not be possible in any ordinary transla-tion."[92] Rather than "carrying across" (that is, translating in its original meaning) the Yiddish text to the English-language reader, Green strives to transport the reader back—not only in time and place but also in language. Thus, in *On Foreign Soil* the ostensibly impossible act of translation reverses direction and gradually un-does itself, in an effort to do nothing less than reverse the currents of the recent his-tory of Yiddish and its speakers.

Translations of Yiddish literature in the postvernacular mode evince a radical transformation of the language's symbolic meaning and of translation's role in modern Jewish life. Here the use of Yiddish, no longer a language of daily life, is highly self-conscious, especially as a tenacious signifier of Jewishness. Moreover, translation itself is charged with a special cultural onus: as Green explains in the in-troduction to his exceptional translation, the mission of these efforts is ultimately concerned with extralinguistic and extraliterary issues of maintaining and actualizing Jewish identity: "Many contemporary Jews share a strong sense of pride and affection towards the Yiddish language. But short of learning to speak Yiddish, how are they to translate such feelings into action?"[93]

All translations are, in a sense, transmigrations as well. But postvernacular translations into Yiddish do not convey the reader beyond the distinctive core of Yiddish culture, as vernacular translations into the language do. Instead, they bring the reader back into it, forging bridges between Yiddish and the reader's literacy in other languages and cultures. As exercises in negotiating cultural frontiers, postvernacular translations situate the act of translation itself as central. The translator's hand is not meant to go undetected in these works; on the contrary, it is meant to be the focus of attention. For in these works one observes a transformative act in which Yiddish is not lost, but found, and the foundational role that translation plays in creating Yiddish culture is renewed and, inevitably, remade.

CHAPTER FOUR

YIDDISH AS PERFORMANCE ART

I am at a conference held in an American city in the early 1990s. In the lobby of the building where the proceedings are about to begin, participants mill about, chatting. Among them are two people who greet each other in Yiddish:

"*Sholem-aleykhem!*" [Hello!]

"*Aleykhem-sholem!*" [Hello!]

"*Nu, vos makhstu?*" [So, how are you?]

"*Gants gut, un du?*" [Pretty good, and you?], and so on.

Why does this conversation catch my ear—and eye? There is nothing extraordinary about the content of the exchange; it is a very routine give-and-take of salutations. This is a Jewish academic conference, where Yiddish language, literature, and culture are not only topics of discussion but are also sometimes discussed in sessions convened in Yiddish. The two people conversing are both scholars of Yiddish and have known each other for many years. Each grew up in a Yiddish-speaking home, though nowadays, I believe, they teach and conduct most of their daily affairs in English. What engages my attention is the manner of their conversation. They are speaking rather too loudly for this sort of casual, intimate exchange; they are standing a bit too far apart from one another; their gestures are a little too broad. They're not simply having a conversation in Yiddish; they're HAVING A CONVERSATION IN YIDDISH. They want others around them to notice. Indeed, it seems that they aren't only conversing (and perhaps not really conversing at all); they are performing. I notice them, and so does a friend standing beside me. I nudge him with my elbow and nod toward the pair. He gives me a piqued look and mutters, "Show-offs!"

This moment has lodged in my memory, I think, because it speaks to the distinctively performative nature of postvernacular Yiddish. In the decades following World War II a simple exchange of greetings in Yiddish has increasingly become something that is not to be taken for granted—not even at a Jewish event where there are plenty of Yiddish speakers. There is in this moment a heightened awareness of using Yiddish as a language of conversation, both on the part of the speakers—who have made a deliberate, if impromptu, choice to exchange greetings in the language—and on the part of observers, who find the exchange something to take note of and evaluate. Slight as this instance may seem, it exemplifies a pervasive development in postvernacular Yiddish culture. In this new semiotic mode for the language, every utterance is enveloped in a performative aura, freighted with significance as a *Yiddish* speech act quite apart from the meaning of whatever words are spoken.

MIMESIS IN CRISIS

While Jewish self-consciousness regarding Yiddish speech dates back to the Haskalah, its significance today is shaped most powerfully by the Holocaust. The implications of this catastrophe for Yiddish are but a part of the Holocaust's manifold repercussions in Jewish life during the past six decades. Besides posing compelling theological, political, and aesthetic challenges, the Holocaust has disturbed widely held assumptions about how to enact Jewishness.

In the 1990s Jewish historian Haym Soloveitchik addressed this issue as he scrutinized a striking transformation that had taken place during his lifetime within his own community of Orthodox Ashkenazim in America. In the decades since World War II, Soloveitchik observed the advent of a "new and controlling role that texts now play in contemporary religious life," superceding a long-standing notion that "the Ashkenazic community saw the law as manifesting itself in two forms: in the canonized written corpus (the Talmud and [later rabbinic] codes), and in the regnant practices of the people. Custom was the correlative datum of the halakhic system [i.e., the corpus of rabbinic laws governing traditional Jewish life]. And, on frequent occasions, the written word was reread in light of traditional behavior." What has been lost, Soloveitchik argued, is the transmission of a religious way of life that was "mimetic, imbibed from parents and friends, and patterned on conduct regularly observed in home and street, synagogue and school." Mimetic learning of halakhah has been replaced, "abruptly and within a generation, [by] a rich literature of religious observance, [which] focuses on performances Jews have engaged in . . . for thousands of years." Since then, "traditional conduct, no matter how venerable, how elementary, or how closely remembered, . . . can no longer hold its own against the demands of the written word."[1]

Soloveitchik's sense of the loss of mimesis is worth interrogating. Even so, it prompts considerations of a similar perception of mimetic rupture implicated in the postwar decline in vernacular use of Yiddish, especially as a spoken language, among Ashkenazim (be they Orthodox, secularist, or somewhere in between) and the concomitant expansion of postvernacular Yiddish.[2] This shift in language use and its meaning is manifest in diverse cultural phenomena that entail innovations as well as losses. Daily Yiddish newspapers, for example, once widely read in major centers of Jewish population around the world, are now a thing of the past, though weekly newspapers and a range of periodicals in the language continue to appear in the Americas, Europe, Israel, and elsewhere. There are also new trends in Yiddish-language pedagogy and in Yiddish literary activity, both in the original language and in translation, as discussed in previous chapters. But it is in performance, I argue, that postvernacular Yiddish is manifest most extensively and provocatively.

The mode of performance has a particular primacy in what Benjamin Harshav terms the "semiotics of Yiddish," wherein the symbolic value of the language, regardless of its use, signifies orality and vernacularity:

In the twentieth century, Yiddish has been used for many kinds of discourse, often quite contradictory to whatever might be its "inherent" or accepted nature. This "oral" and popular language has been successfully harnessed to impressionist prose, historiography, linguistic and statistical research, political propaganda, and "ivory tower" poetry. Nevertheless, in social perception, the language did carry a cluster of characteristic features, developed in its unique history and crystallized in its modern literature. The very fact that native speakers may assign such emotive qualities to the language, rather than seeing it as a neutral vehicle for communication, speaks for itself.[3]

Given the primacy of orality in the meta-meaning of Yiddish, the postwar attrition of Yiddish vernacularity is manifest most acutely in speech. What has been in decline is not merely the number of speakers or the extent of Yiddish discourse, but the unselfconscious, seemingly inevitable use of Yiddish as a full language (as op-

קול ששון וקול שמחה קול חתן וקול כלה

The Jewish Book Center
of The Workmen's Circle
cordially invites you to attend
the model wedding of

The illustrious khosn   The praiseworthy kale
Kalmen Azriel & **Frumke Reyzl**
may his light shine   may she live long

On the eighteenth of November, 1995
26 Kheshvan 5756
at 45 East 33rd Street
Kaboles Ponem at 8:00 p.m. • Khupe at 8:15 p.m.
Kosher dinner and Klezmer dance to follow

A re-enactment of a wedding in Eastern Europe
conducted in Yiddish with English explanations

General admission $15 • WC members $10 • Students $7
Group Discounts Available
For more information, call (212) 889-6800, ext. 285

דער ייִדישער ביכער צענטער פֿאַרבעט אײַך,
איר זאָלט קומען זיך משׂמח זײַן
אויף דער כּמו-חתונה פֿון

קלמן-עזריאל • מיט • פֿרומקע-רייזל

במזל טוב ובשעה טובה ומוצלחת
מוצאי″ק אור לכ″ו חשוון תשנ″ו
אין אַרבעטער-רינג
קבלת-פּנים: 8:00 אין אָוונט
חופּה: 8:15 אין אָוונט
נאָך דער חופּה: סעודת-מיצווה און טענץ

Bilingual announcement of a model East European Jewish wedding conducted in Yiddish "with English explanations," presented by the Workmen's Circle, New York, 1995. This performance offered a complex configuration of mimesis, fusing elements of ritual, theater, and pedagogy. Attendees, who were charged admission, were configured as both insiders and outsiders and as a hybrid of tourists, theatergoers, students, and community members.
Courtesy of the Workmen's Circle/Arbeter Ring.

posed to isolated Yiddishisms embedded in another language) for routine conversation among Jews. What does this loss connote? Jews still talk to one another, after all. But fewer do so in the traditional languages of the Jewish diaspora—not only Yiddish, but also Judezmo (Judeo-Spanish), Yahudic (Judeo-Arabic), and Yavonic (Judeo-Greek), among others. Their use signifies a particular kind of social speech: internal, intimate, unofficial, the distinctive voice of centuries-old minority diaspora communities.[4] The decline in the routine use of Yiddish and of other diasporic Jewish languages, especially in spoken form, are both consequences and symbols of other losses: ruptures in intergenerational continuity and the erosion of Jewish sociocultural distinctiveness. Consequently, the decline of these Jewish vernaculars challenges long-cherished notions of the tenacity of diaspora Jewry's "portable culture" and of Jewishness as a manifestly comprehensive way of life.

Like the decline of halakhic transmission through mimesis among Orthodox Ashkenazim, the attrition of vernacular Yiddish speech has given way to new forms of cultural communication. Along with the shift from Yiddish to English, Hebrew,

Russian, Spanish, French, German, and so forth as the languages of daily life for most Ashkenazim, there has also been the advent of engagements with Yiddish that are other than vernacular. These encompass a great diversity of practices with regard to genre, setting, and community, as well as their symbolic investments in Yiddish. At the same time, all these postvernacular activities have something in common, in that they are newly self-aware of their use of Yiddish, especially in its oral form. Increasingly, Yiddish speech must be willed into existence, constructed and monitored with unprecedented deliberateness. It has become, therefore, more of a performance in its very nature.

Postvernacular Yiddish performances are often characterized as exercises in cultural salvage. Describing one popular example of this phenomenon, Ruth Ellen Gruber observes that "playing *kleʒmer* and Yiddish music in Germany and Poland represents a symbolic attempt to right wrongs: to reconstitute Jewish culture destroyed in the Holocaust, to 'bring back,' to 'resurrect,' to 'heal.' "[5] Postvernacular performances seek to span other breaches in Ashkenazic experience as well, including those wrought by emigration, linguistic assimilation, and religious reform. Consider, for example, "The Singing Table: A Music Celebration of the Hasidic Tish," presented at the Eldridge Street Synagogue, a Lower East Side architectural landmark, in November 2003. At this public program, musicians Michael Alpert, Lisa Mayer, and Sruli Dresdner promised to "evoke Jewish Eastern Europe with an intimate evening of new and old-world Hasidic music at which audience members become guests at candle-lit tables. All share in the freylekh [happy] and transcendent nigunim [melodies] learned from family and community, plus stories of mothers, fathers, and other ancestors." The presentation was part of the synagogue's "Lost & Found Music Series, which extends our preservation mission, reclaiming Jewish musical forms that are at risk of disappearing and presenting them to a general audience."[6]

The sentiments invoked by this and similar events suggest that they are part of an unprecedented project in cultural restoration (in the above example, encompassing music, language, spirituality, family life, and synagogue architecture).[7] Yet such performances can also be understood as part of a larger trajectory in the history of Ashkenazic Jewry defined not in terms of continuity but rather as a sequence of disruptive encounters with secular Western performance culture. Extending back almost two centuries before World War II, this trajectory situates recent postvernacular Yiddish performances not as examples of endurance but as the latest in a series of challenges that modernity has posed to Yiddish culture, provoking transformations in the performance of Yiddish and in its symbolic value.

Beginning in Berlin in the latter half of the eighteenth century, the Haskalah stigmatized Yiddish speech as inimical to this movement's project of realizing the modern, Westernized Jew. Yiddish became an object of parody and satire in performance among both *maskilim* and non-Jewish Germans. The former wrote scathing satirical plays in Yiddish using the language as a weapon against itself and its speakers. Among the latter, Yiddish-inflected German speech (known as *mauscheln*) became a stock feature of comic performances mocking the integrationist efforts of German Jewish parvenus.[8] By contrast, in the final decades of the nineteenth century the Yiddish theater inaugurated by Abraham Goldfaden quickly emerged as an epitome of secularization and modernity—a "civilizing agency par excellence"—for Yiddish-speaking masses in Eastern Europe and in immigrant centers, especially New York.[9] A common theme in many of the dramas these theaters presented was the challenge posed by modern life to the traditional Yiddish-speaking world. This challenge was repeatedly performed on the Yiddish stage at the same time that it was being enacted by the Yiddish theater as a public institution.

Concurrently, Yiddishists' visions of a Jewish diaspora nationalism centered on their vernacular engendered unprecedented uses of Yiddish in performance in political culture, trade union activities, youth movements, classrooms, and on the street. As these practices imbued Yiddish with new symbolic value as a defining force of Jewish nationhood, they also demanded instrumental innovations, such as the creation of new terminology and the promotion of orthographic, lexical, and grammatical standards. Consequently, Yiddishism invited a new kind of attention to the nature of the language as a vehicle of political ideology in performance. Thus, Nathan Birnbaum's opening address at the landmark conference on Yiddish held in Czernowitz in 1908 was scrutinized in the Russian-language Jewish journal *Rasʒvet* (Dawn) for the manner of his delivery as well as the content of his remarks. Noting that Birnbaum—who, though he played a leading role in convening the conference, was not a native Yiddish speaker—read "his first speech in Yiddish fluently from his notes," *Rasʒvet* reported that "his expressions [are] pure Yiddish. Recognizable on occasion are pedantries of speech and a polished style. He reads his speech in the Galician dialect."[10]

This project of transforming Yiddish into a language for enacting Jewish modernism engendered distinctive developments among immigrant Jews in the United States. During the first decades of the twentieth century, America's Yiddishist organizations created new rites, such as the *driter seyder* (third seder), a communal Passover celebration, inaugurated in the 1930s, and new institutions, especially *shules* (afternoon and weekend schools) and summer camps, where an array of performances (including skits, plays, recitals, and concerts) played leading roles in the realization of a secular culture organized around Yiddish.[11] In Soviet Russia, Yiddish, the official language of the state's Jewish national minority, was used to enact a wide array of performances of the revolutionized Jewish citizen in arenas ranging from early childhood education to the creation of the Jewish Autonomous Region of Birobidzhan. Prominent among these efforts were government-sponsored Yiddish theaters, celebrated in their day for artistic innovation (and that, during Stalinist purges, became a prime target of liquidation).[12] Simultaneously, Zionist Hebraists in Palestine rejected Yiddish as part of their enactment of the "new Jew," whose repudiation of the diaspora included the forging of a new Jewish vernacular. Here acts of deriding and erasing Yiddish culture became symbolic performances in themselves.

After World War II, innovations in performing Yiddish culture are found not only among those Jews who have largely abandoned it as a vernacular but also among hasidim, who have maintained its use as a daily language most extensively. During this period hasidic and other ultra-Orthodox communities have expanded traditional uses of Yiddish in performance—such as writing and staging new plays with religious themes not only on Purim but also at other times of the year—and have created new ones, notably the use of Yiddish in song lyrics by artists of "Orthodox pop" music.[13]

Soloveitchik characterizes postwar Ashkenazic life as marked by "the end of the East European heritage of self-evident Jewishness."[14] In the wake of the perceived breakdown of mimetic tradition, Orthodox observance has, he argues, altered and, in some instances, abandoned long-standing practices of cultural transmission through the performance of everyday life. At the same time, new modes of performance in the traditional vernacular of Ashkenaz are flourishing among secular as well as observant Jews, among non-Ashkenazic Jews and non-Jews as well as the descendants of Yiddish speakers. These new, postvernacular uses of Yiddish are often vaunted as acts of cultural endurance in the face of adversity. However, like the new, text-based culture of Orthodox observance, they are better understood as innovative cultural negotiations, responsive to the profound ruptures in Jewish life wrought by the Holocaust and other twentieth-century upheavals that have left Jewish mimesis in an apparent state of crisis. Indeed, by simultaneously imitating and transforming Yiddish vernacularity, these innovations in Yiddish performance problematize the very notion of Ashkenazic mimesis.

Performance of *Kheyder,* an antireligious play "based on the classic Yiddish writers," at the Belorussian State Yiddish Theater in Minsk, some time during the interwar years. The letters on the backsides of the three performers in the foreground spell the word *kosher.*
Courtesy of the Archives of the YIVO Institute for Jewish Research, New York.

A LANGUAGE OF FESTIVALS

In January 2002 the most recent issue of *Der Bay* (acronym for Bay Area Yiddish) arrived in the mail. Then in its twelfth year, this newsletter is published by Philip "Fishl" Kutner of San Mateo, California (Kutner also runs a related website, www.derbay.org). Inside *Der Bay* are eight pages of listings of lectures, concerts, plays, meetings, conferences, and so on, all involving, in one way or another, the Yiddish language. (The newsletter itself is mostly in English, with some items in romanized Yiddish.) A Yiddish club in New Orleans reports its upcoming production of a "homegrown" play. There are reports on Jewish music festivals in Amsterdam and Munich, on activities at the Vilnius Yiddish Institute, and on monthly seminars at the Medem Library in Paris. Yiddish club meetings in Los Angeles and Chicago, Gainesville, Florida, and Mt. Laurel, New Jersey, are also posted. An index of articles that appeared in *Der Bay* during 2001 lists reports from Mexico, South Africa, and Australia, as well as a feature on "Hoosier Mame-loshn." On the back page is a discussion of proper Yiddish terminology for playing tennis. Among the *"oystsugn fun briv in der redaktsye"* (excerpts from letters to the editor), a woman in Toronto enthuses that "things seem to be jumping re Yiddish all over the world."[15]

This and similar listings in the Jewish press, in various organizational brochures, and on Internet bulletins and websites evince a lively, if mutable, international Yiddish culture now being realized in a wide variety of performances that are held, in one place or another, almost every day of the year. These events are not only distinct from those of the traditional Jewish festival calendar—aside from their largely secular nature, the inventory of Yiddish cultural events changes from year to year, and they variously appeal to a considerable spectrum of audiences with regard to region, generation, and ideology. They are also significantly different from the array of secular Yiddish performances—plays, concerts, conferences, rallies, lectures, and so on— that flourished during the first half of the twentieth century throughout Europe and the Americas. Typically, these contemporary events take place in social environments in which Yiddish is no longer a primary vernacular or, sometimes, not a vernacular at all, and they often entail the use of one or more other languages in their execution. Diverse as they are, these are performances of Yiddish in the postvernacular mode.

Yiddish is thus not the language in which these events are usually facilitated, the language used to advertise them or used by event organizers to communicate with those planning to attend or even with one another. Frequently it is not the language one hears most at these events, whether in welcoming remarks made by presenters or in casual conversation among audiences. Rather, Yiddish is primarily reserved for restricted moments of performance by selected performers. More than a symptom of diminished fluency in the language, this development reflects a distinctly postvernacular esteem for Yiddish as a language of special performative worth. In these contexts Yiddish is not regarded as a vehicle for routine communication, as the equivalent of other vernaculars. Rather, the language is prized for its exceptional ability to voice cultural distinctiveness associated not with the here and now but with Jewish life remote in time, place, and sensibility, doing so in formally concentrated and affectively intense performances. Indeed, it is a distinction of postvernacular Yiddish events that, rather than the language serving as the instrument of performance, its utterance is, at least in part, the performance's objective itself.

For some observers this phenomenon is a cause for concern. In an editorial published in the *Forward* during the fall of 2000, Yiddish author and journalist Boris Sandler stated:

[it] is a bitter paradox of Yiddish today, that it has been transformed from a daily language into a language of celebrations and festivals. What one sees from the outside is not even the language itself, only its shining, joyous outer mantle. What lies beneath—the depths of our literature and culture and the spiritual treasure of our people—remains hidden, like a Torah scroll under a lavishly decorated covering. Only the most stubborn and devoted of our people remove the beautiful outer garment to unravel the yellowed parchment and intone their prayer.[16]

Although he is writing in a secular Jewish newspaper and addressing what is essentially a concern of secular Jewish culture, Sandler draws his metaphor from religious tradition, comparing vernacular Yiddish to the rolled parchment on which the text of the Torah is traditionally written. In likening Yiddish festivals, by contrast, to the decorative cloth mantles with which Torah scrolls are covered in Ashkenazic synagogues, he invokes the distinction between *klekoydesh* (holy objects, such as the Torah scroll, whose sanctity is inherent) and *tashmishe kdushe* (ritual appurtenances, such as Torah mantles—i.e., items that "service, enclose, or activate holy objects" and that "attain their sanctity only in use").[17]

Sandler invokes this traditional ritual hierarchy to distinguish levels of secular linguistic and cultural experience: the authenticity of vernacular Yiddish is equated with the most venerated embodiment of scripture (both the form and content of the Torah scroll are sacred); festivals, in contrast, likened to Torah mantles, have a lesser, contingent worth. Often decorated with embroidery and other ornamentation, these mantles are more visually engaging than the austere, inscribed parchments they envelop, but their own substantive value is adventitious, indicating the enclosed scroll's sanctity.

The implications of Sandler's metaphor extend beyond dismissing festivals as "mere ornament," for it also points up a disquieting challenge facing Yiddishists. Vernacular Yiddish, he suggests, lacks the facile, eye-catching, popular appeal of festivals; it is prized and, moreover, understood only by a limited number of true devotees. Therefore, like the text of the Torah, Yiddish needs to be translated and interpreted by a scholarly elite for general audiences. Insufficiently literate in Yiddish, the Jews flocking to these festivals encounter the traditional vernacular of Ashkenaz—for many in the audience, the native tongue of their forebears—"from the outside."

Sandler is far from the first to decry this development. In 1911 Moyshe Olgin observed that Russian Jewish intellectuals, including those who professed support for Yiddish, did not speak the language at home with their families. They regarded it as a language to be used in public, in formal, ideologically self-conscious undertakings, but not for routine use in private. These intellectuals treated Yiddish as "holiday attire, put on to be seen by others."[18] And yet Yiddish festivals and similar events bemoaned by some are regarded by others as "cultural performances par excellence." Barbara Kirshenblatt-Gimblett characterizes festivals generally as "multisensory, multifocus" events, involving an elaborate, sometimes totalizing transformation of an encapsulated environment and a saturation of the senses. Festivals offer the visitor the diffuse riches of everyday life in a concentrated time and place. As such, they are widely regarded as an ideal point of entry to cultures for tourists seeking to encounter another way of life in the form of an "experience"—a term that "indexes an engagement of the senses, emotions, and imagination."[19]

Thinking of Yiddish festivals as tourist productions is especially provocative, for it positions Jews, who make up the majority of the audiences at most of these events, as visitors in what is ostensibly their own cultural terrain. While this notion might well dismay Sandler and those of like mind, it is exemplary of what anthropologist Marjorie Esman has termed "internal tourism," that is, tourist activities that enable one to visit one's "own people." Writing about contemporary Cajun culture in Louisiana, Esman regards performances on the "tourist stage" as benefiting both locals and visitors by facilitating "ethnic preservation," thereby providing Cajuns with a bulwark against acculturation and reinforcing cultural distinctiveness.[20] However, the suggestion that tourist productions simply "preserve" culture is far from unproblematic. Esther Romeyn and Jack Kugelmass term such events as Wisconsin's Holland Festival, Festa Italia, and Belgian Days "festivalizations" of sites of ethnic and national memory. In this postmodern form of tourist culture, they argue, " 'place' is packaged as an 'experience' " so compelling that "the packaged version of the 'real' displaces reality itself."[21]

Moreover, the notion of Jews attending Yiddish festivals as "internal tourists" has especially challenging topical implications—for what, exactly, is their destination? In addition to a wide array of actual geographic locations—whether São Paulo, Strasbourg, or Safed, a synagogue in the New Jersey suburbs, a castle in Weimar, or a kosher resort hotel in the Laurentians—there is the shared virtual destination of Yiddishland, the imaginary realm defined by the use of Yiddish. As efforts to conjure some notion of this Yiddish utopia, Yiddish festivals and related cultural events entail highly inventive transformations of time and place. In doing so, these events constitute a particularly provocative case of what performance theorist

The *Nayeh Velt Malakh* (New World Angel), leading the Ashkenaz Parade, which marks the conclusion of the Ashkenaz Festival. Toronto, 1999.
Photograph by Robert Bernecky. Copyright © Robert Bernecky 2004.

Richard Schechner terms "restoration of behavior," for in Yiddish festivals a variety of actual, "indicative" sources (i.e., what Yiddish culture once was) as well as mythic, "subjunctive" ones (what Yiddish culture might have been or may yet be) inform the performances. These events, in turn, look both backward and forward in time to a wide range of possibilities with regard to what is being "restored" in performance.[22] It is quite possible, therefore, that for each audience member at any given festival a different vision of Yiddishland is being realized (or challenged).

Toronto's biennial Ashkenaz festival, first held in 1995, exemplifies this phenomenon by employing the traditional term for Yiddish-speakers' original European cultural domain in naming this "festival of new Yiddish culture." Here Yiddish simultaneously signifies both retrospection—"I see [Yiddish] as a precious legacy, . . . a thousand-year-old language and culture which contains the essence of our collective soul," writes Rosalie Sharp, president of the festival's board of directors, in the 1999 festival program—and innovation: "Sparking new artistic creation is . . . a central ASHKENAZ theme," states the festival's artistic director, musician David Bookbinder.[23]

The multivalent agenda of the Ashkenaz Festival is realized most tellingly in its use of Toronto's geography as a symbolic space for performing Yiddish culture in the form of a pageant that traverses space, time, and sensibility. Most events of the weeklong festival take place at Harbourfront Centre, the city's downtown water-front complex of performance and exhibition spaces (and frequently the site of other ethnic cultural programs). However, the festival culminates with an "Ashke-naz Parade," described as follows in the festival brochure:

> Beginning in Kensington Market's Bellevue Square Park, the swirling spectacle of music, colour and community celebration winds through the bustling market streets, arriving at the steps of the Anshei Minsk shul [a synagogue founded in 1916 by immigrants from Minsk]. Then, with the Nayeh Velt Malakh (our "new world" angel) leading the way . . . , the Parade takes over the streets and dances in jubilant procession down Spadina Avenue [once the commercial center of Toronto's Yiddish-speaking immigrant community] for a finale at Harbourfront Centre.[24]

The inventive spirit of the parade, which is the brainchild of the Ashkenaz Fes-tival's organizers, is extended to festival participants. Before the parade begins, the public is invited to work with the artists in charge of the event "to build anything from Yiddish-inspired hats and festive *schmattes* [here meaning "glad rags"], to giant puppets, banners and flags."[25] With this event, Toronto's streets and public spaces become the staging ground for a self-styled, celebratory reenactment of im-migration, both that of Jews from Eastern Europe to North America and of Yid-dish from the vernacular of immigrant community life to the symbolic center of a postimmigrant culture of ethnic heritage. The performance facilitating this sym-bolic transmigration does not so much draw on any precedent of public procession among Yiddish-speaking Jews (with the possible exception of political rallies) as it is indebted to the idioms of North American ethnic parades and avant-garde street theater.

Enacting the meta-value of Yiddish at festivals and cultural programs often draws on external cultural sources as it reflects the sensibilities and needs of new-comers to Yiddish. Consider, for example, the range of images used to articulate the meaning of Yiddish language and culture in promotional material for "The Art of Yiddish: Cultural Nourishment for a New Age," a "two-week immersion in the liv-ing language" offered in December 2000 by Yiddishkayt Los Angeles. In a brochure featuring a palm tree against a "sky" of Yiddish text on its front, the program char-acterizes Yiddish as "the DNA of Ashkenazic Jews—embedded in every word and untranslatable expression is the historic code and continuity of a complex and enduring culture." Elsewhere in the brochure, works of Yiddish theater, film, music, and literature are offered to potential participants as "accessible, timeless legacies," and the program as a whole is characterized as "unique and inspiring."[26] Here Yiddish is nature *and* nurture, art *and* science, as well as old and new, local and exotic, singular and enduring, inscrutable and accessible.

Because fluency in Yiddish is increasingly less common, those who stage festivals and other events celebrating Yiddish culture cannot assume that participants' devotion to the language's secondary, symbolic level of meaning is matched by their competence in Yiddish at its primary level. These Yiddish performances address this challenge by implementing strategies pursued in other postvernacular cultural undertakings discussed in previous chapters. Like literary projects, many contemporary Yiddish performances rely on code-switching, translating, and anthologizing to forge new meanings for Yiddish and to engage new audiences. These events also frequently draw on pedagogical practices and idioms of the classroom.

Performances of plays, poems, songs, folktales, and the like are mainstays of contemporary Yiddish cultural events, but in these venues, Yiddish-language texts seldom stand on their own. As a rule, their presentation entails translation into a local vernacular by means of a variety of devices: explanatory comments delivered during the performance or in program notes, wholesale translating of Yiddish (sometimes involving simultaneous translation heard on headphones or projected as supertitles), or bilingual performances of texts originally written only in Yiddish.[27] Translation has thus become intrinsic to postvernacular Yiddish performance.

These code-switching practices are different from the bilingualism of immigrant and second-generation entertainments, such as songs performed by the Barry Sisters, Mickey Katz, or Menashe Skulnik, which were popular among American Jews during the middle decades of the twentieth century. In those earlier performances, the code-switching between Yiddish and English assumed a bilingual audience, and the humor those performances produced celebrated the listeners' cultural competence in these two languages and cultures. Rather, translation practices in postvernacular performances assume a lack of Yiddish fluency, and the interplay between Yiddish and the language(s) of translation is therefore largely devoid of the speech play inherent in earlier bilingual comedy.

Moreover, postvernacular performances tend to separate the semantic value of Yiddish from its other semiotic registers. The primacy of its form over its content in many of these presentations renders Yiddish as something more akin to music than a language, to be appreciated as a signifier of affect or as an aesthetic experi-

Jenny Romaine (as Glückel), Roberto Rossi (as her first husband, Chaim), and their twelve children (puppets by Clare Dolan), in Great Small Works' *The Memoirs of Glückel of Hameln/Zikhroynes Glikl,* directed by Jenny Romaine, created and conceived by Jenny Romaine, Adrienne Cooper, and Frank London, performed in Toronto in 1999. This adaptation of a seventeenth-century Yiddish memoir, written by a Jewish woman living in northern Germany, was performed in a mixture of English and Yiddish. At performances of the play in New York City's LaMaMa E.T.C. the following year, bilingual lyrics to the production's songs were sold as broadsides to the audience.
Photograph by N. Bereket. Courtesy of Great Small Works.

ence of sound play. Thus, Moni Ovadia, a popular performer of Yiddish cabarets throughout Italy in the 1990s, explains, "It doesn't matter that the audience doesn't understand the words. What's important is that they hear the sound and cadences of Yiddish."[28] (In this regard, postvernacular performances in Yiddish resemble stagings of plays in sign language for hearing as well as deaf audiences; to the former, "the language of the deaf [is] presented as art," and deafness itself serves as an emotionally charged metaphor within the drama.)[29]

In addition to code-switching with other languages, the translation of Yiddish at postvernacular events can entail complementing or replacing Yiddish speech with one or more other activities, such as singing, dancing, or playing musical instruments. These activities heighten the affective significance assigned to the language or provide analogies for its expressiveness through performance genres in which the audience has greater fluency. Sometimes this practice entails assigning "Yiddish-ness" to nonverbal genres of performance with only a tangential connection to the language—for example, "Yiddish dance" (i.e., traditional East European Jewish folk dance), which is both performed and taught (in English) at KlezKamp, an annual Yiddish Folk Arts Program established in 1984, among other venues.[30] The American modern dance company Pilobolus also explored the possibility of translating Yiddish into movement in "Davenen" (Praying). This 2001 dance, set to an original composition by the Klezmatics (a klezmer band started in New York in 1986), grew out of an idea to choreograph a piece based on Leo Rosten's popular book *The Joys of Yiddish*.[31]

In such postvernacular performances Yiddish is embodied rather than uttered. The language functions mainly, sometimes solely, at the symbolic level, invoking an erstwhile shared ethnic knowledge base and sensibility in an effort to make this accessible, despite the lack of linguistic fluency and cultural literacy in the audience. Thus, musician Henry Sapoznik, founder of KlezKamp, explains in a prefatory note to his 1999 history of klezmer that, in his work, the term *Yiddish* "denotes not only the language but the society and culture served by it. *Yiddish music*, then—be it folksongs, theater compositions, the singing of cantors, even instrumental music—refers to what has been recognized as music by *yidishe oyern* (Jewish ears), long the arbiters of what gains entry into the soundscape of *Yiddishkayt*."[32] By focusing on the ears rather than the mouth, Sapoznik shifts the agency of defining Yiddish culture from production to reception.

Another consequence of the diminishing ranks of fluent Yiddish speakers is the professionalization of uttering Yiddish at postvernacular cultural events by actors, musicians, teachers, and lecturers (who may themselves not be native speakers of the language). As a result, pedagogy is frequently imbricated with entertainment and other modes of performance at Yiddish festivals, in effect teaching audiences what the pleasures of Yiddish culture are even as they are engaged in its appreciation. Musician Adrienne Cooper writes of her experiences performing at the 1992 Jewish Cultural Festival in Cracow, "The audiences are intelligent, attentive, and very malleable. They respond to everything, participate actively, adapt to each of the diverse performances. For Andy Statman's trio, they listen with the fixed attention of a jazz audience; for Shlomo Carlebach, they are flower children wannabees; for the Klezmatics—rock and rollers. . . . You can feel their effort from the stage."[33]

Conversely, Yiddish educational programs make extensive use of what might conventionally be thought of as "entertainment" activities—folksinging sessions, screenings of vintage Yiddish films, walking tours of Jewish neighborhoods—as

Poster announcing the International Yiddish Festival in Cracow, 1990. Performers came from Amsterdam, Boston, Jerusalem, Paris, Saarbrücken, Stockholm, Tel Aviv, Warsaw, Wuppertal, and Zurich. Designed by Janusz Wrzeniski. Courtesy of the Jewish Culture Festival in Cracow.

part of their instruction. At events such as the Jewish Music Institute's KlezFest London 2002, pedagogy and entertainment were strategically linked: according to its promotional material the event began with a six-day "Crash Course in Yiddish," employing a "first-class international faculty" to "introduce the language to newcomers [and to] refresh the memory of those who remember it from childhood," followed by "five days of instrumental, ensemble, song and dance workshops and performances, as well as sessions on Yiddish theatre, poetry, film, humour, history and folklore" taught by "the most renowned and inspiring teachers and musicians from Europe and America."[34]

The conjoining of pedagogy and entertainment in postvernacular Yiddish performances is epitomized by the emergence, since the mid-1970s, of *klezmorim* as public authorities on prewar East European Jewish culture—a phenomenon that would have no doubt astonished their professional forebears a century ago. Marginal figures in East European Jewish society before World War II, klezmorim are now prominent cultural spokespeople, enacting representations of that society on stages around the world. Unlike prewar Eastern Europe's klezmorim, who performed a client-driven repertoire at weddings and other celebrations for both Jews and non-Jews in their communities, many contemporary klezmorim are primarily concert and recording artists. Their musicianship, typically centered more exclusively on a repertoire defined as "Jewish," is largely the result of their own research and composition and frequently includes the performance of Yiddish songs, both vintage and original. (The incorporation of Yiddish folk and theater songs into what had been instrumental performances is also an American-led innovation of the last quarter-century.) Indeed, these musicians are largely responsible for the shift in definition of the term *klezmer* from its original meaning in Yiddish as "musician" to a genre of Jewish music defined by a new kind of musicianship, which casts its cultural gaze forward as well as backward. Thus, one performer, Alicia Svigals, has characterized the contemporary klezmer scene as part of a larger search for "new ways to negotiate our Jewishness in America."[35]

Svigals, a founding member of the Klezmatics, argues that contemporary klezmorim have moved beyond resurrecting a "lost" repertoire and are now taking on the same role of serving as a cultural avant-garde that rock musicians have played in the West since the 1960s. At the same time, she notes, most American klezmorim today are middle-class, college-educated Jews, and they come to klezmer after having been trained in other musical styles (classical, rock, jazz, Balkan, bluegrass, etc.). Consequently, she posits, they bring a high level of self-awareness to their musicianship and show a great propensity to discussing their work and its meaning in public—whether by writing historical studies of klezmer music (including more than one doctoral dissertation) or personal artistic manifestos, or by providing written and oral commentary on their performances, both live and recorded.[36]

Thus, revivalist groups such as the Boston-based Klezmer Conservatory Band routinely frame their performances with explanations situating individual musical numbers in historical and cultural contexts unfamiliar to their audience. Sometimes they even incorporate pedagogy within a number—for example, by teaching audiences the words to a Yiddish song as they perform it.[37] At the same time, this band appeals to audience members for information about the music that it has been performing since 1980. Referring to the audience during a 2001 concert at New York's Avery Fischer Hall as *meyvens* (anglicized Yiddish for "experts"), bandleader Hankus Netsky commented, "Some of you have known this music longer than we have." With this observation, he solicited support for the Klezmer Conservatory

Foundation, which "welcomes the donation of *klezmer* manuscripts, Yiddish sheet music, radio transcriptions, oral histories, interviews, and Yiddish *klezmer* recordings to its collection."[38] Reflecting on this informational give-and-take between performers and their audiences, Svigals suggests that klezmer groups construct an imaginary vision of cultural continuity from the early twentieth century, when "every Jewish wedding supposedly had a klezmer group playing traditional dances that everyone knew how to do." The Klezmatics, she notes, are also inspired by an imagined continuity of a different sort: if there hadn't been a Holocaust, she posits, "there would be Yiddish rock bands today, playing the kind of music we play."[39]

Even as they strive to restore a traditional repertoire, postvernacular Yiddish performances transform the cultural resources of the past. As is the case with assembling collections of literary translations, the practice of anthologizing discrete works in performance creates new cultural entities by virtue of their selection and juxtaposition. Among the most common examples of this practice in contemporary Yiddish performance are the diverse repertoires of songs heard in solo and choral recitals or in amateur sing-alongs, which frequently place numbers as disparate as hasidic songs of mystical devotion and anarchist anthems of agit-prop side by side.[40] Such performances are quite different from the repertoires of traditional Jewish singers in prewar East Europe, which were often less eclectic in content but more culturally diverse, since these singers were typically multilingual.[41] Yet far from provoking conflicts, the great range of these contemporary repertoires is savored precisely for their ideological variety, because the singers and audiences come together as celebrants of Yiddish as the embodiment of Ashkenazic heritage. The Jewish People's Philharmonic Chorus, for example, founded in New York City in 1923 (as the Freiheit Gezang Farein), was originally associated with the *Morgen-Freiheit*, a Communist Yiddish newspaper published in New York. Long since independent of any political affiliation, the chorus today performs a repertoire of "two centuries of Yiddish song . . . , the voices of sweatshop laborers, immigrants, mothers, partisans, *khalutsim* [Zionist pioneers], *tumlers* [jokesters] and lovers . . .—all in our warm, eloquent *mame-loshn*."[42]

These Yiddish repertoires acquire a new value defined by the nature of their anthological projects. Yiddish singer Wolf Krakowski exemplifies this transformation on his recordings *Transmigrations: Gilgul* (1996) and *Goyrl: Destiny* (2002).[43] A child of Holocaust survivors born in a Displaced Persons camp in Austria and raised in Sweden and Canada, Krakowski performs a Yiddish repertoire that includes traditional folksongs and the works of acclaimed composers of modern Yiddish song both before and after World War II, such as Mordecai Gebirtig, Szmerke Kaczerginski, and Sholom Secunda, as well as his own compositions. The lyricists in Krakowski's repertoire range from religious writers (Rabbi Abraham Isaac Kook, Aaron Zeitlin) to secular theater artists (Bernardo Feuer, Max Perlman). Krakowski articulates and extends the diversity of his repertoire through his musicianship, offering performances accompanied by an international array of instruments—balalaika, steel guitar, bouzouki, Dobro, saxophone, steel drum, doumbek, maracas—and in styles inflected by country, rock, blues, tango, and reggae, thereby situating Yiddish song within the cultural hybridity of contemporary world music.

In this regard, Yiddish concerts and sing-alongs, as well as other anthological performances of Yiddish texts, function like museums, presenting a selection of cultural fragments whose juxtaposition enables attendees to experience a cultural expanse ranging over generations and across continents. In these performances, collections of songs (or of poems, stories, folktales, proverbs, jokes, etc.) limn the dimensions of Yiddish culture as a totalized "world." Elided in these enterprises are the nuances of Ashkenazic subcultures, the dynamics of their history, and the complexities of their erstwhile multilingual and multicultural contacts. But what is gained is an ameliorating vision of Yiddish as constant and comprehensive.

If Yiddish, in the postvernacular mode, has become a language of festivals, then it has done so as part of a distinctive project of the postwar era to reconstitute Yiddish as something other than a language of daily life. Postvernacular performances have transformed Yiddish into a signifier of a bygone way of life that can be sampled as an "experience." In this process, the language's primary, vernacular level of significance is diminished, fragmented, and mediated, while its secondary, symbolic values expand and proliferate. Indeed, postvernacular performances have become a proving ground for testing the extent to which Yiddish can sustain these diverging vectors of meaning.

THE CALL TO YOUTH

In November 2000 I received the following announcement via email:

THE YIDDISH-"SVIVES"
A NEW YUGNTRUF PROJECT
We warmly invite all Yugntruf members and Yiddish-speaking friends to take part in Yugntruf's new Yiddish SVIVES (groups).
What are the SVIVES?
The SVIVES are groups of 6 to 10 people who meet at least every other week.

What is the goal of the SVIVES?

The goal of the SVIVES is to create a place where people can SPEAK Yiddish and also ENRICH their Yiddish.

Why do we need the SVIVES?

Yiddish will cease to be a living language (outside the Ultra-Orthodox community) if nobody speaks Yiddish and if nobody raises children in Yiddish. Through the SVIVES we plan to encourage people to speak Yiddish more often and better. . . . At the SVIVES, the main objective is to speak a good Yiddish. Topics for discussion are determined in advance. The SVIVES meet regularly, and the SVIVE members have the opportunity to build relationships with each other that will help to create a Yiddish language community.

What happens at a SVIVE meeting?

—We constantly remind ourselves that our goal is to speak a good Yiddish.

—We discuss the language of a text (article, story, etc.) that all have read in advance (yes, there's homework for the SVIVE!)

—We learn new expressions and idioms, and try to use them in our own Yiddish.

—We act out scenes from plays.

—We seek all kinds of games in order to use Yiddish and have fun.

—We sing. . . .

WE INVITE YOU ALL TO JOIN THE SVIVES!

COME AND HELP TO CREATE A YIDDISH-SPEAKING COMMUNITY!

SET UP YOUR OWN SVIVE—WE'LL HELP YOU![44]

The post–World War II decades have witnessed not only extensive abandonment of Yiddish as a vernacular but also organized reactions against this trend. Among the array of contemporary Yiddishist groups, the organization known as Yugntruf (Yiddish for "call to youth") distinguishes its commitment to the language by insisting on the primacy of maintaining Yiddish as "a living language."[45]

Founded in New York City in 1964, Yugntruf's membership numbered over one thousand households as of 2004. The majority (over eight hundred) are in the United States (about half of whom are in the New York metropolitan area); the others are located in twenty-six other countries, including Australia, Brazil, Canada, England, France, Germany, Israel, Italy, Japan, Mexico, Russia, and Uruguay.[46] Yugntruf publishes a journal, maintains a website, and sponsors a children's play group, a writers' workshop, a housing database for those looking to live near other Yiddish speakers, conversation groups, as well as a changing roster of activities, most of which take place in New York and all of which are conducted in Yiddish.

From its inception, Yugntruf's commitment to speaking Yiddish has been conceived as an act of cultural persistence, demanding vigilance and rigor on the part of its members. Yugntruf's constitution, published in the second issue of its eponymous journal, bears this out, providing its constituents not merely with a set of bylaws but also with a manifesto offering a rationale for speaking Yiddish and investing Yiddish speech acts with powerful extralinguistic significance.

Yugntruf's constitution begins by identifying Yiddish as "more than simply a means of linguistic expression" for its members, who all know two or more languages. Rather, it is "a symbol of ethnic identification" and of "Jewish creativity," linking its speakers across time (the thousand-year history of Ashkenaz) and space (the global geography of the Ashkenazic diaspora). Yugntruf characterizes its devotion to Yiddish as an expression of a commitment to ethnicity (*folkstimlekhkeyt*, which can also mean "populism"), which in turn is characterized as a rejection of "careerism and snobbism." Moreover, this commitment is defined as an act of justice, redressing cultural wrongs: "For hundreds of years Yiddish has been the stepchild of the Jewish people—ignored, discriminated against, persecuted by outsiders and by our own people." Not only has the language been victimized by Nazism and Stalinism, but "the indifference, ignorance, and even self-hatred of millions of Jews . . . have brought the Yiddish language to its current state" of crisis.[47]

Yugntruf's response to this sense of crisis centers on a commitment to Yiddish vernacularity. Like Moyshe Olgin a half-century earlier (and anticipating Boris Sandler's recent concerns by several decades), Yugntruf's founders decried the devolving of Yiddish into a language reserved for special occasions: "One of the dangers that threatens Yiddish from within . . . is a tendency to reduce [it] to a language of songs and recitations, graduation ceremonies and Hanukkah or Purim parties. Yiddish has always been and must remain . . . not only a holiday language, but also an everyday language."[48] However, maintaining Yiddish as a vernacular is understood as requiring "work" on the part of Yugntruf members, who must continue to study and practice the language. The deliberateness of this effort is naturalized by characterizing it as akin to an ecological phenomenon: "A plant that receives no water or food withers. So, too, the intellect withers if all that it has to live on is the mental nourishment of childhood and elementary education."

Most important, the constitution asserts, is that "a member of Yugntruf does not say one thing and do another." Paying lip service to the idea of supporting Yiddish while persisting in speaking other languages is untenable. For Yugntruf, a commitment to Yiddish is a commitment to its performance; "saying" is one with "doing." Indeed, Yugntruf's Yiddishism exemplifies philosopher J. L. Austin's foundational

"Sha! Di eltern hern. Redt yidish!" (Shh! Our parents can hear. Talk in Yiddish!) Cartoon by Jim Kaplin of Baltimore, published in *Yugntruf* in 1984.
Courtesy of Yugntruf.

definition of performative speech: "The issuing of the utterance is the performing of an action—it is not . . . just saying something." But while Austin sought to distinguish performative utterances (e.g., marriage vows, bequests, wagers) from what he termed constative ones, Yugntruf's agenda elides any such distinction. Speaking in Yiddish—which its members acknowledge as an elective act on their part—is in itself the performance of maintaining Yiddish as a living language. Therefore, regardless of what is said, saying it in Yiddish is an enactment of the conviction that "saying" can "make it so."[49]

As the organization's name proclaims, youth figures strategically in Yugntruf's articulation of its mission. The older generation of Yiddish speakers (i.e., those born before World War II), laments Yugntruf's constitution, is "tired" and content with maintaining a linguistic status quo. Young Yiddishists are called on to "contribute new energy" to the task, which entails not merely preserving but "raising Yiddish to new heights." This progressive appeal to youth is also, in a sense, retrospective. The model for Yugntruf is the organized youth culture that flourished among Jews in interwar Eastern Europe. At that time an array of youth movements provided vital social, cultural, and political communities for Jews in their teens and early twenties. Usually linked to an adult political organization, these youth movements represented the splintered array of ideologies espoused by interwar East European Jews: religious and secular, Zionist and anti-Zionist, left-wing and right-wing, integrationist and separatist, Yiddishist and Hebraist. Modeled on the *Wandervogel* movement that had emerged in turn-of-the-twentieth-century Germany, Jewish youth organizations promoted ideological indoctrination through an array of activities that had come to define European youth culture: outings, athletic competitions, public debates, amateur theatricals, and the like. Some of the activities that Yugntruf currently sponsors—lectures, recitals, reading circles, picnics, and hikes—evoke this prewar European culture. But the nature of the activities is of secondary importance; their ultimate value is that they are conducted in Yiddish.

Yugntruf's youth-movement model does not simply hearken back to an Old World Jewish cultural heyday as remembered by the organization's founding advisors, who grew up in interwar Eastern Europe. Its "call to youth" is also a symbolic statement that positions Yiddish not as a dying language, known only by a dwindling, elderly population, but as a language of eternal youth. This position, which challenges prevailing notions of the postwar state of Yiddish, also requires stretching the definition of youth: as Yugntruf explains on its website (in Yiddish and English), most of its members "are in their 20s, 30s, and 40s; but we also have many older members who feel young at heart and who want to help keep Yiddish active among the younger generation."

Unlike the Jewish youth movements of interwar Eastern Europe, Yugntruf espouses no particular religious or political ideology. On the contrary, it proudly announces that "its members are of all ideological persuasions."[50] In this regard, the movement is also distinguished from most American Yiddishist organizations, founded by immigrants in the first half of the twentieth century, which were variously tied to socialist, communist, anarchist, Territorialist, or Labor Zionist movements. Instead, Yugntruf articulates its commitment to Yiddish—in particular, the use of Yiddish as a spoken language—as its ideology. Thus, while it positions itself as an alternative to postvernacularity, Yugntruf is similarly devoted to Yiddish as a cultural end rather than a means.

Moreover, while Yugntruf articulates its mission as a project of cultural maintenance, it is, in large measure, an exercise in cultural subversion. Just as Yugntruf defies conventional notions of the mortality of Yiddish or of what constitutes youth, the organization regularly challenges prevailing notions of where, when, how, by whom, and about what topics Yiddish might be spoken. For example, in March 2000 Yugntruf sponsored a reading at the Columbia University Bookstore at which author Michael Skakun, a member of the organization, discussed his recently published book, *On Burning Ground: A Son's Memoir*.[51] Skakun read excerpts from the book in English, but his comments and discussion with the audience were conducted entirely in Yiddish. Rather than Yiddish being the language of a text that then must be translated and discussed in another language, as is often the case in literature classes or public lectures on Yiddish culture, here it was employed as the language for explicating a work written in English. The bookstore setting proved a strategic venue. The discussion took place amid curious onlookers, who had come to the store to shop, some of whom doubtless had no idea what language was being spoken at the event. But for Yugntruf members, this enactment of a Yiddish discussion in a public venue where English is hegemonic framed the event as an act of linguistic tenacity.

Or consider Yugntruf's pre-Passover shopping expedition to Boro Park, the largest hasidic neighborhood in Brooklyn, held the following month. Members of the organization (who, while they range in their religious convictions from ardent secularism to Orthodoxy, typically have limited, if any, contact with hasidim) visited a variety of shops to purchase food, books, and other items, as well as to engage salespeople and other locals in Yiddish. The results of this effort were varied; some salespeople began conversing with these obvious outsiders to the community in English but, once engaged, switched to Yiddish. Several hasidim expressed approval of the organization's efforts to maintain Yiddish, though they occasionally offered these sentiments in English. But other salespeople persisted in responding in English to the Yugntruf members. In these cases, the hasidim refused to relinquish Yiddish from its postwar role in their community as a language that articulates the separation of hasidim from other Jews who are less (or differently) observant of religious traditions. At no time, however, did the members of Yugntruf abandon their use of Yiddish when speaking among themselves or with the hasidim. Here, too, the venue for this event was strategic, with the hasidic milieu playing a complex role. On the one hand, it was attractive as an environment in which Yiddish is indigenous; on the other, the members of Yugntruf refused to compromise their own distinctive commitment to speaking Yiddish when confronted with resistance from some hasidim, thereby defying local notions of who might speak the language and to what end.

Yugntruf's most elaborate exercise in fostering Yiddish as a living language occurs during *yidish-vokh* (Yiddish Week), its end-of-summer retreat, convened annually since 1976. Described by its current organizer, Binyumen Schaechter, as "half kibbutz, half Woodstock," *yidish-vokh* evinces a relatively low intensity of performance, compared to Yiddish festivals or folk arts programs, which typically offer a densely packed schedule of recitals, concerts, lectures, plays, and so on. While there are a few such presentations at *yidish-vokh*, they are not undertaken by a separate, professionalized class of performers. Moreover, these performances are secondary to the event's main intent, which is to provide participants with an opportunity to inhabit a thoroughly Yiddish-speaking milieu. To quote from recent promotional material for *yidish-vokh* (distributed in Yiddish and English):

Participants in the *yidish-vokh* are singles, couples and Yiddish-speaking families. . . . Seniors are also welcome. . . . All activities are in Yiddish, including sports, folk-dancing, yoga, lectures, discussions, literary readings, campfire singing, talent show, concerts, films, Yiddish classes for the advanced beginner and organized programs for children. . . . The *yidish-vokh* is a real community, in which our members give the lectures, lead discussions and workshops. . . . Many at the *yidish-vokh* have made lifelong friends; some have married each other and now return every summer![52]

Organized activities at *yidish-vokh* include those specific to Yiddish (e.g., group reading and discussion of works of Yiddish literature, Yiddish folksinging, presentations on Yiddish terminology or the latest developments in Yiddish-language computer software), as well as Jewish culture more generally (studying *mishnayes* [early rabbinic commentaries on the Bible] or Sabbath meditation), plus general activities (playing baseball, learning to crochet or to dance the bolero), all conducted in Yiddish.[53] Paralleling this variety of activities is the diversity of the participants, whom *yidish-vokh* vaunts as intergenerational, international, as well as ideologically diverse, ranging from Orthodox to secular (and including some non-Jews)—all united by their devotion to Yiddish as a spoken language. At the same time, a tacit hierarchy exists among the participants, defined by their degree of fluency in Yiddish as well as the base of their knowledge of it (native speakers versus those who have acquired the language through study, speakers of a prewar East European dialect versus speakers of *klal-yidish*, or Standard Yiddish).

For all participants, though, maintaining Yiddish as the language of routine conversation proves to be an effort that continually tests the program's quotidian ideal. Indeed, *yidish-vokh* constitutes a deliberate performance of vernacularity that is quite different from actual routine behavior and speech, in which language use is generally much less self-conscious. The distinction is apparent from the start of *yidish-vokh*. Among the materials provided to participants on arrival, along with a schedule of activities and a map of the campgrounds (both in Yiddish), are a two-page list of common food terms in Yiddish, glossed from English, and a twelve-page list of sports and leisure terminology. During the weeklong event, conversations frequently become pedagogical; in the midst of discussions people stop to correct their own grammar as well as that of others and ask or explain how to say something properly in Yiddish.

Moreover, the need to communicate or to express oneself sometimes conflicts with and even overpowers the commitment to speaking in Yiddish—certainly when talking with the staff of the camp where *yidish-vokh* is held, since none of them is fluent in Yiddish. (Indeed, some staffers during the summer of 2000, when I attended, were young adults on summer working internships from Eastern Europe, and so there was, at times, an odd resonance with an Old World interethnic dynamic between Yiddish-speaking Jews and Poles or Russians). A few participants at *yidish-vokh* have been known to sneak off into nearby woods to converse in other languages—and when discovered, stammer apologies in Yiddish. And some children attending *yidish-vokh* with their families occasionally rebel against their parents by publicly refusing to speak Yiddish. This rebellion is significantly different from, say, that of an American-raised child of immigrants refusing to speak Yiddish with parents who know no other language as well as they do their mother tongue. The children at *yidish-vokh* are often the youngest of multigenerational families of Yiddishists and figure as ideal models of language maintenance in the face of the pervasive language shift away from Yiddish among American Jews. Like their parents, these children are fluent not only in Yiddish but also in English, and often in other languages as well. For such children to speak a language other than Yiddish openly at *yidish-vokh* constitutes a flouting of their parents' ideological commitment to Yiddishism. Thus, *yidish-vokh*, which seems, at first, to be the least intensively performative of Yiddish cultural events, is in fact a constant, tenacious performance of Yiddish vernacularity by all involved. Indeed, the boundless performativity of *yidish-vokh* calls to mind the desires of avant-garde artists, from dadaists to Fluxus, to subvert the conventions of theatrical performance and bring a new, transformative consciousness to the "art of living" in a state of "permanent creation."[54]

Why the desire to utter Yiddish, as it becomes increasingly a postvernacular language? It is not merely, or even primarily, motivated by a wish to communicate, which is why form so often prevails over content in postvernacular Yiddish performances. Rather, it expresses an aspiration to participate in a wide-ranging cultural project of the imaginary, in which one inhabits an existence, regardless of where one lives or what one is doing, that is thoroughly marked as Jewish in a Yiddish idiom. This is not necessarily a matter of striving to become "more Jewish" religiously, culturally, or intellectually (especially as one need not be a Jew to wish to do this). It is ultimately a subjunctive, rather than substantive, enterprise, rooted in a desire to experience singing, speaking, or even simply hearing Yiddish *as if* it were one's communal vernacular. This, in turn, would mean that one would be someone other than who one is, and, moreover, that the recent history of Yiddish-speaking Jewry would have been something other than what it has been. (Writing about similar practices among folk musicians seeking "to find new or renew old musical resources," musician R. Murray Schafer characterizes such efforts as representing "a desire to transcend the present tense.")[55]

Consequently, postvernacular Yiddish performance entails not merely speaking or hearing Yiddish, but "experiencing" Yiddish as a delimited, totalizing, intensive, multisensory event that entails affective as well as (and sometimes instead of) intellectual or ideological engagement. Hence the importance of music, dance, and spectacle in postvernacular Yiddish performances, as well as the extension of bodily engagement with Yiddish to other senses: taste, for example, is employed in savoring the traditional East European Jewish foods frequently served or sold at Yiddish cultural events.

Although postvernacular Yiddish culture is, to a considerable degree, a response to a shared sense of cultural loss, participants in this enterprise are engaged in a variety of discrete, sometimes incompatible projects. Hasidim employ innovative means of maintaining Yiddish in order to sustain its post-Holocaust role as a marker of their particular approach to piety (this in addition to the long-standing role of Yiddish in hasidism as the expressive language of a vernacular Jewish spirituality). Jews who are not traditionally observant are frequently attracted to Yiddish as a hallmark of Jewish alterity, the language variously signifying diaspora nationalism (as opposed to Zionism), secular ethnicity (as opposed to religiosity), matriarchy (as opposed to a traditionally male-centered culture), and radicalism or queerness (as opposed to conventionally heteronormative Jewish respectability). For some *baley-tshuve* (Jews living nontraditional or nonreligious lives who decide to become observant), learning Yiddish is part of a larger personal project of (re)turning to religious tradition. For some non-Jews, speaking Yiddish offers the tantalizing prospect of inhabiting a culture that is not only "other" but also "lost." For Germans and Poles, in particular, learning Yiddish can be a project of cultural reparation.

Though postvernacular performances are typically couched in retrospective meta-language that speaks of their value as a continuation or retrieval of the quotidian Ashkenazic past, they are in fact innovative acts that transvalue Yiddish as an exceptional experience. Singing, reciting, lecturing, or even conversing in Yiddish is no longer something one simply does (as presumably had once been the case). Rather, it is something one elects and arranges to do, one rehearses, studies, and appreciates; Yiddish speech has been professionalized, aestheticized, academized, and ritualized. Rather than regarding this development simply as a loss, in which Yiddish has devolved into a kind of denatured *lieu de mémoire*, I find it both more useful and more encouraging to view the semiotic disparities of postvernacular Yiddish as defining a distinctive cultural enterprise in its own right.[56]

Indeed, even though the desires that prompt them might never be completely fulfilled, postvernacular Yiddish performances prove to be an especially productive mode of cultural creativity. These performances can flourish independent of a vernacular base and can be highly contingent, existing in a limited time, place, and scope; they rely more on a sharing of affect or sensibility than on a common fluency or ideology. Most important, in these performances one witnesses the powerful act of cultural transformation enacted live—a factor especially important in the case of Yiddish, which is so often characterized as dying or otherwise linked with Jewish cultural demise. Implicit in every contemporary Yiddish performance, therefore, is a test of linguistic viability.

The ground of loss against which all recent Yiddish performances are figured, albeit often implicitly, demonstrates the "value of absence" that Jacques Derrida argues is inherent in communication, which he links with mimesis and remembrance: "The sign is born at the same time as imagination and memory, at the moment when it is demanded by the absence of the object for present perception."[57] An awareness of this disparity between creativity and loss, retrospection and innovation, somehow both haunts and animates every Yiddish festival, concert, lecture, and, perhaps, even every Yiddish conversation.

CHAPTER FIVE

ABSOLUT TCHOTCHKE

On a shelf in my office I've accumulated an assortment of objects—coffee mugs, refrigerator magnets, lapel buttons, knickknacks, board games, toys, snack canisters, cocktail napkins, greeting cards, and other items—all bearing one or more Yiddish words. Nearby sits a stack of comic Yiddish-English dictionaries; in a drawer is a growing collection of T-shirts also featuring one or more Yiddishisms. Friends and relatives have given me some of these objects; I've come across others in stores, catalogs, and online, and I've encountered more such items in the homes and offices of colleagues and acquaintances.

One might easily dismiss these objects as frivolous or in questionable taste, but I've come to appreciate their value as artifacts that embody some of the transmigrations of Yiddish language and culture that have taken place since World War II. Indeed, their lowbrow silliness belies the complexity of their value as artifacts. These objects, all mass-produced items made or sold in the United States at some time since the late 1940s, prompt a provocatively rich array of insights on several counts: as materializations of spoken language, as works of Americana and Judaica, as artifacts of a Yiddish culture strikingly different from that of the prewar era. Their analysis reveals a fundamental transformation of Jewish notions of vernacularity in response to signal shifts in language use and, moreover, in the symbolic value invested in language. By fixing the meta-value of the language in objects that are themselves part of a new, postwar American Jewish vernacular material culture, my collection of Yiddish realia epitomizes postvernacularity.

SEMIOTIC SOUVENIRS

Objects inscribed with Jewish words or even with individual letters of the *alefbeys* comprise an important component of traditional Jewish material culture. In addition to ritual objects *(tfiln,* for example), items such as goblets, dishes, utensils, boxes, cloth bags and covers are thus marked as Judaica—as are articles of clothing, furniture, even buildings—not by dint of their form or of any other symbol or ornament but by the presence of Jewish letters.[1] The items in my collection of Yiddish realia, which comprises but a small part of this larger inventory of Judaica, are distinguished by the particular semiotics of their use of the language, which is characteristically postvernacular in nature—invoking, yet apart from, Yiddish as a language of daily life.

Thus, the semiotic feature of these items that one most likely notices first is the fact that typically the Yiddish is rendered in the Roman alphabet rather than in the *alefbeys.* This extensive use of romanization might be understood as a symptom of or concession to diminished Yiddish literacy (and to Jewish cultural literacy more generally), but it can also be seen as a proactive transformation of the written language. Romanization makes the language more widely accessible, at least phonetically, to the many Jews and non-Jews who have some familiarity with Yiddish but don't know how to read it in its original alphabet.[2] The use of Latin letters also facilitates the integration of Yiddishisms into English or other languages written in the Roman alphabet. At the same time, romanized Yiddish terms frequently appear on the items in my collection in typefaces that imitate the calligraphic curves and large serifs of the traditional *alefbeys.* This device marks the words as distinctively Jewish while integrating them into a more widely familiar communicative code. The use of these fonts thus resembles "kosher-style" cuisine, preserving manner while altering, even subverting, substance.

But the most telling semiotic feature of my collection of Yiddish realia is their atomization of Yiddish. Whether offering one or more isolated terms or presenting Yiddishisms embedded in English-language texts, these artifacts consistently present Yiddish as something less than a whole language. Indeed, a key implication of these objects is that Yiddish cannot be thought of as a complete semiotic system but rather, as a postvernacular language, as inherently fragmentary.

The atomization of Yiddish can occur even when its fullness is invoked, as is the

Jewish Mood Cube, 1970s.

case of the Yiddish version of Magnetic Poetry, one of a series of languages other than English in the "World Series" of these popular refrigerator magnet sets (other languages include French, German, Italian, Spanish, and Sign Language). The "Mini Dictionary" accompanying CHUTZPA (impertinence), a set of poetry magnets that supplements the basic Yiddish edition of Magnetic Poetry, states, "Yiddish is a complete language full of dramatic expressions." Yet while the six-hundred or so words that appear in these two sets include such colorful terms as "ongepotshket" (made a mess [of]), "bashert" (destined), and "gotenyu" (Dear God), one has to struggle to write simple, ordinary sentences with them; they don't, for example, provide such basic elements of the language as all pronouns or prepositions or most modal verbs.[3] A comparison with word lists of similar length—proposed vocabularies for beginning students in American secular Yiddish schools during the 1940s—is instructive. Whereas the lexical inventories prepared for the schools focus on basic, denotative terms for common, quotidian phenomena, the words in the Magnetic Poetry sets dwell on the extreme, the particularist, and the richly connotative.[4]

The encounter with Yiddish that these magnet sets proffer marks it as both less than and more of a language—limited and fragmentary on one hand, aestheticized and charged with affect on the other hand. *"Di kunst fun an anderer shprakh lernen iz aleyn poezie, "* reads a sentence in not quite grammatically correct Yiddish on the box of the basic Yiddish set of Magnetic Poetry: "The art of learning another language is itself poetry." But these magnets don't come with instructions in basic Yiddish usage; they invite improvisational play rather than methodical learning. Each word has a concentrated value understood as inherently artful, which will become further intensified in the creation of poetry—a specialized form of language that thrives on density, affect, word play, and the flouting of formal conventions of narrative prose or conversation. Thus, a mock warning label on the Yiddish Magnetic Poetry package (which appears on other sets as well) cautions that within are "loaded words: This box contains highly unstable language, which may accidentally result in powerful imagery. Users are warned that breaking the seal of this container will trigger an expansion of perception and creativity, and could result in permanent life change."[5]

As this "warning" suggests, the individual Yiddish words in these sets are like charged subatomic particles, endowed with a new energy by having broken free from the stable structures of a full vernacular code. Being magnetic, they are at liberty to attach themselves anywhere, in any fashion. And their endlessly recombinant, artful play ultimately promises to enliven and transform another language—English—whose vernacular primacy is implicit as the language of the packaging and in the use of romanization on the magnets themselves.

Many of the other objects in my collection reinforce this notion of Yiddish words as highly charged linguistic fragments by offering isolated Yiddish terms within an English-language text. For example, I have acquired a number of greeting cards for birthdays and other occasions, such as the following:

[Front of card:] It's a simcha [happy occasion]!
Can there be a better date to tummel [revel] and to celebrate?
[Inside of card:] Mazel [luck] and glick [happiness] on your Birthday![6]

In these cards, Yiddish is offered as an implicitly vestigial code, whose semiotic completion is now dependent on other, full, vernacular languages. There is, then, an inherent retrospection to these objects; even items in current production might be seen as mementos evoking a time and place when Yiddish functioned as a self-sufficient language of daily life.

A Yiddish word, then, is like a curio—or, as a 1998 vodka ad suggests, an "Absolut Tchotchke"—a decorative piece (with some kind of retro, perhaps kitschy, appeal) that is suited to collection, display, contemplation, and discussion rather than any utilitarian purpose. Indeed, the Yiddish realia I've been collecting epitomize

Advertisement for Absolut Vodka, 1998.
Courtesy of TBWA.

what literary scholar Susan Stewart characterizes as a key aspect of souvenirs in general, which are "by definition always incomplete." Stewart argues that the souvenir "must remain . . . partial so that it can be supplemented by a narrative discourse, . . . which articulates the play of desire."[7] Here, the metonymic nature of the material object reinforces the fragmentary quality ascribed to Yiddish. The narratives that complete these isolated Yiddishisms situate them in discourses that are often deceptively simple, given their modest form. But by their very nature, they can offer powerfully, if tacitly, ambivalent statements about Jewish culture through language play and the play between language and materiality.

YIDDISH AS FETISH

The inscribing of Yiddish onto objects displayed, used, and especially worn can endow them with the power of a fetish, characterized by anthropologist William Pietz as a "composite fabrication," consisting not only of "material elements" but also of "desires and beliefs and narrative structures establishing a practice." The fetish is invested with "the power to repeat its originating act of forging an identity of articulating relations between certain otherwise heterogeneous things." The symbolic power of the fetish as it relates to the "embodied status of the individual"[8] is exemplified by T-shirts imprinted with Yiddish words—including one bearing the word *yidish* itself (in the *alefbeys*), which has been available for years from Yugntruf, as well as another T-shirt, recently sold by the Workmen's Circle, which features the text of a Yiddish dictionary (actually, of course, a fragment of one). The wearer of these and other similar T-shirts embodies the language, taking on whatever symbolic value he or she has invested in Yiddish and, by extension, in its speakers.

Significantly, the wearer does so without necessarily uttering a word of Yiddish him- or herself. Vernacularity is replaced here by the putting on (and taking off) of a symbolic second skin—a behavior that invokes, and yet is quite different from, a polyglot's code-switching. Rather, these T-shirts are an example of ethnic branding, transforming the Yiddish word into a logo for folkhood. Historian Marilyn Halter suggests that this has become a widespread practice in the "new ethnicity" of the late twentieth century, in which people "construct their [ethnic] identities through purchase."[9] In this sense, some of these Yiddish items are also totemic artifacts—that is, they situate Yiddish (or Jewishness more generally) within a parallel array of identities similarly materialized: caps emblazoned with "Kiss me, I'm Italian," T-shirts that say "Black is Beautiful," bumper stickers reading "It's exciting to be Estonian," and so forth. Others, however—such as lapel buttons that read "Marcel Proust Is a Yenta [here: gossip]" or "St. Patrick Spoke Yiddish" playfully trouble the distinct and parallel linguistic and ethnic categories that they invoke.

While sporting these items is generally a voluntary, celebratory gesture on the part of the wearer, the various T-shirts, caps, and lapel buttons with Yiddish on them have a distinctive resonance with the history of stigmatizing Jews through dress, especially their enforced racial branding in Nazi-occupied Europe, where many were required to wear yellow, six-pointed stars, usually inscribed with the word *Jew* in German, Dutch, or French. In light of this recent history, a Jew wearing Yugntruf's *yidish* T-shirt embodies an implicit act of defiance—flouting both anti-Semites out to stigmatize Jews and those Jews who prefer not to wear their ethnicity on their

Lapel button, 1960s.

sleeves (or chests). Conversely, a T-shirt bearing the word SHLEPPERS (haulers) has very different implications when worn by the many non-Jewish employees of the eponymous New York City moving company—suggesting, perhaps, the embrace of Yiddish as a code shared by New Yorkers of all ethnic backgrounds.[10]

Pietz notes that fetishes are of particular interest since they articulate cultural relations forged "in singular moments of 'crisis' in which the identity of the self is called into question [or] put at risk."[11] In light of this notion, we should consider what sense of crisis in identity might engender the attraction to Yiddish realia, and how these objects facilitate responses to these definitional moments. To do so requires scrutinizing not merely the objects themselves but also the contexts of their acquisition, display, and use, their involvement in people's lives. Especially important, given that these are items of mass production, are instances of their use that demonstrate a shared sensibility. As an acquirer of these items, I enter into a tacit relationship—however attenuated, ironized, or contrarian it may be—with a (largely unknown) community of fellow collectors.

OBJECTS OF RITUAL

Most of the items I have been collecting have no explicit ritual use in the conventional sense, especially as it is understood in traditional Jewish life. Yet many of them do have an oblique connection to ritual through the modes of play, transgression, mockery, and inversion. Yiddish words seldom appear on Jewish ritual objects, which are much more likely to bear inscriptions in Hebrew. The most popular Jewish ritual object inscribed in Yiddish, albeit implicitly, is doubtless the *dreydl,* a small, four-sided top used by Ashkenazic children to play games of chance during Hanukkah. Each side of the *dreydl* bears a different letter of the *alefbeys.* These letters stand for Yiddish words, which determine the fortune of the players as they ante up coins, nuts, buttons, or candies and take turns spinning the *dreydl.* For example, if the *dreydl* lands with the letter *giml* (G) face up, this indicates the word *gants* (all), and the player takes the entire ante; if *hey* (H) turns up, the player takes *halb* (half), and so on.[12] Significantly, this most widely familiar materialization of Yiddish in traditional Jewish culture is associated with a ritual rooted in Ashkenazic custom rather than rabbinic law, with play, and with behavior that is transgressive, though sanctioned (games of chance are traditionally permitted only during Hanukkah). And it is also telling that formal explanations of the *dreydl* in modern sources usually state that the letters stand for a Hebrew sentence—*Nes gadol haya sham* (A great miracle happened there)—thereby obscuring their Yiddish origins while elevating the status of this gambling toy to a token of piety.[13]

Conversely, the mock-ritual role of some of the items that I have been collecting emerges when they are juxtaposed with traditional ritual objects, which are usually inscribed with one or more words in Hebrew. Thus, one might regard the "mah jongg mavin [expert]" mug—these words, printed in red on the side of a white coffee cup in Roman letters, appear below a drawing of a Chinese dragon—as a kind of mock *kidesh* (ritual wine) cup, which "sanctifies" the Chinese gambling game within American Jewish ritual life.[14] Or consider the implications of the "Mr. Mahzel" figurine, created by comedian Morey Amsterdam in 1962. Even without its inscription, this comical statuette of an Orthodox Jewish man is a transgressive figure, flouting the traditional ban on making idols and verging on Jewish caricature. The Yiddish/English name on the figure's base consolidates and extends the provocative playfulness of this object, inscribing it as a talisman of Jewish luck.

The parodic link between the legitimate and the mock in these objects is hardly an innovation of contemporary American Jewish culture. It recalls what Dan Miron has identified as the "antifolklore" of East European maskilic Yiddish writers of the nineteenth century. Here, too, is what Miron calls a "cultural paradox," rooted in "contradictory attitudes" toward the language and an "equivocal attitude" toward folkways. By making the ritual and material culture of traditional East European Jewry the subject of their satires, *maskilim* preserved folkways even as they mocked and sought to eradicate them. These texts also derive "extraordinary vivacity from

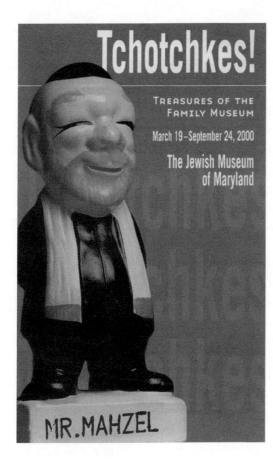

Mr. Mahzel figurine, as featured on the cover of the brochure for "Tchotchkes! Treasures of the Family Museum," an exhibition of American Jewish collectibles presented by the Jewish Museum of Maryland in 2000.
Courtesy of the Jewish Museum of Maryland. Copyright © Stonehouse Design.

the counterpoint of the most heavily destructive caricaturistic satire, on the one hand, and an almost childlike delight in artistic play on the other."[15] One might, therefore, see these mocking Yiddish artifacts as works created within a Yiddish "tradition" of satirical preservation and destruction that by the end of World War II was more than a century in the making.

MATERIALIZING LANGUAGE PLAY

Just as nineteenth-century *maskilim* often articulated their satirical associations with Yiddish by juxtaposing it against the other languages in their milieu, the objects in my collection generally express mockery through language play that takes place not within Yiddish but in the movement back and forth between Yiddish and English. This can be seen most simply and directly in a gift that the National Yiddish Book

Center gave to donors in the late 1990s. This item—a wooden yo-yo inscribed with *oy oy* in the *alefbeys* on one side and OY OY in Latin letters on the other side—concretizes language play rooted in the inverse relationship of reading Yiddish from right to left as opposed to reading English from left to right. (Note, however, that the mirror-play of *oy oy* and "yo-yo" works in its romanized form but not in the *alefbeys*.) Imprinting these words on an actual yo-yo deftly materializes the interlinguistic playfulness; as a premium from the NYBC, this item celebrates a delight in the notion that Yiddish and English can have reciprocal semantic value. At the same time, it obliquely acknowledges the primacy of English as the facilitator of Yiddish culture for most supporters of the organization—even with regard to the language's quintessential diphthong.

A similar visualization of English/Yiddish interlingual play can be seen in the logo of the *Forward*, an English-language weekly Jewish newspaper inaugurated in 1990 by the publishers of the *Forverts*, a Yiddish daily from 1897 until 1986, when it became a weekly. Printed on tote bags, coffee mugs, and refrigerator magnets, the logo shows the word *Forverts*, written in the *alefbeys*, gradually morphing into the English word *Forward*. Emblematic of the transformation of this venerable secular Jewish newspaper, this logo evokes the double-edged implications of translating Yiddish into English more generally, simultaneously connoting language loss and cultural transformation read as continuity.

A more elaborate form of language play is inscribed on another materialized bilingual pun: the Yiddishe Cup—a coffee mug that plays on the Yiddish idiom *a yidisher kop* (literally, "a Jewish head," referring to Jewish cultural literacy or sensibility). There are several versions of this item; one that I own, given to me in the 1980s, translates "a yiddishe cup" as "a smart person." It also features nine other Yiddish terms with English glosses. These range from straightforward definitions—"maven" = "expert"; "nudnick" = "pest"—to translations that are deliberately playful: "naches" (joy) = "grandchildren"; "gishmock" (tasty) = "Jewish cooking"; "mechitanista" (female co-in-law) = "opposition"; "mishpoocha" (family) = "cousins club."

These objects require knowledge of both Yiddish and English (as well as the American Jewish culture they signify) for appreciating their humor. They exemplify the bilingual humor of immigrant cultures, in which the alternation from one language to another is "not the result of incompetence or illiteracy" but rather constitutes a celebration "of considerable skill in the manipulation of the available linguistic resources."[16] Some of the mock glosses that appear on the Yiddishe Cup are also typical of postvernacular Yiddish culture, in which ordinary Yiddish words ac-

Refrigerator magnet with the *Forward* logo, around 1990.

quire new meaning as markers of Jewish ethnicity. Thus, in full, vernacular Yiddish, Italian or Chinese food can be just as *geshmak* as Jewish cooking, but such is not the case here. Rather, in the supervaluated Jewishness of postvernacular Yiddish, what the language evokes is *yidisher tam* (Jewish flavor). At the same time that the Yiddishe Cup celebrates immigrant Jewish culture, another less felicitous meaning is suggested by its materiality, though I doubt that this is intentional: by implicitly reducing Yiddish cultural literacy to a handful of words, has a *yidisher kop* become, in the postvernacular culture, an empty vessel?

THE MOCK MODE

The limited number of words on it notwithstanding, the Yiddishe Cup is part of a genre of Yiddish mock dictionaries, such as the "Dictionary of Basic Yiddish," printed on a folded souvenir card given to diners at Sammy's Roumanian Steak House on New York's Lower East Side. This dictionary includes the following among its thirty-eight definitions:

MICKVEH [ritual bath]: A Kosher aquacade
OI VAY [Oh, woe!]: April 15th
BRIS [circumcision ritual]: Getting tipped off.[17]

Though this and similar comic texts are formatted like dictionaries, rather than giving equivalent glosses of Yiddish terms into English, they offer comically bogus definitions. Knowing the disparity between the proper meanings of these terms and the mock glosses is the basis of their humor. These faux glosses indicate the divergent meta-values that Yiddish has acquired, especially in a postimmigrant American context, as both a comic "marker of social immobility" and an "affirmation of ethnic origin."[18] These mock definitions skew one set of meanings as they reveal others, thereby probing the ambiguous affective responses generated by linguistic upheaval and breakdown of cultural barriers. Yiddish mock dictionaries appear in print, on sound recordings, and online. Mock dictionaries can also be found on such ephemera as cocktail napkins and business cards, a further flouting of the notion of the language as substantial. Indeed, the full inventory of Yiddish mock dictionaries produced in America since World War II well outnumbers that of legitimate Yiddish-English dictionaries.

At the same time that they defy the idea of Yiddish as a fully viable and expressive vernacular, Yiddish mock dictionaries also transgress traditional cultural boundaries, with titles such as *Yiddish for Yankees* and *Every Goy's Guide to Common Jewish Expressions.*[19] Or consider *The Chinese-Kosher Cookbook*, *The Italian-Kosher Cookbook*, and *The French-Kosher Cookbook*, first published in 1963, which link mock definitions of Yiddish (e.g., "GAN EDEN [paradise]: A Miami Beach retirement community") with the cross-cultural culinary travesty of recipe names such as "Matzoh Brei Foo Yong," "Flanken Pizzaiola Alla Shmendrick," and "Knish Lorraine."[20] Such works presume Yiddish as a code of Jewish exclusivity, its use not only limited essentially to Ashkenazim but also serving as an instrument and a signifier of Jewish difference. In exposing the Jews' "secret language" to the public, the authors of these comic dictionaries focus on key areas of the lexicon. Besides culturally specific terminology (words associated with Jewish belief, ritual, and custom, especially foodways), they emphasize the immoderate—in particular terms dealing with emotional extremes—and the unmentionable, notably words related to sex and elimination. This shift in language usage and semantic value was observed by Uriel Weinreich in the early 1950s. As a language such as Yiddish in postwar America "los[es] its main communicative role," he wrote, it seems "destined to acquire peculiar connotations and be applied to special functions," especially "comic associations." One also sees a selective "borrowing of its lexical elements," in particular,

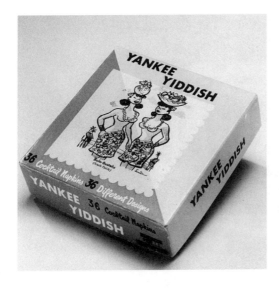

Yankee Yiddish Cocktail Napkins, created by cartoonist Lawrence Lariar in 1953. Each design offers mock glosses of Yiddish terms in the form of English-language puns. For example, "Menschen" (people) is translated as "a ten room ranch house"—that is, a mansion.

"colorful idiomatic expressions . . . with strong affective overtones, whether endearing, pejorative, or . . . obscene."[21] The focus on these terms in one comic Yiddish dictionary after another suggests shared understandings of the meta-value of the language as an index of divergent modes: of sentiment and, at the same time, of the carnivalesque, that is, the inherently subversive, transgressive, emotive, and appetitive, centered on the lower half of the body.

CONSUMING THE CARNIVALESQUE

While quite a few materializations of Yiddish reflect this particular meta-meaning of the language, the phenomenon is epitomized by two objects in my collection that link snacking with Yiddish as a signifier of excess and vulgarity—enabling one, literally, to consume Yiddish as carnivalesque: Mashuga [crazy] Nuts, produced in San Francisco, and the Alter Caulker, distributed by Herman Nut Company of Omaha, Nebraska. What makes Mashuga Nuts a material Yiddish artifact is not the contents—pecans coated with a cinnamon-flavored meringue—but the container, which is covered with Jewish-English idioms and Yiddish terms, from the "Gonif [thief] proof seal" on the top to its manufacturer's label: "Delivered by Schlemiels [bumblers] on Wheels for Mashuga Nuts, Inc.," which was "founded in 1992 (but for you, 1889)." Indeed, the Yiddishisms and comic Jewish banter on the Mashuga Nuts canister mark the enclosed delicacies both as faux-ethnic (there is a bogus fam-

GEFILTE fish plastic ornament.
Copyright © EvolveFISH.com 2004.

ily history of Old World immigrants who ostensibly originated the recipe) and as genuinely excessive, indulgent, and transgressive—a snack food that materializes Jewish madness. Similarly, with the Alter Caulker, "food for the caulking impaired," what matters is not the contents but the container, or rather, the juxtaposition of the two—chocolate-covered cashew nuts inside a transparent caulking-gun refill tube. Here is a Yiddish vulgarism (*alter kaker*, literally, "old shitter"; cf. English "old fart") materialized, linking the language with a mockery of the gastrointestinal woes of the elderly.

One of the most subversive uses of Yiddish in material form is produced by a non-Jewish enterprise: the GEFILTE fish, a plastic ornament available from F.I.S.H. (Freethinkers In Service to Humanity), an organization based in Colorado Springs "dedicated to countering the destructive aspects of [Christian] religious zealotry."[22] This is a variation on the familiar Christian symbol of a fish, typically inscribed with ΙΧΘΥΣ (the Greek word for "fish"), which began to appear as a decorative symbol widely seen on car bumpers (as well as on jewelry, T-shirts, etc.) in the United States in the 1960s.[23] The GEFILTE fish flouts Christian fundamentalism, as does its subversive predecessor, the DARWIN fish. (Also sold by F.I.S.H., this features the same silhouette, inscribed with the famous evolutionist's name and sporting two feet.) The GEFILTE fish, however, assails fundamentalism not with natural science but with Yiddish ethnicity in the form of one of its quintessential delicacies and, less obviously, with Jewish piety (the careful observer will spot an "O-U" symbol—the sign of the Orthodox Union's approval of food products as kosher—which appears near the fish's tail).[24]

OBJECT LESSONS

In the inventory of Yiddish realia there are, of course, plenty of items that are not in mock mode. Some are tokens of secular Yiddish culture at its most earnest, including busts, lapel buttons, and even a card game, all of which commemorate Yiddish literati of the past as cultural heroes.[25] Other items, especially mugs, aprons, magnets, or food products (e.g., "Bubbie's [Grandmother's] Pure Kosher Dills"), employ the language as a sign of sentimentality that pay tribute to a Jewish grandparent as the progenitor of Ashkenazic heritage. Still others, which can be found especially among *khareydim*, use Yiddish as a signifier of traditional Ashkenazic piety. These range from pot holders and other kitchenware marked *fleyshik* (containing meat), *milkhik* (containing dairy products), and *pareve* (food that contains neither meat nor dairy products) to adhesive stickers given as rewards to children in ultra-Orthodox day schools. One of these says "I Davened *geshmak!*" (a hybrid of English and Yiddish meaning "I prayed well!"), printed against a colorful, op-art spiral; another, depicting a young hasidic boy and inscribed *"Ikh bin dray yor alt!"* (I am three years old!), is used to mark the celebration of a boy's *opshern* (first haircut), after which he is obligated to wear a yarmulke, *peyes* (sidelocks), and *arbekanfes* (undergarment with ritual fringes).

The full range of Yiddish realia demonstrates the language's various subcultures, distinguished by how they use the language and the value they assign to it, responsive to their respective desires. Therefore, the extensive inventory of material Yiddish culture in the mock mode is especially compelling. While the impetus for sentiment and piety in post-Holocaust Yiddish culture is readily apparent, what motivates fixing the language as an emblem of the mock and the carnivalesque? What cultural desires does this practice reflect, and what does it reveal about the nature of postvernacular Yiddish among some American Jews of the immigrant and postimmigrant generations?

Consider two of the more elaborate artifacts in my collection, box games produced in the mid-1960s and mid-1990s. Each game comprises a self-contained culture in miniature, through rules that define players' roles and govern their interactions, as well as through the games' cards, tokens, and so on, which materialize virtual environments. Their reliance on mockery and humor notwithstanding, these items are, as historian Johan Huizinga observed more generally about such games, a form of play marked by "an element of seriousness." Even as they appear to flout the idea, these games aspire to what anthropologist Clifford Geertz identifies as "deep play," symbolically charged activity that "provides a metasocial commentary" and through which people "tell themselves about themselves." "More than a game," such activities "tell us less what happens than . . . would happen if, as is not the case, life were art and could be as freely shaped by styles of feeling."[26]

The earlier of the two games, called *Chutzpah*, was created by What-Cha-Ma-Call-It, Inc., of Mount Vernon, New York, and produced by Hobbit Toys and Games of Kalamazoo, Michigan, in 1967. Modeled on *Monopoly*, *Chutzpah* requires its players to work their way around a game board that situates them in a contemporary American Jewish milieu of middle-class comfort (on its box *Chutzpah* is subtitled "the game of the good life"). The game is marked as such by references to geographic settings (the Catskills and Miami), activities (getting one's nose fixed, joining a country club), and acquisitions (a mink stole, wall-to-wall carpeting). Although these are by no means exclusively the provenance of postwar American Jewish bourgeoisie, invoking this wide array of phenomena as markers of this community occurs repeatedly in mock Yiddish dictionaries and in satiric American Jewish fiction of the era. *Chutzpah* also indexes American Jewish life by its liberal use of Yiddishisms, which appear on the game board and instruction cards and are glossed in a mock dictionary inside the box. Some of these vaunt a comically Judeocentric view of America, for example: "NACHES [joy]: a little town in Tennessee [i.e., Natchez] where they have Halavah [sesame candy] Plantations." Read against *Monopoly*, *Chutzpah* is true to its name, constituting a celebration of brazen American Jewish self-assertion. (The box also boasts, "If you got Chutzpah—you can do anything!") The game embodies a postimmigrant, post-Holocaust sensibility that also pervades American Jewish comic performances of the period, such as the stand-up routines of Lenny Bruce and the "Jewish new-age" films of Mel Brooks, Sidney Lumet, and Carl Reiner, which often rely similarly on Yiddish words as signposts of an economic, geographic, social, and cultural journey, and in doing so offer a sense of attachment as well as a sense of distance.[27]

A generation later, Yiddish likewise appears as a sign of both the carnivalesque and the mock mode in a 1995 box game called *Look at the Schmuck on That Camel*, designed by Wilbur Pierce of Philadelphia and produced by the Avalon Hill Game Company, based in Baltimore.[28] The game's provocative name, which provides a visual icon as well as thematic focus for the game, is derived from a joke that appears in Leo Rosten's 1968 book, *The Joys of Yiddish*. (The most widely familiar of comic Yiddish dictionaries, it has also become the most "authoritative," frequently cited as a legitimate source of Yiddish philology.) In the joke in question, a lonely Jewish widower in Miami Beach asks for advice on making friends. Someone suggests he get a camel and ride it up and down the street, since this would be a sure way to

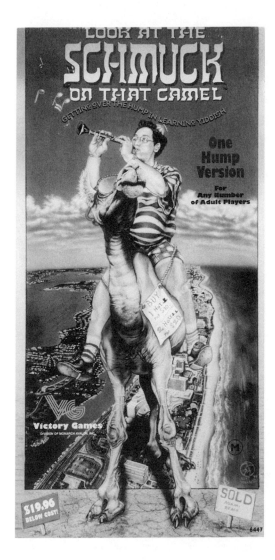

Look at the Schmuck on That Camel, board game created by Wilbur Pierce, 1995.
Courtesy of Wilbur Pierce.

attract attention. The man does so, creating quite a stir. Then, one day his camel is gone. The man calls the police to report his loss and is asked to describe the animal, which he can do only in the vaguest of terms. When asked the sex of the camel, however, he is positive that it was a male. He reassures the police, "Every time and every place I was riding on that camel, I could hear people yelling: 'Hey, look at the *shmuck* [slang for "penis" and for "boor"; cf. English "prick"] on that camel!' "[29]

A comparison of these two games provides one measure of American Yiddish cultural literacy over the course of a generation. *Chutzpah* employs Yiddishisms throughout and provides a mock dictionary to gloss them, thereby assuming that this practice is familiar to players. But the play itself focuses, like *Monopoly,* on acquiring and spending money in pursuit of "the good life." In *Look at the Schmuck on That Camel,* acquiring familiarity with the basic as well as the comic meanings of Yiddish words is the end, rather than a means, of the game. (Indeed, it promises, on its box cover, to assist players in "getting over the hump in learning Yiddish.") To play, participants select one of over one hundred cards, each of which gives a Yiddish word followed by a choice of definitions. For example:

BULVON

1. Ox.

2. Erudition.

3. Oaf.

4. Capable of moving a brick wall.

5. Missing a neck.

6. When the Matador loses.

The answers include the "correct" definition—"oaf"—and connotative glosses—"ox" (figuratively), "capable of moving a brick wall," "missing a neck"—as well as wrong answers that include a bilingual pun ("when the Matador loses"—i.e., the bull won). These cards are supplemented by an audiotape featuring two songs in English (with many embedded Yiddish words) that elaborate on the camel joke ("There goes that schmuck on a camel, Bouncing on his two-humped mammal") and offer a model of Yiddish pronunciation and intonation. Also included in the game box is a brochure featuring "Camelite products: articles of faith and practice," which can be ordered from the makers of the game. All these items (including a coffee mug, jewelry, T-shirts, and other garments) feature the game's logo of a man riding a camel. They are described as "anti-Schmuck amulets [that] will protect you from all camel riders who block your promotion, stifle your creativity, sue you in court, date your girlfriend, keep you waiting in line, say 'no' to good ideas, reject your proposals and spill soup on your suit."

Look at the Schmuck on That Camel materializes the sensibility of one stratum of American Yiddish culture as it passes from the children of Yiddish-speaking immigrants, who came of age in the middle decades of the twentieth century, to the next generation. Here the first generation's comical inventories of Yiddish terms, placed in context through jokes—a practice epitomized by Rosten's popular book—

become the implied prooftexts for the next generation's elaborations on a mock Yiddish heritage that is understood as inherently fragmentary, parodic, and carnivalesque. For the children of immigrants, this bilingual humor emerged from their parents' experience of negotiating between the languages of the Old and New Worlds and demonstrates a mastery of the linguistic and cultural challenges of immigration. For subsequent generations, however, the hybridized, comic language that emerged in immigrant humor is received as the code of ethnicity itself and therefore needs to be learned as such. Thus, the rules for *Look at the Schmuck on That Camel* describe it as a "game to teach initiates, or the uninitiated" Yiddish language and culture.[30] In the course of this transmission of a mock heritage, the meta-value of Yiddish acquires new properties—such as attaining the magical power of an amulet—even as it is further displaced from vernacular literacy.

Thus, members of the postimmigrant generations preserve this mock heritage by perpetuating a limited Yiddish vocabulary in its modes of ridicule and carnival. They elaborate this heritage not by expanding the repertoire of Yiddishisms or bilingual jokes but rather by inventing materializations of them. This change suggests that sites of cultural creativity and networks of distribution have shifted from language-based activities, such as code-switching and joke-telling, to new arenas of contact and expertise, including merchandising and consuming.

Or, in the case of the 1999 Off-Broadway comedy *Oy!* by Rich Orloff, the task of learning the meanings of Yiddishisms as they figure in contemporary American Jewish life is rendered as a stage work. A series of comic sketches, *Oy!* enacts the meanings of a highly selective inventory of Yiddish words: "kvell" ("take pride in") "macher" ("big shot"), "nudge" ("pester"), "chutzpah" ("brazen nerve"), "oy" ("a word with many meanings"), "kibbitz" ("converse"), "yenta" ("busybody"), "kvetch," ("complain"), "traif" ("unkosher").[31] As staged by the Melting Pot Theatre Company, each sketch began with actors displaying the letters spelling the key word in question (in romanization) on a clothesline strung across the stage, thereby materializing Yiddishisms as scenery. Here, too, Yiddish signals a Jewish sensibility that is both elusively connotative and widely accessible. Use of the language indicates ethnicity, in literary scholar Werner Sollors's terms, both "by descent" and "by consent."[32] Thus *Oy!* begins with "Word Play," a sketch in which a gentile secretary newly employed in an otherwise all-Jewish law firm struggles to master the Yiddishisms they use with one another—terms that, one character explains, "can't be learned from a dictionary." Even so, the production's program includes a glossary, though noting that "some of the definitions describe the usage more than the literal meanings of the words" and reassuring audience members, "don't worry . . . there won't be a quiz."[33]

The performance of this mock mastery of the language is also implicit in Yiddish realia in mock mode. Like many other novelty items, these are jokes incarnate, with Yiddish words and the language play that they engender functioning as punch lines. In addition, as is the case with spoken jokes generally, these items require a social context for performance and appreciation. A prime social context for the appearance of these objects is gift giving, which links them to marking special occasions and articulating interpersonal relationships, especially, in the case of Yiddish realia, intergenerational ones. Such social occasions provide opportunities for giving voice to Yiddish (albeit in highly fragmented, mock form), whether reading aloud the bogus definitions and jokes in comic dictionaries, instruction cards for games, or bilingual puns on snack canisters. Indeed, these objects and texts often stimulate oral delivery or invite discussion (the instructions inside the lid of *Chutzpah* end thus: "In case you have any questions about how to play the game—argue! Don't call us, we'll be in Miami.") Oral engagement with these objects might well prompt elaborations on the participants' own initiative, such as recalling other jokes, anecdotes, or Yiddish idioms.

The voicing of these objects will, of course, vary widely, according to the composition of those assembled—whether they comprise an all-Jewish group or a mix of Jews and non-Jews, a unigenerational group or an intergenerational one. The last example is of special interest, for as gag gifts—mock offerings of a mock heritage—passing between generations, these items intimate ambivalent feelings about inheriting Yiddish language and Jewish vernacularity. Giving one of these items might be understood as a gesture of cultural homage, on the one hand, and as a tacit acknowledgment of cultural breakdown on the other. At the same time, these lowbrow, sometimes salacious, materializations reinforce associations of Yiddish with the vulgar in its multiple meanings, especially when the vitality of Jewish vulgarity has appeared to be endangered and, at the same time, attractive. This was doubtless part of the appeal of these items in the first post-Holocaust decades, when, for many, living with questions about identity "in a state of useful discontent was," according to Irving Howe, "perhaps what it . . . meant to be a Jew."[34]

More recent examples of materializing Yiddish often seem to celebrate the previous generation's cultural anxieties about the language as a heritage to be adopted as well as spoofed, admired as well as derided. Jennifer and Victoria Traig's 2002 book *Judaikitsch: Tchotchkes, Schmattes, and Nosherei*, offers an array of ludic crafts projects and recipes (including the "Borscht Belt," the "Neil Tzedakah Box," and the "Poi Vey Pineapple Mold") as both a continuation of and a corrective to earlier Jewish material culture. Claiming that "ever since that unfortunate incident with the golden calf, Judaism has shied away from the plastic arts," the authors demonstrate "what might happen if Martha Stewart was abducted by a tribe of trailer-park rabbis." At the same time, the Traigs position "Jewish kitsch" within "a long and proud history." Noting that "the word *tchotchke* is around 500 years old," they explain that East European immigrant Jews "brought their kitschy tchotchkes with them" on their journeys to America, to the displeasure of "more established" German Jews. Lowbrow "tchotchkes"—and, by implication, the Yiddish language—are thus historicized as inimical to "*kultur,* or high art," eventually giving way to the authors' sensibility of camp (which, they explain, "can only be described as arched-brow").[35]

Along with the insights that Yiddish realia prompt regarding their symbolic value—their linguistic and cultural playfulness, their sociohistorical timeliness—we must also consider the attraction of their materiality. Materializing language offers the promise of concretizing the most evanescent of cultural enterprises. In the case of Yiddish in post–World War II America, these objects ostensibly stabilize the language during a state of manifold upheaval. The nature of its speech community, its lexicon, its semiotics, its relationship to other languages, are all in flux. In doing so, these items fix the language as a sign of linguistic and cultural tenacity.

In this respect, the inventory of Yiddish artifacts should be considered alongside two of the most ambitious of recent material efforts to preserve Yiddish culture: erecting the new headquarters of the National Yiddish Book Center on the campus of Hampshire College in Amherst, Massachusetts, and the NYBC's project to create digital scans of the full inventory of Yiddish literature, enabling customers to order new copies of thousands of titles, printed and bound on demand. These two undertakings, equally impressive in scale, offer complementary responses to the challenge of saving old Yiddish books by separating their contents from their materiality.

The NYBC's new headquarters, which opened in 1997, are built around large, open stacks, with row upon row of shelves holding thousands of vintage volumes. According to the building's architect, Allen Moore, this was planned so that there would be nothing separating the books from the visitor, who would "be able to smell them!" As a result, "the books are going to come across as being real and alive, and the mustiness will suggest that Yiddishkeit has been forgotten for a long time but now it's coming into the light and being taken care of by young people."[36] In contrast, the NYBC's digital scanning of Yiddish books, begun in 1998, preserves their literary content while removing it from its original material form. Reproduced on acid-free paper, the NYBC's reprints are bound in covers of uniform design, thereby encompassing what may eventually be the full inventory of modern Yiddish literature within a single imprint: the Steven Spielberg Digital Yiddish Library.[37] (The project's major funder is Spielberg's Righteous Persons Fund, thereby linking the preservation of Yiddish books and Holocaust remembrance.)

Vintage Yiddish books, while generally in poorer physical condition than new reprints, nonetheless have their original covers and often bear the signs of prior use—inscriptions, book plates, marginalia, even stains and tears—that endow them with the aura of a bygone way of life. The open stacks at the heart of the NYBC's headquarters capitalize on this aura, transforming literary volumes from a wide array of publishing venues into a massive gathering of votive objects, to be encountered with the nose as much as the eye. These Yiddish books remain powerful cultural catalysts, though their mode of engagement has shifted radically—away from informational or aesthetic encounters with individual books (and away from the cultural specificity of Yiddish as well, since old books tend to smell much the same regardless of the language in which they are written) and toward an affective, visceral experience of books en masse. Drawing on the powerful association of smell with memory, inhaling the aroma of abandoned Yiddish books is meant to evoke a lost culture as well as its retrieval. Indeed, the books' very presence on shelves in the NYBC, surrounded by its young staff, transforms them into symbols of resurrection.

Powerful cultural desires are embodied in all these materializations of Yiddish language. This is not only the case in the NYBC's devotion to Yiddish as a form of Jewish high culture, however populist and even sentimental that might at times be; it also holds for the lowbrow Yiddish realia in mock mode that I have been collecting. All these materializations concretize the semiotic transformation of Yiddish inherent in postvernacularity, privileging the language's symbolic meanings over its vernacular value. The significance of these artifacts is therefore in flux, even as they strive to secure meaning. As with any artifact, their meaning relies on the cultural literacy of those who own them and engage with them, posing a special challenge for younger generations who are further removed from the vernacular culture that engendered these items. For through them, these generations encounter Yiddish as a curio—a fragment of a whole with which they are unfamiliar, a souvenir of experiences that they have never had.

CHAPTER SIX

WANTED DEAD OR ALIVE?

"Some say Yiddish is dead, it hardly lives outside the classroom or archives. We don't
know if we are part of a revival or are assisting at a slow death."

    —S. L. WISENBERG, *Holocaust Girls*, 2000

"Y2K = Yiddish: The Second Millennium."

    —DAVID BRAUN, 2000

Hovering around postvernacular Yiddish in all its manifestations are questions regarding the language's viability. More often than not, contemporary Yiddish culture is assessed—even by some of its champions—according to the widespread notion that the language is moribund. So pervasive is this notion that at the turn of the
twenty-first century it also haunts those, such as S. L. Wisenberg—a young American author studying Yiddish in continuing-education classes—who are seeking
ways to engage with the language and make it part of their lives.[1] In response, some
Yiddishists—among them David Braun, who taught Yiddish language at Harvard
University in 2000—vigorously, and at times provocatively, insist in its viability.[2]

HAVING THE LAST WORD

The trope of Yiddish as a dead or dying language is not new, of course. It has not only
been reiterated in the wake of the Holocaust; it has been voiced since the turn of the
previous century. In 1899 Leo Wiener questioned the viability of Yiddish in his pioneering study of modern Yiddish literature. While characterizing the language as "not
an anomaly, but a natural development," Wiener also saw its imminent passing as inevitable, especially in the United States: "In America [Yiddish] is certainly doomed to

extinction. Its lease of life is commensurate with the last large immigration to the new world. In the countries of Europe it will last as long as there are any disabilities for the Jews, as long as they are secluded in Ghettos and driven into Pales."[3] Though writing about Yiddish literature at a moment of its fervent efflorescence, Wiener positioned his study near what he saw as the language's inevitable denouement.

Such a paradox is not unique to outsiders to the Yiddish-speaking milieu such as Wiener. Even as the "sweatshop" poet Morris Rosenfeld helped to forge modern Yiddish literature, he predicted its demise, writing in 1897 that Yiddish "has no future" in America and that "within twenty-five years . . . even the best works in this language will only be literary curiosities. . . . Woe to those who are unable to utter their thoughts and feelings in a living tongue."[4] And, of course, opponents of Yiddish—such as the staunch Hebraist Ahad ha-Am (né Asher Ginsberg), writing in 1902—argued that

> this Jargon, though it is to-day the language of most Jews, is gradually being forgotten all over the world. . . . In America, where the Jargon and its literature are most flourishing (save the mark!), it is in reality only the language of the older generation, which brought it from Europe. . . . If not for the yearly inrush of Jargon-speaking immigrants, there would not be a vestige of the language left in the New World. . . . Even in its native countries—Russia, Galicia, and Roumania—the Jargon is being driven to the wall by the language of the country. . . . There is therefore no doubt that before long Yiddish will cease to be a living and spoken language.[5]

Similar sentiments continued to be expressed in the early decades of the twentieth century. To cite but one example, in 1928 the *Jewish Tribune,* an English-language weekly published in New York, editorialized that celebrations marking the twentieth anniversary of the Czernowitz conference on Yiddish "will not convince an unpartisan observer that the Yiddish tongue will achieve immortality," and the editors repeated their conviction that it was "difficult to view the future of Yiddish in America optimistically."[6]

As enduring and widespread as the notion of its fatality is in the discourse on modern Yiddish, this is no more than a trope; it is not inevitable that the language be discussed in these terms. Assessing the state of Yiddish in the past century, especially since the Holocaust, calls for other, more discerning paradigms. At the same time, the pervasiveness of this one demands that it be interrogated, for speaking of the language as moribund has become part of modern Yiddish culture in itself. What does it mean, for example, that Wiener and Rosenfeld characterized Yiddish as dying just as the language was facilitating cultural achievements in literature, journalism, and politics of a scope unprecedented in Jewish history? Indeed, only a few years after they—and Ahad ha-Am—predicted the imminent demise of Yiddish in America, Henry James would characterize the "Yiddish world" of New York's Lower East Side as "vast," deeming the language he heard spoken in its cafés to be "the agency of future ravage" of "our language as literature has hitherto known it." In the same time and place, what James saw as endangered was not Yiddish, but rather his own native tongue: "Whatever we shall know it for, certainly, we shall not know it for English."[7]

The trope of Yiddish as moribund follows several generations of denunciations of the language by advocates of the Haskalah; but though they characterized Yiddish as a deformed language and as unhealthy for its speakers, they did not question its vitality. On the contrary, the *maskilim* who repudiated Yiddish considered its vigor to be part of the problem that it posed for Ashkenazim. To describe it as near death at the turn of the twentieth century marks a telling shift in the discourse surrounding Yiddish. The language then enjoyed an unprecedented number of speakers and a growing recognition of its importance to Jews symbolically as well as instrumentally. At the same time, its status as a centuries-old fixture of East European Jewish life was destabilized in new ways—by mass immigration from the Romanov and Habsburg empires, by the advent of a small but influential linguistic assimilation into Russian or German, and by the widespread radicalization of East European Jews.[8] The trope of Yiddish as dying may well have emerged in response to these cultural and political transmigrations or to some other sense of crisis among Yiddish speakers, but it was not due to a sense of this community's imminent disappearance.

Discussing the death of Yiddish would therefore seem to entail something very different in the wake of World War II, which witnessed the massacre of about half the world population of Yiddish speakers and the destruction of their centuries-old cultural center in Eastern Europe. During the past six decades it has become a commonplace to speak of Yiddish language and culture as being murdered, along with millions of Jews, by Hitler. Yet the postwar discourse of Yiddish as a dying or dead language is not simply a response to the Holocaust. Indeed, some observers have posited that Yiddish would have become obsolescent in Eastern Europe even had there been no Holocaust. Sociologist Celia Heller, for example, argued that, "had Poland not been defeated and had Jews lived on there, within two or three generations Polish would have probably replaced Yiddish as their predominant language."[9]

Other postwar observers have taken on the discourse of the language's death more obliquely and playfully. Among the dozens of Yiddish-language poems about

Yiddish written during this period are works that use the power of versifying in the language to defy or ironize claims of its demise. In his 1965 poem "To Africa," for example, the Soviet poet Avraham Gontar tells his grandchild that he plans to go to Africa to buy a parrot and teach it to speak Yiddish. Then, well after he and his grandchildren (whose command of the language is in decline) are long gone, an "aged linguist" will capture the parrot, which can live "three centuries or so," and will learn to speak Yiddish from the bird.[10] Most famously, Isaac Bashevis Singer regularly reminded his English-speaking audiences that, when it came to the well-being of Yiddish, there was a significant difference between a dead language and a dying one. On receiving the Nobel Prize for literature in 1978, Singer drolly explained why he wrote in Yiddish: "I like to write ghost stories, and nothing fits a ghost better than a dying language. The deader the language, the more alive is the ghost. Ghosts love Yiddish; they all speak it."[11] Nevertheless, in his speech at the award ceremony in Stockholm, the author felt compelled to state that "Yiddish has not spoken its last word"—though he uttered these words in English, after beginning his speech in Yiddish.[12]

The trope of Yiddish as a dying or dead language has therefore proved something other than a sociolinguistic assessment both before and after the Holocaust. It has served, instead, as a discursive frame for addressing the shifting stature and significance of Yiddish in modern Jewish life. The resilience of the trope at the turn of the twenty-first century demonstrates just how much it remains an issue of contention and the extent to which the trope is understood to have meaningful implications for the intellectual, political, psychological, and even moral well-being of the Jewish people.

Thus, in 1998 literary scholar and psychoanalyst Janet Hadda argued that ardent Yiddishists' "tenacity and pluckiness do not bestow immortality" on the language, and that these devotees simply "cannot bear to acknowledge that an era has ended." In their commitment to the continuity of the language they are, in fact, "mourning its death throes," though, like someone who cannot accept the loss of a loved one, they are denying its demise. While acknowledging that such "denial is a powerful psychological tool" and can help cushion the initial impact of an intolerable blow, Hadda argues that those who persist in refusing to accept the passing of Yiddish culture as it once flourished in prewar Eastern Europe cannot move beyond despair toward a psychologically salubrious "reorganization."[13]

Similarly, author and translator Hillel Halkin recently felt compelled to revisit the "great language war" between modern Hebrew and Yiddish that raged during the first decades of twentieth century to reassert the triumph of what he deems the

The YIDDISH THEATRE will
be very much alive
this Fall!

דעם הארבסט אין דעם יידישן
טעאַטער וועט זיך טאָן אויף
טיש און אויף בענק!

Promotional brochure for the 2002 season of the Folksbiene, a New York–based
Yiddish theater company that has performed annually since 1915. Here, the Yiddish
theater's vivacity is celebrated as a sign of its continued viability.
Courtesy of the Folksbiene Yiddish Theatre, Zalmen Mlotek, executive director.

"right side" (i.e., Hebrew) over the "wrong side" (Yiddish). Even as he rehashes its
disputes, he notes that this war was waged not by modern Jewish literature's greatest luminaries but by "ideologues" and "literary hacks." Nonetheless, Halkin judges
the Yiddishism of yore to have been a "catastrophic misjudgment" that also has had
a lingering influence on "the voguish sentimentality of much of the current revival
of interest" in Yiddish.[14] (Halkin's rearguing of this erstwhile debate inspired the
ire of at least one reader of his essay, published in *Commentary* in 2002; she responded that "continuing to argue for the old mistakes, as Mr. Halkin does, is to
wage war against the phantoms of history. The exercise now seems perverse.")[15]

The trope of Yiddish as moribund has, of course, prompted its converse. Yiddishists such as Joshua Fishman exhort fellow devotees to "never say die!" (this
being the title of his 1981 compendium of articles about "a thousand years of Yiddish life and letters") and to insist on the vitality of the language and its culture.[16]
In his own evaluation of the trope of Yiddish as dying, Fishman shifts the moral
onus onto its advocates: "Much of the claim that Yiddish is dead merely reflects how
dead it is to the claimants and how dead *they are* to its continued speakers." In this
trope Fishman sees evidence of more than Jewish polemics, attributing it to a general societal trend "from intimate community to megalopolis," in which loss of a
language is indicative of a larger humanistic loss.[17]

Such apprehensions are voiced repeatedly in the growing scholarly attention to
language loss as a global phenomenon. While sharing an urgent concern about the
imminent disappearance of dozens of the world's languages, linguists disagree

about how to define languages that no longer have a viable speech community. Some do prefer to characterize them as dying, arguing that "to say a language is dead is like saying a person is dead"; others, though, prefer to speak of "language loss," noting that "languages are not entities and it can be seriously misleading to make them the subjects of active verbs."[18]

Yet however this phenomenon might be termed, it clearly does not apply to Yiddish today. While its number of speakers is now perhaps less than one-tenth of what it was before World War II, hundreds of thousands of people still speak, read, and write Yiddish, producing in it books, periodicals, plays, websites, audio and video recordings, and of course continuing to use it in daily life both for routine communication and in more structured and specialized settings, be it a *gemore shier* in an ultra-Orthodox yeshiva or a secular concert of Yiddish songs. Indeed, while the overall scope of Yiddish six decades after World War II is much reduced, there are signs of linguistic stability and growth—as a language spoken and written among Ashkenazic *khareydim* and as a language studied and performed among less traditionally observant and secular Jews, as well as a noteworthy number of non-Jews.

That the trope of Yiddish as dying or dead has endured for over a century despite sweeping changes in the fortunes of the language, positive as well as negative, makes it clear that this notion has become an autonomous cultural phenomenon; like a specter, it has taken on a "life" of its own. Moreover, this trope addresses—as meta-discussions of language so often do—extralinguistic concerns. While speaking of a language as dying (or thriving) is inherently metaphoric, since the language is likened to a human or other living being, analogizing Yiddish language and human life has a special historical resonance.

Traditional sources have characterized linguistic consciousness as a feature of Jewish life since ancient times.[19] Nevertheless, the nature of that consciousness changed profoundly as a consequence of the Haskalah, when the issue of language—written and spoken, sacred and profane, official and vernacular, ideal and actual—came to the fore of realizing Jewishness in the modern Western world. This was true not only for the array of Europe's Jewish cultural and political progressives but also for defenders of Orthodoxy, who were inevitably compelled to address the challenges of modernity.

Yiddish thus became the subject of a new kind of attention that problematized its status as the traditional vernacular of Ashkenaz, whether among advocates of the language or among its detractors. Yiddish came under scrutiny as a negative model among those who wished to leave it behind for an established European national language or who longed to replace it with a new vernacular, be it Jewish (modern

Hebrew) or internationalist (Esperanto). At the same time, the champions of Yiddish also subjected it to unprecedented consideration, as they too sought a new culture realized through linguistic innovation.

In this new attention to the significance of language in modern Jewish life, Yiddish came to signify a diasporic communality that extended across the globe and back in time for several centuries. At the turn of the twentieth century Yiddishists transformed this valuation of the language into the basis of a political ideology, arguing that Yiddish, its culture, and its speakers were, in effect, tautological. Thus, Y. L. Peretz exhorted his fellow Yiddishists at the 1908 Czernowitz conference: "[There is] a Jewish nation; its language is Yiddish. And this is the language in which we wish to . . . fashion our culture, to awaken our soul, and to unite with one another across all nations and all epochs."[20] This ideological model, which projected a Jewish dominion implemented and sustained through language, resonated powerfully with extensive daily practice, transvaluing vernacularity as national consciousness.

The foundation on which Yiddishism rested was shaken severely by the upheavals, culminating in genocide, of the middle of the twentieth century. But beyond the extensive loss of life, large-scale geographical relocations, and sweeping new political and social orders lay fundamental transformations of how Jews might conceptualize the interdependency of peoplehood, culture, and language. Therefore, when people now speak of Yiddish as moribund, they invoke the language symbolically to address, albeit obliquely, the sense of a breach in Jewish cultural or social continuity at its most elemental level.

Pronouncing Yiddish as dying at the turn of the previous century addressed a sense of unprecedented and sweeping change in the Yiddish-speaking world, in which use of this vernacular was expanding rapidly and, at the same time, experiencing widespread destabilization and contestation. Invoking the trope of Yiddish as moribund today implicitly invokes this erstwhile debate. It is, therefore, a nostalgic gesture, intimating a desire to recall, and perhaps even to reenter, a discourse in which the union of Jewish language, culture, and people was once an urgently meaningful idea—for this idea has since come undone.

It is essential to take this change into account when seeking an alternative discourse for assessing the current state of Yiddish. In particular, one needs to consider possibilities other than the Yiddishist models of the first half of the past century, which championed a vision of Yiddish as a full national language that emulated the major languages of Europe—having a comprehensive vocabulary, standardized orthography and grammar, implemented in its own high-cultural apparatus (press, theater, schools, political organizations, etc.). Using such a model as the measure of

Yiddish viability runs the risk of deeming anything less—be it the delimited and exclusivist nature of the Yiddish now used by *khareydim,* the predominantly passive engagement that performers and humanities scholars often have with the language, the fragmentary and sentimentalized or vulgarized Yiddish of many amateurs—as illegitimate or as a failure. Doing so also obviates the opportunity to consider how these and still other forms of engagement with Yiddish figure in contemporary Jewish life and how they are transforming both the language and its significance in the post-Holocaust era. Therefore, scholars (and others contemplating the state of Yiddish) need to consider a variety of engagements with Yiddish that accommodates a range of proficiencies, agendas, and sensibilities. At the same time they must recognize that Yiddish has crossed a monumental threshold in its long history, marked by the loss of its millions of East European speakers in the Yiddish "heartland."

TOWARD A NEW YIDDISH?

In fact, during the past several decades alternative models have been proposed for assessing the current state of Yiddish or conceptualizing its future. They are offered forthrightly as theoretical projections and also emerge implicitly from new cultural practices. Some of these models directly challenge widely held assumptions about Yiddish being in decline and, in doing so, flout conventional notions of what could be considered Yiddish culture—or even what might constitute the language itself.

Several writers have outlined new paradigms for conceptualizing Yiddish language and literature within large-scale prescriptions for contemporary Jewish culture, which they also regard as standing at a significant threshold. For example, in a recent essay entitled "Outwitting History," Aaron Lansky, founder of the National Yiddish Book Center, proposed that Jews view Yiddish literature as "our Mishna"—that is, as a finite corpus that can serve as a "bridge between epochs." Just as in the Talmud the Aramaic Gemara supercedes, yet is indebted to, the older Hebrew Mishna, Lansky argues, Yiddish "can play a similar role" in contemporary Jewish letters, "as a repository of history and sensibility, a key to dialectical process, and a wellspring for continued Jewish literary creativity—in English, Spanish, Russian, Hebrew, or whatever language we speak." This subsequent literary activity "cannot exist in any meaningful way without reference to what came before."[21]

Lansky's model resembles, and may even be inspired by, what Cynthia Ozick termed "New Yiddish" in 1970. With this term Ozick posited an English-language culture "that is centrally Jewish in its concerns and thereby liturgical in nature. Like old Yiddish before its massacre by Hitler, New Yiddish will be the language of multitudes of Jews: spoken to Jews by Jews, written by Jews for Jews. And, most necessary of all, New Yiddish, like old Yiddish, will be in possession of a significant literature capable of every conceivable resonance." New Yiddish, then, is a cultural project in which Jews will "rethink ourselves in America" and "preserve ourselves by a new culture-making."[22]

Literary scholar David Roskies might well consider Ozick's and Lansky's cultural and linguistic rethinking of Yiddish to be examples of what he has termed "creative betrayal"—a "dynamic" he sees running though Yiddish narrative practices, in which "each generation of modern Jews" experiences "some kind of negotiated return" to a "forgotten past" of Jewish literary traditions.[23] Roskies offers both a critique of what Ozick terms "new culture-making" and a model of his own by implicitly situating the multivalent dynamics of modern Yiddish culture within the traditional Jewish rubric of *tshuve* (repentance, particularly with regard to religious observance). Deeming current Yiddish culture to be the remnants of a "lost art"—"What remains of this folk culture are Yiddish theater melodies without their lyrics, a few vulgarisms in the mother tongue, a religion stripped of its stories and superstitions, and a reinvented folklore that tries to pass for the real thing"—Roskies presents his model as a corrective response, similar in this regard to Hadda's urging Yiddishists toward *Trauerarbeit*, the task of grieving.[24]

These models call much-needed attention to the importance of invention in modern Jewish culture, thereby challenging the simplistic notion of continuity as sameness, which haunts the trope of Yiddish as dead or dying. At the same time, they rely on time-honored paradigms for discussing Yiddish culture, centering their approaches on modern literature (as do Hadda's and Halkin's assessments of Yiddish) and linking modern Yiddish culture, one way or another, with religious tradition. But how might one frame a discussion of the state of Yiddish today and its future possibilities to accommodate the full range of Yiddish culture, including its many nonliterary practices—notably performances, from casual, impromptu joke-telling to elaborately planned festivals—not to mention the efforts of those who eschew modern literature or who resist linking Yiddish culture with religiosity?

Indeed, some of the contemporary phenomena marginalized by these theoretical models might be considered "the real thing"—that is, they might be examined as paradigmatic Yiddish cultural practices true to their own time and constituency rather than as obstinately vestigial efforts to be measured against the Yiddish past. Regarding these phenomena in this light reveals how they generate their own provocative models for conceptualizing Yiddish in the post-Holocaust era, further expanding and complicating its spectrum of possibilities.

Consider, for example, Chaim Weiser's 1995 volume *Frumspeak: The First Dictionary of Yeshivish*, which documents this fusion of English, Yiddish, modern Hebrew, and Loshn-koydesh (in particular, the traditional Hebrew and Aramaic terminology of rabbinical scholars) spoken by men and boys in American yeshivas in the post–World War II era. Emerging as an exigent language for talmudic study among English-speaking students learning from Yiddish-speaking teachers, Yeshivish has become an established vernacular, Weiser argues, used beyond the confines of the classroom. He demonstrates the linguistic possibilities of Yeshivish by rendering in it not only examples indigenous to the Yeshivish world (such as an excerpt from the introduction to *Sefer Chofetz Chaim*, a key ethical text of modern yeshiva culture) but also Shakespeare soliloquies and such quintessentially American texts as the Pledge of Allegiance and Lincoln's Gettysburg Address: "Be 'erech a yoivel and a half ago, the meyasdim shtelled avek on this makom a nayia malchus with the kavana that no one should have bailus over their chaver, and on this yesoid that everyone has the zelba zchusim."[25]

Weiser raises the question of whether Yeshivish merits being termed a language per se as opposed to something more limited in scope. In this regard Yeshivish might be considered a variety of what linguist David Gold termed "Jewish English," which he defined as a "cluster of lects whose common characteristics are (1) their chief component is English, (2) they are used by Jews, and (3) each lect is an adequate expression of its users' Jewish experiences."[26] (Gold, writing in 1985, is not the first to identify or name this phenomenon. In 1928 H. B. Wells proposed in the journal *American Speech* that "American Yiddish will within a very a few years lose its identity . . . , will turn into Judeo-English," and eventually this, too, will "expire quietly.")[27] However, in his review of *Frumspeak*, Sam Weiss argues that Weiser underrecognizes the role of Yiddish in Yeshivish, not only lexically, noting that its use of Loshn-koydesh terms is largely rooted in the Yiddish idiom, but also syntactically, since many Yeshivish constructions using English words are calques of Yiddish locutions—for example, "come on to [from the Yiddish *onkumen tsu*], 'resort to.' " Weiss suggests that, in light of the paucity of English in some of the samples of Yeshivish Weiser provides, it might be better considered "a Yiddish, rather than an English, patois."[28]

However one may wish to categorize it, Yeshivish is clearly indebted to vernacular Yiddish while at the same time remaining distinct from it, in terms of both its linguistic composition and its sociolinguistic profile. The fact that Weiser sees it as meriting its own lexicon and grammar indicates an emerging consciousness about Yeshivish as a distinct code that cannot be comfortably subsumed within either En-

Promotional card for the all-female "klezbian ensemble" Isle of Klezbos, New York, 2001.
Designed by Lisa M. Kelsey.
Courtesy of Isle of Klezbos.

glish or Yiddish. It may also reflect an awareness that, besides figuring as a component of the lexicon and grammar of Yeshivish, Yiddish contributes to its secondary semiotic value, albeit ambivalently, marking Yeshivish as part of the tradition of Ashkenazic rabbinic scholarship and, at the same time, as a break in Ashkenazic vernacularity.

A quite different model for conceptualizing Yiddish after the Holocaust is suggested by Queer Yiddishkeit, a term applied to a cluster of discrete cultural phenomena of recent years, in which Jews, most of them Americans born after World War II who identify as gay, lesbian, or bisexual, explore links between queer and Yiddish cultures. These include the undertakings of educator and performer Hinde Ena Burstin (who has taught a course called "Yidish far Lezbiankes" [Yiddish for Lesbians] in Melbourne, Australia), performance artist Sara Felder, filmmaker Diane Nerwen, journalist Alisa Solomon, poet Yermiyahu Aharon Taub, and musicians who are members of the Klezmatics or the Isle of Klezbos, among others. Though these writers and performers work in an array of cultural genres, their efforts all analogize queer and Yiddish sensibilities—often tacitly, though sometimes, as in the case of Solomon, directly.

In a 1997 essay published in *Davka*, a magazine dedicated to "Jewish cultural revolution," Solomon acknowledges that the notion of "Yiddishkeit as hospitable to queers" is a construct of recent vintage, made by a particular constituency. Nevertheless, she characterizes this idea as an outgrowth of an inherent "affinity between queerness and Yiddishkeit." To demonstrate, she enumerates parallels between the two sensibilities: diasporism; rootless cosmopolitanism; a penchant for transgression, border-crossing, and being proudly, defiantly different; standing as a challenge to broader societies' sense of "certitude and power." In citing these parallels Solomon energizes and validates the existence of Queer Yiddishkeit. Indeed, enumerating and extending the analogy becomes an enactment of Queer Yiddishkeit in itself, which Solomon characterizes as "a post-modern marriage."[29]

Whereas Yeshivish involves Yiddish as a linguistic component, in Queer Yiddishkeit the language often figures more as a sensibility.[30] This practice entails a deliberate, often aestheticized, engagement with the secondary, symbolic value of Yiddish that can range well beyond its primary value as an instrument of communication. And rather than contributing some semiotic value seen as inherent in the language, as is the case with its role in Yeshivish, Yiddish becomes meaningful in Queer Yiddishkeit as a result of its provocative juxtaposition against queerness.

Not everyone finds this juxtaposition felicitous; one case in point is Ruth Wisse, who implicates Queer Yiddishkeit in her critique of much of contemporary Yiddish culture:

> These days, Jewish (and non-Jewish) spokesmen for gays and lesbians, feminists and neo-Trotskyites freely identify their sense of personal injury with the cause of Yiddish. They thereby commit a double fault, occluding the moral assurance and tenacity of Yiddish culture in its own terms and, by attributing value to weakness, retroactively defaming the Jewish will to live and to prosper. A student who seeks in this debased image of Yiddish a substitute for Jewish civilization as a whole not only traduces the past but can become, himself, a caricature.[31]

For Wisse, the "queering" of Yiddish, analogous to what she deems its misappropriation by the New Left, perverts both its authentic cultural past and the possibility of a healthy Jewish future. Yet other Jewish Studies scholars find that "Jewishness and queerness . . . utilize and are bound up with one another in particularly resonant ways" that are "not only theoretical" but also have "profound implications for the ways in which Jewish and queer bodies are lived."[32] Thus the juxtaposition can be seen not merely as legitimate but also as productive both in theory and in practice. The phenomenolization of Queer Yiddishkeit in particular suggests the value of queer theory as a model for thinking about modern Yiddish culture, past and present. As a poststructuralist conception, queer theory challenges the notion of cultural definitions (such as heterosexuality and homosexuality) as essential and calls for interrogating the implications of definitional terminology, boundaries, and taxonomies. Queer theory also places a special value on alterity as an energizing, rather than destructive, mode of culture.[33]

The most provocative implications for modern Yiddish culture posed by queer theory are the alternatives that it proposes to a biological model of intergenerational cultural transmission. These alternative models contest traditional Jewish concepts of cultural and communal continuity, which are rooted in heterosexual reproduction and family life, and are assumed as normative in almost all discussions of the maintenance of Yiddish. Joshua Fishman writes that what Yiddish requires to continue flourishing is a "bounded life-style of its own at the home-neighborhood-community level," such as one finds among some ultra-Orthodox Ashkenazim, especially in New York and Jerusalem. The alternative—"exposure to . . . Yiddish in college courses, in theater presentations, in song recitals, in readings of translations and at commemorative events—is both too little and too late, . . . regardless of the intellectual and entertainment merits of such exposure." In this context, Fishman laments, "Yiddish . . . , for all of its esthetic and intellectual variety, ingenuity and refinement, is now fated to remain the language of small and intergenerationally non-continuous coteries of devotees, each generation of which will scramble to find its own intellectual heirs." However, among *khareydim*, "the continuity of Yiddish . . . is limited only by the birth rate of its members, since each member's own children are his or her heirs."[34]

This argument not only disregards the considerable empirical sociolinguistic evidence that children's language is not so simply or exclusively determined by that of their parents; it also discounts the contribution made by other forms of social contact to cultural, and therefore linguistic, vitality—including the vitality generated by "scrambling" in response to discontinuity. In queer culture, generationality is articulated not in terms of the biological relationship of parents and children but (as is also the general pattern of modern Western youth culture) by coming-of-age cohort groups. Hence, cultural identity is more a matter of when and where one grows up rather than into what family one is born. In both youth culture and queer culture, authority figures are not parents and teachers but peers and leaders selected by the cohort community, including figures encountered only indirectly, such as authors, performers, or political figures. The temporal distance between generations of queers or of youth—a decade at most— is, therefore, much shorter than the one-quarter to one-third of a century between biological generations. Consequently, intergenerational discontinuity is not simply more prevalent in these cohort-based cultures but is valued as an energizing force. Instead of the ideal image of culture as an enduring inheritance passed from parents to children, the queer paradigm of culture is that of a dynamic proving ground, its constancy comprising an ongoing breaking down and rebuilding among closely differentiated cohorts.

This is an apt model for understanding the transmigrations of modern Yiddish culture not only in the post-Holocaust era but since the late nineteenth century—if not, perhaps, even earlier. Although Yiddish culture is often vaunted as a "golden chain" forged by an unbroken succession of biological generations, it might be better understood in the modern era as proceeding through cohort generations, manifest in youth movements, political parties, trade unions, literary circles, educational institutions, various immigrant, refugee, and survivor associations, and so on.[35] Moreover, the history of Yiddish culture is replete with moments when abrupt demise adjoins transformative renewal. Even as Yiddishists champion the intergenerational continuity of language use as an ideal, it is worth remembering that during the past century this has been the exception rather than the rule for Yiddish. In this regard, the history of modern Yiddish culture prior to the Holocaust not only has telling losses—for example, the fact that none of the children of S. Y. Abramovitsh, Sholem Aleichem, or Y. L. Peretz spoke Yiddish—but also reveals illuminating gains. Thus, the Jewish political polemicist Nathan Birnbaum, the Bundist ideologist Vladimir Medem, and the Yiddish linguist Max Weinreich were all Jews who did not learn Yiddish as their mother tongue but mastered it later in life.

As members of Jewish subcultures, speakers of Yeshivish and those engaged in Queer Yiddishkeit seem poles apart; nevertheless, they have in common an approach to Yiddish that is distinctively postvernacular. Perceived as being somewhere on a spectrum between English and Yiddish, Yeshivish challenges conventional notions of the borders of Yiddish as a discrete language. The hybridity of Yeshivish encourages considering it not as *either* one language *or* another, but as *both* one *and* the other—and, therefore, as something else as well. As Yeshivish challenges, albeit implicitly, the conventional integrity of Yiddish as a complete and distinct language, Queer Yiddishkeit contests established notions of what constitutes Yiddish culture and the nature of its transmission among its constituency. Both as practice and as theory, Queer Yiddishkeit suggests that Yiddish may thrive not as a language but as a sensibility, and not through a resilient commitment to Jewish continuity as it is conventionally understood, but through a tenacious discontinuity that, far from resisting disruption, thrives on it.

"WHAT DO WE MEAN BY YIDDISH, ANYWAY?"

One telling factor uniting all the aforementioned discussions and practices of contemporary Yiddish culture, diverse as they may be, is that they are American phenomena, reflecting America's postwar role as the largest and most influential diaspora Jewish community. Despite sentiments of a century ago that it was at the vanguard of Yiddish's demise, the United States is now home to the greatest extent and variety of Yiddish cultural productivity—in some instances, importing back to older European centers the scholarship and cultural creativity of the pre-Holocaust Ashkenazic Old World. At the same time, the vitality of American Yiddish culture in the post-Holocaust era has been enriched immeasurably by scholars, performers, writers, and other cultural activists who have come from places abroad, including Canada, Australia, Latin America, Europe, Israel, and, more recently, the former Soviet Union. With respect to contemporary Yiddish—and, perhaps, contemporary Jewish culture generally—America is perhaps better understood as the nexus of a new, highly mobile, international cultural diaspora than as the locus of a geographically bounded culture. Or perhaps it is best understood, as Sander Gilman writes, as "a permanent frontier in which peoples enter and mix and change and confront one another, producing a constantly new and revitalizing culture."[36]

Indeed, more than a geographical shift, the postwar recentering of Yiddish culture in America entails fundamental changes in the conceptualization of language, culture, identity, and their interrelation, which has implications for Yiddish internationally. Unlike Soviet or Israeli Yiddish cultures, which have been shaped to a considerable degree by state language policies (even as forces to be resisted), American Yiddish culture has been forged largely in a linguistic open market, albeit one in which English is hegemonic. (The importance of America for world Jewry after World War II is also due, in no small part, to the rise of English in the postwar era to the stature of "a true world language" on an unprecedented scale. Although their embrace of English was not inevitable, in using the language Jews—living not only in officially Anglophone countries but elsewhere as well—have largely followed a trend encompassing much of the globe.)[37]

So powerful is English as a pervasive cultural force in American life that, suggests literary scholar Marc Shell, Anglophone America's understanding of itself entails not merely "forgetting language difference" but even "partly suppressing the category of 'language' itself."[38] America's constellation of languages is uniquely configured, shaped not only by the dominant force of English but also by distinctively labile patterns of multilingualism and protean notions of how language relates to identity. Similarly, contemporary American culture is distinguished by its plastic approach to ethnic identity, wherein an essentialized understanding of ethnicity as something fixed, inevitable, and determined by biological descent has increasingly given way to notions of "symbolic" and "voluntary" ethnicity (despite—or perhaps owing to—the fact that race continues to be regarded as an intractable social category).[39]

These developments challenge long-held postulates that the interrelation of language, culture, and identity is organic and mutually definitional—a notion running through Western scholarship in an unbroken line "from Herder and Humboldt to Benjamin Lee Whorf" but that scholars working in different disciplines have challenged in the postwar era. Thus, Whorf's hypotheses of a culturally driven linguistic relativism and linguistic determinism, which he formulated in the decade before World War II, have been superseded by a linguistics built on the fundament of Noam Chomsky's universalist theories of language, in which "the true issue is now one of 'grammaticality' " rather than meaning—or, for that matter, one of performance, social context, or other contingent elements of language.[40] Conversely, scholarly conceptualizations of culture that are clearly indebted to structural linguistics—such as Clifford Geertz's definition of culture as "an historically transmitted pattern of meanings embodied in symbols, a system of inherited conceptions expressed in symbolic forms by means of which men communicate"—are being questioned.[41] Philosopher Régis Debray argues that, among scholars of culture generally, "the paradigm of Language" has "passed out of fashion" and "is yielding pride of place, via the cognitive sciences, to a new philosophy of mind."[42] Their divergences notwithstanding—indeed, precisely because of them—such theoretical developments testify to the enduring challenge of positioning language in relation to culture, and especially of providing a model that explains the nature of their apparent interdependency as many people experience it. In the case of Yiddish, the implications are especially charged, given its considerable history as a language credited with defining, sustaining, or embodying the life of its speakers, without—and often despite—political aegis, geographical turf, or social esteem.

Yiddish in its cultural heyday of the half century preceding World War II would therefore seem to provide a case study par excellence for exploring the relationship of language, culture, and peoplehood. Certainly the writings of Yiddishists and their various cultural projects offer compelling examples of the vernacular's power to define and sustain a sense of communality, extended to nationalist dimensions, in the face of the geographical challenges of diaspora and the lack of recognition or support of a sovereign state, not to mention the divisive contentions within the Yiddish-speaking world. Yet I would argue that the case of Yiddish becomes much more revealing in the postwar era, when assumptions—not only those of Yiddish ideologists but also those of many "ordinary" members of the Yiddish-speaking world—about the definitional interrelation of Yiddish language, its culture, and Ashkenazic Jewry have been profoundly challenged.

The undoing of these assumptions was a result not only of there being different languages at play, new cultural activities, and major shifts in Jewish geography and demographics. Nor was it due to a resolution of the "language war" that had been waged in the pre-Holocaust era; rather, the present rules of linguistic engagement have rendered the erstwhile casus belli moot. In the post–World War II era language no longer informs Jewish culture or defines Jewish peoplehood in the same ways that it once did. Modern Hebrew has not taken over the role of Yiddish in its pre-war configuration, nor has English or any other language spoken by Jews done so. Modern Hebrew's place in Jewish life is determined primarily by its status as the official language of the State of Israel; as such, Hebrew defines Israeli, rather than Jewish, vernacular culture. (In fact, the use of modern Hebrew is often key to making this cultural distinction.) English, the vernacular language that now links most Jews internationally, positions Jewish communications very differently than Yiddish ever did or could. Yiddish has not disappeared, nor has its value been rendered obsolete, but the tautology of language, culture, and people that it once evoked for the majority of world Jewry is no more.

Far from devaluing Yiddish, however, the undoing of this tautology has transformed the very nature of the language's worth, often endowing it with greater significance, and at times with higher esteem, than it enjoyed before World War II. The disruption of language, culture, and people as mutually definitional has likewise stimulated new configurations of these elements, thereby providing new opportunities for redefining Yiddish, especially in the postvernacular mode. Indeed, postvernacularity can be understood as a response to the demand for a new ordering of language, culture, and peoplehood. This effort entails renegotiating their meanings, individually as well as in relation to one another, in light of both recent innovations and powerful historical precedents. Central to this transformation are desires not simply to abandon Yiddish and all that it represents but to find some way to continue enjoying what George Steiner characterizes as the "psychic, poetic benefits" of a different language.[43] Such benefits are not without problems or easily won. Literary scholar Doris Sommer notes that living with different languages can "trouble the assumption that communication should be easy," but she adds that this "discomfort demands . . . creativity" and that appreciating it calls for "a new sentimental education to develop a taste for unfinished pieces."[44]

From the analysis of contemporary Yiddish culture in the preceding chapters, several general observations about this language in the postvernacular mode emerge. First, *the acquisition of Yiddish is not undertaken as inevitably as it once was*—even among those who learn it as a language of home from their parents. Increasingly, learning Yiddish is a deliberate practice; it is taken up not simply for the instrumental value of being able to understand, speak, read, write, or perform in the language but as a meaningful form of cultural engagement in itself. Once assumed to be essentially mimetic, an automatic part of Ashkenazic childhood, learning Yiddish now centers on new cultural practices, often among adults. These innovations epitomize diverging trends in contemporary Jewish culture generally: on the one hand, textbooks and other instructional materials provide more exacting standards of proper usage than mimetic learning does; on the other, "immersion" language classes strive to provide the student with an intensive "experience" of Yiddish, extending beyond the classroom to include field trips, concerts, folk dancing, and the like.

Contrary to established definitions of its legitimacy as the equal of other languages, *Yiddish in the postvernacular mode is not necessarily thought of, or even valued, as a separate, complete language.* Its partial, restricted use, including frequent atomization into a limited inventory of individual idioms and words (and even fragments of words), suggests that Yiddish is esteemed for its difference from, rather than its similarity to, other languages. This notion can be understood as enriching rather than impoverishing Yiddish culture by opening up its linguistic boundaries, thereby enabling a variety of engagements with the language other than conventional fluency. Or, in the case of hasidic use of Yiddish, the language's limitations are understood as strengthening, rather than weakening, its signifying power as a language of a distinctly pious community.

Indeed, as the value of Yiddish as a whole language declines, the esteem of its fragments increases. Exemplified by the fetishizing of individual Yiddishisms in American Jewish material culture of the past half-century, Yiddish terms in isolation can take on additional meaning, their Yiddishness variously signifying Jewish particularism (the proselytizing organization Jews for Jesus has occasionally made strategic use of Yiddish words on the cover of some of its brochures), an affective intensity associated with ethnicity ("This isn't just a family—it's a *mishpokhe*," I once overheard someone enthuse at a gathering of his relatives), or the carnivalesque (exemplified by the widespread notion among those not fluent in Yiddish that its utterances are inherently histrionic, comic, salacious, or ironic). As a vernacular, Yiddish is becoming more heterologous—that is, regarding Yiddish as a full language for routine communications is increasingly at odds with the notion that it bears an intrinsic secondary level of meaning (of insularity, tradition, loss, alterity,

Fotocomic's "Kosher" set of "talking stickers" provides an assortment of Yiddish, Hebrew, and English expressions as humorous captions that can be adhered to snapshots. Copyright © Fotocomic, 80 E. 46th St., Hialeah FL 33013, 1986.

etc.). Conversely, postvernacular Yiddish grows more homologous, the limited, fragmentary use of the language conforming with its charged signification of a cultural incompleteness of some kind.

The atomization of Yiddish has also expanded the potential for reconceptualizing it as a semiotic system, in which its signifiers might be inflections, melodies, gestures, or objects more than (or even instead of) words. Or it can be conceived as a sensibility, engaged solely at the symbolic, "meta-" level of meaning. The implication of these developments is profound and, for some, very unsettling: they suggest that Yiddish culture does not require Yiddish fluency or, for that matter, any use of Yiddish at all. At the same time that these developments flout traditional notions of fluency, they create new possibilities for what might constitute Yiddish literacy. Thus, klezmorim demonstrate their status as Yiddish cultural authorities primarily by virtue of their musical expertise rather than by their traditional Jewish knowledge or practice of piety or by being well versed in modern Yiddish literature, folklore, or linguistics (although some klezmorim do have these skills as well). Conversely, vernacular Yiddish behavior has become performative. As other performance genres stand in for Yiddish vernacularity, speaking Yiddish has become an end in itself, and hence has been professionalized, becoming something akin to an art form.

Therefore, *rather than reaffirming Jewish identity, postvernacular Yiddish radically transforms it.* In doing so, postvernacularity liberates Yiddish from the fate of expiring with its dwindling population of native speakers born in Eastern Europe before World War II. Increasingly, Yiddish is learned as something other than a first language, sometimes taken up well after early childhood, thereby challenging the conventional definition of a "native" tongue. Postvernacularity flouts other established notions of identity: Yugntruf suspends the consequences of aging by identifying Yiddish speakers as forever young. Both Yeshivish and Queer Yiddishkeit challenge the traditional gendering of Yiddish, the former incorporating it into an all-male code, the latter claiming the alterity of Yiddish as an emblem of Jewish affinity for an "alternative" sexuality. This queering of Yiddish further suggests that as a modern cultural phenomenon it defies, rather than supports, traditional Jewish notions of familial and communal solidarity, thriving instead in alternative social configurations defined by the endlessly turbulent dynamic of coming of age.

Moreover, *Yiddish no longer serves as a marker of Ashkenazic or even Jewish cultural and demographic boundaries.* In some instances—notably, the use of Yiddish by *khareydim*—Yiddish divides rather than unites Ashkenazim, with use of the language intentionally marking internal distinctions in belief and stringency of practice. Besides reinforcing the use of Yiddish as a language of religious study, this new semiotic value of Yiddish has facilitated an innovative leisure culture for *khareydim*, ranging from board games for children to suspense fiction for adults. At the same time that its traditional population of speakers has abandoned the language in large numbers, Yiddish has become more available than ever before to non-Ashkenazic Jews and non-Jews. Their engagement ranges from using the handful of Yiddishisms that are part of the speech of many New Yorkers or Israelis, whatever their background, to the linguistic expertise of a considerable number of performers and scholars around the world. It is now even possible to find Yiddish culture realized in former centers of Ashkenazic civilization in Europe without the involvement of Ashkenazim (or Jews of any kind) themselves. Here, again, we encounter a disquieting mix of losses and gains.

Many of the cultural practices in which this dissolution of longstanding definitional boundaries marked by Yiddish takes place—notably in tourism, performance, and the academy—are of recent vintage. At the same time, the testing of boundaries has a long history in Yiddish culture; it can be traced through the history of the language itself and through the practice of translating into and from Yiddish. In the postvernacular mode, the act of translation takes readers not only away from Yiddish culture but also toward it and, in some instances, can even embody it.

This amulet, purchased in a souvenir shop in Israel in 2000, fuses traditional Mizrahi and Ashkenazic folkways for warding off the evil eye. The *hamsa*, a stylized hand shape used by North African Jews as a talisman, is inscribed with the Yiddish prophylactic phrase *tfu-tfu-tfu*.

As a postvernacular language, whose meta-meaning supercedes its value as a system for quotidian communications, *Yiddish has shifted from a cultural means to a cultural end*. Yiddish has become a topic of discussion more than an instrument of discussion. In the post-Holocaust era even the vernacular use of Yiddish has become an increasingly deliberate, self-conscious act, subsumed (or, at least, inflected) by the postvernacular mode. Absent the organicist or instinctual properties attributed to a native or first language, postvernacular Yiddish depends on a cultural motive of some kind for its existence. Consequently, language play, including ludic code-switching between Yiddish and another language, proves to be vital to the engagement with Yiddish in the postvernacular mode. No longer regarded as inevitable, or even as necessary, knowing Yiddish is a matter of election, of will—even for *khareydim*, and even for Yiddishists. ("Yes, Ashkenazi Jews can live without Yiddish, but I fail to see what the benefits thereof might be," writes Joshua Fishman, adding, "May God preserve us from having to live without all the things we *could* live without.")[45]

The notion of Yiddish as thriving in response to social and cultural change is hardly new. In his history of the language, Max Weinreich situates the ability to accommodate change by means of "vertical legitimation" as an inherent property of Ashkenazic culture. By such means "the golden chain is forged," leading back to the Talmud, the ultimate precedent for "a sanctioned constitutional procedure of change."[46] Yet the diverse phenomena of postvernacular Yiddish seem to test the very limits of what ties language to culture and of what constitutes the community connected one way or another to Yiddish, prompting some observers to ask, "What do we mean by Yiddish, anyway?"[47]

In contrast to Weinreich's notion of vertical legitimation—an "unceasing adjustment to constantly changing times," yet within a greater commitment to the "maintenance of the continuity of the Jewish community"—postvernacularity underscores the presence and the value of discontinuity as a productive force in Jewish culture.[48] The case of postvernacular Yiddish is replete with breaks along both diachronic and synchronic vectors. That there are those who believe Yiddish to be approaching or to have already reached its terminus reflects the prevalent notion that the continuity of Yiddish across time, however tumultuous it has been, has at last been dealt a fatal blow. Those calling for a "new Yiddish" of some kind—including linguistic and literary activity in other languages, wherein Yiddish is maintained as a meta-linguistic sensibility—seek an alternative to this finality as a way to sustain a sense of cultural vitality expressed in terms of continuity. Yet it is possible for vitality to emerge from discontinuity as well.

Thus, Gennady Estraikh characterizes a trend that he sees among some contemporary Yiddish writers as a "post-golden chain" phenomenon. Terming them "Esperantists," he distinguishes those writers who are drawn to Yiddish not because it embodies Ashkenazic heritage, but rather because they are "escapists trying to find a cultural oasis amid the dominant mass culture." For some of these writers, Yiddish serves as a "trans-rational language" or a *"zaum"* (that is, the "abstruse language" of Russian Futurism). Estraikh argues that, especially for the poets among these writers who have learned Yiddish as adults, it affords them "the possibility of writing in a language whose vocabulary is not burdened with irrelevant associations from the poets' everyday life and, as such, these words sound fresh, pristine and, in general, appropriate for describing the 'alien world' of poetry."[49] Following the trajectory of this model, Yiddish might become, in effect, an "imagined language." Loosed from its vernacular moorings and its literary and cultural heritage, Yiddish would gain infinite artistic potential to probe the limits of "tolerable linguistic deviance" and make its art out of "the disruptive force of linguistic slippage," as in James Joyce's *Finnegan's Wake* or Gertrude Stein's *Tender Buttons*.[50]

Jonathan Boyarin speaks more encouragingly about the synchronic discontinuity of contemporary Yiddish, arguing that "we must begin with the fragmentation of our language and encourage the possibilities of the various fragments." Modern Yiddish culture has always been polyvalent, but in the post-Holocaust era the differences among various Yiddish subcultures are seen not in terms of adjacent bands on a broad spectrum but as disparate, incomplete shards of a former whole. Boyarin invokes Peretz Markish's compelling image of a mirror shattered on a stone as a metaphor for this discontinuous state, which Boyarin also characterizes as "so many fragmented Torah-sparks of Yiddish that we study among others."[51] In fact, the various contemporary Yiddish subcultures do look to one another as points of reference and even, at times, influence. Not only does the Yiddish of today's hasidim figure as a compelling model of an imagined Ashkenazic past and as an exemplar of contemporary Yiddish vernacularity for those who are less traditionally observant or are outside the Jewish community altogether; American hasidim are also known on occasion to attend secular Yiddish theater productions, seeking inspiration for their own theatricals, and to consult Uriel Weinreich's *Modern English-Yiddish Yiddish-English Dictionary.*

That the discontinuities of Yiddish in the post-Holocaust era can stimulate cultural creativity points up the importance of self-consciousness in the postvernacular mode. The deliberate and reflexive nature of so much of contemporary Yiddish culture may mark it as suspect in the eyes of some observers, as a painful consequence of the loss of an "automatic" traditional Ashkenazic vernacularity, or even as inimical to "authentic" *yidishkeyt*. However, these properties might also be seen as an inevitable consequence of the Yiddish-speaking world's encounters with modernity and perhaps even as a development that now enables and enhances, rather than hinders, cultural innovation. Such self-awareness allows one to account for and accommodate the disparities and contradictions of Yiddish in the postvernacular era; it facilitates the essential ability to look both forward and backward in time, within Jewish cultural borders as well as beyond them. Self-consciousness demands not only an open mind with regard to contemporary Yiddish culture but an informed one as well. Therefore, self-consciousness can also serve as a check on the vectors of diachronic and synchronic discontinuity as they probe the limits of metalanguage, by prompting important questions about the implications of the dissolution of Yiddish into a handful of words or about that quality of a Yiddish culture

"O.K., who said 'Mazel tov?'"

Cartoon by Peter Steiner, published in *The New Yorker* on June 17, 2002.
Copyright © *The New Yorker* Collection, 2002. Courtesy Peter Steiner from cartoonbank.com. All Rights Reserved.

that is completely divorced from the Yiddish language, from Jewish traditions, or from Jews.

Finally, there is a need to consider discussions about Yiddish, such as the one I have offered in this book, as a distinct cultural phenomenon, not to be conflated with or judged against similar discussions undertaken in Yiddish. Discussions about Yiddish in another language underscore the extent to which it has become a meta-language, often standing in for extralinguistic interests—Jewish cultural and de-mographic continuity, Jewish memory, Jewish authenticity, Jewish heritage, Jewish alterity. These discussions are, inevitably, at some remove from un–self-reflexive use of the language itself, but as such they can afford a perspective on Yiddish that perhaps cannot be seen so readily from within. Nor should this distance be thought of simply as a one-way street moving away from Yiddish. These discussions can also encourage new approaches to the language, stimulating desires to renegotiate the distance between its pasts and one's present, and opening up prospects for more adventures with Yiddish in the future.

∎ ∎ ∎

On a summer evening in 2003 I attend a meeting in Manhattan, organized by Yugntruf, to hear about the current state of Yiddish in Israel from Assaf Galai, a founding member of Hemshekh-dor (Generation of Continuity). This group of young Israelis has drafted a manifesto in which they call on their fellow Israelis to reconnect with Ashkenazic heritage and to recognize the value of Yiddish as a resource for Israeli Jews today. Hemshekh-dor argues that this rethinking of their identity as Israelis will not only be to their own benefit but will have a positive impact their on relations with Palestinians and the Arab world.[52]

Yugntruf's corresponding secretary, Sholem Berger, who has convened the meeting, interviews Galai in Yiddish about Hemshekh-dor, its goals, and related issues concerning Yiddish in Israel. At times Galai struggles to formulate his answers in Yiddish; Berger and others in attendance politely help him out with the vocabulary he gropes for. (Galai is in New York to study at the Yiddish Summer Program run by YIVO at Columbia University.) At times it isn't clear to me whether Galai can't fully articulate the rationale behind his quest for Ashkenazic heritage in its traditional language, which he is in the process of learning, or whether the ideas themselves are still somewhat inchoate.

Therefore it is simultaneously a frustrating event and an inspiring one for me (and, I think, for at least some of the others who attend the meeting). Although it is the evening's common language, Yiddish is not its vernacular. Rather, Yiddish serves as the catalyst for engagement, linking the conversation with a larger, imagined project, borne out of desires to reconfigure the roles of language and culture in a radically redefined sense of self. The conversation with Galai would proceed much more easily in Hebrew or, perhaps, English, but then it would lose a revealing stratum of meaning.

Galai and his cohorts bring the youthful energy of dissatisfaction with the status quo to their quest for Yiddish, a desire that has animated modern Yiddish culture for generations. Their grand, sweeping desires collide with the painstaking challenge of mastering Yiddish at the turn of the twenty-first century—but rather than proving to be a frustration, it animates and directs the members of Hemshekh-dor. Yiddish is not a dead end for them but more like a detour or scenic route, one that brings the traveler unexpected discoveries along the way. Indeed, to find his way "back" to Ashkenaz, Galai has traveled a circuitous path, from Israel (where he studies Yiddish at Bar-Ilan University) to New York and then back again. As he traverses oceans and continents, Galai also leaps across temporal boundaries and ideological epochs, his transmigrations moving him away from one sense of home to bring him closer to another, looking backward to move forward. It is a journey, as he characterizes it, "to Yiddishland."

NOTES

INTRODUCTION

1. In 2001 the sociolinguist Joshua A. Fishman estimated that there were about 250,000 Yiddish speakers in the United States, approximately the same number in Israel, and another approximately 100,000 elsewhere in the world. Paul Glasser, email message to author, 14 May 2003. Fishman discusses the challenge of determining the number of Yiddish speakers in "How Many Jews Speak Yiddish?" (in Yiddish), *Afn shvel* 316 (October–December 1999): 22.

2. See Miriam Isaacs, "*Haredi, Haymish* and *Frim:* Yiddish Vitality and Language Choice in a Transnational, Multilingual Community," *International Journal of the Sociology of Language* 138 (1999): 9–30; Lewis H. Glinert, "We Never Changed Our Language: Attitudes to Yiddish Acquisition among Hasidic Educators in Britain," *International Journal of the Sociology of Language* 138 (1999): 31–52; Fishman, "How Many Jews Speak Yiddish?" 22.

3. Based on a keyword search for "Yiddish" of UMI Proquest Digital Dissertations (www.lib.umi.com/dissertations). See Jeffrey Shandler, "The State of Yiddish Studies: Some Observations and Thoughts," *Conservative Judaism* 54, no. 4 (summer 2002): 69–77.

4. Ruth R. Wisse, "Yiddish: Past, Present, Imperfect," *Commentary* 104, no. 5 (November 1997): 37, 39.

5. Ashkenaz, the biblical term (Genesis 10:3) with which Jews designated German lands during the Middle Ages, subsequently came to identify a distinctive diaspora Jew-

ish cultural tradition (including liturgy, holiday customs, foodways, and language) and its community of practitioners. Ashkenazim eventually became the majority Jewish population in Europe and, later, around the world.

6. Gersh Kuntzman, "Subway Learns Joy of Yiddish," *New York Post*, 13 May 2004.

7. Charlotte Yiddish Institute (mailing), March 2004. See also Jon G. Auerbach, "They Can't Spell It, Can't Pronounce It and Don't Get It: So Why Does Every Tom, Dick and Herschel Use Yiddish? If You Do, Too, Mazel Tov," *Wall Street Journal*, 2 June 1988.

8. Joshua A. Fishman, "The Sociology of Yiddish: A Foreword," in *Never Say Die! A Thousand Years of Yiddish in Jewish Life and Letters* (The Hague: Mouton, 1981), 1.

9. Translation of the couplet from Joachim Neugroschel, ed. and trans., *No Star Too Beautiful: An Anthology of Yiddish Stories from 1382 to the Present* (New York: Norton and Co., 2002), xiv. On the couplet itself, see Dov Sadan, "The Oldest Rhyme in Yiddish" (in Yiddish), *Di goldene keyt* 47 (1963): 158–59.

10. Benjamin Harshav, *The Meaning of Yiddish* (Berkeley and Los Angeles: University of California Press, 1990), 91.

11. See Jerold C. Frakes, *The Politics of Interpretation: Alterity and Ideology in Old Yiddish Studies* (Albany, N.Y.: SUNY Press, 1989).

12. Jeffrey A. Grossman, *The Discourse on Yiddish in Germany from the Enlightenment to the Second Empire* (Rochester, N.Y.: Camden House, 2000), 24–25.

13. Steven E. Aschheim, *Brothers and Strangers: The East European Jew in German and German Jewish Consciousness* (Madison: University of Wisconsin Press, 1982), 8.

14. Sander L. Gilman, *Jewish Self-Hatred: Anti-Semitism and the Hidden Language of the Jews* (Baltimore: Johns Hopkins University Press, 1986), 18, 312.

15. George Steiner, *After Babel: Aspects of Language and Translation*, 3rd. ed. (Oxford and New York: Oxford University Press, 1998), 89.

16. For example, in *Di kremerkes, oder Golde Mine di broder agune* (The Female Shopkeepers, or Golde Mine, the Abandoned Wife of Brody) (Vilna, 1865), Dik glosses *rundung* (surroundings) as *svive* (4), *laydenshaft* (passion) as *tayve* (8), and *protses* (trial) as *mishpet* (30).

17. Christopher Hutton, "Normativism and the Notion of Authenticity in Yiddish Linguistics," in *Field of Yiddish: Studies in Language, Folklore, and Literature, Fifth Collection*, ed. David Goldberg (Evanston, Ill.: Northwestern University Press, 1993), 14.

18. "*Undzer tsikhtik loshn*" (Our Well-kept Tongue), in Yankev Glatshteyn, *Gedenklider* (Memorial Poems) (New York: Farlag yidisher kemfer, 1943), 82–84.

19. See Jeremy Eichler, "Klezmer's Final Frontier," *New York Times*, 29 August 2004.

20. *Brave Old World: Beyond the Pale* (Hamburg: Pinorrekk Musikverlag, 1993), 5, 30–31 (compact disc booklet). Used with permission of Michael Alpert. The English translation of the song lyrics is Alpert's. In the booklet, the lyrics are printed in Yiddish in the *alefbeys*, romanized according to a German orthography and translated into both

German and English. I have romanized the Yiddish lyrics here according to the YIVO standard.

21. At the same time, linguists occasionally call attention to the role of Yiddish as a formative element of modern Israeli Hebrew. See, for example, Ghil'ad Zuckermann, *Haivrit kemitos: aẕ eẕo safa haisraelim medabrim?* (Hebrew as Myth: So What Language Do Israelis Speak?) (Tel Aviv: Am Oved, forthcoming).

22. See Joshua A. Fishman and David E. Fishman, "Yiddish in Israel: A Case-Study of Efforts to Revise a Monocentric Language Policy," *International Journal of the Sociology of Language* 1 (1974): 125–46.

23. See, for example, Zerubovl (Jacob Vitkin), "We Accuse and Demand Responsibility!" (in Yiddish), in *Yidish in erets yisroel* (Yiddish in the Land of Israel), 1936, reprinted in Fishman, ed., *Never Say Die!*, 297–311. For a broader discussion of this issue, see Arye Leyb Pilowsky, *Tsvishn yo un neyn: yidish un yidish-literatur in Erets-Yisroel, 1907–1948* (Between Yes and No: Yiddish and Yiddish Literature in Palestine, 1907–1948) (Tel-Aviv: Veltrat far yidish un yidisher kultur, 1986).

24. "Compromise Settles Fight Over Showing of Initial Yiddish Talkie in Tel Aviv," *Jewish Daily Bulletin* (New York), 30 September 1930.

25. See Mordecai Kosover, *Arabic Elements in Palestinian Yiddish: The Old Ashkenaẕic Jewish Community in Palestine, Its History and Its Language* (Jerusalem: Rubin Mass, 1966).

26. Mordkhe Tsanin, "About the Yiddish Bulletins of the Eichmann Trial" (in Yiddish), *Jewish Daily Forward*, 16 April 1961.

27. *A Homage to Yiddish: Special Session of the Knesset Dedicated to the Yiddish Language and Yiddish Culture* (Jerusalem: World Council for Yiddish and Jewish Culture; Association of Yiddish Writers and Journalists in Israel, 1993), 3–4 (English); cf. 3–4 (Hebrew), 25–26 (Yiddish).

28. Leo Rosten, *The Joys of Yiddish* (New York: McGraw-Hill, 1968), xxi. If this joke is told in Yiddish, then the double meaning of the word *yidish*—as both "Yiddish" and "Jewish"—would be juxtaposed against the word *yid* (Jew) more explicitly. As told here in English, the contested tautological relationship between language and people is less directly articulated.

29. I was told this joke by Naomi Prawer Kadar in New York in about 1990.

30. Efrat Shalom, "The Great Yiddish Comeback," *Haaretẕ*, 18 May 2003 (English edition online at www.haaretzdaily.com). See also Sore-Rohl Shekhter, "Young Sabras Cling to Yiddish" (in Yiddish), *Forverts*, 15 August 2003; Ruti Roso, "The New Ashkenazim" (in Hebrew), *Ma'ariv*, 14 September 2004 (English edition online at www.maarivintl.com); Kobi Vaytser, "Ashkenazic and Proud!" (in Yiddish), *Forverts*, 23 September 2003.

31. "The Aria 'Rachel'," in *Cantors in Yiddish: Arias, Operetta, Folk Songs, and Chassidic Songs by Famous Cantors*, audiocassette, no. IMC 1110, Israel Music, n.d. Though undated, this is apparently an early post–World War II recording. Koussevitzky, a renowned

cantor in Warsaw before World War II, immigrated to the United States in 1947; he continued performing into the 1960s and died in 1966. Singing this aria in Yiddish, which was once a frequent practice among Ashkenazic cantors (a performance of "Di arye 'Rokhl' " by Yosef Shlisky is also included in *Cantors in Yiddish*) is in itself a provocative act, since the translation appears to "restore" the aria to the "original" language of its Jewish protagonist (the opera is set in fifteenth-century Constance). The translation thereby underscores the tension between the style and milieu of French grand opera and this opera's historical subject of anti-Semitism in Europe at the end of the Middle Ages.

32. Max Weinreich, *History of the Yiddish Language*, trans. Shlomo Noble (Chicago: University of Chicago Press, 1980), 280.

33. Harshav, *The Meaning of Yiddish*, 119, 122, 123.

34. The estimated number of Czech speakers on the eve of World War II is 8,500,000; Dutch speakers estimated at 10,000,000; and Greek speakers at 5,500,000. Henry Oswald Coleman, "Language," in *1938 Britannica Book of the Year*, ed. Franklin H. Hooper and Walter Yust (Chicago: Encyclopaedia Britannica, 1938), 380.

35. Leo Wiener, *The History of Yiddish Literature in the Nineteenth Century* (New York: Charles Scribner's Sons, 1899), 12.

36. See D. A. Eliashevich, *Pravitel'stvennaia politika i evreiskaia pechat' v Rossii, 1797–1917, ocherki istorii tsenzury* (Government Policy and the Jewish Press in Russia 1797–1917: An Historical Overview of Censorship) (St. Petersburg and Jerusalem: Mosty kul'tury/Gesharim, 1999).

37. See, for example, Eugene C. Black, "Lucien Wolf and the Making of Poland: Paris, 1919," in *From Shtetl to Socialism: Studies from Polin*, ed. Antony Polonsky (London: Littman Library of Jewish Civilization, 1993), 277–78; Rick Kuhn, "The Jewish Social Democratic Party of Galicia and the Bund," in *Jewish Politics in Eastern Europe: The Bund at 100*, ed. Jack Jacobs (New York: New York University Press, 2001), 134.

38. Joshua Rubenstein and Vladimir P. Naumov, eds., *Stalin's Secret Pogrom: The Postwar Inquisition of the Jewish Anti-Fascist Committee* (New Haven, Conn.: Yale University Press, 2001), 231.

39. Khayem S. Kazdan (Chaim Kazdan), "An Important Task" (in Yiddish), in *Fragn fun dertsiung: Zamlheft* (Questions of Pedagogy: Collected Essays) (Vilna: Farlag "TsYShO," March 1940), 9–10.

40. Maks Vaynraykh (Max Weinreich), "After the War Our Yiddish Language Will Not Be the Same as It Is Now" (in Yiddish), *Jewish Daily Forward*, 28 December 1941.

41. Bernard Goldstein, *The Stars Bear Witness*, trans. Leonard Shatzkin (New York: Viking, 1949), 277.

42. Jonathan Sarna, *American Judaism: A History* (New Haven, Conn.: Yale University Press, 2004), 274.

43. Nathan Glazer, *American Judaism*, 2nd rev. ed. (1957; repr., Chicago: University of Chicago Press, 1989), 108.

44. Sammy Levenson, *Meet The Folks: A Session of American-Jewish Humor* (1946; repr., New York: Citadel, 1951), 119, 121, 108.

45. Clyde Haberman, "The Oys of Yiddish (Ignore at Your Peril)," *New York Times*, 22 October 2000.

46. See Michael Berenbaum, *The World Must Know: The History of the Holocaust as Told in the United States Holocaust Memorial Museum* (Boston: Little, Brown, 1993), 92.

47. Samy Feder, "The Yiddish Theater of Belsen," in *Theatrical Performance during the Holocaust: Texts, Documents, Memoirs*, ed. Rebecca Rovit and Alvin Goldfard (Baltimore: Johns Hopkins University Press, 1999), 157. This memoir was originally published in *Belsen* (Tel Aviv: Irgun Sheerit Hopleita Me'Haezor Habriti, 1957).

48. Joseph Leftwich, ed., *The Golden Peacock: A Worldwide Treasury of Yiddish Poetry* (New York: Thomas Yoseloff, 1961), 20.

49. See, for example, Glatshteyn's poems "Reyd" (Speech), 167, and "An os" (A Letter of the Alphabet), 172, in *Dem tatns shotn* (Father's Shadow) (New York: Farlag "Matones," 1953); "Bloyz kol" (Only Voice), 78, and "Di freyd fun yidishn vort" (The Joy of the Yiddish Word), 203–206, in *Di freyd fun yidishn vort* (The Joy of the Yiddish Word) (New York: Der kval, 1961).

50. From "Yiddish," in Abraham Sutzkever, *Selected Poetry and Prose*, trans. Barbara and Benjamin Harshav (Berkeley and Los Angeles: University of California Press, 1991), 214. Copyright © 1991 The Regents of the University of California, used with permission of the University of California Press.

51. Memo from Samuel Norich, "Forward Association Constitutional Purposes and Objects," 11 February 2002, 2. According to Norich, the Forward Association adopted a mission statement in 2003 that it "exists to promote and strengthen Jewish peoplehood, Yiddish culture, and social and economic justice" (Norich to author, 28 May 2003).

52. David Lowenthal, *The Heritage Crusade and the Spoils of History* (Cambridge: Cambridge University Press, 1988), 5.

53. See, for example, Elenore Lester, "Yiddish Comes out of the Shtetl," *New York Times Magazine*, 2 December 1979, 192–98; Ron Avery, "Oy Vey, Such a Language: Yiddish Making a Comeback in the U.S.," *Philadelphia Daily News*, 8 May 1990.

54. "Two New Yiddish Journals by and for Young People!" (in Yiddish), *Forverts*, 14 February 2003, 13.

55. J. Hoberman and Jeffrey Shandler, "The Media That 'Speak Your Language': American Yiddish Radio and Film," in Hoberman and Shandler, eds., *Entertaining America: Jews, Movies and Broadcasting* (Princeton, N.J.: Princeton University Press, 2003), 104.

56. "Daf Hashavua: Talmudic Seminar in the Air" (mailing) (Elizabeth, N.J.: Jewish Educational Center), 2003.

57. David Michael, "Commentary: Connections between Yiddish and Hip-Hop Music" (transcript), *Morning Edition*, National Public Radio, 29 November, 2002. Copyright © NPR® 2002. Any unauthorized duplication is strictly prohibited.

58. David A. Hollinger, *Postethnic America* (New York: Basic Books, 1995), 6.

59. For a range of case studies, see Joshua A. Fishman, ed., *Can Threatened Languages Be Saved? Reversing Language Shift, Revisited: A 21st Century Perspective* (Clevedon, Eng.: Multilingual Matters, 2001).

60. Albert Memmi, *The Liberation of the Jew*, trans. Judy Hyun (New York: Orion Press, 1966), 182; "Argon," in Primo Levi, *The Periodic Table*, trans. Raymond Rosenthal (New York: Schocken, 1984), 3–20.

61. On Powell's knowledge of Yiddish, see, for example, Zellig Bach, "Exclusive Interview in Yiddish with Colin Powell," *Mendele: Yiddish Literature and Language* 5.137 (11 October 1995), item 1, http://shakti.trincoll.edu/~mendele/vol05/vol05.137. The Urban Legends Reference Pages validates the claim that "as a teenager, U.S. Secretary of State Colin Powell learned to speak Yiddish while working in a Jewish-owned baby equipment store in New York," www.snopes.com/glurge/powell.htm. On Madonna singing in Yiddish, see, for example, "The Singer Madonna Also Sings Yiddish Songs!" (in Yiddish), *Forverts*, 30 July 2000. The discussion of non-Jews' comprehension and use of Yiddish is wide-ranging and has continued throughout the twentieth century; for example, it is mentioned by Sholem Aleichem in his fiction (e.g, his 1902 story "Di groyse behole fun di kleyne mentshelekh" [The Great Confusion of the Little People]), by Chaim Zhitlowski in his memoirs (discussed in chapter 1 of this book), and by H. L. Mencken in his *The American Language: A Preliminary Inquiry into the Development of English in the United States* (New York: Knopf, 1919). As a running issue in the United States, see, for example, Leo Robbins, "How Many Yiddish Words Do *You* Know?" *Jewish Daily Forward*, 16 May 1926; Wallace Markfield, "The Yiddishization of American Humor," *Esquire* (October 1965): 114, 115, 136; Lillian Mermin Feinsilver, *The Taste of Yiddish* (Cranbury, N.J.: Thomas Yoseloff, 1970); Sol Steinmetz, *Yiddish and English: A Century of Yiddish in America* (Tuscaloosa: University of Alabama Press, 1986).

62. See, for example, Andrew Dalby, *Language in Danger: The Loss of Linguistic Diversity and the Threat to Our Future* (New York: Columbia University Press, 2003).

63. See Barbara Kirshenblatt-Gimblett, "The Folk Culture of Jewish Immigrant Communities: Research Paradigms and Directions," in *The Jews of North America*, ed. Moses Rischin (Detroit: Wayne State University Press, 1987), especially 86–89.

64. A very different trajectory for Yiddish over the course of the twentieth century can be traced by centering the analysis elsewhere, especially in Palestine/Israel or Russia/the Soviet Union. On the former, see Pilowsky, *Tsvishn yo un neyn;* on the latter, see Gennady Estraikh, *Soviet Yiddish: Language Planning and Linguistic Development* (Oxford: Clarendon, 1999).

65. A telling example of this is found in the publications of ArtScroll, a Jewish press based in Brooklyn and established in the mid-1970s, which provides an extensive inventory of texts, including *sforim* (sacred works), for Orthodox Jews whose native language is English. See Jeremy Stolow, "Communicating Authority, Consuming Tradi-

tion: Jewish Orthodox Outreach Literature and Its Reading Public," in *Religion, Media and the Public Sphere,* ed. Birgit Meyer and Annelies Moors (Bloomington: Indiana University Press, forthcoming).

1. IMAGINING YIDDISHLAND

1. Michael Chabon, "Guidebook to a Land of Ghosts," *Civilization* (June/July 1997): 67–69; idem, "The Language of Lost History," *Harper's,* October 1997, 32–33.

2. These illustrations appear only in the *Civilization* version of the essay. Katchor is no stranger to inventing landscapes; see, for example, the unnamed retrograde urban setting of his *Julius Knipl, Real Estate Photographer: Stories* (Boston: Little, Brown, 1996) or *The Jew of New York* (New York: Pantheon, 1998), an imaginary work about Jewish life in the state during the nineteenth century. Katchor has also designed murals for the core exhibition of the National Yiddish Book Center.

3. Chabon, "Guidebook," 67–69.

4. Beatrice Weinreich, interview by author, YIVO Institute, New York, November 1998.

5. Even more provocative, perhaps, are more recent Yiddish phrase books for speakers of German, Italian, and Japanese. See Arnold Groh, *Jiddisch Wort für Wort* (Yiddish Word for Word) (Bielefeld, Ger.: Verlag Peter Rump, 1997); Davide Astori, *Parlo Yiddish: Manuele di Conversazione* (I Speak Yiddish: Conversation Guide) (Milan: Antonio Vallardi, 2000); K. Ueda, *Idisshugo jō yō: 6000-go* (6,000 Commonly Used Yiddish words) (Tokyo: Daigaku kan rin, 1993).

6. Elisheva Schwartz, "Yiddish Spoken Here" (letter to the editor), *Harper's,* January 1998, 8. Other letters, including a response by Beatrice Weinreich, appear in *Civilization* (Aug./Sept. 1997): 15. See also Janet Hadda's discussion of *Say It in Yiddish* and of Chabon's article in her essay "Yiddish in Contemporary American Culture," in *Yiddish in the Contemporary World: Papers of the First Mendel Friedman International Conference on Yiddish* (Oxford: LEGENDA European Research Centre, University of Oxford, 1999), 93–105.

7. Chabon offered something of an apology in a presentation entitled "Dangerous Territory: Misadventures in Yiddishland," presented at the conference "Yiddish on the American Scene," University of California, Los Angeles, 29 October 2000, which I attended. While insisting that a Yiddish phrase book for travelers serves "no imaginable purpose," he admitted to discovering from the heated response to his essay that there is a "virtue in its uselessness" as an act of cultural defiance. Since then, Chabon has apparently begun to conjure a Yiddishland of his own. In an interview published in 2002, he reported working on "a thriller set in an alternate reality where . . . there's a Yiddish-speaking Jewish state in lower Alaska." See Meryl Gordon, "Child's Play," *New York,* 9 September 2002.

8. Although I don't remember who said this or exactly when he or she said it, I do recall that the comment, made in Yiddish, was greeted with a burst of applause.

9. The term *Yid(d)ishland* does appear in the glossaries of two recent French publications: "Yidishland (Y): désigne la vaste aire géographique et culturelle dans laquelle se parlait le yiddish" in *Mille ans de cultures ashkenazes* (One Thousand Years of Ashkenazic Culture), ed. Jean Baumgarten et al. (Paris: Liana Levi, 1998), 626; and "Yiddishland: vaste aire géographique ou territoire linguistique et culturelle du yiddish," in *Lituanie juive 1918–1940: Message d'un monde englouti* (Lithuanian Jewry 1918–1940: Message from a Vanished Land), ed. Yves Plasseraud and Henri Minczeles (Paris: Editions Autrement, 1996), 283.

10. Uriel Weinreich, *Modern English-Yiddish Yiddish-English Dictionary* (New York: McGraw-Hill, 1968), 573/220.

11. Nakhmen Mayzil, ed., *Briv un redes fun Y. L. Perets* (Letters and Speeches of Y. L. Peretz) (New York: YKUF, 1944), 139. Peretz continues to explain that he, in contrast to Sholem Aleichem, writes for himself, for his own pleasure. The term *zhargon*, sometimes used as a synonym for Yiddish in the late nineteenth century (including by Sholem Aleichem), appears to be used here in a derogatory sense. Elsewhere in the letter, Peretz uses the term *yidish*.

12. Benjamin and Barbara Harshav, *American Yiddish Poetry: A Bilingual Anthology* (Berkeley and Los Angeles: University of California Press, 1986), 22. Ruth Wisse makes a similar assertion in her discussion of *The Penguin Book of Modern Yiddish Verse*, the 1987 anthology of Yiddish poetry she co-edited with Irving Howe and Chone Shmeruk: "The homeland of Yiddish poetry is where the Jewish people makes its home." Ruth R. Wisse, *What Shall Live and What Shall Die: The Makings of a Yiddish Anthology*, Annual Rabbi Louis Feinberg Memorial Lecture in Judaic Studies, 12 (Cincinnati: University of Cincinnati, Judaic Studies Program, 1989), 26.

13. J. Hoberman, *Bridge of Light: Yiddish Film Between Two Worlds* (New York: Schocken, 1991), 5.

14. Abraham Burg, "Yiddish Is the Language of Life," *A Homage to Yiddish: Special Session of the Knesset Dedicated to the Yiddish Language and Yiddish Culture* (Jerusalem: World Council for Yiddish and Jewish Culture; Association of Yiddish Writers and Journalists in Israel, 1993), 10 (English), 8 (Hebrew), 32 (Yiddish).

15. On the Yiddishland Cafe, see, for example, the electronic journal *Mendele: Yiddish Literature and Language*, 8.042 (13 August 1998), item 6, http://shakti.trincoll .edu/~mendele/vol08/vol8.042. For Yiddishland Records, see www.yiddishland records.com; for Yugntruf, see www.yugntruf.org.

16. George Steiner, "Our Homeland, the Text," *Salmagundi* 66 (Winter/Spring 1985): 4–25; Czesław Miłosz, "Moja wierna mowo / My Faithful Mother Tongue," *The Separate Notebooks*, trans. Robert Hass and Robert Pinsky et al. (New York: Ecco Press, 1984), 192–93. (The poem's colophon reads, "Berkeley, 1968.")

17. On *doikeyt* and the concept of diaspora nationalism generally, see Ezra Mendelsohn, *On Modern Jewish Politics* (Oxford and New York: Oxford University Press, 1993).

18. Khayem Zhitlovski (Chaim Zhitlowski), *Geklibene verk* (Selected Works), ed.

Yudel Mark (New York: CYCO, 1955), 321–23. This essay was first printed in *Yidishe velt* in 1913, with the subtitle "How I Became a Yiddishist."

19. Benedict Anderson, *Imagined Communities: Reflections on the Origin and Spread of Nationalism*, rev. ed. (London: Verso, 1991), 6.

20. As cited in Chimen Abramsky, "The Biro-Bidzhan Project, 1927–1959," in *The Jews in Soviet Russia since 1917*, 3rd ed., ed. Lionel Kochan (Oxford and New York: Oxford University Press, 1978), 71.

21. Robert Weinberg, *Stalin's Forgotten Zion: Birobidzhan and the Making of a Soviet Jewish Homeland* (Berkeley and Los Angeles: University of California Press/Judah L. Magnes Museum, 1998), 59.

22. At the same time, the symbolic value of Birobidzhan for Yiddish-speaking Jews living outside the Soviet Union may be more in keeping with Yiddishlands as exercises in the cultural imaginary. Gennady Estraikh notes, in particular, that the left-wing American Yiddishist summer camp Kinderland, located in Hopewell Junction, N.Y., used to stage imaginary visits to Birobidzhan for campers in a remote, forested corner of the campgrounds. "Ingathering of the Proletarian Exiles: Soviet Jewish Nation Building in the Crimea, Ukraine, and Birobidzhan" (paper presented at the Second Annual Berkeley Yiddish Conference, University of California, Berkeley, 24 May 2004).

23. Jenna Weissman Joselit, "The Jewish Way of Play," in *A Worthy Use of Summer: Jewish Summer Camping in America*, ed. Jenna Weissman Joselit and Karen S. Mittelman (Philadelphia: National Museum of American Jewish History, 1993), 14.

24. The founders of Camp Yidishland explain that the name was selected so that the camp would serve as a "firm bulwark against the great, disruptive force of assimilation that assails our offspring, our continuity." See *30 yor gezelshaft far yidish-veltlekhe shuln in Argentine, 1931–1961: yovl-oysgabe* (Thirty Years of the Society for Secular Yiddish Schools in Argentina, 1931–1961: Anniversary Edition) (Buenos Aires, October 1961), n.p.

25. On Catalan, see Robert Hughes, *Barcelona* (New York: Knopf, 1992); on Welsh, see John Aitchison and Harold Carter, *Language, Economy and Society: The Changing Fortunes of the Welsh Language in the Twentieth Century* (Cardiff: University of Wales Press, 2000).

26. Yankev Botoshanski, "A Demonstration in the Capital of 'Yiddishland' " (in Yiddish), *Literarishe bleter*, no. 34 (589) (23 August 1935): 543.

27. Lucy S. Dawidowicz, *From That Place and Time: A Memoir, 1938–1947* (New York: Norton, 1989), 100–101. See also Cecile Kuznitz, "On the Jewish Street: Yiddish Culture and the Urban Landscape in Interwar Vilna," in *Yiddish Language and Culture: Then and Now*, Studies in Jewish Civilization 9, ed. Leonard Jay Greenspoon (Omaha, Nebr.: Creighton University Press, 1998), 65–92.

28. Y. Slovatski (Juljusz Słowacki), *Der foter fun farpestikte* (The Father of the Lepers), trans. L. Popik (1938; repr. Tel Aviv: Farlag "Eygns," 1973), 4.

29. Yitskhok Grudberg, "A Declining City in Yiddishland" (in Yiddish), *Literarishe bleter*, no. 2 (713) (7 January 1938): 26.

30. See, for example, Shmuel Rozhansky, ed., *Antologye: yidish in lid* (Anthology: Yiddish in Poetry) (Buenos Aires: Literatur-gezelshaft baym YIVO in Argentine, 1967), which includes 169 such poems by seventy-four poets.

31. The full text of the poem appears in *Di lider fun Avrom Reyzen in tsvelf teyln* (The Poems of Abraham Reisen, in Twelve Sections) (New York: Shulsinger Brothers, 1951), 264.

32. A. Almi, "Yidish," in *Far yidish: a zamlbukh* (For Yiddish: An Anthology), ed. S. Edberg (New York: National Council of Young Israel, 1930), 59–60.

33. Sidra DeKoven Ezrahi, *Booking Passage: Exile and Homecoming in the Modern Jewish Imagination* (Berkeley and Los Angeles: University of California Press, 2000), 14, 10.

34. Leon Feinberg, *Yidish: poeme* (Yiddish: A Narrative Poem) (New York: Shaulzakh druk, 1950), 1.

35. Jack Kugelmass and Jonathan Boyarin, eds., *From a Ruined Garden: The Memorial Books of Polish Jewry* (New York: Schocken, 1983), 2.

36. Marvin Herzog et al., *The Language and Culture Atlas of Ashkenazic Jewry*, vol. 1, *Historical and Theoretical Foundations* (Tübingen: Max Niemeyer, 1992), vol. 2, *Research Tools* (1995), vol. 3, *The Eastern Yiddish-Western Yiddish Continuum* (2000).

37. Uriel Weinreich, "Mapping a Culture," *Columbia University Forum* 6, no. 3 (1963): 17 (emphasis original).

38. Weinreich, "Mapping a Culture," 17–19.

39. Abraham Joshua Heschel, *The Earth Is the Lord's: The Inner World of the Jew in Eastern Europe* (New York: Farrar Straus Giroux, 1978), 15.

40. On more recent efforts to consider the territoriality of the Ashkenazim, see Neil G. Jacobs and Joseph C. Loon, "The Geography of Ashkenaz: On the Development of an Ethno-Geographic Information System (EGIS)," *Shofar* 10, no. 4 (summer 1992): 6–30.

41. According to Szonja Komoroczy, *Handl erlikh* was created by a Hungarian Hasid who took his inspiration from a Hungarian board game, *Gazdálkodj Okosan* (Deal Wisely), an anticapitalist version of *Monopoly* created in the 1950s. The creator of *Handl erlikh* was inspired to adapt the Hungarian game to teach hasidic, rather than communist, values. Szonja Komoroczy, "Hungarian Yiddish after the Holocaust" (paper presented at the International Conference on Yiddish after the Holocaust, Oxford Centre for Hebrew and Jewish Studies, 2003).

42. *Handl erlikh* (board game).

43. One of these penalty cards reads: "You conversed with each other in English! Speaking Yiddish separates us from gentiles!" The penalty for this transgression is losing three turns. On another penalty card, the speaker of modern Hebrew is denounced as a Zionist.

44. *Kfitsas haderekh*, Kiryas Tahsh, Canada, 1996–97 (board game).

45. Gérard Silvain and Henri Minczeles, *Yiddishland* (Corte Madera, Calif.: Ginko Press, 1999), 7, 33. The book was originally published under the same title in a French-language edition by Hazan (Paris) earlier in 1999. For further discussion of this volume,

see my review, "Postcards from a Land That Never Was," *Forward* (English-language edition), 28 January 2000.

46. Silvain and Minczeles, *Yiddishland*, 7, 9, 11, 30.

47. Silvain and Minczeles, *Yiddishland*, 7.

48. "Abraham Sutzkever" (in Yiddish), *Yedies fun YIVO/YIVO News* 170 (Winter 1986/87): 14.

49. Anita Norich, "Yiddish Literary Studies," *Modern Judaism* 10, no. 3 (October 1990): 300. See also Naomi Seidman, *A Marriage Made in Heaven: The Sexual Politics of Hebrew and Yiddish* (Berkeley and Los Angeles: University of California Press, 1997), 135.

50. Ezrahi, *Booking Passage*, 4.

51. Michael Wex, *Born to Kvetsh* (New York: St. Martin's Press, forthcoming).

52. Gennady Estraikh and Mikhail Krutikov, eds., *The Shtetl: Image and Reality: Papers of the Second Mendel Friedman International Conference on Yiddish* (Oxford: Legenda, 2000), 5.

53. Email to Jeffrey Shandler from Nikolai Borodulin, 6 November 2003. Borodulin, Assistant Director of the Center for Cultural Jewish Life of the Workmen's Circle in New York City, began offering these programs in 1997.

54. "The New Home of the National Yiddish Book Center," *The Book Peddler/Der pakn-treger* 19 (Summer 1994): 8, 29, 30.

55. The naming of the NYBC as a "national" institution breaks with a precedent set by older Yiddishist organizations, which more frequently name themselves as *alveltlikhe* (international), rather than *natsyonale*, when they wish to articulate broadness of scope.

56. Email to Jeffrey Shandler from Eric Gordon, 20 September 1998.

57. Barbara Kirshenblatt-Gimblett, *Destination Culture: Tourism, Museums, and Heritage* (Berkeley and Los Angeles: University of California Press, 1998), 149.

58. The production, a pastiche of popular Yiddish and Hebrew songs, was conceived and staged by Szymon Szuriej, the theater's artistic director.

59. An irony compounding the complex transvaluing of languages in this production was the fact that most audience members, at the performance I attended, listened to simultaneous translation into Polish via headsets.

60. "Literary and Folkloristic Yiddish Tour of Ukraine" (in Yiddish), *Yidish-velt: Informatsye-buletin fun veltrat far yidisher kultur* no. 7 (Winter 2000): 6.

61. Dan Miron, "The Literary Image of the Shtetl," *Jewish Social Studies* 1, no. 3 (spring 1995): 3, 4, 7.

62. See www.shtetlfoundation.org.

63. Kirshenblatt-Gimblett, *Destination Culture*, 199.

64. See Steven Eddy Snow, *Performing the Pilgrims: A Study in Ethnohistorical Role-Playing* (Jackson: University Press of Mississippi, 1993).

65. I asked Eliach this question at a public presentation on the Shtetl Museum, convened at City University of New York Graduate Center on 17 December 2003. She said

that it was an interesting question and added, "We are working on it." On this project, see Jeffrey Shandler, "The Shtetl Subjunctive: Yaffa Eliach's Living History Museum," in *Creating and Disseminating Jewish Culture in Eastern Europe,* ed. Benjamin Nathans and Gabriella Safran (Philadelphia: University of Pennsylvania Press, forthcoming).

66. See Ruth Ellen Gruber, *Virtually Jewish: Reinventing Jewish Culture in Europe* (Berkeley and Los Angeles: University of California Press, 2002), chap. 2.

67. See www.ibiblio.org/yiddish/shtetl.html.

68. Barbara Kirshenblatt-Gimblett, "The Electonic Vernacular," in *Connected: Engagements with Media,* ed. George E. Marcus (Chicago: University of Chicago Press, 1996), 34.

69. See www.mendele.net. Mendele was established by Noyekh Miller. It is published by Victor Berg, Miller, and Iosif Vaysman, and Vaysman is its editor.

70. Jonathan Boyarin, "Yiddish Science and the Postmodern," trans. Naomi Seidman, in his *Thinking in Jewish* (Chicago: University of Chicago Press, 1996), 198. Note that Yiddish postings on the Internet do not, as of yet, seem to have evolved the sort of orally based shorthand (e.g., "r u rdg my msg") or new speech-based acronyms (LOL) that have become a commonplace of English-language email and chat room communications.

71. There are programs to facilitate Yiddish communications on the Internet in the *alef-beys,* but their use remains limited. See, for example, Der BlitsBrivnShteler, "the first Yiddish text email discussion list, all in Yiddish letters," at www.shoshke.net/uyip/bbsh.htm.

72. On Yiddish bloggers, see William O'Shea, "The Sharer of Secrets," *Village Voice,* 16–22 July 2003; Sholem Berger, "Yiddish 'Blogs' on the Internet: A Brand New Literary Genre" (in Yiddish), *Forverts,* 12 September 2003, 20.

73. For online access to contemporary Yiddish radio broadcasts, see, for example, *The Forward Hour,* yiddish.forward.com/radio/index.html; and *Dos Yidishe Kol / The Yiddish Voice,* WUNR, Brookline, Mass., www.yiddishvoice.com. For online Yiddish language instruction, see the Dora Teitelboim Center for Yiddish Culture website at www.yiddishculture.org. There are also a number of websites that archive prerecorded Yiddish speech and song. See, for example, the Yiddish Radio Project (http://yiddishradioproject.org), where one can sample mid-twentieth-century American Yiddish broadcasts; the Yiddish American Digital Archive (www.yiddishsong.org), where one can listen to rare vintage recordings of Yiddish songs; the Spoken Yiddish Language Project (www.columbia.edu/cu/cria/currentprojects/Yiddish/Yiddish.html), where one can hear recordings of Yiddish interviews with native speakers from across Eastern Europe collected in the 1960s for the *Language and Culture Atlas of Ashkenazic Jewry.*

74. See www.yugntruf.org.

75. Jonathan Boyarin, "Jewish Geography Goes On-Line," *Jewish Folklore and Ethnology Review* 16, no. 1 (1994): 3–5.

76. Boyarin, "Yiddish Science and the Postmodern," 199–201.

2. BEYOND THE MOTHER TONGUE

1. Rosemond Mitchell and Florence Myles, *Second Language Learning Theories* (London: Arnold, 1998), 13.

2. Max Weinreich, *History of the Yiddish Language*, trans. Shlomo Noble (Chicago: University of Chicago Press, 1980), 256.

3. Ivan G. Marcus, *Rituals of Childhood: Jewish Acculturation in Medieval Europe* (New Haven, Conn.: Yale University Press, 1996), 106, 26.

4. Weinreich, *History of the Yiddish Language*, 270.

5. See also Wilhelm Christian Just Chrysander, *Chrysander's Yiddish Grammar of 1750*, reproduced from the original with introductory remarks by Max Weinreich (New York: YIVO, 1958).

6. On *brivnshtelers*, see Lewis Glinert's introduction to *Mamme Dear: A Turn-of-the-Century Collection of Model Yiddish Letters* (Northvale, N.J.: Jason Aronson, 1997).

7. Tsvi Hirsh Goldshteyn-Gershonovitsh, *Yidish-daytsher moral brivnshteler, in fir teyln* (Judeo-German Moral Letterwriting Manual, in Four Parts), 3rd rev. ed. (Berdichev: Yankev Sheftel, 1890), 4. The title page indicates that ten thousand copies of the book had already been published.

8. On the role of Yiddish orthography as a marker of Yiddishist ideology, see Kalman Weiser, "The 'Orthodox Orthography' of Solomon Birnbaum," *Studies in Contemporary Jewry* 20 (2005): 275–95.

9. Steven J. Zipperstein, *Imagining Russian Jewry: Memory, History, Identity* (Seattle: University of Washington Press, 1999), 41–62.

10. Quoted from *Russkoe slovo* (The Russian Word), 1882, in Gennady Estraikh, *Soviet Yiddish: Language Planning and Linguistic Development* (Oxford: Clarendon, 1999), 11.

11. See Philip Friedman, "Joseph Perl as an Educational Activist and His School in Tarnopol" (in Yiddish), *YIVO-bleter* 31–32 (1948): 157. Writing Yiddish was also taught at a school established by Avram ben Sholem Hacohen in Brody in 1845; see K. S. Kazdan (Chaim Kazdan), *Fun kheyder un "shkoles" biz TsIShO: dos ruslendishe yidntum in gerangl far shul, shprakh, kultur* (From the *Kheyder* and "Russian" School to the C[entral] Y[iddish] S[chool] O[rganization]: Russian Jewry's Struggle over Schooling, Language, Culture) (Mexico: Shloyme Mendelson-fond, 1956), 96.

12. Elias Schulman, *A History of Jewish Education in the Soviet Union* (New York: KTAV, 1971), 20–22.

13. Kazdan, *Fun kheyder un "shkoles,"* 178.

14. See, for example, M. Taytsh and M. Birnboyn, *Folks-shuhle: a lehrbukh far onfanger tsu lezen un shrayben yidish, far shuhlen un hoyz-lehre, ershte heft* (The People's School: A Textbook for Beginners Learning to Read and Write Yiddish, for Schools and Home Study, Part One) (Warsaw, 1908).

15. Moyshe Fridman, *Hayehudiye: a naye metode tsu oyslernen in a gikher tsayt un zeyer*

gring leyenen un shraybn yidish (The Jewess: A New Method for Learning to Read and Write Yiddish Quickly and Easily), pt. 1 (Odessa: Haokhim Bletnitshki, 1904), 4. The book's title implies a female readership, and, in fact, Fridman explains that most of the stories in *Hayehudiye* are "from girls' life, because I expect that this book will mostly be used in girls' schools." Nevertheless, he writes of both male and female students and explains that the book "would certainly do no harm to boys."

16. Y. Pirozhnikov, *Reyshis mikro: a praktishe lehr-bukh in tsvey teyln tsu lernen onfangs-kinder* (Beginning Reading: A Practical Instructional Manual in Two Parts to Teach Young Children) (Vilna: Y. Pirozhnikov, 1906), ii–iii.

17. Y. Klepfish, *Di folks-shprakh* (The People's Language) (Warsaw: Farlag "Progres," 1909–1910), 47.

18. Esther (Maria Yakovlevna Frumkin), *Tsu der frage vegn der yidisher folkshul* (On the Question of the Jewish Public School) (Vilna: Di velt, 1910), 4.

19. Cited in Kazdan, *Fun kheyder un 'shkoles,'* 281.

20. See Kazdan, *Fun kheyder un 'shkoles,'* 329.

21. See Shimen Dubnov (Simon Dubnow), *Fun zhargon tsu yidish un andere artiklen* (From Jargon to Yiddish and Other Articles) (Vilna: Kletskin, 1929); Y. L. Perets (Peretz), "Education" (in Yiddish), in *Y. L. Perets: ale verk* (Y. L. Peretz: Complete Works), vol. 8 (New York: CYCO, 1947), 3–17. Peretz's essay was first published in 1891.

22. Cited in Kazdan, *Fun kheyder un 'shkoles,'* 247–48.

23. Hirsz Abramowicz, *Profiles of a Lost World: Memoirs of East European Jewish Life Before World War II,* ed. Dina Abramowicz and Jeffrey Shandler, trans. Eva Zeitlin Dobkin (Detroit: Wayne State University Press, 1999), 313.

24. David Shneer, "A Revolution in the Making: Yiddish and the Creation of Soviet Jewish Culture," (Phd diss., University of California Berkeley, 2001), 31. See also David Shneer, *Yiddish and the Creation of Soviet Jewish Culture, 1918–1930* (Cambridge: Cambridge University Press, 2004).

25. See Joshua A. Fishman, "Attracting a Following to High Culture Functions for a Language of Everyday Life: The Role of the Tshernovits Language Conference in the 'Rise of Yiddish,' " in *Never Say Die! A Thousand Years of Yiddish in Jewish Life and Letters,* ed. Joshua A. Fishman (The Hague: Mouton, 1981), 369–94.

26. See *Der eynheytlekher yidisher oysleyg: takones fun yidishn oysleyg (6ter oysdruk); Fun folkshprakh tsu kulturshprakh: an iberblik iber der historye funem eynheytlekhn yidishn oysleyg [fun] Mordkhe Shekhter* (The Standardized Yiddish Orthography Rules of Yiddish Spelling [6th ed.]; The History of the Standardized Yiddish Spelling by Mordkhe Schaechter) (New York: YIVO / Yiddish Language Resource Center of the League for Yiddish, 1999).

27. Standardizing and simplifying Yiddish orthography, for example, followed government-instituted reform of Russian spelling in its elimination of redundant letters. Soviet Yiddish orthography's elimination of traditional spelling of Yiddish terms from

Loshn-koydesh was widely regarded (especially outside the Soviet Union) as an extension of the state's rejection of Hebrew as an acceptable Jewish language. See Rachel Erlich, "Politics and Linguistics in the Standarization of Soviet Yiddish," in *Never Say Die!*, ed. Fishman, 688–708, as well as the discussion in Estraikh, *Soviet Yiddish*, 115–40.

28. Christopher Hutton, "Normativism and the Notion of Authenticity in Yiddish Linguistics," in *Field of Yiddish: Studies in Language, Folklore, and Literature, Fifth Collection*, ed. David Goldberg (Evanston, Ill.: Northwestern University Press, 1993), 13.

29. Hutton, "Normativism and the Notion of Authenticity," 27.

30. Shneer, "A Revolution in the Making," 117.

31. See, for example, the discussion of language use among Jewish students in Kiev, according to polls taken in 1909 and 1910 in Estraikh, *Soviet Yiddish*, 16–20.

32. Abramowicz, *Profiles of a Lost World*, 245, 247.

33. Sore Shenirer (Sarah Schenirer), "Jewishness and Yiddish" (in Yiddish), *Beys-Yankev literarisher familyen-zshurnal* 8, no. 71–72 (Sivan, 1931), reprinted in *Never Say Die!*, ed. Fishman, 176. This issue of *Beys-Yankev literarisher familyen-zshurnal* was devoted entirely to the issue of maintaining Yiddish in religious life and in the classroom, proclaiming on its cover a "*khoydesh far yidish un yidishkeyt*" (month for Yiddish and Jewishness).

34. Shneer, "A Revolution in the Making," ix.

35. Estraikh, *Soviet Yiddish*, 29–30.

36. Educational Committee of the Jewish Autonomous Region, *Alefbeys* (Alphabet) (Biro-Bidzhan, 1982).

37. Peter Meyer et al. *The Jews in the Soviet Satellites* (Syracuse, N.Y.: Syracuse University Press, 1953), 545.

38. Meyer et al., *The Jews in the Soviet Satellites*, 285–89.

39. The use of Yiddish as a language of instruction in these schools during the late nineteenth century was an object of contention between East European Jewish immigrants and "uptown" Jews of German background. See Jeremiah J. Berman, "Jewish Education in New York City, 1860–1900," *YIVO Annual of Jewish Social Science* 9 (1954): 272–75.

40. Judah L. Shapiro, *The Friendly Society: A History of the Workmen's Circle* (New York: Media Judaica, 1970), 100–103.

41. Zalmen Yefroykin, "Yiddish Education in the United States" (in Yiddish), *Algemeyne entsiklopedye* (General Encyclopedia), vol. *yidn: hey* (Jews: 5) (New York: Dubnovfond, 1957), 209. See also Mark M. Krug, "The Yiddish Schools in Chicago," *YIVO Annual of Jewish Social Science* 9 (1954): 276–307. Krug's overview of the dynamics of secular Yiddish education from the 1910s to the 1950s, including some discussion of textbooks used in these schools, is instructive for a perspective that is not centered on New York City.

42. For an overview of American Jewish education at this time, see, for example, Israel E. Chipkin, "Twenty-five Years of Jewish Education in the United States," *Amer-*

ican Jewish Yearbook 5697, ed. Harry Schneiderman (Philadelphia: Jewish Publication Society, 1936), 27–116.

43. For example, Yankev Levin's *Di naye yidishe shul: a lernbukh far yidish-onfanger* (The New Yiddish School: A Textbook for Beginners) (New York: Hebrew Publication Company) was first written in 1916; a sixteenth edition was published in 1939.

44. Jenna Weissman Joselit, *The Wonders of America: Reinventing Jewish Culture, 1880–1950* (New York: Hill and Wang, 1994), 92–93.

45. Leon Elbe, *Di yidishe shprakh: a yidish lehr-bukh mit bilder in tsvey opteylungen far onfanger un hekhere talmidim* (The Yiddish Language: An Illustrated Yiddish Textbook in Two Parts for Beginners and Advanced Students), 3rd ed. (New York: M. Gurevitsh bukhhandlung, 1918), ix.

46. For example, Yekhiel Shtern reports that, at the beginning of the twentieth century, on a child's first day of *kheyder* in Shtern's native town of Tishevits (Tyszowce), children learned the letters *shin* (Sh), *dalet* (D), *yud* (Y), *alef* (silent consonant), *mem* (M), and *sof* (S) and to read with the newly learned letters the sentence *Shaday emes* (Almighty God [is] truth). See Shtern, *Kheyder un besmedresh* (*Kheyder* and *Besmedresh*) (New York: YIVO, 1950), 12. See also Diane Roskies, "Alphabet Instruction in the East European Heder: Some Comparative and Historical Notes," *YIVO Annual of Jewish Social Science* 17 (1978): 21–53.

47. See, for example, Raphael Gutman, *Yidish* (Yiddish), pt. 1 (New York: Hebrew Publishing Company, 1934); Yankev Levin, *Der onfanger* (The Beginner), pt. 1 (New York: Farlag "yidishe shul," Hebrew Publishing Company, 1922); Dvoyre Tarant, *Mayn yidish bukh* (My Yiddish Book), vol. 1 (New York: Farlag fun dem yidishn fraternaln folks-ordn, 1944); Herman J. Waldman, *Yidish far onfanger* (Yiddish for Beginners) (Boston, 1935).

48. Steven Pinker, *The Language Instinct: How the Mind Creates Language* (New York: HarperCollins, 1995), 32.

49. The word *mame-loshn* also invokes the traditional gendering of Yiddish as feminine and often signifies in particular the archetypal East European Jewish mother. See Naomi Seidman, *A Marriage Made in Heaven: The Sexual Politics of Hebrew and Yiddish* (Berkeley and Los Angeles: University of California Press, 1997), 31.

50. See, for example, Tarant, *Mayn yidish bukh*; Dvoyre Tarant and Betsalel Friedman, *Kinder* (Children) (New York: Internatsyonale arbeter ordn, 1931).

51. See, for example, Yoysef Mlotek, *Yidishe kinder* (Jewish Children), vol. 1 (New York: Educational Department of the Workmen's Circle, 1959), 29, in which the sentence *"Shabes kumen nit di kinder in shul"* is meant to be glossed as "On Saturdays the children don't come to school" and not "On the Sabbath, the children don't come to the synagogue" (although the implication is not, I think, accidental). The earlier lesson in Jewish secularism, *shul* means "school" and not "synagogue," serves as the foundation for a new lesson: *Shabes* means "Saturday" and, implicitly, does not mean "the Sabbath."

52. See, for example, Yitskhak Katsenelson, *Mayn yidish bukh* (My Yiddish Book), pt. 1 (New York: Hebrew Publishing Company, 1923); Yitskhak Shpira, *Mayn bukh: a*

leyen- un ibungs-bukh farn ershtn lernyor (My Book: A Reader and Exercise Book for the First Year of Study) (New York: Central Committee of the Jewish Folk Schools of the Jewish National Workers' Alliance and Poale Zion-Zeire Zion in the United States and Canada, 1944).

53. Another example of this is *Cartilla Escolar Antifascista* (Primer for the Antifascist Schoolchild), published in 1937 by Jesús Hernández, Ministry of Public Education in the Republic of Spain. This primer "combined phonetics with politics, identifying the military struggle against fascism with the cultural fight against ignorance." See Julian Rothstein and Mel Gooding, eds., *ABZ: More Alphabets and Other Signs* (London: Redstone Press, 2003), 79.

54. Betsalel Friedman, *Arbeter shul* (Workers' School) (New York: Farlag internatsyonale arbeter ordn, 1934), 145, 112, 46.

55. Tarant, *Mayn yidish bukh*, 156–57; Y. Kaminski, *In der heym un in der shul: a lernbikhl far onheybers* (At Home and At School: A Textbook for Beginners) (New York: Educational Committee of the Workmen's Circle, 1951), 110–11.

56. Khayem Bez (H. B. Bass), *Shprakh un dertsiung: metodik un program fun yidish-limed in der elementar-shul* (Language and Education: Methodology and Programming for the Study of Yiddish in the Elementary Grades) (New York: Bildungs-komitet fun Arbeter-ring, 1950), 5.

57. Yankev Levin, *Der nayer onfanger: lernbukh tsu lernen kinder leyenen, shraybn un redn yidish, ershter teyl* (The New Beginner: Textbook for Teaching Children How to Read, Write, and Speak Yiddish, Part One) (New York: Farlag "yidishe shul," 1945), v–vi. This is a revised version of Levin's *Der onfanger*, first published in 1922 (see note 47). The question of what to call Yiddish when it is no longer a mother tongue—and, moreover, how to conceptualize it—continues to concern Yiddish-language educators. See, for example, the discussion on the Internet listserv *Mendele: Yiddish Literature and Language* during late August 1998, vols. 8.043, 8.044, 8.045, and 8.046, http://shakti .trincoll.edu/~mendele/toc08.htm.

58. The larger question of how to teach Yiddish to the descendants of American Jewish immigrants is addressed in a collection of essays by Israel Steinbaum, David Bridger, and Yudel Mark in their discussion of creating a standard vocabulary for beginning students in Yiddish classes. Dovid Bridzhen, Yisroel Shteynboym, and Yudel Mark, *Der vokabular farn onheyber-klas in der amerikaner yidisher shul* (The Vocabulary for the Beginning Class in the American Yiddish School) (New York: YIVO, 1944), English summary, 75–78. While Bridger argues for modeling the instruction of Yiddish to American Jewish children on the teaching of foreign languages, Mark challenges the assumption underlying this approach, "because bilingualism may appear in various degrees and a modicum of the Yiddish language is found even in homes where the child speaks English to his parents" (76).

59. Dvoyre Tarant, *Mayn alefbeys* (My Alphabet) (New York: IWO, 1937).

60. Tarant, *Mayn yidish bukh*, 3. The words *a shul* also appear written in the *alefbeys*, next to where they are romanized. This text's notes to the teacher explain (in Yiddish) that "this book is structured according to the principal of introducing the child to Yiddish through English" (158).

61. Alexander M. Dushkin and Uriah Z. Engelman, *Jewish Education in the United States: Report of the Commission for the Study of Jewish Education in the United States*, vol. 1 (New York: American Association for Jewish Education, 1959), 20.

62. Yoysef Mlotek, *Yidishe kinder* (Jewish Children), vol. 1, 2nd ed. (New York: Educational Department of the Workmen's Circle, 1971), 5, 9.

63. Sandra Postman, *The Yiddish Alphabet Book* (Palo Alto: P'nye Press, 1979), 1. Similarly, Richard Michelson's children's book, *Too Young for Yiddish* (Watertown, Mass.: Taelwinds, 2002), explains that it is "bound 'back to front' to share an aspect of Yiddish culture with you" (3). The book contains a glossary of twenty-two Yiddish terms used (in romanization) in the story.

64. Hirsh-Dovid Katz, "Enriching the Yiddish Language of Hasidic Children" (in Yiddish), *Forverts*, 17 April 1998, 15. See also Dovid Katz, *Words on Fire: The Unfinished Story of Yiddish* (New York: Basic Books, 2004), 379–91.

65. An exception is the case of Lubavitcher (Habad) hasidim, who issued a Yiddish primer at the end of World War II: Y. Y. Lifshits, *Unzer bukh: a ler-bukh far yidish* (Our Book: A Yiddish Textbook) (Brooklyn: Merkos L'inyonei Chinuch, 1945). A tenth edition of the book was published in 1983. This suggests a relationship to Yiddish among Lubavitcher hasidim different from that of other hasidim, which may be linked to additional factors that distinguish this community, in particular, its commitment to outreach to less observant Jews.

66. See Miriam Isaacs, "*Haredi, Haymish* and *Frim:* Yiddish Vitality and Language Choice in a Transnational, Multilingual Community," *International Journal of the Sociology of Language* 138 (1999): 9–30.

67. See, for example, Bruce Mitchell, "A Bibliography of Yiddish Literature for Haredi Children and Young Adults," *Yiddish* 13, no. 2–3 (2003): 139–51.

68. "Introduction" (in Yiddish), in *Oylem umloye: entsiklopedye far yugnt* (The World and All That's in It: Encyclopedia for Youth), vol. 4 (Jerusalem and Lakewood, N.J.: Toras Chaim, 1999), 5.

69. *Di yidishe shprakh, undzer tsirung: Lern leyen bukh* (The Yiddish Language, Our Jewel: Textbook [and] Reader), pt. 1, rev. ed. (1982; repr., Brooklyn: Ohel Torah, 2002), 2. Like the Lubavitch primer *Unzer bukh* (see note 65), this workbook also assumes prior literacy in Hebrew with *nikudes*. One of the few hasidic publications primarily concerned with teaching Yiddish grammar is S. Mandl et al., *Bleterheft 8: der, di, dos* (Workbook 8: Masculine, Feminine, Neuter) (Brooklyn: Beys Rokhl d'Satmar, 1976). This is a coloring book, one of a series issued by the Beys Rokhl Schools run by the Satmarer hasidim, that teaches the gender of common nouns.

70. A. Fram et al., *Yidish leyenbukh far lererin* (Yiddish Reader for the Female Teacher) (Brooklyn: Bais Rochel Publishing, 1977). For a discussion of hasidic pedagogical materials for girls, including this text, see Jeffrey Shandler, "Beyond the Mother Tongue: Learning the Meaning of Yiddish in America," *Jewish Social Studies* 6, no. 3 (2000): 112–15.

71. See, for example, George Jochnowitz, "Bilingualism and Dialect Mixture Among Lubavitcher Hasidic Children," *American Speech* 43 (1968): 182–200; Solomon Poll, "The Role of Yiddish in American Ultra-Orthodox and Hassidic Communities," *YIVO Annual of Jewish Social Science* 13 (1965): 125–52.

72. Asher Pen, *Yidishkeyt in Amerike: a vegvayẓer tsu dem gaystikn yidishn lebn in Amerike in der tsveyter helft fun 20stn yorhundert* (Jewishness in America: A Guide to Jewish Intellectual Life in America in the Second Half of the Twentieth Century), vol. 1 (New York: Shulsinger Bros., 1958), 477.

73. Such is the observation of linguist Lewis Glinert with regard to the use of Yiddish among *khareydim* in England; see his "We Never Changed Our Language: Attitudes to Yiddish Acquisition among Hasidic Educators in Britain," *International Journal of the Sociology of Language* 138 (1999): 31–52.

74. Isaacs, *"Haredi, Haymish and Frim,"* 16, 22, 16.

75. David Lowenthal, *The Heritage Crusade and the Spoils of History* (Cambridge: Cambridge University Press, 1988), 13.

76. Katz, "Enriching the Yiddish Language of Hasidic Children," 22.

77. Katz also notes a special list of words considered "elevated, literary," including *koleges* (colleagues), *yuristn* (judges), *khaos* (chaos), *portret* (portrait), and *entuẓiaẓm* (enthusiasm). This last word is glossed in *Mayles* as *"hislayves,"* indicating that the child is expected to be more familiar with this Loshn-koydesh term than with the synonymous anglicism.

78. "Letters to the Editor" (in Yiddish), *Mayles* 6, no. 68 (2002): 3.

79. Leonard Prager, "Yiddish in the University," *Jewish Quarterly* 22, nos. 1–2 (1974): 31–40; reprinted in *Never Say Die!*, ed. Fishman, 529, 538 (emphasis original).

80. For a further discussion of *College Yiddish*, see my foreword to Uriel Weinreich, *College Yiddish: An Introduction to the Yiddish Language and to Jewish Life and Culture*, fiftieth anniversary ed. (New York: YIVO Institute, 1999), 1–7.

81. Prager, "Yiddish in the University," 541.

82. Uriel Weinreich, *College Yiddish: An Introduction to the Yiddish Language and to Jewish Life and Culture* (New York: YIVO, 1949), 7–8.

83. Weinreich, *College Yiddish* (1949), 30.

84. Two websites that document colleges and universities where Yiddish is currently taught are http://carla.acad.umn.edu/lclt/access.html (Less Commonly Taught Languages) and http://sunsite.unc.edu/yiddish/school (Shtetl). Richard Brod and Bettina J. Huber, "Foreign Language Enrollments in United States Institutions of Higher Edu-

cation, Fall 1995," *ADFL Bulletin* 28, no. 2 (winter 1997), lists 656 students enrolled in Yiddish language courses, ranking Yiddish as eleventh among 124 less commonly taught languages in size of enrollment. The number of institutions offering these courses is not given.

85. Prager, "Yiddish in the University," 532.

86. Alicia Svigals, "Why We Do This Anyway: Klezmer as Jewish Youth Subculture," *Judaism* 47, no. 1 (winter 1998): 48.

87. *Yidish la-universitah* (Yiddish for the University), a Hebrew-language edition of Uriel Weinreich's *College Yiddish*, was published by YIVO in conjunction with Magnes Press in Jerusalem in 1977. The first book of its kind in modern Hebrew, it marks an important landmark in the dynamics of Yiddish pedagogy in Israel.

88. Monika Adamczyk-Garbowska, "Is There a Place for Yiddish in Poland's Jewish Revival?" in *Yiddish in the Contemporary World: Papers of the First Mendel Friedman International Conference on Yiddish*, ed. Gennady Estraikh and Mikhail Krutikov (Oxford: Legenda, 1999), 63.

89. "The Third Annual Vilnius Program in Yiddish" (brochure), 2000, 9.

90. Pierre Nora, "Between Memory and History: *Les Lieux de Mémoire*, " *Representations* 26 (Spring 1989): 7–25.

91. *The Vilnius Yiddish Institute Newsletter*, email, Vilnius, Lithuania, March 2003.

92. See Seidman, *A Marriage Made in Heaven*, 103.

93. Yudel Mark, "Changes in the Yiddish School," in *Jewish Education in the United States: A Documentary History*, ed. Lloyd P. Gartner (New York: Teachers College Press, 1969), 188. Mark's piece was originally published in *Jewish Education* 19, no. 1 (fall 1947): 321–39.

3. FOUNDED IN TRANSLATION

1. Richard J. Fein, *The Dance of Leah: Discovering Yiddish in America* (Rutherford, N.J.: Fairleigh Dickinson University Press/New York: Cornwall Books, 1986), 26.

2. Homi K. Bhabha, *The Location of Culture* (London: Routledge, 1994), 38.

3. See Nehemiah 8:8.

4. The interrelation of Hebrew and Yiddish is especially well illustrated by the tales of hasidic leader Nahman of Bratslav, which were first published in a bilingual edition in 1815/16, several years after the author's death and almost a decade after he told the earliest of these stories to his followers. Typical of hasidic storytelling, these tales were related orally in Yiddish and recorded (here, by Nathan Sternhartz) in Hebrew. Scholars have noted both the interrelation of the two languages (for example, the influence of Yiddish narrative idioms on the Hebrew) and their divergences (notably, the greater capacity of the Hebrew to convey mystical connotations). See the introduction to *Nahman of Bratslav: The Tales*, ed. and trans. Arnold J. Band (New York: Paulist Press, 1978), especially 43–48.

5. Max Weinreich, *History of the Yiddish Language*, trans. Shlomo Noble (Chicago: University of Chicago Press, 1980), 5, 248.

6. On this literature, see Khone Shmeruk, *Sifrut yidish: perakim letoledotiah* (Yiddish Literature: Aspects of Its History) (Tel Aviv: Porter Institute for Poetics and Semiotics, Tel Aviv University, 1978), or the Yiddish version of this work, *Prokim fun der yidisher literatur-geshikhte* (Jerusalem: Hebrew University/Tel Aviv: Farlag I. L. Peretz, 1988).

7. Weinreich, *History of the Yiddish Language*, 315.

8. Israel Zinberg, *A History of Jewish Literature*, trans. Bernard Martin, vol. 7, *Old Yiddish Literature from Its Origins to the Haskalah Period* (Cincinnati: Hebrew Union College Press/New York: Ktav Publishing House, 1975), 47–48 (emphasis original).

9. Weinreich, *History of the Yiddish Language*, 277.

10. Zinberg, *History of Jewish Literature*, 125; Weinreich, *History of the Yiddish Language*, 276.

11. For a discussion of what she terms the "sexual-linguistic system" of Ashkenaz, see Naomi Seidman, *A Marriage Made in Heaven: The Sexual Politics of Hebrew and Yiddish* (Berkeley and Los Angeles: University of California Press, 1997).

12. See Chava Weissler, *Voices of the Matriarchs: Listening to the Prayers of Early Modern Jewish Women* (Boston: Beacon Press, 1998).

13. Zinberg, *History of Jewish Literature*, 185.

14. Nancy Sinkoff, *Out of the Shtetl: Making Jews Modern in the Polish Borderlands* (Providence, R.I.: Brown Judaic Studies, 2004), 172. Lefin's Yiddish translation of Ecclesiastes, accompanied by a brief commentary in Hebrew, was written by 1788 and then circulated in manuscript but not published until 1873. Lefin subsequently translated Proverbs into Yiddish (published in 1814) and also drafted unpublished, and lost, Yiddish renderings of Psalms, Job, and Lamentations. On the controversy over Lefin's Yiddish renderings of the Bible, see chapter 4 of Sinkoff's book.

15. The advertisement appears on the back cover of the following translation: Viktor Hugo, *Der letster tog fun a farurteyltn [Le Dernier Jour d'un Condamné]*, trans. A. Beylin (London: Farlag "Progres," 1910).

16. Farlag un bukhhandlung B. A. Kletskin, *Ilustrirter katalog* (Illustrated Catalog) (Warsaw: B. A. Kletskin, March 1925). The catalog lists titles published by Kletskin as well as those issued by other presses that Kletskin sold. Some of these translations were widely read by Jewish youth in interwar Poland. For examples, see "A. Greyno," "Forget-me-not," and "Esther," in *Awakening Lives: Autobiographies of Jewish Youth in Poland before the Holocaust*, ed. Jeffrey Shandler (New Haven, Conn.: Yale University Press, 2002), 51–112, 123–40, 321–43. For a general discussion of the significance of reading to the lives of this generation of Polish Jews, see the introduction to *Awakening Lives*, xxvi–xxxvii.

17. As evidence of the popularity of Maupassant in Yiddish in the early twentieth century, the National Yiddish Book Center reports that as of 2004 it had received 611

sets of these translations (compared to 439 sets of the collected works of Sholem Aleichem); see http://yiddishbookcenter.org.

18. Ellen Kellman, *"Dos yidishe bukh alarmirt!* Towards the History of Yiddish Reading in Inter-War Poland," *Polin* 16 (2003): 219, 223, 230.

19. "Yehoash's Introduction" (in Yiddish), *Haroyes tsum tanakh fun Yehoyesh* (Notes to Yehoash's translation of the Hebrew Bible) (New York: Yehoash Farlag Gezelshaft, 1949), 1.

20. Dzshek London (Jack London), *Di shtime fun blut* (The Call of the Wild), trans. M. Olgin (New York: Farlag "Nay-tsayt," 1919), vii.

21. Yohan Volfgang Gethe (Johann Wolfgang von Goethe), *Verther's laydn* (Werther's Sorrows), trans. S. Yudson (Solomon Judson), 2nd ed. (New York: Literarishe farlag, 1910), 9.

22. As cited in Yaakov Ariel, *Evangelizing the Chosen People: Missions to the Jews in America, 1880–2000* (Chapel Hill: University of North Carolina Press, 2000), 91. For a discussion of Einshprukh's *Der bris khadoshe* and other New Testament translations, see 88–92.

23. Sukanta Chaudhuri, *Translation and Understanding* (Oxford and New York: Oxford University Press, 1999), 14–15.

24. While the original Yiddish versions of Kvitko's books had press runs of three thousand, their Russian-language translations were printed in editions of five hundred thousand. See David Goldberg, "Fantasy, Realism, and National Identity in Soviet Yiddish Juvenile Literature: Itsik Kipnis's Books for Children," in *Field of Yiddish: Studies in Language, Folklore, and Literature, Fifth Collection*, ed. David Goldberg (Evanston, Ill.: Northwestern University Press, 1993), 165.

25. Walter Benjamin, "The Task of the Translator," in *Illuminations: Essays and Reflections*, ed. Hannah Arendt, trans. Harry Zohn (New York: Schocken, 1969), 73.

26. Comparing the translation of Yiddish literature into English with efforts to render this literature into other languages is instructive. See, for example, Mikhail Krutikov, "Soviet Yiddish Literature of the 1960s-80s and its Russian Translations," in *Yiddish in the Contemporary World: Papers of the First Mendel Friedman International Conference on Yiddish*, ed. Gennady Estraikh and Mikhail Krutikov (Oxford: Legenda, 1999), 73–91. On Yiddish literature translated into Polish, see Monika Adamczyk-Garbowska, "Is There a Place for Yiddish in Poland's Jewish Revival?" in *Yiddish in the Contemporary World: Papers of the First Mendel Friedman International Conference on Yiddish*, ed. Gennady Estraikh and Mikhail Krutikov (Oxford: Legenda, 1999), 66–68. On the translation of Yiddish literature into German, see Jeffrey A. Grossman, *The Discourse on Yiddish in Germany from the Enlightenment to the Second Empire* (Rochester, N.Y.: Camden House, 2000), 5–6; and Leslie Morris, "The Translation of Issac Bashevis Singer's *Gimpel der Narr* Appears in the Federal Republic of Germany," in *Yale Companion to Jewish Writing and Thought in German Culture, 1096–1996*, ed. Sander L. Gilman and Jack Zipes (New Haven, Conn.: Yale University Press, 1997), 742–48. For a comparative case study of Yiddish literature

rendered into several languages, see, for example, Teodor Gutsmans, "Sholem Aleichem in the Source Languages: Notes on Translations of 'The Pot' in Ukrainian, German, Hebrew, English, and Russian" (in Yiddish), in *For Max Weinreich on His Seventieth Birthday: Studies in Jewish Languages, Literature, and Society* (The Hague: Mouton, 1964), 477–99.

27. Leo Wiener, *The History of Yiddish Literature in the Nineteenth Century* (New York: Charles Scribner's Sons, 1899), xi.

28. *Yiddish Tales*, trans. Helena Frank (Philadelphia: Jewish Publication Society, 1912), 6.

29. Sholom Aleichem, *Jewish Children* (New York: Knopf, 1926), 6.

30. Chaudhuri, *Translation and Understanding*, 15, 17.

31. Joseph Leftwich, ed., *The Golden Peacock: An Anthology of Yiddish Poetry* (Cambridge, Mass.: Sci-Art Publishers, 1939), xxi, xxii, xxiv.

32. Chaim Lieberman, *The Christianity of Sholem Asch: An Appraisal from the Jewish Viewpoint* (New York: Philosophical Library, 1953), 1, 7.

33. Anita Norich, "Sholem Asch and the Christian Question," in *Sholem Asch Reconsidered*, ed. Nanette Stahl (New Haven, Conn.: Beinecke Rare Book and Manuscript Library, 2004), 255, 251.

34. Norich, "Sholem Asch and the Christian Question," 251, 264.

35. Lieberman, *The Christianity of Sholem Asch*, 3.

36. Norich, "Sholem Asch and the Christian Question," 265.

37. In his bibliography of research sources for Sholem Aleichem, Uriel Weinreich lists *The World of Sholom Aleichem* under the heading "criticism" but notes that "rather than supplying a background for Sholom Aleichem's works from external sources, this book draws most of its evidence from within Sholom Aleichem's works. It thus provides no perspective for the evaluation of Sholom Aleichem as a creative person or for his works as portraits of anything but themselves." Uriel Weinreich, "Sholom Aleichem (1859–1916): Principal Research Sources," in *The Field of Yiddish: Studies in Yiddish Language, Folklore and Literature*, ed. Uriel Weinreich (New York: Linguistic Circle of New York, Columbia University, 1954), 284.

38. Maurice Samuel, *The World of Sholom Aleichem* (New York: Knopf, 1943), 3, 6–7.

39. See Barbara Kirshenblatt-Gimblett, "Imagining Europe: The Popular Arts of American Jewish Ethnography," in *Divergent Centers: Shaping Jewish Cultures in Israel and America*, ed. Deborah Dash Moore and Ilan Troen (New Haven, Conn.: Yale University Press, 2001), 167–169.

40. For a more extended analysis of Sholem Aleichem in English translation, see Jeffrey Shandler, "Reading Sholem Aleichem from Left to Right," *YIVO Annual* 20 (1991): 305–32.

41. Sholom Aleichem, *Stories and Satires*, trans. Curt Leviant (New York: Thomas Yoseloff, 1959), 13–14.

42. Sholom Aleichem, *Selected Stories of Sholom Aleichem* (New York: Random House, 1956), vi–ix.

43. Seth L. Wolitz, ed., *The Hidden Isaac Bashevis Singer* (Austin: University of Texas Press, 2001), xiv.

44. See, for example, Cynthia Ozick's 1969 short story, "Envy; or, Yiddish in America," in *The Pagan Rabbi and Other Stories* (New York: Dutton, 1983); Bruce Davidson's 1974 film, *Isaac Singer's Nightmare and Mrs. Pupko's Beard;* and Dvorah Telushkin, *Master of Dreams: A Memoir of Isaac Bashevis Singer* (New York: William Morrow, 1997).

45. Eli Lederhandler, *New York Jews and the Decline of Urban Ethnicity, 1950–1970* (Syracuse, N.Y.: Syracuse University Press, 2001), 76.

46. Naomi Seidman, "Elie Wiesel and the Scandal of Jewish Rage," *Jewish Social Studies* 3, no. 1 (fall 1996): 14–16. The evolution of Abraham Joshua Heschel's *The Earth Is the Lord's: The Inner World of the Jew in Eastern Europe* (New York: Henry Schuman, 1950) from Yiddish originals offers another interesting example of the consequences of shifting languages and audiences in post-Holocaust writing. See Jeffrey Shandler, "Heschel and Yiddish: A Struggle with Signification," *Journal of Jewish Thought and Philosophy* 2 (1993): 245–99.

47. Irving Howe and Eliezer Greenberg, eds., *A Treasury of Yiddish Stories* (New York: Viking, 1954), 1. I discuss this and other anthologies of Yiddish literature in English translation in greater detail in "Anthologizing the Vernacular: Collections of Yiddish Literature in English Translation," in *The Anthology in Jewish Literature*, ed. David Stern (Oxford and New York: Oxford University Press, 2004), 304–23.

48. Howe and Greenberg, *A Treasury of Yiddish Stories*, 3, 12.

49. Compare, for example, Rosenfeld's boosterish Yiddish-language poems, "Yidish" (Yiddish) and "Ir fregt oyb yidish iz a shprakh" (You Ask If Yiddish Is a Language), in *Moris Roȥenfeld: oysgeklibene shriftn* (Morris Rosenfeld: Selected Works), ed. Shmuel Rozhanski (Buenos Aires: YIVO, 1962), 97–98, 135–36, with his English poem, "I Sing and Sing," in Ezekiel Lifschutz, "Morris Rosenfeld's Attempts to Become an English Poet," *America Jewish Archives* (1970): 128.

50. On the case of Brenner, see Yael Chaver, *What Must Be Forgotten: The Survival of Yiddish in Zionist Palestine* (Syracuse, N.Y.: Syracuse University Press, 2004).

51. See Shmuel Werses, "S. An-ski's 'Tsvishn tsvey veltn (Der Dybbuk)' / 'Beyn Shney Olamot (Hadybbuk)' / 'Between Two Worlds (The Dybbuk)': A Textual History," in *Studies in Yiddish Literature and Folklore*, Research Projects of the Institute of Jewish Studies, Monograph Series 7 (Jerusalem: Hebrew University, 1986), 99–185.

52. See Isaak Euchel, *Reb Henoch, oder: Woß tut me damit. Eine jüdische Komödie der Aufklärungȥeit* (Reb Henoch, or: What Can One Do? A Jewish Enlightenment Comedy), ed. Marion Aptroot et al. (Hamburg: Buske, 2004).

53. On *Yekl*, see Aviva Taubenfeld, " 'Only an "L" ': Linguistic Borders and the Immigrant Author in Abraham Cahan's *Yekl* and *Yankel der Yankee*," in *Multilingual America: Transnationalism, Ethnicity, and the Languages of American Literature*, ed. Werner Sollors (New York: New York University Press, 1998), 144–65. On *Call It Sleep*, see

Hana Wirth-Nesher, "Between Mother Tongue and Native Language: Multilingualism in Henry Roth's *Call It Sleep,*" *Prooftexts* 10 (1990): 297–312.

54. Hana Wirth-Nesher, "Language as Homeland in Jewish-American Literature," in *Insider/Outsider: American Jews and Multiculturalism,* ed. David Biale, Michael Galchinsky, and Susannah Heschel (Berkeley and Los Angeles: University of California Press, 1998), 220.

55. Irena Klepfisz, *A Few Words in the Mother Tongue: Poems Selected and New (1971–1990)* (Portland, Ore.: Eighth Mountain Press, 1990), 218, 228, 230. Copyright © 1990 by Irena Klepfisz, reprinted with permission of Irena Klepfisz and Eighth Mountain Press.

56. John Hollander, *Picture Window: Poems* (New York: Knopf, 2003), 38.

57. Jacqueline Osherow, "Ch'vil Schreibn a Poem auf Yiddish," in *Jewish American Literature: A Norton Anthology,* ed. Jules Chametzky et al. (New York and London: Norton, 2001), 1132–33. Used with permission of Jacqueline Osherow.

58. Cynthia Ozick, *Bloodshed and Three Novellas* (New York: Knopf, 1976), 9.

59. Cynthia Ozick, "Envy; or, Yiddish in America," 32. "Envy" was first published in *Commentary* (November 1969): 33–53.

60. Ozick, "Envy," 53, 74.

61. Ozick, "Envy," 59.

62. See, for example, Chametzky et al., *Jewish American Literature,* 857.

63. I heard Ozick offer this explanation of her story's origins at a public program entitled "A Language of One's Own?" held at the City University of New York Graduate Center, 26 April 1999. The program, which also included remarks by playwright Tony Kushner and literary scholar Benjamin Harshav, was presented in conjunction with the Forward Association.

64. Ozick, "Envy," 70.

65. Translation by the author, with the kind assistance of Gitl Schaechter-Viswanath.

66. Ozick, "Envy," 83.

67. Khane Norikh (Anita Norich), "Winnie the Pooh Speaks in Yiddish" (in Yiddish), *Forverts,* 25 August 2000.

68. Customer review of *Vini-Der-Pu,* "Who's this book for, anyway?" www .amazon.com, 7 March 2001.

69. Wilhelm Busch, *Max und Moritz auf jiddish: Eine Bubengeshchichte in sieben Streichen/Shmul un Shmerke: A mayse mit vayse-khevrenikes in zibn shpitselekh* (Max and Moritz in Yiddish: A Juvenile History in Seven Tricks), trans. Shmoyl Naydorf (Charles Nydorf) and Leye (Elinor) Robinson (Nidderau: Verlag Michaeli Naumann, 2000); Heinrich Hoffman, *Der Struwwelpeter: Lustige Geschichten un drollige Bilder/Pinye shtroykop: vitsike mayses mit komishe bilder* (Struwwelpeter: Jolly Stories with Comical Pictures), trans. Shmoyl Naydorf (Charles Nydorf) and Elinor Robinson (Nidderau: Verlag Michaeli Naumann, 1999); Antoine de Saint-Exupéry, *Der kleyner prints: yidish* (The Little Prince in Yiddish), trans. Shloyme Lerman (Nidderau: Verlag Michaeli Nau-

mann, 2000); Eric Carle, *Der ʒeyer hungeriker opfreser* (The Very Hungry Caterpillar), trans. Marcia Gruss Levinsohn (Silver Spring, Md.: Jewish Educational Workshop, 1996); *Di kats der payats: The Cat in the Hat by Dr. Seuss in Yiddish,* trans. Sholem Berger (New York: Twenty-fourth Street Books, 2003).

70. Marie B. Jaffe, *Gut Yuntif, Gut Yohr: A Collection in Yiddish of Original Holiday Verses and Popular English Classics in Translation* (1965; repr., New York: Citadel Press, 1991). Yiddish-language versions of Gilbert and Sullivan operettas include *Der Yiddisher Pinafore* and *Der Yiddisher Mikado,* adaptations by Al Grand and Bob Tartell, Yiddish lyrics by Al Grand and Miriam Walowitz, both of which were recorded by the Gilbert & Sullivan Light Opera Company of Long Island in 1994. Grand has also written *A Tuml in Beʒdin* (Commotion in Court), a Yiddish version of *Trial by Jury,* and *Di Yam Gaʒlonim* (The Pirates), a Yiddish version of *The Pirates of Penʒance.* The latter was published as *Di Yam Gaʒlonim,* based on Gilbert and Sullivan's *The Pirates of Penʒance,* Yiddish book and lyrics by Al Grand (Cedarhurst, N.Y.: Tara Publications, 1988).

71. For example, *Eydlshteyner un ash* (Melbourne: Scribe Publications, 1997), Romek Mokotow's Yiddish translation of Arnold Zable, *Jewels and Ashes* (New York: Harcourt Brace, 1994). In a prefatory note, Mokotow explains that, shortly after the original English-language publication of this account by a child of Holocaust survivors of his search for his parents' East European past, "I felt that it had to be translated into Yiddish for those for whom it isn't possible to read the book in the original" (n.p.).

72. *Kalevala: folks epos fun di finen* (Kalavala: The Finnish National Epic), trans. Hersh Rosenfeld (New York: Martin Press, 1954), 13.

73. Meir Kutshinski, as cited in the preface to Samuel Beket (Beckett), *Dos vartn af Godo* (Waiting for Godot), trans. Gisela Skilnik (Tel Aviv: I. L. Peretz Publishing House, 1980), 8. Kutshinski's review originally appeared in Yiddish newspapers published in Buenos Aires and São Paulo.

74. Susan Bassnett, *Translation Studies,* 3rd ed. (London: Routledge, 2002), 11.

75. Y. Esterman, " 'The Little Prince'—How Did It Wind Up in Yiddish?" (in Yiddish), *Forverts,* 13 April 2001.

76. Paolo Rónai, "Alexander ille Lenardu: The Man Who Taught Winnie-the-Pooh to Speak Latin," *Américas* 13, no. 8 (August 1961): 21.

77. Doreen Carvajal, "Now It's Haydl-Didl in 'Vini-der-Pu,' " *New York Times,* 29 July 2000.

78. The conclusion of the *Bove-bukh* gives 5267 (1507) as the date of composition; the earliest known published edition appeared in Isny in 1541.

79. Zinberg, *History of Jewish Literature,* 75.

80. Ruth R. Wisse, *The Modern Jewish Canon: A Journey through Language and Culture* (New York: Free Press, 2000), 289. See also "From 'The Love Song of J. Alfred Prufrock,' " trans. Isaac Rosenfeldt [sic], as well as Barbara Mann's English translation

of this Yiddish rendering, in *Princeton University Library Chronicle* 63, nos. 1–2 (autumn 2001–winter 2002): 264–65.

81. Isaac Asimov, foreword to *Di Yam Gazlonim,* 3.

82. A key difference between the Yiddish-English parodies of Borsht Belt entertainers such as Mickey Katz and the Yiddish versions of Gilbert and Sullivan is the treatment of music. In Katz's musical numbers, the bilingual text is performed to a musical accompaniment that is "Judaized" through instrumentation and ornamentation that signals American Jewish celebration music of the mid-twentieth century. Typically, the songs are interrupted by a musical intermezzo that suddenly breaks into a *freylekhs* or other typical Ashkenazic wedding dance numbers. The Yiddish versions of Gilbert and Sullivan, however, do not alter the music; Judaization takes place entirely in the text. A telling study of Gilbert and Sullivan as a vehicle for parody could be made by comparing the Yiddish Gilbert and Sullivan operettas with *The Hot Mikado,* a jazz version with an all-black cast staged in 1939, and *Pinafore!,* a gay version of the Gilbert and Sullivan classic, staged in 2003.

83. Grand, *Di Yam Gazlonim,* 16.

84. In a prewar Yiddish version of Max und Moritz, Episode Four is simply omitted; see Vilhelm Bush (Wilhelm Busch), *Notel un Motel: zeks shtifer-mayselekh, fray baarbet in yidish durkh Yoysef Tunkel* (Notel and Motel: Six Mischievous Tales, Freely Adapted by Yoysef Tunkel) (Warsaw: Farlag Brider Levin-Epshteyn un shutfim, 1920).

85. Chaudhuri, *Translation and Understanding,* 56.

86. Will Eisner, *An opmakh mit Got* (A Contract with God), trans. Bobby Zylberman (Amsterdam: Stripantiquariaat Lambiek, 1984).

87. Irving Howe, "Strangers," in *Selected Writings 1950–1990* (San Diego: Harcourt Brace Jovanovich, 1990), 330 (emphasis original). The essay first appeared in *Yale Review* 66, no. 4 (summer 1977): 481–500.

88. George Ross, " 'Death of a Salesman' in the Original," *Commentary* 11, no. 2 (February 1951): 184.

89. Falk Zolf, *On Foreign Soil,* vol. 1, trans. Martin Green (Winnipeg: Benchmark Publishing, 2000), 21.

90. Zolf, *On Foreign Soil,* 207.

91. Zolf, *On Foreign Soil,* 355.

92. Zolf, *On Foreign Soil,* back of dust jacket.

93. Green, introduction to Zolf, *On Foreign Soil,* 3.

4. YIDDISH AS PERFORMANCE ART

1. Haym Soloveitchik, "Rupture and Reconstruction: The Transformation of Contemporary Orthodoxy," *Tradition* (Rabbinical Council of America) 28, no. 4 (1994): 64–69. For another discussion of this phenomenon, see Menachem Friedman, "Life Tradition and Book Tradition in the Development of Ultraorthodox Judaism," in *Judaism*

Viewed from Within and from Without: Anthropological Studies, ed. Harvey E. Goldberg (Albany, N.Y.: SUNY Press, 1987), 235–56.

2. The perceived loss of mimesis among Orthodox Jews and the decline of vernacular Yiddish are interrelated phenomena, given that Yiddish was the daily language in which the majority of Orthodox Ashkenazim communicated through daily conversation, study of sacred texts, popular religious literature, and journalism, for centuries before the Holocaust. See Soloveitchik, "Rupture and Reconstruction," 83–84.

3. Benjamin Harshav, *The Meaning of Yiddish* (Berkeley and Los Angeles: University of California Press, 1990), 91.

4. Modern Israeli Hebrew, as an official, state-promoted language, is something different—indeed, it has been argued that Hebrew is not a Jewish language per se. See Uzzi Ornan, "Hebrew Is Not a Jewish Language," in *Readings in the Sociology of Jewish Languages,* ed. Joshua A. Fishman (Leiden, Netherlands: E. J. Brill, 1985), 22–24.

5. Ruth Ellen Gruber, *Virtually Jewish: Reinventing Jewish Culture in Europe* (Berkeley and Los Angeles: University of California Press, 2002), 194.

6. Email announcement from Michael Alpert, 2 November 2003. Alpert intimates a playful approach to this performance of restoration by noting, parenthetically, that "any connection to Halloween or El Dia de los Muertos, lehavdl [forgive the comparison], is purely coincidental, though not unacknowledged."

7. Similarly, the history of Yiddish theater has conventionally been told in terms of a cultural continuum, linking *purimshpiln* (Purim plays), performed as early as the sixteenth century in Central Europe, with the modern secular Yiddish theater inaugurated by Abraham Goldfaden in Romania in the 1870s. See, for example, Nahma Sandrow, *Vagabond Stars: A World History of Yiddish Theater* (New York: Harper and Row, 1977).

8. On Haskalah dramas, see Dan Miron, *A Traveler Disguised: The Rise of Modern Yiddish Fiction in the Nineteenth Century* (New York: Schocken, 1973); Israel Zinberg, *A History of Jewish Literature,* vol. 7, *Old Yiddish Literature from Its Origins to the Haskalah Period,* trans. Bernard Martin (Cincinnati: Hebrew Union College Press/New York: Ktav Publishing House, 1975). On *mauscheln,* see Sander Gilman, *Jewish Self-Hatred: Anti-Semitism and the Hidden Language of the Jews* (Baltimore: Johns Hopkins University Press, 1986).

9. Nina Warnke, "Immigrant Popular Culture as Contested Sphere: Yiddish Music Halls, the Yiddish Press, and the Process of Americanization, 1900–1910," *Theatre Journal* 48 (1996): 323. On Goldfaden, see Alyssa Quint, "The Botched Kiss: Avraham Goldfaden and the Literary Origins of the Yiddish Theatre" (PhD diss., Harvard University, 2002).

10. As cited in Joshua A. Fishman, *Ideology, Society, and Language: The Odyssey of Nathan Birnbaum* (Ann Arbor, Mich.: Karoma, 1987), 191.

11. On the third seder, see Anita Schwartz, "The Secular Seder: Continuity and Change among Left-Wing Jews," in *Between Two Worlds: Ethnographic Essays on American Jewry,* ed. Jack Kugelmass (Ithaca, N.Y.: Cornell University Press, 1988), 105–27.

12. In particular, the death in January 1948 of Shloyme Mikhoels, the leading actor of the Soviet Yiddish stage, in an automobile "accident" now known to have been a state-planned assassination, has come to be regarded as a harbinger of Stalin's eventual liquidation of Soviet Yiddish culture that year. See Joshua Rubenstein and Vladimir P. Naumov, *Stalin's Secret Pogrom: The Postwar Inquisition of the Jewish Anti-Fascist Committee* (New Haven, Conn.: Yale University Press, 2002).

13. See Mark Kligman, "On the Creators and Consumers of Orthodox Popular Music in Brooklyn," *YIVO Annual* 23 (1996): 259–93.

14. Soloveitchik, "Rupture and Reconstruction," 90.

15. *Der Bay* 12, no. 1 (January 2002), letters to the editor. The newsletter's name is also a play on the Yiddish word *derbay,* meaning "at present."

16. Boris Sandler, "The Paradox of Yiddish," *Forward* (English-language edition), 1 December 2000, 9. An earlier version of Sandler's essay appears as an unsigned editorial in the Yiddish edition of the *Forward,* see "Yiddish in the Council of Europe" (in Yiddish), *Forverts,* 17 November 2000.

17. Samuel Heilman, "Jews and Judaica: Who Owns and Buys What?" in *Persistence and Flexibility: Anthropological Perspectives on the American Jewish Experience,* ed. Walter P. Zenner (Albany, N.Y.: SUNY Press, 1988), 263. Note that Sandler does not invoke the traditional esteem accorded torah ornaments, as *hider hamitsve*—that is, the enhancement of the fulfillment of a commandment.

18. Moyshe Olgin, "The Yiddish Language in Our Private Life" (in Yiddish), *Fragn fun lebn* (Questions from Life), 1911, reprinted in *Never Say Die! A Thousand Years of Yiddish in Jewish Life and Letters,* ed. Joshua A. Fishman (The Hague: Mouton, 1981), 552.

19. Barbara Kirshenblatt-Gimblett, *Destination Culture: Tourism, Museums, and Heritage* (Berkeley and Los Angeles: University of California Press, 1998), 61, 57, 138.

20. Marjorie R. Esman, "Tourism as Ethnic Preservation: The Cajuns of Louisiana," *Annals of Tourism Research* 11 (1984): 451–67.

21. Esther Romeyn and Jack Kugelmass, "Community Festivals and the Politics of Memory: Postmodernity in the American Heartland," in *The Small Town in America: A Multidisciplinary Revisit,* ed. Hans Bertens and Theo D'haen (Amsterdam: VU University Press, 1995), 197, 201, 200.

22. See Richard Schencher, *Between Theater and Anthropology* (Philadelphia: University of Pennsylvania Press, 1985), chap. 2.

23. "Ashkenaz: A Festival of New Yiddish Cultures" (program), Toronto, 1999, 5, 9.

24. "Ashkenaz" (program), 14. Kensington Market was a major center of Jewish community life in Toronto from the 1920s until the community moved to northern suburbs after World War II. At the turn of the millennium Anshei Minsk was the only synagogue in downtown Toronto holding daily prayer services.

25. "Ashkenaz" (program), 15.

26. "The Art of Yiddish: Cultural Nourishment for a New Age," presented by UCLA Extension and Yiddishkayt Los Angeles, (brochure), Los Angeles, 2000, n.p.

27. See, for example, Adrienne Cooper and Zalmen Mlotek, *Ghetto Tango: Wartime Yiddish Theater*, compact disc (New York: Traditional Crossroads, 2000), in which Yiddish songs originally composed and sung in ghettos where Polish Jews were confined by German forces during World War II are performed in versions that mix the original texts with English translations according to a variety of code-switching strategies.

28. Gruber, *Virtually Jewish*, 63.

29. Leah Hager Cohen, "Deafness As Metaphor, Not Gimmick," *New York Times*, 23 August 2003.

30. From its inauguration until 1999, KlezKamp was convened in one of the few remaining kosher resort hotels in the Catskills. After a hiatus of several years, KlezKamp returned to the Catskills in 2003.

31. Rachel Donadio, "A Prayer for the Mind-Body Problem," *Forward* (English-language edition), 20 July 2001.

32. Henry Sapoznik, *Klezmer!: Jewish Music from Old World to Our World* (New York: Schirmer, 1999), xv (emphasis original).

33. Adrienne Cooper, "Notes from a Concert Journal," *Jewish Folklore and Ethnology Review* 15, no. 1 (1993): 13.

34. *Mendele: Yiddish Literature and Language* 11.025 (16 March 2002), http://shakti .trincoll.edu/!mendele/vol11/vol11.025.txt.

35. Alicia Svigals, "Why We Do This Anyway: Klezmer as Jewish Youth Subculture," *Judaism* 47, no. 1 (185) (winter 1990): 44. On the history of klezmer, especially its "revival" during the past quarter-century, see Steve Rogovoy, *The Essential Klezmer: A Music Lover's Guide to Jewish Roots and Soul Music, from the Old World to the Jazz Age to the Downtown Avant-Garde* (Chapel Hill, N.C.: Algonquin Books, 2000); Sapoznik, *Klezmer!*; Mark Slobin, *Fiddler on the Move: Exploring the Klezmer World* (Oxford and New York: Oxford University Press, 2000); Gruber, *Virtually Jewish*, pt. 4.

36. Doctoral dissertations on klezmer by klezmorim include Hankus Netzky, "Klezmer in Twentieth Century Philadelphia" (PhD diss., Wesleyan University, 2004); Joel Rubin, "The Art of the Klezmer: Improvisation and Ornamentation in the Commercial Recordings of New York Clarinetists Naftule Brandwein and Dave Tarras 1922–1929" (PhD diss., London: City University, 2001).

37. For example, at a live performance on May 2, 1993, in Boston, the Klezmer Conservatory Band's lead vocalist, Judy Bressler, taught audience members to sing the Yiddish folksong "Tumbalalayka." See *The Klezmer Conservatory Band Live!: The Thirteenth Anniversary Album*, compact disc no. 3125, Rounder Records, 1993.

38. "The Klezmer Conservatory Foundation" (brochure), Somerset, Mass., n.d. I acquired a copy of the brochure at the band's concert in Avery Fischer Hall, 23 December 2001.

39. Alicia Svigals, telephone interview with author, New York, 14 November 2000.

40. Consider, for example, the repertoire in three Yiddish song anthologies compiled by Eleanor Gordon Mlotek and Joseph Mlotek, issued by the Workmen's Circle in New York: *Mir Trogn a Geẓang: The New Book of Yiddish Songs* (1972), *Pearls of Yiddish Song* (1988), and *Songs of Generations: New Pearls of Yiddish Song* (n.d.).

41. For example, the repertoire of Mariam Niremberg, a native of Brześć nad Bugiem, Poland, included songs in Yiddish, Polish, Russian, Ukrainian, Hebrew, and (after her emigration to Canada), English. See *Folksongs in the East European Tradition: From the Repertoire of Mariam Nuremberg,* sound recording, Global Village Music/YIVO Institute, 1986.

42. The Jewish People's Philharmonic Chorus, fundraising letter, New York, December 2002.

43. Wolf Krakowski, *Transmigrations: Gilgul,* compact disc no. TZ 7150, Tzadik, 2001, originally released by Kame'a Media in 1996; Wolf Krakowski, *Goyrl: Destiny,* compact disc no. TZ 7166, Tzadik, 2002. See Alex Lubet, "*Transmigrations:* Wolf Krakowski's Yiddish Worldbeat in its Socio-Musical Context," *Polin: Studies in Polish Jewry* 16 (2003): 297–312.

44. Yugntruf, "Di yidish-svives," email announcement, 12 November 2000 (emphases original). The literal meaning of the term *svive* in Yiddish is "environment, surroundings, milieu." As is the case with almost all email announcements from Yugntruf, the text was distributed in romanized Yiddish and English.

45. See also Rakhmiel Peltz, *From Immigrant to Ethnic Culture: American Yiddish in South Philadelphia* (Stanford, Calif.: Stanford University Press, 1998), for the author's account of a Yiddish conversation circle he organized and studied involving senior citizens in an immigrant and second-generation ethnic enclave.

46. Sabina Brukner to Jeffrey Shandler, email, 18 April 2004. Statistics are based on Yugntruf's mailing list, which counts the number of households, rather than individuals.

47. This and all following citations from "The Constitution of the Yugntruf Movement" (in Yiddish), *Yugntruf,* no. 2 (winter 1965): 6–7.

48. The Yiddish text reads "*dos loshn nit nor fun yontef, nor oykh fun vokh*" (7). *Fun vokh* (literally, "of the week[day]"), evokes the Yiddish word *vokhedik* (workaday, vernacular).

49. J. L. Austin, *How to Do Things with Words,* ed. J. O. Urmson and Marina Sbisà, 2nd ed. (Cambridge, Mass.: Harvard University Press, 1975), 6–7.

50. See www.yugntruf.org/arraynfir.html.

51. Michael Skakun, *On Burning Ground: A Son's Memoir* (New York: St. Martin's Press, 2000).

52. Binyumen Schaechter, "A WEEK IN YIDDISH-LAND!," email announcement, 12 June 2000.

53. The one activity not conducted in Yiddish at *yidish-vokh* is group religious worship, which, of course, is conducted in Hebrew, with Ashkenazic pronunciation. Yugn-

truf has also extended its devotion to Yiddish to a commitment to *mineg-Ashkenaz* (the traditional religious customs of Ashkenazim) by conducting a workshop on how to conduct a Passover seder in the Ashkenazic pronunciation. Yugntruf, email announcement, 12 March 2001.

54. Robert Filliou, *Permanent Creation (Instead of Art)*, n.d. See Ken Friedman's discussion of core Fluxus ideas, including Filliou's notion of the "unity of art and life," in his "Fluxus and Company," in *The Fluxus Reader*, ed. Ken Friedman (Chichester: Academy Editions, 1998), 237–53.

55. R. Murray Schafer, *The Soundscape: Our Sonic Environment and the Tuning of the World* (1977; repr., Rochester, Vt.: Destiny Books, 1994), 91.

56. Pierre Nora, "Between Memory and History: Les Lieux de Mémoire," *Representations* 26 (Spring 1989): 7–25.

57. Jacques Derrida, *Margins of Philosophy*, trans. Alan Bass (Chicago: University of Chicago Press, 1982), 312, 314.

5. ABSOLUT TCHOTCHKE

1. Several examples of this can be seen in Norman Kleeblatt and Vivian Mann, *Treasures of the Jewish Museum* (New York: Universe Books, 1986), in which works of Judaica are contrasted with similar non-Jewish items, the primary distinction of the former being their inscription with words or letters in the *alefbeys;* see 38–39, 44–45, 56–57, 62–63, 132–33, 146–47.

2. The use of romanization on these objects, and in related items (especially comic dictionaries, which use it exclusively), ought to be considered in light of other examples of printing Yiddish in Latin letters—for example, Yiddish newspapers published in Displaced Persons camps in the immediate post–World War II years, when there was no *alefbeys* type available in Europe—and arguments made to render Yiddish in Latin letters as a matter of language policy, whether by Chaim Zhitlowski in America in the 1920s, or by Soviet Yiddishists during the 1920s and 1930s.

3. *CHUTZPA: Magnetic Poetry Supplemental Kit: Yiddish* (Minneapolis: Magnetic Poetry, 1997). In addition, some words included in these two magnet sets are (at least arguably) not Yiddish, for instance, *safta* (modern Hebrew for "grandmother") *kibosh*, and *deli*. Their inclusion suggests various notions of what might "belong" within the lexicon of a Jewish vernacular, irrespective of their appearance in Yiddish dictionaries. By comparison, the other foreign-language sets in this series offer a more conventional, quotidian vocabulary, akin to the basic set of magnetic poetry in English.

4. See Yisroel Shteynboym, Dovid Bridzher, and Yudel Mark (Israel Steinbaum, David Bridger, and Yudel Mark), *Der vokabular farn onheyber-klas in der amerikaner yidisher shul* (The Vocabulary for the Beginners' Class in the American Yiddish School) (New York: YIVO, 1944).

5. *Magnetic Poetry: World Series, Yiddish Edition* (Minneapolis, Minn: Magnetic Poetry, 1993).

6. Birthday card, Designer Greetings, Staten Island, N.Y., purchased 1999.

7. Susan Stewart, *On Longing: Narratives of the Miniature, the Gigantic, the Souvenir, the Collection* (Durham, N.C.: Duke University Press, 1993), 136.

8. William Pietz, "The Problem of the Fetish, I," *RES* 9 (Spring 1985): 7–8, 10.

9. Marilyn Halter, "Longings and Belongings: Yiddish Identity and Consumer Culture," in *Yiddish Language and Culture: Then and Now*, Studies in Jewish Civilization 9, ed. Leonard Jay Greenspoon (Omaha, Nebr.: Creighton University Press, 1998), 189.

10. "New York talk may have its roots in German or Yiddish," argues Robert Hendrickson in *New Yawk Tawk: A Dictionary of New York City Expressions* (New York: Checkmark Books, 1998), xv, noting that H. L. Mencken made this observation in *The American Language* (first published in 1919). A recent feature in *Time Out New York* identified, among "the things you gotta do before you can call yourself a real New Yorker," the need to "incorporate a lexicon of Yiddish terms into your vocabulary." "Essential New York," 13–20 November 2003, 16–17.

11. Pietz, "The Problem of the Fetish," 12.

12. There are alternate versions of rules for playing *dreydl*. For example, whereas *giml* is most frequently understood as standing for *gants* ([take] all), others report that it stands for *gib* (give, i.e., add to the ante). See Marvin Herzog et al., *The Language and Culture Atlas of Ashkenazic Jewry*, vol. 2 (Tübingen: Max Niemeyer, 1992), question 193:020.

13. See, for example, Isidor Margolis and Sidney L. Markowitz, *Jewish Holidays and Festivals* (Secaucus, N.J.: Citadel Press, 1962), 55.

14. For another example of American Jewish material culture that situates mahjongg as a "Jewish game," see *Getting Comfortable in New York: The American Jewish Home, 1880–1950* ed. Susan L. Braunstein and Jenna Weissman Joselit (New York: The Jewish Museum, 1990), fig. 66.

15. Dan Miron, "Folklore and Antifolklore in the Yiddish Fiction of the *Haskala*," in *Studies in Jewish Folklore: Proceedings of a Regional Conference of the Association for Jewish Studies Held at the Spertus College of Judaica, Chicago, May 1–3, 1977*, ed. Frank Talmage (Cambridge, Mass.: Association for Jewish Studies, 1980), 220–22, 232.

16. Barbara Kirshenblatt-Gimblett, *Traditional Storytelling in the Toronto Jewish Community: A Study in Performance and Creativity in an Immigrant Culture* (PhD diss., Indiana University, 1972), 337.

17. Sammy's Roumanian Steak House, "Dictionary of Basic Yiddish," souvenir card, New York, n.d. For a discussion of this artifact in context, see Jack Kugelmass, "Green Bagels: An Essay on Food, Nostalgia, and the Carnivalesque," *YIVO Annual* 19 (1990): 57–80.

18. Esther Romeyn and Jack Kugelmass, *Let There Be Laughter!: Jewish Humor in America* (Chicago: Spertus Press, 1997), 78–79.

19. Martin Marcus, *Yiddish for Yankees: Or, Funny, You Don't Look Gentile* (Philadelphia and New York: Lippincott, 1968); Arthur Naiman, *Every Goy's Guide to Common Jewish Expressions* (New York: Ballantine, 1981). The front cover of the latter reads, under the title, "Also recommended for Jews who don't know their punim [face] from their pupik [navel]." Here, the non-Jewish reader serves as the "kind of permission" for the mock dictionary, not dissimilar to the role of women as model readers of early Yiddish literature that was, in fact, for women and men who were like women in their lack of Jewish literacy, as discussed in chapter 3 of this book.

20. These books have been reprinted numerous times, including in one volume: see Ruth and Bob Grossman, *The New Kosher Cookbook Trilogy* (Secaucus, N.J.: Castle Books, 1985).

21. Uriel Weinreich, *Languages in Contact* (1953; repr., The Hague: Mouton, 1966), 95.

22. See http://evolvefish.com/about.htm.

23. See Colleen McDannell, *Material Christianity: Religion and Popular Culture in America* (New Haven, Conn.: Yale University Press, 1995), chap. 8.

24. Closer inspection also reveals that the GEFILTE fish is dead: its eye is filled with an "X" and its tongue hangs out. Given the agenda of the creators of the GEFILTE fish, this, too, appears to mock the original referent as a Christian symbol of life. However, F.I.S.H. also sells a variant of the GEFILTE fish that is not "dead" and sports a six-pointed Star of David as its eye.

25. Leyzer Ran, *Fun Elye Bokher biz Hirsh Glik: kortn leksikon* (From Elye Bokher [Elijah Levita] to Hirsh Glik: Card Lexicon) (New York: Vilner farlag, 1963). This "learn and play" card game features one hundred cards commemorating four hundred years of Yiddish literature; an instruction booklet explains rules for various games that can be played with the deck. Both cards and booklet are entirely in Yiddish.

26. Johan Huizinga, *Homo Ludens: A Study of the Play-Element in Culture* (Boston: Beacon, 1955), 198; Clifford Geertz, *The Interpretation of Cultures* (New York: Basic Books, 1973), 412, 448, 450.

27. See J. Hoberman, "Flaunting It: The Rise and Fall of Hollywood's 'Nice' Jewish (Bad) Boys," in J. Hoberman and Jeffrey Shandler, eds., *Entertaining America: Jews, Movies and Broadcasting* (Princeton, N.J.: Princeton University Press, 2003), 220–43.

28. According to Halter, "Longings and Belongings," this game was also distributed in the mid-1990s by Pierce, then the proprietor of Einstein's, an unusual "museum with price tags" in downtown Philadelphia, specializing in "ethnic merchandise of all kinds," including Yiddish artifacts and other Judaica. Halter reported at the time that "there is such a great demand" for the game and its accompanying cassette "that they can't keep enough on the shelf" (192).

29. The full joke appears in Leo Rosten, *The Joys of Yiddish* (New York: Simon & Schuster, 1968), 361–62 (emphasis original).

30. Most of the items listed on the brochure of "Camelite" products are given the Yiddish dismissive prefix "*shm-*": for example, "schmug," "tee schmirt," "schmear-rings," etc. Golf balls bearing the "Schmuck on That Camel" logo are named "putts," a pun on another Yiddish vulgarism for penis. Typical of other highly selective comic Yiddish lexicons, the one hundred or so Yiddish words included in the game consist mostly of culturally specific terms (e.g., *mikveh* [ritual bath], *payess* [sidelocks]), kinship terms (*bubba* [grandmother], *schviger* [mother-in-law]), food terms (*khrane* [horserad-ish], *latke* [pancake]), insults (*foiler* [idler], *schlepper* [slowpoke]), and obscenities. This last category focuses mostly on male genitalia (including three vulgarisms for penis), while insults often single out females (*yachneh, yenta* [both of which connote a coarse or vulgar woman], *shiksa* [a derogatory term for a non-Jewish woman]), suggesting a gendered point of view for the game's creator and implied players.

31. Glosses as per *Oy!: A New Comedy,* program, Melting Pot Theatre Company, New York, 1999, n.p.

32. See Werner Sollors, *Beyond Ethnicity: Consent and Descent in American Culture* (Oxford and New York: Oxford University Press, 1986).

33. *Oy!: A New Comedy* (program), n.p.

34. Irving Howe, *World of Our Fathers: The Journey of the East European Jews to America and the Life They Found and Made* (New York: Harcourt Brace Jovanovich, 1976), 642.

35. Jennifer Traig and Victoria Traig, *Judaikitsh: Tchotchkes, Schmattes, and Nosherei* (San Francisco: Chronicle Books, 2002), 8, front jacket flap, 8, 10, 11. *Judaikitsh* features a glossary of Yiddish and Hebrew terms, labeled "Hebonics" (118), offering conven-tional, rather than mock, definitions. Play takes place in the craft projects and their names, more often involving non-Jewish cultural referents such as "Jewshi" and "Spice Girls Spice Box."

36. Kenneth Turan, "The Architect," *The Book Peddler/Der pakn-treger* 19 (Summer 1994): 33–34.

37. NYBC reprints feature the logo of "the *goldene pave,* or golden peacock, . . . a traditional symbol of Yiddish creativity," on their spine and title page. The reprints were originally issued as paperback books. The illustration on the cover of all these reprints, designed by Paul Bacon, features a montage of images, including traditional shtetl fig-ures and architecture as well as images of immigrant life in America (a pushcart peddler, tenements, etc.). Beginning in 2003 the NYBC switched from paperback to plain cloth-cover reprints with library bindings.

6. WANTED DEAD OR ALIVE?

1. See S. L. Wisenberg, *Holocaust Girls: History, Memory and Other Obsessions* (Lincoln: University of Nebraska Press, 2000), 84–90. A flyer advertising Wisenberg's book at the 2002 Annual Modern Language Association Conference in New York featured "Yiddish you can use at the MLA: A handy-dandy guide to being post-postmodern." The list of twelve terms (credited to Dr. Khane-Faygl Turtletaub) included "deconstruction: di funandernemung" and "performative: aroysredevdik."

2. Braun passed a note to me bearing his "Y2K" message during a session of the 32nd Annual Association for Jewish Studies Conference, in Boston, 2000.

3. Leo Wiener, *The History of Yiddish Literature in the Nineteenth Century*, 2nd ed. (New York: Herman Press, 1972), 24, 10–11.

4. Cited in Ezekiel Lifschutz, "Morris Rosenfeld's Attempts to Become an English Poet," *America Jewish Archives* (1970): 124. The original text of the letter appears in *Moris Rozenfelds Briv* (Morris Rosenfeld's Letters), ed. Y. Lifshits (Buenos Aires: YIVO, 1955), 38–39. Rosenfeld was, in fact, writing to Leo Wiener. The poet was Wiener's protégé, and Wiener arranged for the English-language publication of Rosenfeld's poetry. Rosenfeld, in turn, was an important informant for Wiener in his study of American Yiddish literature. On their relationship, see Alisa Braun, "Becoming Authorities: Jews, Writing, and the Dynamics of Literary Affiliation, 1890–1940" (PhD diss., University of Michigan, Ann Arbor, forthcoming).

5. Ahad Ha-'Am, "The Spiritual Revival," in *Selected Essays by Ahad Ha-'Am*, trans. Leon Simon (Philadelphia: Jewish Publication Society, 1912), 282. The essay was "originally an address delivered before the general meeting of Russian Zionists at Minsk, in the summer of 1902" (253).

6. Editorial, *Jewish Tribune*, New York, 24 August 1928.

7. Henry James, *The American Scene* (1907; repr., New York: Charles Scribner's Sons, 1946), 138–39.

8. See Gennady Estraikh, *Soviet Yiddish: Language Planning and Linguistic Development* (Oxford: Clarendon, 1999), 5–20.

9. Celia Stopnicka Heller, *On The Edge of Destruction: Jews of Poland Between the Two World Wars* (New York: Columbia University Press, 1977), 66. See also John Myhill, *Language in Jewish Socety: Towards a New Understanding* (Clevedon, U.K.: Multilingual Matters, 2004), 136–40.

10. Abraham Gontar, "Keyn Afrike" (To Africa), in *Antologye: yidish in lid* (Anthology: Yiddish in Poetry) ed. Shmuel Rozhansky (Buenos Aires: Literatur-gezelshaft baym YIVO in Argentine, 1967), 180–81.

11. As cited in Paul Kresh, *Isaac Bashevis Singer: the Magician of West 86th Street* (New York: Dial Press, 1979), 418.

12. Isaac Bashevis Singer, *Nobel Lecture* (New York: Farrar Straus Giroux, 1978), 9.

13. Janet Hadda, "Yiddish in Today's America," *Jewish Quarterly* 170 (Summer 1998): 34–35. The essay was subsequently posted on *Mendele* (vol. 8.153, 13 May 1999), where it generated extensive and passionate discussion. See, for example, *Mendele: Yiddish Literature and Language* 9.006 (23 May 1999), http://shakti.trincoll.edu/~mendele/vol08/vol8.153.txt and http://shakti.trincoll.edu/~mendele/vol09/vol09.006.txt.

14. Hillel Halkin, "The Great Jewish Language War," *Commentary* 114, no. 4 (December 2002): 54, 53, 55.

15. Adina Cimet, letter to the editor, *Commentary* 115, no. 3 (March 2003): 4.

16. Joshua A. Fishman, ed., *Never Say Die! A Thousand Years of Yiddish in Jewish Life and Letters* (The Hague: Mouton, 1981).

17. Joshua A. Fishman, "The Lively Life of a 'Dead' Language or 'Everyone Knows That Yiddish Died Long Ago,'" *Judaica Book News* 13, no. 1 (fall/winter 1982–83): 10 (emphasis original).

18. Andrew Dalby, *Language in Danger: The Loss of Linguistic Diversity and the Threat to Our Future* (New York: Columbia University Press, 2003), x; David Crystal, *Language Death* (Cambridge: Cambridge University Press, 2000), 1.

19. For example, a Midrash explains that the rescue of Hebrew slaves from Egyptian bondage is attributed, in part, to their maintenance of their own language (Mekhilta de-Rabbi Ishmael, Bo, Parasha 5).

20. Y. L. Peretz, in *Di ershte yidishe shprakh-konferents: barikhtn, dokumentn un opklangen fun der tshernovitser konferents 1908* (The First Yiddish Language Conference: Reports, Documents, and Repercussions from the Czernowitz Conference of 1908) (Vilna: YIVO Institute for Jewish Research, 1931), 76. Note that the same word in the Yiddish original of this text—*yidish*—is here rendered as both "Yiddish" and "Jewish."

21. Aaron Lansky, "Outwitting History," *Pakntreger* 32 (Spring 2000): 19. See also *Outwitting History: The Amazing Adventures of a Man Who Rescued a Million Yiddish Books* (Chapel Hill, N.C.: Algonquin Books, 2004).

22. Cynthia Ozick, "Toward a New Yiddish," in *Art and Ardor* (New York: Knopf, 1983), 174. In her prefatory remarks to this published version of her essay, originally a talk delivered at the Weizmann Institute in Rehovoth, Israel, Ozick added that she was "no longer so tenderly disposed to the possibility of a New Yiddish—which was, anyhow, an invention, a literary conceit calculated to dispel pessimism" (151–52). See, in comparison, Janet Hadda, who recently termed contemporary Yiddish culture (excluding that of the *khareydim*) "neo-Ashkenaz" in her essay, "Imagining Yiddish: A Future for the Soul of Ashkenaz," *Pakntreger* 41 (Spring 2003): 15.

23. David Roskies, *Bridge of Longing: The Lost Art of Yiddish Storytelling* (Cambridge, Mass.: Harvard University Press, 1995), 4, 9.

24. Roskies, *Bridge of Longing*, 2.

25. Chaim M. Weiser, *Frumspeak: The First Dictionary of Yeshivish* (Northvale, N.J.: Jason Aronson, 1995), xxxiii.

26. David Gold, "Jewish English," in *Readings in the Sociology of Jewish Languages,* ed. Joshua A. Fishman (Leiden: E. J. Brill, 1985), 280.

27. H. B. Wells, "Notes on Yiddish," *American Speech* 4 (1928): 66.

28. Sam Weiss, "A Jewish Language in the Making," *International Journal of the Sociology of Language* 138 (1999): 185.

29. Alisa Solomon, "Notes on Klez/Camp," *Davka* 1, no. 3 (winter 1997): 29–31.

30. Raymond Williams notes that sensibility first becomes an important term in critical thinking in the mid-eighteenth century, meaning "a conscious openness [and] . . . consumption of feelings"; by the early twentieth century sensibility comes to refer to "a whole activity, a whole way of perceiving and responding, not to be reduced to either 'thought' or 'feeling,' " serving especially as "a key word to describe the human area in which artists worked and to which they appealed." See his *Keywords: A Vocabulary of Culture and Society,* rev. ed. (Oxford and New York: Oxford University Press, 1983), 281–82.

31. Ruth R. Wisse, "Yiddish: Past, Present, Imperfect," *Commentary* 104, no. 5 (November 1997): 38.

32. Daniel Boyarin, Daniel Itzkovitz, and Ann Pellegrini, eds., *Queer Theory and the Jewish Question* (New York: Columbia University Press, 2003), 1.

33. See Steven Seidman, ed., *Queer Theory/Sociology* (Oxford: Blackwell, 1996), especially the essays by Ki Namaste and Barry D. Adam.

34. Joshua A. Fishman, *Yiddish: Turning to Life* (Amsterdam: John Benjamins Publishing, 1991), 77.

35. The term *di goldene keyt* (the golden chain) emerged as a modernist metaphor of diasporic Jewish continuity with Y. L. Peretz's 1907 play of that name. Abraham Sutzkever chose this as the name of the Yiddish literary quarterly that he inaugurated in Israel in 1949.

36. Sander L. Gilman, *Jewish Frontiers: Essays on Bodies, Histories, and Identities* (New York: Palgrave Macmillan, 2003), 29.

37. David Crystal, *English as a Global Language* (New York: Cambridge University Press, 1997), 1.

38. Marc Shell, "Babel in America: Or, The Politics of Language Diversity in the United States," *Critical Inquiry* 20, no. 1 (fall 1993): 127.

39. Herbert Gans, "Symbolic Ethnicity in America," *Ethnic and Racial Studies* 2 (1979): 1–20; Mary C. Waters, *Ethnic Options: Choosing Identities in America* (Berkeley and Los Angeles: University of California Press, 1990).

40. George Steiner, *After Babel: Aspects of Language and Translation,* 3rd ed. (Oxford and New York: Oxford University Press, 1998), 89, 108.

41. Clifford Geertz, *The Interpretation of Cultures: Selected Essays* (New York: Basic Books, 1973), 89.

42. Régis Debray, *Transmitting Culture,* trans. Eric Rauth (New York: Columbia University Press, 2000), 118.

43. Steiner, *After Babel*, 58.

44. Introduction, *Bilingual Games: Some Literary Investigations*, ed. Doris Sommer (New York: Palgrave Macmillan, 2003), 11.

45. Fishman, "The Lively Life of a 'Dead' Language," 10 (emphasis original).

46. Max Weinreich, *History of the Yiddish Language*, trans. Shlomo Noble with Joshua A. Fishman (Chicago: University of Chicago, 1980), 207, 209.

47. For example, Hadda, "Imagining Yiddish," 14. See also Maria Damon, "Talking Yiddish at the Boundaries," *Cultural Studies* 5, no. 1 (January 1991). In seeking to conceptualize "the idiomatic fog that is Yiddish," Damon describes her "exegetical 'mining' activities" as being "fueled by an admittedly essentialist and wishfully cultivated instinct that where there's a Jew there must be some sort of Jewish consciousness, and language, for one trained in literary analysis, is the key. As for the question 'who gets to be Jewish?'—who gets to claim any sort of cultural authenticity—we could—and do—talk about that forever" (16–17).

48. Weinreich, *History of the Yiddish Language*, 210.

49. Gennady Estraikh, "Has the 'Golden Chain' Ended? Problems of Continuity in Yiddish Writing," in *Yiddish in the Contemporary World: Papers of the First Mendel Friedman International Conference on Yiddish*, ed. Gennady Estraikh and Mikhail Krutikov (Oxford: Legenda, 1999), 129, 124, 127, 128–29. Estraikh distinguishes Elinor Robinson among these poets as "the only 'Esperantist' whose debut was welcomed by Sutzkever" (128). Robinson's verse includes the poem "Vos bistu?" (What Are You?), which the Yiddishist journal *Afn shvel* published with a lengthy English glossary of abstruse terms used in the poem (*Afn shvel* 318 [April–June 2000], 6).

50. Jed Rasua and Steve McCaffery, eds., *Imagining Language: An Anthology* (Cambridge, Mass.: MIT Press, 1998), x.

51. Jonathan Boyarin, "Yiddish Science and the Postmodern," trans. Naomi Seidman, in *Thinking in Jewish* (Chicago: University of Chicago Press, 1996), 198–99. The image of "a shpigl af a shteyn" (a mirror on a stone) appears in Markish's poem "Brokhshtiker" (Shards); it appears in (and provides the name for) Khone Shmeruk's anthology, *A shpigl af a shteyn: antologye poezye un proze fun tsvelf farshnitene yidishe shraybers in Ratn-farband* (A Mirror on a Stone: Anthology of Poetry and Prose by Twelve Murdered Soviet Yiddish Writers) (Tel Aviv: Farlag Y. L. Perets, 1964), 489. The poem also appears, along with an English translation by Leonard Wolf, in *The Penguin Book of Modern Yiddish Verse*, ed. Irving Howe, Ruth R. Wisse, and Chone Shmeruk (New York: Viking Penguin, 1987), 376–77.

52. Sholem Berger distributed a Yiddish translation that he had prepared of the Hemshekh-dor manifesto (the text was originally written in Hebrew) at the meeting, which was held in Berger's Manhattan apartment on July 30, 2003.

INDEX

Note: Italicized page numbers indicate figures.

Abramovitsh, Sholem Yankev, 41, 54, 98, 111, 190. *See also* Mendele Moykher-Sforim
Abramowicz, Hirsz, 69, 70, 71–72
Absolut Vodka, 158, *159*
Adamczyck-Garbowska, Monika, 88
Advertising and advertisements, 4, *35*, *88*, 99, *129*, *142*, 158, *159*, *181*, *187*
Aesop, fables of, 95
agricultural colonies, Jewish, 37, 38, 39. *See also* Birobidzhan
Ahad ha-Am (Asher Ginsberg), 178, 179
Ainu, 23
alefbeys (Jewish alphabet): ideology and, 79; learning, 62, 76–78, 218n46, 220n60; on objects, 162, 164. See also romanization
Aleichem, Sholem. *See* Sholem Aleichem
Alexander II (czar), 12
Almi, A., 41

Aloni, Shulamit, 10
Alpert, Michael, 8–9, 130, 204–5n20, 230n6
Alter Caulker, 167, 168
American Association for Jewish Education, 81
American Speech (journal), 186
Amsterdam, Morey, 162
Anderson, Benedict, 37
Anshei Minsk (synagogue, Toronto), 138, 231n24
Ansky, S., 111
anthologizing: of literature, 105, 109–10; of music and songs, 144–45, 233n40; performance strategies of, 139
anti-Semitism, 7, 12, 105
Antwerp, 46
Arabs, 11
Arbeter Ring. *See* Workmen's Circle
Argentina, 38, 39, 42, 211n24
Arthur (king), romance of, 95
artifacts. *See* material culture

Artisbashev, Mikhail, 99
"Art of Yiddish, The" (program),
    138–39
ArtScroll (press), 208–9n65
Asch, Sholem, 103, 105–6
Aschheim, Steven, 7
Ashkenaz Festival (Toronto), 137–38
Ashkenazim (diasporic Jewish commu-
    nity): definition of, 203–4n5; geo-
    graphic range of, 6; relation to Yid-
    dish of, 3–4, 11, 12, 95, 138–39; use of
    Yiddish by 128–30, 196
Asimov, Isaac, 120–21
Association of Former Residents of
    Dobrzyn-Golub, 43
Austin, J. L., 147–48
Australia, 16, 20, 82, 133, 146, 187, 191
Austria, 39, 40
Avalon Hill Game Company, 170
Azuma, Chika, 60

Bacon, Paul, 237n37
Balagan [Chaos] (film), 21
baleytshuve (Jews returning to religious
    observance), Yiddish and, 153, 182, 196
Baram, Nir, 11
Bar-Ilan University, 202
bar mitzvah, Yiddish speeches at, 74–75
Barry Sisters (musicians), 139
Beckett, Samuel, 110, 228n73
Bellow, Saul, 112, 120
Benjamin, Walter, 104
Ben-Yehuda, Eliezer, 90
Ber, Yosl, 52
Berdychiv, 52
Bergen-Belsen, theater troupe of, 18
Berger, Sholem, 117, 118, 201–2, 241n51
Beyond the Pale (recording), 8–9, 204n20
Beys Rokhl schools, 83, 220n69
Beys Yaakov schools, 69, 72
Bez, Khayem, 79–80
Bhabha, Homi, 93
Bialik, Hayyim Nahman, 111

Bible, Hebrew: language for studying,
    84; translations of, 93, 98, 99–100,
    223n14. See also Tsenerene
bilingualism/multilingualism: of au-
    thors, 110–13; code-switching and, 92;
    as definitional Jewish practice, 92–93;
    internal Jewish, 5–6, 62, 93; interwar
    changes in, 71–72; language play in,
    163–65, 193–94; in performances, 139;
    and translation, 110–16; Yiddish peda-
    gogy and, 62–63, 219n58
Binshtok, Yehude-Leyb, 98
Birnbaum, Nathan, 131, 190
Birobidzhan, 37–38, 72, 132, 211n22
Bloomgarden, Solomon (Yehoash),
    99–100
Boiberik (summer camp), 38
Bookbinder, David, 137
books and bookstores, 83, 149–50,
    175–76. See also National Yiddish
    Book Center
Borodulin, Nikolai, 50–51
Boro Park (Brooklyn), 3, 33, 46, 150
Botoshanski, Yankev, 39–40
Bove-bukh (Book of Buovo), 119–20
Boyarin, Jonathan, 43, 54, 56, 57–58, 199
Bratslav, 52
Braun, David, 177
Brave Old World (klezmer band), 8–9,
    204–5n20
Brazil, 41, 146
Brenner, Joseph Hayyim, 111
Bressler, Judy, 232n37
Bridger, David, 219n58
brivnshtelers (letter-writing manuals), 63
Brooks, Mel, 170
Bruce, Lenny, 170
Budapest, 46
Buloff, Joseph, 122
Bund. See Jewish Workers' Bund
Buovo d'Antona, 119–20
Burg, Abraham, 10, 34
Burstin, Hinde Ena, 187

Busch, Wilhelm, 117
Byron, Lord (George Gordon), 99

Cahan, Abraham, 112
Canada, 39, 41, 146. *See also* Montreal; Toronto
Cantors in Yiddish (recording), 11–12, 205–6n31
Carle, Eric, 117
Carlebach, Shlomo, 141
Casting (film), 21
Catalan, 39
Cat in the Hat, The, 117, *118*
Chabon, Michael, 31–34, 209n7
Charlotte Yiddish Institute, 4
Charney (Shmuel Niger), 92
Chaudhuri, Sukanta, 103, 122
Chekhov, Anton, 122
children: as focus of Yiddishists, 67, 68–69; language learning of, 189; and parents' use of Yiddish, 152, 172–3; stickers for, 169; toys for, 162, 164, 235n12. *See also* games; schools
children's literature: hasidic publications of, 83–85; in Soviet Union, 103, 224n24; translations of, 116–19, 121, 122. *See also* instructional manuals and primers
Chofetz Chaim. *See* Hafez Hayyim
Chomsky, Noam, 192
Christianity: Asch's novels about, 105–6; symbol of, mocked, 168, 236n24. *See also* New Testament
Chrysander, Wilhelm Christian Just, 63
Chutzpa (poetry magnets), 157
Chutzpah (game), 170, 171–72, 174
Cirker, Hayward, 32
Civilization (periodical), 31–33, 209n2
code-switching: as definitional Jewish activity, 92, 93–94; in literature, 111; performance strategies of, 139; in song lyrics, 232n27. *See also* bilingualism/multilingualism; translations

College Yiddish, 86, 222n87
Columbia University, 33, 149–50, 201
Commentary, 181
conferences: of Jewish teachers in Vilna, 68; Yiddish used at, 126–27, 238n1; of YIVO (1935), 39–40. *See also* Czernowitz Yiddish Conference
cookbooks, 166, 174–75
Cooper, Adrienne, *140*, 141
Cracow: in board game, 46; Jewish festival in, 141, *142*
creative betrayal, concept of, 185
cultural autonomy: Versailles Treaty provisions for, 13; of Yiddish in interwar Poland, 40
culture: immigrant, 73–75, 172–73; Mizrahi, 11, *197*; neo-Ashkenaz, 239n22; queer, 189–90. *See also* Jewish culture; language/culture/identity interrelations; material culture; Yiddish culture
Czech, 206n34
Czernowitz, 46
Czernowitz Yiddish Conference, 131, 178, 183

Damon, Maria, 241n47
dance, as "Yiddish," 141
Davilman, Barbara, *60*
Davka (magazine), 187
Dawidowicz, Lucy, 40
daytshmerish (overreliance on literary German), 7–8
Debray, Régis, 192
Defoe, Daniel, 99
deep play, concept of, 169
Der Bay (Bay Area Yiddish newsletter), 133–34
Derrida, Jacques, 154
diaspora: hasidic, post–WWII, 82; Jewish languages and, 129; mapping of, 45; nationalism, 36; poetic visions of, 40–42; position of U.S. in, 16, 73, 191;

diaspora *(continued)*
    Yiddish as signifier of, 11, 39, 49–50,
    87–88, 183. See also *doikeyt*; immi-
    grants and immigration; national con-
    sciousness and nationalism
Dickinson, Emily, 117
dictionaries. *See* mock dictionaries; *Mod-*
    ern English-Yiddish Yiddish-English
    Dictionary; phrase books
Dik, Isaac Meyer, 7, 98, 204n16
dissertations: on klezmer, 143, 232n36; on
    Yiddish, 2
Dobrzyn, map of, *43*
doikeyt ("hereness"), 36
Dostoyevsky, Fyodor, 99
Dover Publications, 31–34
Dresdner, Sruli, 130
dreydl (top), 162, 235n12
driter seyder (third seder), 131
Dubnow, Simon, 68
Dutch, 160, 206n34
Dybbuk, The (drama), 111
Dzhankoiia, 38

Eastern Europe: evoked on websites, 54;
    Jewish education in, 64–66, 69–73; Jew-
    ish youth movements in, 148–49; place
    of Yiddish in, 16, 26, 27, 35–36, 39, 42,
    47; "radical Judaization" of, 52–53; re-
    membrance of Jewish past in, 53,
    107–10, 130, 142–44; Yiddish instruction
    in, 71–72, 87–89; Yiddish translations in,
    99–100. *See also* Hungary; Latvia;
    Lithuania; Poland; Romania; Russia;
    shtetl; Soviet Union; Ukraine
education. *See* instructional manuals and
    primers, Yiddish; schools; Yiddish-
    language pedagogy
Efros, Mirele, *52*
Eichmann, Adolf, 10
Einspruch, Henry, 101–2
Eisner, Will, 122, *123*
Elbe, Leon, 75, *77*

Eldridge Street Synagogue (NYC), 130
Eli, Ovadia, 10
Eliach, Yaffa, 53, 213–14n65
Eliot, T. S., 120
encyclopedias, 83
England, 38, 46, 142, 146, 221n73
English language: dominance of, in U.S.,
    191–92; isolated Yiddish terms in, 156,
    158; in Jewish education, 74, 76–78,
    81, 164; literary translations into Yid-
    dish from, 98, 99, 101, 116–21; in rela-
    tion to Yiddish, 78–79, 81, 111, 129,
    133–34, 149–50, 163–65, 179, 208n61;
    as world language, 191; Yiddish trans-
    lated into, 103–10, 112
Entin, Joel, 75
"Envy; or, Yiddish in America" (short
    story), 114–16
Esman, Marjorie, 136
"Esperantists," as kind of Yiddish writer,
    198–99
Esperanto, 12, 39
Ester-Rokhl Kaminska State Yiddish
    Theater, 52
Estonian language, 89
Estraikh, Gennady, 50, 72, 198–99, 211n22
ethnicity: immigrant humor as code of,
    172–73; logos for, 160; as voluntary vs.
    biological, 173, 191–92; Yiddish in re-
    lation to, 147, 165
Euchel, Isaac, 111
exile: as theme in literature, 41; Yiddish
    as emblem of, 11. *See also* diaspora
"experience": use of term, 136; Yiddish
    in performance as, 139–40
Ezrahi, Sidra, 41, 49

Fareynikte, 68
Farlag B. A. Kletskin (publisher), 99
Farlag "Progres" (publisher), 99
Feder, Samy, 18
Fein, Richard, 92
Feinberg, Leon, 41, *42*

Felder, Sara, 187
festivalization, concept of, 136
festivals, 135–38
fetishes, Yiddish-inscribed objects as, 160–61, 194
Feuer, Bernardo, 145
films: use of Yiddish in, 20–21; Yiddish, attack on, 9–10; Yiddish, as constituting Yiddishland, 50–51
Finkel, Emmanuel, 21
Finnish language, 117
F.I.S.H. (Freethinkers In Service to Humanity), 168, 236n24
Fisher, Dorothy Canfield, 105
Fishman, Joshua A.: on learning Yiddish, 197–98; on number of Yiddish speakers, 203n1; on vitality of Yiddish language, 181, 189; on Yiddish culture, 70
fish symbols, 168, 236n24
Fitzgerald, Edward, 99
folklore: preserved/mocked by Haskalah, 162–63; valuations of Yiddish in, 10–11, 61
Folksbeine (theater company), 181
folkshprakh (vernacular language): defined, 13; vs. kulturshprakh, 70–71. See also vernacular languages
Folkspartey, 68
food: at cultural events, 153; and material culture, 167–68, 174; in Yiddish folkways, 44, 93; Yiddish terms for, 151, 164–65, 166–67. See also cookbooks
Forverts (Yiddish-language weekly), 20, 116–17. See also Forward, Forward Association, Jewish Daily Forward.
Forward (English-language weekly): logo of, 164, 165; on Yiddish language, 134–35. See also Forverts, Forward Association, Jewish Daily Forward.
Forward Association, 19–20, 207n51, 227n63. See also Forverts, Forward, Jewish Daily Forward.

France, 39, 146. See also Paris
Frank, Helena, 105
Frankfurt, 46
Freethinkers In Service to Humanity (F.I.S.H.), 168, 236n24
Freiheit Gezang Farein (Yiddish chorus), 144
French language, 54, 98, 99, 103, 109, 111, 117, 130, 157, 160
Fridman, Moyshe, 66, 215–16n15
Frumkin, Maria Yakovlevna, 67
Frumspeak (Weiser), 186

Galai, Assaf, 201–2
games: creators of, 170, 212n41; gender and, 237n30; language play in, 169–73, 174; as mapping projects, 46–47; sales of, 236n28; about Yiddish literature, 169, 236n25
Garnett, Constance, 122
gay and lesbian Jews. See Queer Yiddishkeit
Gebirtig, Mordecai, 144
Geertz, Clifford, 169–70, 192
gefilte fish: customs of preparing, 44; in ornament, 168, 236n24
gender: in education, 74, 84 (see also girls' education); games and, 237n30; literacy and, 95–98; Yeshivish and, 186–87, 196; of Yiddish as "mother tongue," 218n49. See also queer theory
generational differences: in attitudes toward Yiddish, 11; cartoon on, 148; gift giving and, 174; in queer and youth cultures, 189; rebellion related to, 152; use of, in humor, 17–18; Yiddish pedagogy and, 79–80, 219n58
gentiles. See non-Jews.
geography: of games, 46–47, 170; homeland and, 35–40; mapping projects and, 43–50; "official" languages linked to, 44; playing Jewish, 56; as symbolic space in performance, 137–38. See also Yiddishland

German language: Jewish schools taught in, 65; and *mauscheln* (Yiddish-inflected), 131; as model for national language movements, 7–8; marking of Jews in, by Nazis, 160; poetry magnets in, 157; relation of Yiddish to, 6–7, 8–9, 95, 111, 129, 179; on Yiddish list-serv, 54; Yiddish literary translations of, 99, 101, 117, 121; Yiddish literature translated into, 103, 224n26; Yiddish phrase book in, 209n5. See also *dayt-shmerish*

Germany: Jews as outsiders in, 6–7; klezmer in, 8–9, 130; role of Yiddish in, post-WWII, 2, 130, 153; youth movement in, 148; Yugntruf members in, 146

Gilbert and Sullivan operettas, Yiddish versions of, 120–22, 228n70, 229n82

Gilman, Sander, 7, 191

Ginsberg, Asher (Ahad ha-Am), 178, 179

girls' education: primers for, 83–84, 215–16n15; schools for, 69; Yiddish and religion in, 72, 83–84

Glatshteyn, Yankev, 8, 19, 115

Glazer, Nathan, 16

Glik, Hirsh, 18–19

Glinert, Lewis, 221n73

glossaries, 157, 173, 210n9, 237n35. *See also* instructional manuals and primers, mock dictionaries

Goethe, Johann Wolfgang von, 101

Gogol, Nikolai, 99

Gold, David, 186

goldene keyt, di (the golden chain), 190, 198, 240n35

Goldfaden, Abraham, 131, 230n7

Goldshteyn-Gershonovitsh, Tsvi-Hirsh, 63

Gontar, Abraham, 180

Gordon, Eric, 51

Grade, Chaim, 110

grammar, Yiddish, 63, 70–71, 220n69

Grand, Al, 120–21, 228n70

Great Small Works (theater company), 140

Greek, 206n34. *See also* Judeo-Greek

Green, Martin, 123–24

Greenberg, Eliezer, 109–10

Greenberg, Uri-Zvi, 111

Gross, Milt, 112

Grossman, Jeffrey, 7

Groyser kundes, Der (The Big Prankster, magazine), 14, 100

Gruber, Ruth Ellen, 53, 130

Grudberg, Yitskhok, 40

Gruss, Marcia, 117

Gubalnik, Dovid, 40

Gujerati, 44

Haberman, Clyde, 18

Hadda, Janet, 180, 185, 239n22

Hafez Hayyim: in board game, 47; writing of (*Sefer Chofetz Chaim*), 186

Halévy, Jacques Fromenthal, 11, 205–6n31

Halkin, Hillel, 180–81

Halter, Marilyn, 160, 236n28

Handl erlikh (Deal Honestly, game), 46–47, 212n41

Harper's Magazine, 32–33

Harshav, Barbara, 34

Harshav, Benjamin, 6, 12, 34, 128, 227n63

Harvard University, 177

hasidim: interaction with other Yiddish speakers, 150, 199; Lubavitcher (Habad), 220n65; postwar communities of, 82; role of Yiddish for, 46, 85, 153, 194, 203n2; Satmar, 83; story-telling by, 222n4; Yiddish-language pedagogy of, 82–85. See also *kharey-dim*

Haskalah (Jewish Enlightenment): de-bates on Yiddish translations in, 98; educational experiments of, 65; folk-ways preserved/mocked by, 162–63;

Yiddish disparaged by, 7, 12, 64, 65, 131, 179; Yiddish literacy and, 63–64, 95

"Hebonics," 237n35

Hebrew language: as Jewish language, 193, 230n4; as mother tongue, 90; phrase book of, 31; rabbinic vs. modern, 23; relation to Yiddish, 9–11, 48–50, 81–82, 129, 180–81, 222n4, 233–34n53; ritual objects inscribed with, 162; shift from vernacular to scriptural use of, 23; Soviet rejection of, 216–17n27; study of, 16, 69; 86–87; translations of Yiddish literature in, 103; Yiddish as formative element of, 205n21. See also Loshn-koydesh

Heller, Celia, 179

Hemshekh-dor (Generation of Continuity, organization), 201–2, 241n51

Hendrickson, Robert, 235n10

Herder, Johann Gottfried von, 6–7, 192

heritage: mock, characteristics of, 172–73; productions of, 51–52, 53; subversion of, 78; translations and, 107–10; Yiddish as object of, 75, 79–82

Herman Nut Company, 167

Hernández, Jesús, 219n53

Heschel, Abraham Joshua, 46, 226n46

Hester Street (film), 20

Hiawatha (poem), 99

hip-hop, 21–22

Hitler, Adolf, 179

Hobbit Toys and Games, 170

Hoberman, J., 34

Hoffman, Heinrich, 117

holidays, as occasions for speaking Yiddish, 135–36, 147. See also rituals.

Hollander, John, 113

Hollinger, David, 22

Holocaust: accounts of, 21, 109, 228n71; book preservation linked to, 176; catastrophic effects of, 15–16, 26, 72, 81, 184; literary translation in context of,

104, 108-10, 117–19; memorial to, 10, 19; Yiddish in relation to, 8, 14–15, 18–19, 42–44, 127, 179. See also Nazis

homeland: implications of Yiddishland for, 35–40, 49–50; language linked to, 34–35

L'homme est une femme comme les autres [English version: *Man Is a Woman*] (film), 21

Howe, Irving, 109–10, 122, 174

Hugo, Victor, 99, 223n15

Huizinga, Johann, 169

Huljet (klezmer band), 9

Humboldt, Wilhelm von, 6–7, 192

humor: carnivalesque in, 167–68; in crafts and recipes, 174–75, 237n25; language play in, 92, 93, 139, 163–65; of mock dictionaries, 165–67; of mock-ritual objects, 162–63; in stand-up comedy, 170; valuations of Yiddish in, 10–11. See also language play; mockery; playfulness

Hungarian language, 12

Hungary, 46, 212n41

Hurvits, S., 78

Hutton, Christopher, 8, 71

Ibsen, Henrik, 103

identity: extralinguistic issues in, 124–25; fetishes in relation to, 160–61; in Israel, 11; questioning, 174, 201–2; transformed in postvernacular Yiddish, 196; translation as factor in, 92. See also language/culture/identity interrelations

ideology: commitment to Yiddish as, 149; in instructional manuals and primers, 78–79, 219n53; standardization of language and, 8. See also Yiddishism (ideology)

imagined communities, concept of, 37

immigrants and immigration: bilingual humor of, 164–65; cultural impact of,

immigrants and immigration (*continued*)
73–75; symbolic reenactment of, 138;
symbolic value of language for, 35;
teaching about, 79–80, 219n58; viability of Yiddish linked to, 178. *See also*
diaspora; exile
Indonesian language, 31
Instant Yiddish (recording), *24*
instructional manuals and primers, Yiddish: by Christian humanists, 63;
college-level, 86–88; early twentieth-
century, 65–67, 215–16n15; English
used in, 80–82, 220n60; examples of,
64, 77, 78; for hasidim, 83–85, 220n65;
ideological nature of, 67, 78–79,
219n53; for letter writing, 63; parody
of, *60*; pedagogical reform and, 80–81;
poetry in, 79–81; postwar changes in,
81–82; for U.S. Yiddish schools,
74–82. *See also* glossaries; mock dictionaries; phrase books
International Workers Order (IWO), 74,
79, 80–81
International Yiddish Festival (Cracow),
142
Internet: orally based shorthand on,
214n70; as "virtual Jewish world,"
53–58; Yiddish archived on, 214n73
Ireland, 2
Irish language, 23
Isaacs, Miriam, 83, 84
Isle of Klezbos (klezmer band), 187
Israel: attitudes about Yiddish in, 9–11,
19, 34, 191, 201–2; college-level Yiddish instruction in, 87, 222n87; establishment of, 16; Hebrew as official lan-
guage of, 49, 193; Yugntruf members
in, 146. *See also* Jaffa; Jerusalem; Ris-
hon LeZion; Tel Aviv
Italian, 157, 209n5. *See also* Judeo-
Italian
Italy, 2, 23, 146
IWO. *See* International Workers Order

Jacobs, Ken, 20
Jaffa, 48
Jaffe, Marie, 117
Jakobson, Roman, 86
James, Henry, 179
Japan, 2, 146
Japanese, 209n5
Japan Yiddish Club, *55*
Jerusalem, 82
Jewish Anti-Fascist Committee, 14
Jewish Commissariat, 70
Jewish Cultural Festival (Cracow), 141
Jewish culture: as found in translation,
92; invention's importance in, 185;
Jews as tourists of, 136–37; linguistic
consciousness in, 182–83; loss of
mimesis in, 127–32. *See also* Yiddish
culture
Jewish Daily Forward (Yiddish-language
daily), 15, 99. See also *Forverts, For-
ward,* Forward Association
Jewish English, definition of, 186
Jewish Museum of Maryland, *163*
Jewish Music Institute, 142
Jewish National Fund, 49–50
Jewishness: language in realizing,
182–83; mimetic transmission of,
127–30; modern definitions of, 12; par-
adigm shift of, from "Judaism," 16;
Yiddish in relation to, 14–15, 48–50,
124–25
Jewish People's Fraternal Order
(JPFO), 79, 80–81
Jewish People's Philharmonic Chorus
(NYC), 144
Jewish studies (academic), 85–91,
188–89, 221–22n84
Jewish Theological Seminary of Amer-
ica, 87–88
Jewish Tribune (English-language
weekly), 178
Jewish Workers' Bund, 36, 67–68
Jews: cultural center of, 16, 26, 27, 42, 47;

as cultural middlemen, 105; and discussion of language use, 11–13, 98; immigration of, 73–74; impact of Holocaust on, 15–16; as outsiders in German culture, 6–7; paradigm shift from Jewishness to Judaism of, in U.S., 16; youth movements of, 148–49. *See also* Ashkenazim; *baleytshuve*; hasidim; *khareydim*; Mizrahi culture

Jews for Jesus (organization), 194

Joselit, Jenna, 38, 74–75

Joyce, James, 199

Joys of Yiddish, The, 10–11, 141, 170–72

JPFO. *See* Jewish People's Fraternal Order

Judaism, paradigm shift from "Jewishness" to, 16. *See also* religion and religiosity, Jewish

Judaization: of music, 229n82; in translations, 119–22

Judeo-Arabic, 23, 129

Judeo-Aramaic, 23

Judeo-English, definition of, 186

Judeo-Greek, 129

Judeo-Italian, 23

Judezmo (Judeo-Spanish), 129

Judson, Solomon, 101

Kaczerginski, Szmerke, 144–45

Kadar, Naomi Prawer, 205n29

Kadushin, Hirsh, 18

Kafka, Franz, 109

Kalevala (Finnish epic), 117

Kaplan, Yisroel, 48

Kaplin, Jim, *148*

Karen, Rea, 50

Karnilova, Maria, *24*

Katchor, Ben, 32, 209n2

kats der payats, Di (trans. of *The Cat in the Hat*), 117, *118*

Katz, Dovid, 82, 85, 221n77

Katz, Mickey, 139, 229n82

Kazdan, Chaim, 14–15, 65

Kazin, Alfred, 107–8

Kellman, Ellen, 99

Kelsey, Lisa M., 187

Kfitses haderekh (Shortcut, game), 46–47

Khalkha, 44

khareydim (ultra-Orthodox Jews): Yiddish as signifier of piety for, 150, 169, 196; Yiddish as vernacular of, 2, 182, 189, 221n73. *See also* hasidim

kheyder (traditional Jewish school), 62, 65, 74, 77. *See also* schools

Kheyder (play), *133*

Khrushchev, Nikita, 72

Kiev, 41, 87

Kinderland (summer camp), 38

Kinder Ring (summer camp), *38*

Kipling, Rudyard, 99

Kirshenblatt-Gimblett, Barbara, 51, 107, 136

kitsch, 175. *See also* material culture

Klepfisz, Irena, 112–13

kleyner prints, Der (trans. of *Le Petit Prince*) 117, 119

KlezFest, 142

KlezKamp, 141, 232n30

Klezmatics (band), 141, 143, 144, 187

Klezmer Conservatory Band (Boston), 143–44, 232n37

klezmer (musician and music): educational role of, 142–44, 195; performed in Germany, 8–9, 130; recordings of, *9*, 204–5n20; use of term, 143

Knesset (Israel), homage to Yiddish in, 10, 34

Kobrin, Leon, 99

Komoroczy, Szonja, 212n41

Kook, Rabbi Abraham Isaac, 145

Koussevitzky, Moshe, 11–12, 205–6n31

Krakowski, Wolf, 144–45

Krug, Mark M., 217n41

Krutikov, Mikhail, 50

Kugelmass, Jack, 43, 136

kulturshprakh (language of high culture), 8, 19, 71, 86

Kushner, Tony, 227n63

Kutner, Philip "Fishl," 133–34

Kutshinski, Meir, 228n73

Kuźnica, 46

Kvitko, Leyb, 103, 224n24

Labor Zionists, 74, 75, 79, 149

language: acquisition of, 76–78, 103, 189–90; acquisition of second, 60–61, 79–82, 86–89; changing role of, 166–67, 192–93; choice of, 11–12, 15, 84–85, 191, 194, 197–98; as heritage, 20, 84, 174–75; homeland linked to, 34–35; immigrant vs. minority, 83; loss of, 20, 25–26, 181–82; oral in relation to written, 54, 62, 93, 94, 95; postvernacular, defined, 22–25; symbolic meanings of, 51–52, 112, 193–94, 213n59. *See also* bilingualism/multilingualism; language/culture/identity interrelations; language play; languages, specific; Yiddish language

Language and Culture Atlas of Ashkenazic Jewry (LCAAJ), 44–46

language/culture/identity interrelations: cohort groups' role in, 189–90; early conceptualizations of, 6; interwar changes in, 71–73; moral character assigned to, 8; postvernacularity's implications for, 23–25; undoing/discontinuity of, 183–84, 192–94; U.S. as context for, 191–92

language play: in advertising, 158, *159*; context for, in U.S., 169–76; in crafts and recipes, 174–75, 237n25; in games, 169–73; of material objects, 157–58, 163–65; of mock dictionaries, 165–67; role of, 197–98; between Yiddish and English, 163–65; of Yiddish and hip-hop, 21–22. *See also* code-switching; humor; playfulness

languages, specific: Ainu, 23; Catalan, 39; Czech, 206n34; Dutch, 160, 206n34; Esperanto, 12, 39; Estonian, 89; Finnish, 117; Greek, 4, 206n34; Gujerati, 44; "Hebonics," 237n35; hip-hop, 21–22; Hungarian, 12; Indonesian, 31; Irish, 23; Italian, 157, 209n5; Japanese, *55*, 209n5; Jewish English, 186; Judeo-Arabic, 23, 129; Judeo-Aramaic, 23; Judeo-English, 186; Judeo-Greek, 129; Judeo-Italian, 23; Judezmo (Judeo-Spanish), 129; Khalkha, 44; Korean, 4; Latin, 119; Navajo, 23; Norwegian, 103; Polish, 4, 12, 35; sign, 140, 157; Spanish, 130, 157, 219n53; Swahili, 31; Twi, 44; Ukrainian, 111; Welsh, 39, Yeshivish, 186–87. *See also* English language; French language; German language; Hebrew language; Loshn-koydesh; Russian language; Yiddish language

Lansky, Aaron, 184. *See also* National Yiddish Book Center

Lao-tzu, 99

Lariar, Lawrence, *167*

lashon ha-kodesh. See Loshn-koydesh

Latin language, 119

Latvia, Yiddish translations in, 99

LCAAJ. See *Language and Culture Atlas of Ashkenazic Jewry*

Lederhandler, Eli, 108

Lefin, Mendel, 98, 105, 223n14

Leftwich, Joseph, 18–19, 105

Lenard, Alexander, 119

Lerman, Shloyme, 117, 119

lesbian and gay Jews. *See* Queer Yiddishkeit

lessons, Yiddish: college-level, 86; first, examples of, *77, 78*; first letters and words in, 75–78, 218nn46,51; in hasidic magazine, 85; in material culture, *17*, 164, 170–72; methodology of, 62, 63, 66, 75–77, 80–82, 86, 219n58, 220n69;

recordings of, *24;* subversive messages in, 67, 77–78, 218n51; use of, in humor 17–18, *60,* 173. *See also* glossaries; instructional manuals and primers; mock dictionaries; phrase books; schools

Levenson, Sammy, 17

Levi, Primo, 23

Leviant, Curt, 107

Levin, Yankev, 80, 219n57

Levita, Elijah, 41, 119–20

Leżajsk, 46

Lilien, Ephraim Moses, *102*

listservs, imagining Yiddishland via, 54–56

literacy, Jewish: earlier notions of, 63–64, 95–96; gendering of, 95–98; ideology fused with, 78–79; impact of translations on, 103–10; inversion of, 66; revolutionized notions of, 98–103, 195; rituals of, 62

Literarishe bleter (Warsaw weekly), 39, 40

literature: American Jewish, 112–16; children's, 83–85, 116–19, 121, 122; world, 98–103, 117. *See also* folklore; poetry; Yiddish literature

Lithuania: interwar Yiddish schools in, 69, *70;* postwar Yiddish education in, 87, 89; Yiddish translations in, 99. *See also* Vilna (Vilnius)

living history museums, 53

Łódź, 46

London, 38, 46, 82, 142

London, Frank, *140*

London, Jack, 101

Longfellow, Henry Wadsworth, 117

Look at the Schmuck on That Camel (game), 170–73, 236n28

Los Angeles, 133, 138–39

Loshn-koydesh (language of holiness): defined, 6; Old Yiddish glosses of, 94; as primary written language, 62; in traditional text study, 93; Yiddish in

relation to, 6, 21, 111. *See also* bilingualism/multilingualism; Hebrew language; Judeo-Aramaic

Lowenthal, David, 20, 84

Lozovsky, Solomon, 14

Lublin, 46

Lumet, Sidney, 170

Lurie, Joseph, 68–69

Madame Jacques sur La Croisette (film), 21

Madonna (singer), 26, 208n61

Maeterlinck, Maurice, 99

Magnetic Poetry, 157–58, 234n3

Malamud, Bernard, 112

mame (mother), in first lesson, 77–*78*

mame-loshn (Yiddish as "mother tongue"): gendering of, 218n49; symbolic value of, 77; use of term, 59–60. *See also* Yiddish-language pedagogy

Manger Prize, 48

mapping projects: in board games, 46–47; in memorial books, 43–44; of Yiddishland, *42,* 49–50. See also *Language and Culture Atlas of Ashkenazic Jewry*

Marcus, Ivan, 62

Mark, Yudel, 90, 219n58

Markish, Peretz, 39, 199, 241n51

Mashuga Nuts, 167–68

maskilim (followers of the Haskalah). *See* Haskalah

material culture: as carnivalesque, 167–68; as fetish, 160–61, 194; language play in, 163–65; merchandising of, 172, 237n30; and ritual, 161–63; words inscribed on, 156–59, 234n1

Maud, Zuni, *14*

Maupassant, Guy de, 99, 223–24n17

Mauriac, François, 109

mauscheln (Yiddish-inflected German), 131

Max und Moritz, 117, 121

Mayer, Lisa, 130

Mayles (Virtues, magazine), 85, 221n77

Mayse-bukh (Book of Tales), 97

Medem, Vladimir, 190

Medem Library, 133

Medzhybizh, 52

Melbourne, 82, 187

Melting Pot Theatre Company, 173

Memmi, Albert, 23

*Memoirs of Glückel of Hameln/
    Zikhroynes Glikl, The, 140*

Mencken, H. L., 235n10

Mendele (listserv), 54–55

Mendele Moykher-Sforim, 40, 54, 110.
    See also Sholem Yankev Abramovitsh

Mendelssohn, Moses, 7

Mexico, 20, 41, 133, 146

Michelson, Richard, 220n63

Mickel, David, 21–22

migration. *See* immigrants and immigration

Mikhoels, Shloyme, 231n12

Miller, Arthur, 122

Milne, A. A., 116, 119

Miłosz, Czesław, 35

mimesis: loss of, 127–32; and memory,
    154

Minczeles, Henri, 47–48

Miriam (poet), 48

Miron, Dan, 52, 162

Mishkowsky, Noah, 65

Mizrahi culture, 11, *197*

Mlotek, Eleanor Gordon, 233n40

Mlotek, Joseph, 233n40

mock dictionaries: example of, 17–18;
    language play of, 165–67; and non-
    Jewish reader, 236n19. See also *Joys of
    Yiddish, The*

mockery: in dictionaries, 165–67; in
    games, 169–73; in language play,
    163–65; motivation for, 169; preserva-
    tion linked to, 162–63

*Modern English-Yiddish Yiddish-English
    Dictionary, 33, 199*

Moisésville, 38

Mokotow, Romek, 228n71

Moliére, Jean Baptiste, 99

Monopoly (game), 46–47, 170, 172,
    212n41

Monsey (New York), 46

Montreal, 41, 46, 82

Moore, Allen, 51, 175

Moore, Clement, 117

Morgen-Freiheit (newspaper), 144

Moscow, Yiddish instruction in, 87–88

Mr. Mahzel figurine, 162, *163*

multilingualism. *See* bilingualism/multi-
    lingualism

Muncacz, 46

museums, 10, 53, 145, *163*

music and music performances: antholo-
    gizing of, 144–45, 233n40; as cultural
    restoration, 130; educational role of,
    142–44, 195; in Germany, 8–9, 130;
    hip-hop, 21–22; Judaization of,
    229n82; "Orthodox pop," 132; record-
    ings of, 8–9, *24*, 34, 204–5n20; as sig-
    nifier of Yiddishness, 141. *See also*
    song lyrics

Myhill, John, 239n9

Nabokov, Vladimir, 110

Nahman of Bratslav, 222n4

national consciousness and nationalism:
    classroom emblematic of, 90; dias-
    pora, 36; imagined communities and,
    37; Yiddish language and, 13, 35–36,
    51, 63–64, 90–95, 131, 183–84

National Defense Education Act, 44

National Public Radio, 21–22

National Yiddish Book Center (NYBC):
    architecture of, 51, 175, 176; core exhi-
    bition of, 209n2; digital scanning at,
    175–76, 237n37; goals of, 2; name of,
    213n55; translations of Maupassant in,
    223–24n17; yo-yo from, 163–64. *See
    also* Aaron Lansky

Navajo, 23

naye dor, Dos (The New Generation), 20

Nayvelt (summer camp), 39

Nazis: Jews marked by, 160; racial linguistics of, 7; Yiddish murdered by, 179. *See also* Holocaust

Nemyriv, 52

Nerwen, Diane, 187

Netsky, Hankus, 143–44

New Jersey, 38, 83, 133

New Left, 188

newspapers and newsletters: decline of (Yiddish), 128; in hasidic neighborhood, *3*; logo of, 164, *165*; romanization of (Yiddish), 234n2; Yiddish cultural events listed in (English), 133–34

New Testament: Asch's novels inspired by, 105–6; translation into Yiddish, 101–2

New Yiddish, theorizing of, 184–90

New York City: hasidim in, 82 (*see also* Boro Park); immigrant enclave in, 38; MetroCard vending machines in, 4; use of Yiddish expressions in, 161, 235n10; in Yiddishland poem, 42

New Yorker, 200

Niger, Shmuel (Charney), 92

Niremberg, Mariam, 233n41

Nit Gedayget (summer camp), 39

non-Jews: relation to Yiddish of, 2, 153, 161, 196, 236n19; Yiddish-speaking, 25–26, 182

Nora, Pierre, 89

Norich, Anita, 105–6, 116–17

Norwegian language, 103

Noy, Dov, 52

NYBC. *See* National Yiddish Book Center

Nydorf, Charles, 117, 121

Odessa, primers published in, 66

Öffentliche Israelitische Hochschule (Israelite Public High School), 65

Olgin, Moyshe, 101, 135–36, 147

Oppenheim, Moritz Daniel, *96*

orality, of Yiddish, 61–62, 127–32

Orloff, Rich, 173

orthography, 63, 70–71, 215n8, 216–17n27. See also *alefbeys;* grammar; romanization

Osherow, Jacqueline, 114

Ostrovski, B., *78*

Ovadia, Moni, 140

Oy! (comedy), 173

Oylem umloye (The World and All That's in It, encyclopedia), 83

Ozick, Cynthia: on New Yiddish, 184–85, 239n22; presentation by, 227n63; on translating Yiddish literature, 114–16

Palestine, Yiddish used in, 9–11, 132. *See also* Israel; Zionists and Zionism

Paley, Grace, 112

Paris, 32, 38, 133

Peltz, Rakhmiel, 233n45

Penn, Ascher, 84

Peretz, Y. L.: anthologizing of, 105; children of, 190; on writing, 210n11; writing of, 40, 98, 111, 240n35; on Yiddish language, 33, 183; on Yiddish-language pedagogy, 68

Pereyaslev, 52

performances: as anthologizing practices, 144–45; approach to, 27–28, 29; as disruptive encounters with Western culture, 130–32; loss of mimesis and, 127–32; motivations for, 152–54; newsletter listings of, 133–34; as pedagogy, 142–44; as restoration, 130–31; and significance for Yiddish culture, 50–51, 126–27, 134–45, 147–48, 150–52, 195; strategies of language use in, 139–45; Yiddish parodied in, 131. *See also* dance; festivals; Gilbert and Sullivan operettas; music and music performances; theater

performative speech, definition of, 148
Perl, Joseph, 65
Perlman, Max, 145
Petit Prince, Le (The Little Prince), 117, 119
photographs, 18, 47–48, *195*
phrase books, 31–34, 209n5, 209n7
Pierce, Wilbur, 170, *171*, 236n28
Pietz, William, 160, 161
pilgrimages, 52, 106
Pilobolus (dance company), 141
Pinker, Steven, 78
Pinye shtroykop, (trans. of *Struwwelpeter*), 117
Pirozhnikov, Y., 66–67
playfulness: about death of Yiddish, 179–80; in material culture, 157–58, 162, 169–70, 174–75, 237n35; in postvernacular Yiddish translations, 122. *See also* deep play; language play
Plimoth Plantation, 53
Poe, Edgar Allan, 99
poetry: about Yiddish, 19, 40–42, 179–80; imagining of Yiddishland in, 40–42; translation as subject of, 112–16; translations of, 105, 117, 119–20; in Yiddish primer, 80–81. *See also* literature; Magnetic Poetry
Poland: interwar government resistance to Yiddish in, 13; interwar state of Yiddish language in, 40, 179; Jewish performance in, postwar, 52, 130, 141, *142*; Jews in, postwar, 16, 72–73; postwar interest in Yiddish in, 87, 88, 153; Yiddish schools in, interwar, 69–70; Yiddish translations in, interwar, 99–100. *See also* Cracow; Łódź; Vilna; Warsaw
Polish, 35, 99, 224n26
political activism: Yiddish as language of, 74, 79, 188; Yiddish-language advocacy and, 67–69. *See also* ideology
postcards, 47–48

postvernacularity: concept of, 4–5, 22–30, 55, 193–203; performative nature of, 127; in postwar Yiddish pedagogy, 82–91; in recent translations into Yiddish, 116–25. *See also* symbolic meanings of Yiddish
Powell, Colin, 26, 208n61
Prager, Leonard, 85, 86, 87
Prague, 46
prayer books, 6, 92. See also *tkhines*
primers. *See* instructional manuals and primers
Project Judaica, 87–88
psycholinguistics, language learning and, 60–61
Purim, plays performed on, 132, 230n7
Puriskevitsh, Gitl, *52*

queer theory, 188–90
Queer Yiddishkeit, 187–88, 190, 196

radio programs, 21–22, 56, 214n73
Raduń, 47
Rashi, 94
Rasʒvet (Dawn, journal), 131
Ravitch, Melekh, 101–2
readers: creating Ashkenazic vernacular community of, 95; critique of American Jewish, 107–8; as distinctive class, 102–3; engendering of, 94–98; erudition of, 97–98; response to Asch's Christian novels, 105–6; revolutionized notions of, 98–103; of Yiddish during Holocaust, 14–15
recordings, 8–9, 11–12, *24*, 34, 204–5n20, 205–6n31
Reiner, Carl, 170
Reisen, Abraham, 40, 65
Reise nach Jiddischland (Journey to Yiddishland, film), 50
religion and religiosity, Jewish: attacks on, 79, *133*; language use and, 95–98, 233–34n53; modern Yiddish culture

linked to, 185; popular vs. elite, 95–98; Yiddish instruction linked to, 72, 79, 83–84, 196, 217n33. *See also* hasidim; Judaism; *khareydim*; *kheyder*; rituals

religious literature: prayer books, 6, 92; Talmud, study of, 21, 84; *tkhines* (petitional prayers), 97; translations of, 94–98; *Tsenerene*, 95–96. *See also* Bible; Loshn-koydesh

Righteous Persons Fund, 176

Rishon LeZion, 53

rituals: bar mitzvah, 74; of inaugurating Jewish literacy, 62; model wedding, *129*; objects related to, 135, 161–62, 231n17; Passover seder, 93, 131; Purim plays, 132, 230n7; reading of scripture in, 93. *See also* Sabbath

Robinson, Elinor, 117, 121, 241n49

Rokhman, Leyb, 48

Romaine, Jenny, *140*

Romania: Yiddish schools in, 72; Yiddish theater in, 230n7

romanization: in bilingual works, 112–13; on the Internet, 54–55; of newspapers, 234n2; in translations, 116–17, *118*, 124–25; of words inscribed on objects, 156–59, 164; of Yiddish Magnetic Poetry, 157–58

Romeyn, Esther, 136

Rosenfeld, Hersh, 117

Rosenfeld, Isaac, 120, 122

Rosenfeld, Morris, 111, 178–79, 238n4

Roskies, David, 185

Ross, George, 122

Ross, Leonard, 112. *See also* Leo Rosten

Rossi, Roberto, *140*

Rosten, Leo, 18. See also *Joys of Yiddish, The*; Leonard Ross

Roth, Henry, 112

Roth, Philip, 112

Rubaiyat of Omar Khayyam, The (trans.), 99

Russia: censorship in, 13; post-Soviet instruction in Yiddish in, 87–88; primers published in, 65; restrictions on Jews and Yiddish language in, 13, 65, 67; and Yiddishland, 36–37; Yugntruf members in, 146. *See also* Soviet Union

Russian Communist Party, 13

Russian language, 12, 65, 69, 72, 99, 103, 111, 130, 179, 224n24, 224n26

Russian Revolution (1905), 67

Russian State University for the Humanities, 88

Rymanów, 46

Sabbath: vs. Saturday, 218n51; women reading on, *96*

Sachs, Nellie, 117

Saint-Exupéry, Antoine de, 117, 119

Sammy's Roumanian Steak House (NYC), 165

Samuel, Maurice, 106–8, 225n37

Sandler, Boris, 134–35, 136, 147

Sapoznik, Henry, 141

Sarna, Jonathan, 16

Say It in Yiddish, 31–34, 209n7

Schaechter, Binyumen, 150

Schafer, R. Murray, 153

Schechner, Richard, 137

Schenirer, Sarah, 72, 217n33

schools: hasidic, 82–85; in interwar Eastern Europe and Soviet Union, 69–73; in nineteenth-century Eastern Europe, 65; in U.S., 73–82, 131–32; Yiddish, forbidden in Russia, 13, 65, 67. *See also* girls' education; instructional manuals and primers; *kheyder*; lessons, Yiddish; universities; Yiddish-language pedagogy

Schreiber, Matthias, 71–72

Scooler, Zvee, *24*

Secunda, Sholom, 145

Seidman, Naomi, 109

Sejmists, 68

self-hatred, 7

Selig, Gottfried, 63

semiotics: of souvenirs, 156–59; of Yiddish, 6, 128, 195

sensibility: analogizing of Yiddish and queer, 187–88; concept of, 240n30; Yiddish as, 190

Seuss, Dr., (Theodore Geisel), 117, *118*

shabes. See Sabbath

Shakespeare, William, 117

Shalom, Efrat, 11

Sharp, Rosalie, 137

Shatsky, Jacob, 117

Shell, Marc, 191

Shilansky, Dov, 10

Shleppers (moving company), 161

Shlisky, Yosef, 206n31

Shmeruk, Khone, 241n51

shmues-krayẓn (conversation clubs), 51

Shmul un Shmerke (trans. of *Max und Moriẓ*), 117, 121

Shneer, David, 70, 71

Sholem Aleichem: children of, 190; comparative translations of, 224–25n26; English translation of, 105, 106–8, 225n37; fictional community of, 38–39; Peretz's description of, 33, 210n11; street named for, 37; writing of, 41, 98, 111

Sholem Aleichem Folks-institut, 74

Shtern, Yekhiel, 218n46

shtetl: exclusively Jewish depiction of, 52–53; Ur-home of Yiddishland, 51; website of, 54

Shtetl Museum (Israel), 53

Shtetl (website), 54

shul (school), in first lesson, 77–78, 218n51, 220n60

signage, public, 37, *38,* 52

sign language, 140, 157

Silvain, Gérard, 47–48

Silver, Joan Micklin, 20

Singer, Isaac Bashevis, 108, 111, 115, 180

Sinkoff, Nancy, 98

Sitarz, Magdalena, 88

S'iẓ geven a nes (It Was a Miracle, musical revue), 52

Skakun, Michael, 149–50

Skilnik, Gisela, 117, 228n73

Skulnik, Menashe, 139

Słowacki, Juljusz, 40

sociolinguistics, language learning and, 61

Sollors, Werner, 173

Solomon, Alisa, 187–88

Soloveitchik, Haym, 127–28, 132

Sommer, Doris, 193

song lyrics: by Michael Alpert, 8–9; anthologizing of, 233n40; English-Yiddish, 139; "Orthodox pop," 132; from Polish ghettos, 232n27; teaching in performance, 143–44, 230n37

South Africa, 133

souvenirs, semiotics of, 156–59

Soviet Union: government oppression of Yiddish in, 13–14, 72–73, 132, 191, 231n12; Jewish Autonomous Region in, 37–38, 132, 211n22; language reform in, 71; Yiddish officially recognized in, 69–70. *See also* Russia

Spanish, 130, 157, 219n53. *See also* Judezmo

Spielberg, Steven, 176

Spinoza, Baruch, 99

Stalin, Joseph, 37, 72, 132, 231n12

stand-up comedy, 170

Stanislavski, Konstantin, 111

Statman, Andy, 141

Stein, Gertrude, 199

Steinbaum, Israel, 219n58

Steiner, George, 34–35, 193

Steiner, Peter, *200*

Steinweg, Gernot, 50

Sternhartz, Nathan, 222n4

Steven Spielberg Digital Yiddish Library, 176

Stewart, Martha, 175

Stewart, Susan, 159
Stowe, Harriet Beecher, 98
Strindberg, August, 99
Struwwelpeter, 117
summer camps, Yiddishist: imaginary travels at, 211n22; naming of, 38–39, 211n24; performances at, 131–32; signage of, *38;* as Yiddishlands, 38
Sutzkever, Abraham, 19, 41, 48, 240n35
Svigals, Alicia, 143, 144
svives (Yugntruf project), 145–46, 233n44
Swahili, 31
symbolic meanings of Yiddish: in American Jewish literature, 112–16; as carnivalesque, 167; as a cultural alternative, 87, 187–88, 196, 198; as defining Jewish nationhood, 36–37, 90, 131 (*see also* Yiddishism); as embodying heritage 75, 79–82, 137–39, 147; as epitomizing diaspora, 11, 39, 49–50, 87–88, 183; in films, 20–21; for hasidim, 46, 82–85; in material culture, *17*, 159, 166–67, 169; orality of, 128; in Palestine and Israel, 9–11; in performances, 130, 136–37, 145, 152–54; in relation to the Holocaust, 8 , 14–15, 18–19, 108-10, 117; transformations of, 12–15, 20, 25–26; translation and, 94, 100, 117–19; vs. vernacular use of Yiddish, 4, 22–23, 138–40, 145. *See also* language play; postvernacularity
Szuriej, Szymon, 213n58

Talmud, language for study of, 21, 23, 84. *See also* religious literature
Tartell, Bob, 228n70
Taub, Yermiyahu Aharon, 187
taytsh, use of term, 95
"Tchotchkes! Treasures of the Family Museum" (exhibit), *163*
teachers. *See* schools
Teitz, Rabbi Mordechai Pinchas, 21
Tel Aviv, 9, 42, 48, 50

Teller, Judd, 111
Territorialism, 39, 68, 149
textbooks. *See* instructional manuals and primers
theater, Yiddish: brochure for, *181*; hasidim attending, 199; history of, 230n7; *khareydim* performing, 2, 132; and modernity, 131–32; in post-WWII Poland, 52; in Soviet Union, 132, *133*; translation strategies of, 139–40
time-out activities, concept of, 51
Time Out New York, 235n10
tkhines (petitional prayers), 97
topography. *See* mapping projects
Toronto: Ashkenaz Festival of, 137–38; Jewish community life in, 231n24, Yiddishland Cafe in, *35*
tours and tourist productions, 52, 136–37. *See also* phrase books
Traig, Jennifer, 174–75
Traig, Victoria, 174–75
translation: approach to, 27, 28; in colonial societies, 103; cultural significance of, 92–94, 101–3, 105, 119–21, 125; debates on, 99–101; exoticism in, 105; as literary subject, 112–16; performance strategies of, 139–41; post-Holocaust implications of, 108–10; postvernacular, into Yiddish, 116–25; as recovering imagined Yiddish originals, 116–25; of scripture and folklore into Yiddish, 94–98; transgression and betrayal in, 105–6; undoing of, 115–16, 124–25; of world literature into Yiddish, 98–103, 117; of Yiddish literature, 103–10; Yiddish as resistant to, 112
Trauerarbeit (task of grieving), 185
"Trip to Yiddishland" (program), 50–51
Trubnik, Yoyne, *64*
Tsenerene, 95–96
Tsentrale Yidishe Shul-Organizatsye (Central Yiddish School Organization), 69

T-shirts, 160, 161
Twain, Mark, 99
Twi, 44
typefaces and fonts: "kosher style," 156; of women's Yiddish, 96. *See also* romanization

Ukraine, 25, 38, 52, 87
Uman', 52
United States: as postwar cultural center for Jews, 16, 26, 82, 190–91; Yiddish schools in, 73–82, 131–32. *See also* New York City
universities, Yiddish instruction in, 2, 28, 82, 85–90, 221–22n84. *See also* dissertations; Jewish studies
University of California, Berkeley, *88*
Urban Peasants (film), 20
Uruguay, 146

vaybertaytsh (Yiddish font for "women's literature"), 96
Veiel, Andres, 21
vernacular languages: education in, 61–62, 66, 68–72, 81; English as, 81, 104; German as model of, 7–8; Hebrew as, 23, 36, 48, 90; in relation to nonvernacular languages, 22–23; role of in imagining Yiddishland, 43–44; translation and anthologizing of, 109–10; Yiddish as, 2, 23, 71, 77, 85, 90, 182, 189, 221n73, 230n2; and Yiddishism, 13, 35–36. *See also* ethnicity; *folkshprakh; mame-loshn;* postvernacularity; Yiddish language
Verne, Jules, 98
Versailles Treaty, 13
Verschik, Anna, 89
vertical legitimation, concept of, 198
Very Hungry Caterpillar, The, 117
Vienna, Yiddish culture in, 40
Vilna (Vilnius): in board game, 46; and interwar Yiddish culture, 39–40; and

interwar Yiddish education, 66, 68, 71–72; and postwar Yiddish education, 87, 89; Yiddishland as exemplified by, 39–40, 42
Vilna Gaon, 46
Vilna Jewish Technical School, 71–72
Vilnius Program in Yiddish, 89
Vini-der-Pu (trans. of *Winnie the Pooh*), 116–17, 119
Vinnytsa, 52
Voyages (film), 21

Walowitz, Miriam, 228n70
Wandervogel movement, 148
Warsaw: on board game, 46; interwar Yiddish publications in, 39, 40, 67; postwar Yiddish instruction in, 87; postwar Yiddish theater in, 52; in Yiddishland poem, 42
websites: imagining Yiddishland via, 53–54, *55*; on Yiddish instruction, 221–22n84
wedding, model, *129*
Weiner, Ellis, *60*
Weinreich, Beatrice, 31–34, 209n7
Weinreich, Max: on internal Jewish bilingualism, 62; on vertical legitimation, 198; on war's impact on Yiddish, 15; on women and Yiddish writing, 96–97; on wordplay, 93; on Yiddish as indigenous possession of Ashkenazim, 12; Yiddish learned by, 190; on Yiddish literacy, 63
Weinreich, Uriel: on shift in language use, 166–67; on Sholem Aleichem, 225n37. See also *College Yiddish; Language and Culture Atlas of Ashkenazic Jewry; Modern English-Yiddish Yiddish-English Dictionary; Say It in Yiddish*
Weiser, Chaim, 186
Weiss, Sam, 186
Weiss, Shevah, 10

Weissler, Chava, 97
Wells, H. B., 186
Welsh language, 39
Wex, Michael, 49
What-Cha-Ma-Call-It, Inc., 170
Whiteman, Adam, *52*
Whitman, Walt, 117
Whorf, Benjamin Lee, 192
Wiener, Leo: Rosenfeld's relationship
    with, 238n4; on Yiddish, 13, 177–79;
    Yiddish anthology of, 105
Wiesel, Elie, 109
Wilde, Oscar, 99
Williams, Raymond, 240n30
Winnie ille Pu (trans. of *Winnie the
    Pooh*), 119
Winnie the Pooh, 116–17, 119
Wirth-Nesher, Hana, 112
Wisenberg, S. L., 177
Wisse, Ruth R., 120, 188, 210n12
Wolf, Leonard, 116, 119
Wolitz, Seth, 108
women, as model Yiddish readers, 95–97.
    See also girls' education
Woodbine (NJ), 38
Workmen's Circle: events of, *5*, 34, *35*,
    129; schools of, 32, 74; song antholo-
    gies of, 233n40; T-shirts of, 160; Yid-
    dish textbooks of, 79, 81–82
World Council for Yiddish Culture, 52
Worms *makhzer*, 6
Wrzeniski, Janusz, *142*
Wyspiański, Stanisław, 99

Yad Vashem museum, 10
Yahudic (Judeo-Arabic), 129
Yavonic (Judeo-Greek), 129
Yehoash (Solomon Bloomgarden), 99–100
Yeshivish: as language, 186–87; Queer
    Yiddishkeit compared with, 190, 196
Yiddish culture: alternative notions of,
    184–90, 239n22; approach to, 25; dis-
    cussed in other languages, 200–201;

dynamics of, 1–4, 93, 190, 198, 240n35;
    geographical conceptions of, 43–50,
    190–91; persecution of, 9–10, 13–15,
    67–68, 132; in relation to Jewishness,
    10–11, 25–26, 48, 152–53; in relation to
    queer culture, 187–90; theorizing
    meaning of, 190–201; translation's
    role in, 114–16, 120–21; undoing as-
    sumptions about, 192–94; in U.S. con-
    text, 16, 73–82, 190–91. *See also* cul-
    ture; Jewish culture; language/
    culture/identity interrelations; mate-
    rial culture; music and music perfor-
    mances; performances; postvernacu-
    larity; schools; theater, Yiddish;
    Yiddish language
Yiddishe Cup, 164–65
Yiddish Folk Arts Program, 141
Yiddishism (ideology): defined, 13, 35;
    reflections on, 183–84, 192–93; *See
    also* Czernowitz Yiddish Conference;
    Fishman, Joshua A.; Zhitlowski,
    Chaim
Yiddishists (Yiddish language advo-
    cates): academic legitimacy and, 85; as
    in denial, 180, 185; early activities of
    64–65; language standards of, 70–71;
    on world literature translations,
    99–100; and Yiddish pedagogy, 67–69,
    90–91. *See also* summer camps, Yid-
    dishist; Yugntruf
Yiddishkayt Los Angeles (public pro-
    gram), 138–39
Yiddishland: approach to, 28; compared
    to Esperanto, 29; definitions of, 33–34,
    39, 47–48, 210n9; display of, 51–53;
    geopolitical implications of, 35–36,
    39–40, 57–58; impact of Holocaust on,
    42–44; on the Internet, 53–57; as Jew-
    ish tourist destination, 136–37; real-
    ized in performance, 50–51; university
    Yiddish programs likened to, 85
Yiddishland Cafe, 34, *35*

Yiddishland Records (recording label), 34

Yiddish language: acquisition of, 59, 191, 194, 197–98; approach to, 27–30; atomization of, 156–59, 194–95; contestation of, 13, 71–73, 85; disparagement of, 7, 12, 64, 65, 85, 131, 179; earliest written sentence of, 6; as extralinguistic phenomenon, 111, 123, 188, 190; fluency in, 4, 47–48, 195; geography of, 5–6, 190–91 (*see also* Yiddishland); German's relationship to, 6–7, 8–9; Hebrew's relationship to, 9–10, 48–50, 180–81, 222n4; Holocaust's impact on, 15–16, 18–19, 72, 86, 108, 117, 127, 130, 132; literary images of, 40–42, 112–16; as mother/native tongue, 69, 71, 77, 89; number of speakers of, 2, 12–13, 15–16, 19, 22–23, 25, 61, 81, 182, 203n1; as official language in Soviet Union, 13–14, 37, 69–70, 132, *133*; orality of, 62, 127–30; reading direction of, 76–78, 164, 220n63; as second language, 79–82; as secret language, 7, 166; standardization of, 8, 63, 70–71, 86, 216–17n27; subversive use of, 67, 87–88, 168; symbolic value of, 8, 14–15, 25–26, 95, 124–25, 131; theorizing meaning of, 190–201; use of, as end in itself, 55, 134, 152–53; viability of, 1–2, 16, 17–18, 19–20, 33, 43, 113–14, 119, 146, 149, 154, 177–84, 198; Yeshivish's relationship to, 186–87. *See also* bilingualism/multilingualism; gender; language play; *mame-loshn*; material culture; performances; postvernacularity; readers; translation; Yiddishism; Yiddishists; Yiddish-language pedagogy; Yiddish speakers; Yiddish words; *yidish*

Yiddish-language pedagogy: approach to, 27, 28; challenges in, 61, 65, 66–69, 70–72, 75–77, 79–81, 90–91, 219n58; college-level, 2, 28, 82, 85–90; in cultural activities, 139, 141–44, 151; in Eastern Europe before WWI, 63–69; games as, 172–73; hasidic approach to, 82–85; vs. Hebrew-language pedagogy, 62–63, 66, 68–69, 79, 81, 82, 86, 90; in interwar Eastern Europe, 69–73; postvernacularity and, 73–74, 81–82, 86–91, 194; in postwar Eastern Europe, 87–89; skepticism about, 59–61; translation as tool in, 113, 123–24; in U.S., 73–82, 83–87, *88*. *See also* instructional manuals and primers; lessons, Yiddish; schools

Yiddish literature: anthologizing of, 105, 109–10; characters from, on stamps, *52*; contemporary, 198–99, 241n49; early examples of, 94–98, *140*; game about, 169, 236n25; about Holocaust, 8, 18–19; and Jewish pedagogy, 75, 81, 87; among *khareydim*, 2; postwar role of, 18–19, 184–85; problematic boundaries of, 110–11; readership of, 62–63, 99, 101, 103, 106–10, 146, 151, 175–76; translations of, 103–10, 123–25; translations of imagined, 116–25; about Yiddish, 19, 40–42, 180; Yiddishland articulated in, 40–42. *See also individual authors*

Yiddish speech: decline of, 128–30, 135–36, 138–39, 141; among hasidim, 46, 153, 203n2, 221n71; hierarchy of, 151; motivations for, 147–50, 152–54; self-awareness in, 127, 130–32 199–202; significance in performances, 131–35, 139–41, 147. *See also* orality, of Yiddish

Yiddish words: on clothing, 160, 161; comic glosses of, 17, 164, 166, *167*, 170, 172; in mock dictionaries, 165–67; objects inscribed with, 156–59, 234n1;

on stickers, 169, *195*; vulgarisms, 168, 237n30. *See also* glossaries

yidish, double meaning of term, 36–37, 205n28, 239n20

Yidishland (summer camp), 39

yisker-bikher (memorial books), *43*, 44, 46, 50

YIVO Institute for Jewish Research: in interwar Poland, 39–40; language standards of, 54–55, 70–71, 116; Project Judaica of, 87–88; Yiddish summer program of, 33, 201

Yugntruf (journal), *148*

Yugntruf (organization): activities of, 146, 149–50, 201–2; constitution of, 147–48; Internet use of, 56; name of, 146; objectives of, 147–50; retreats of, 34, 51, 150–52, 233–34n53; *svives* project of, 145–46; T-shirts of, 160; "Yiddishland" as used by, 34; youthfulness of members, 149, 196

Yunge gvardye, Di (The Young Guard), 20

Zable, Arnold, 228n71

Zangwill, Israel, 105

ʐaum' ("abstruse language" of Russian futurism), 198

Zeitlin, Aaron, 145

ʐeyer hungeriker opfreser, Der (trans. of *The Very Hungry Caterpillar*), 117

ʐhargon ("jargon," i.e., Yiddish), use of term, 33, 63, 66–67, 210n11

Zhitlowski, Chaim, 36–37, 234n2

Zilbermann, Jean-Jacques, 21

Zinberg, Israel, 95, 120

Zionists and Zionism: in American Yiddish schools, 74, 75, 79; Ashkenazi vs. Mizrahi cultures under, 11; conception of place by, 49–50; Soviet responses to, 37–38, 72; Yiddish denounced by, 9–10; on Yiddish-language pedagogy in Eastern Europe, 68–69

Zipperstein, Steven, 65

Zola, Emile, 99

Zolf, Falk, 123–24

Zylberman, Bobby, 122, *123*

Text:	10.25/14 Fournier
Display:	Gotham medium
Compositor:	Binghamton Valley Composition, LLC
Printer and binder:	Thomson-Shore, Inc.